Amazing Agent

art by Shiei

story by Nunzio DeFilippis
and Christina Weir

[CONFIDENTIAL]

VOLUME 008

Amazing Agent
LUNA
VOLUME 8

art by **Shiei**

story by **Nunzio DeFilippis & Christina Weir**

STAFF CREDITS

lettering	**Nicky Lim**
toning	**Ludwig Sacramento**
layout	**Alexis Roberts**
design	**Nicky Lim**
proofing	**Shanti Whitesides**
managing editor	**Adam Arnold**
publisher	**Jason DeAngelis** **Seven Seas Entertainment**

ISBN: 978-1-935934-19-6

Printed in Canada

First Printing: December 2012

10 9 8 7 6 5 4 3 2 1

FOLLOW US ONLINE: *www.gomanga.com*

READING DIRECTIONS

This book reads from *right to left*, Japanese style. If this is your first time reading manga, you start reading from the top right panel on each page and take it from there. If you get lost, just follow the numbered diagram here. It may seem backwards at first, but you'll get the hang of it! Have fun!!

File 40
TERMINUS

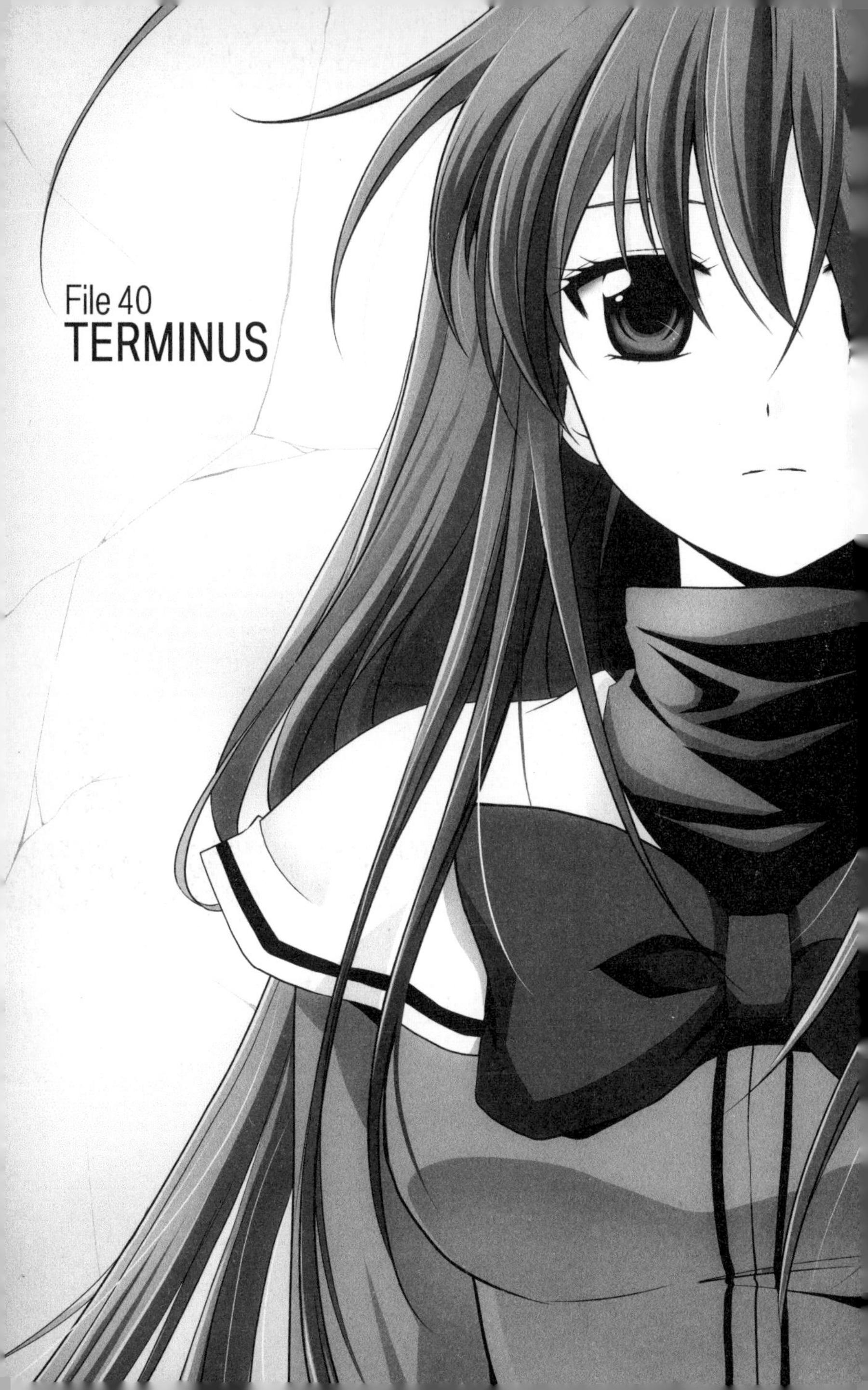

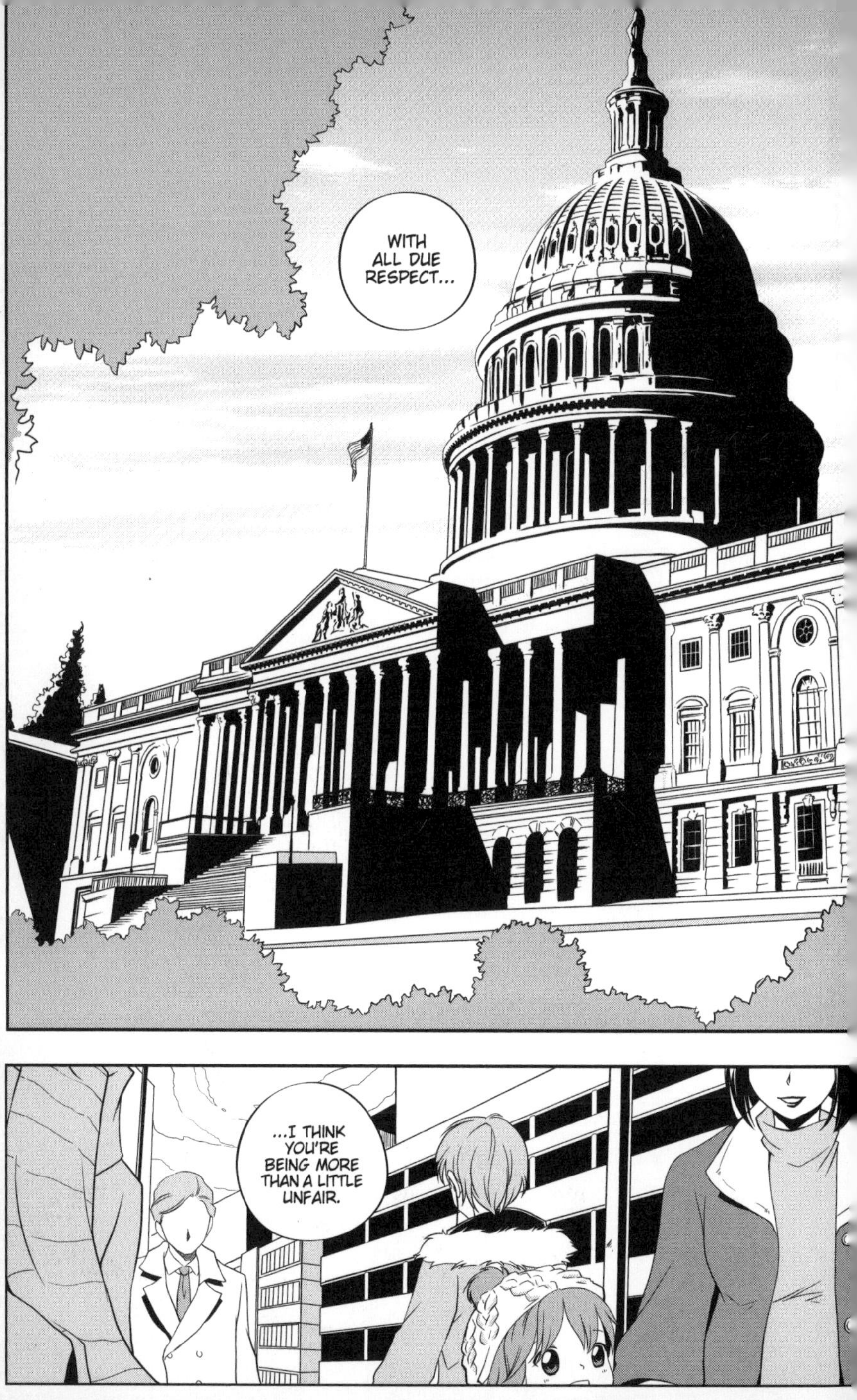
WITH ALL DUE RESPECT...
...I THINK YOU'RE BEING MORE THAN A LITTLE UNFAIR.

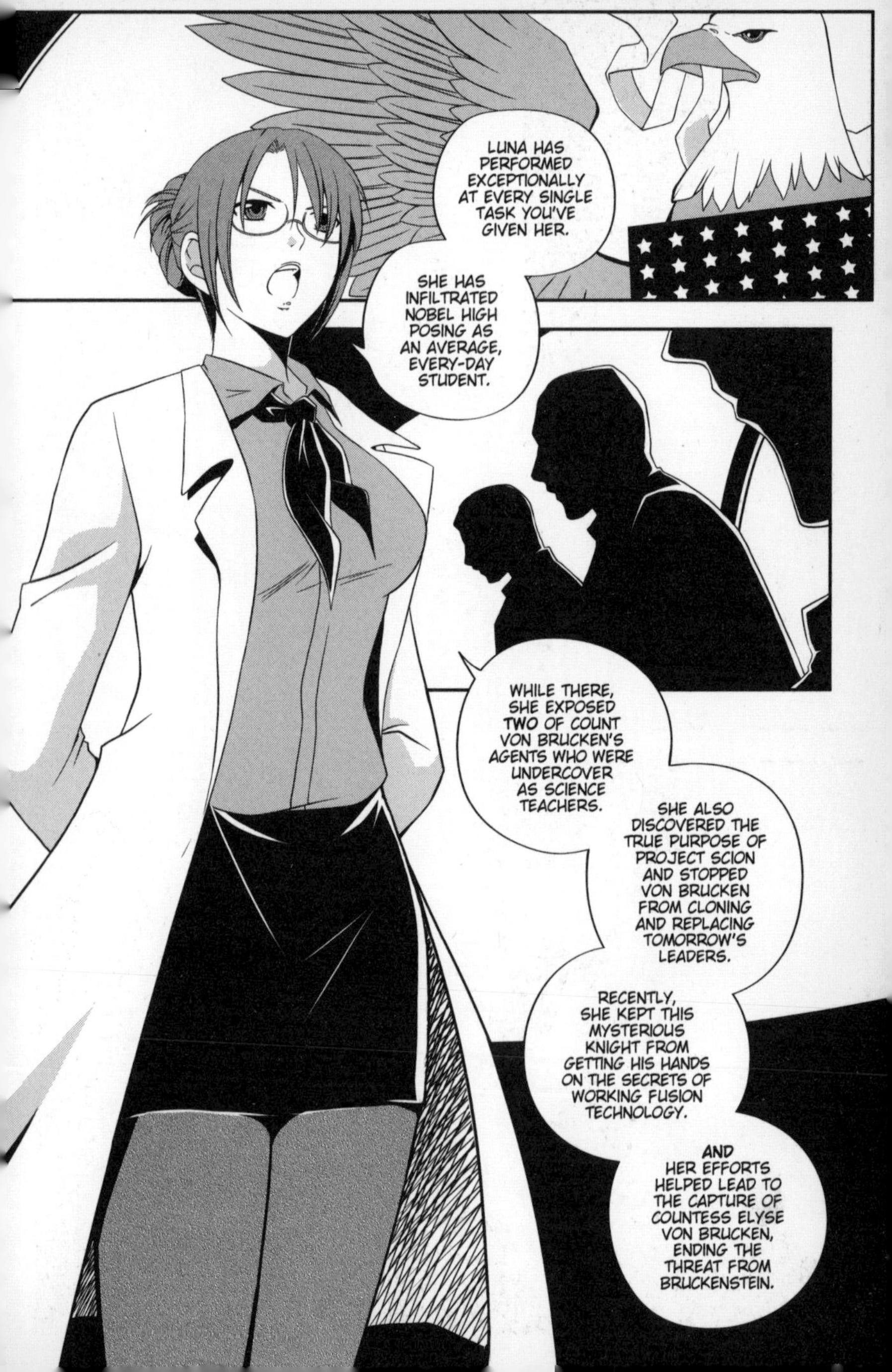
LUNA HAS PERFORMED EXCEPTIONALLY AT EVERY SINGLE TASK YOU'VE GIVEN HER.
SHE HAS INFILTRATED NOBEL HIGH POSING AS AN AVERAGE, EVERY-DAY STUDENT.
WHILE THERE, SHE EXPOSED TWO OF COUNT VON BRUCKEN'S AGENTS WHO WERE UNDERCOVER AS SCIENCE TEACHERS.
SHE ALSO DISCOVERED THE TRUE PURPOSE OF PROJECT SCION AND STOPPED VON BRUCKEN FROM CLONING AND REPLACING TOMORROW'S LEADERS.
RECENTLY, SHE KEPT THIS MYSTERIOUS KNIGHT FROM GETTING HIS HANDS ON THE SECRETS OF WORKING FUSION TECHNOLOGY.
AND HER EFFORTS HELPED LEAD TO THE CAPTURE OF COUNTESS ELYSE VON BRUCKEN, ENDING THE THREAT FROM BRUCKENSTEIN.

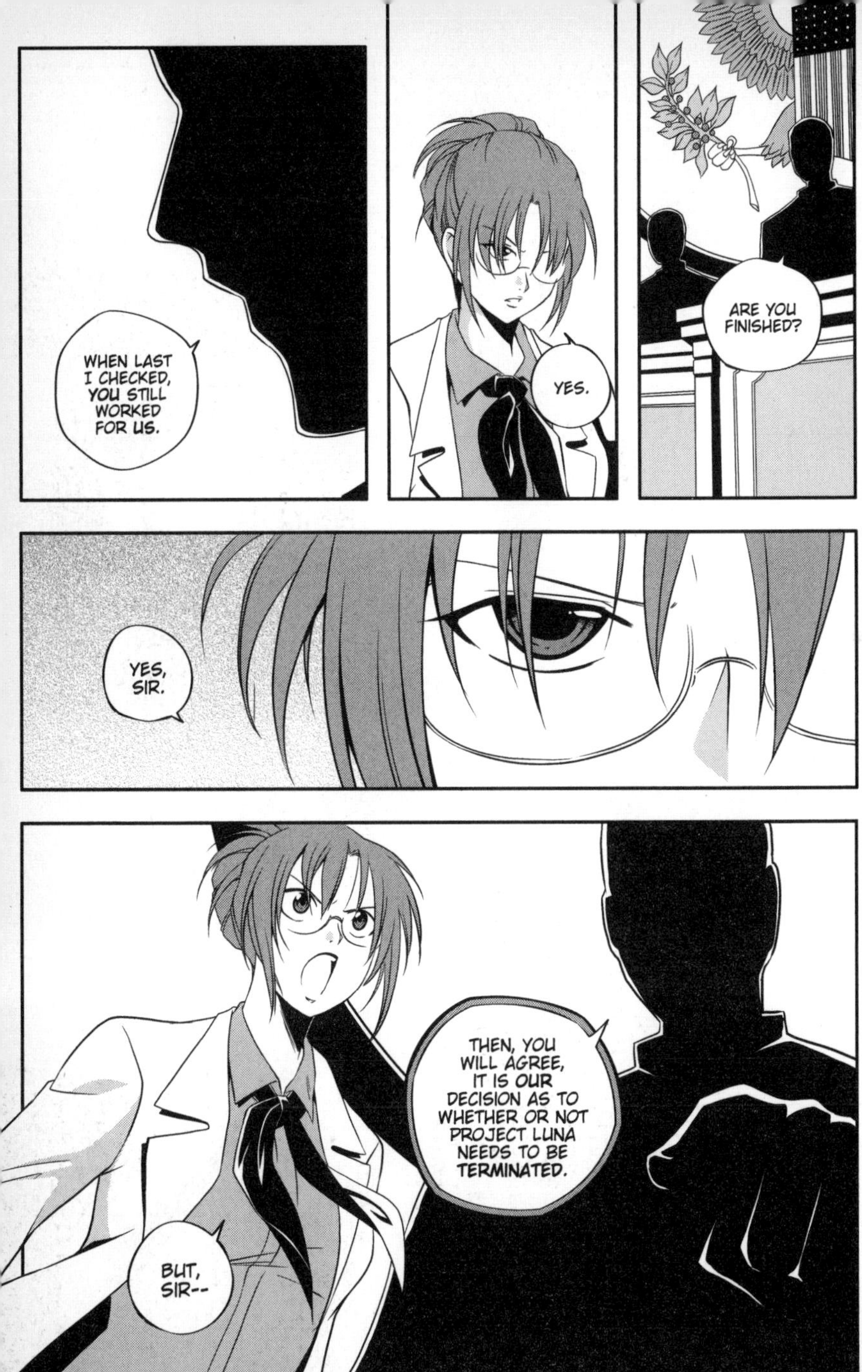
ARE YOU FINISHED?
YES.
WHEN LAST I CHECKED, YOU STILL WORKED FOR US.
YES, SIR.
THEN, YOU WILL AGREE, IT IS OUR DECISION AS TO WHETHER OR NOT PROJECT LUNA NEEDS TO BE TERMINATED.
BUT, SIR--

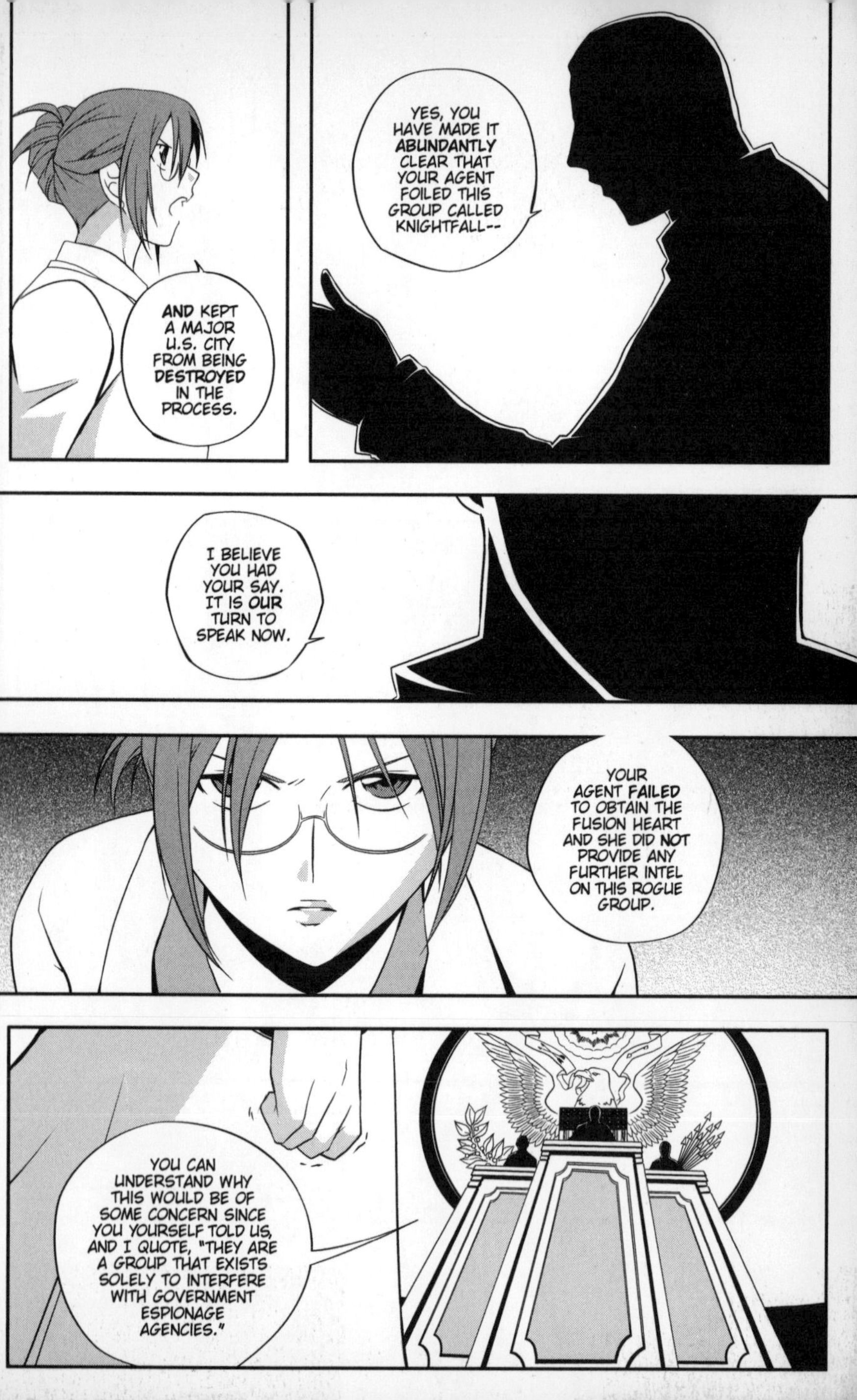
YES, YOU HAVE MADE IT ABUNDANTLY CLEAR THAT YOUR AGENT FOILED THIS GROUP CALLED KNIGHTFALL--
AND KEPT A MAJOR U.S. CITY FROM BEING DESTROYED IN THE PROCESS.
I BELIEVE YOU HAD YOUR SAY. IT IS OUR TURN TO SPEAK NOW.
YOUR AGENT FAILED TO OBTAIN THE FUSION HEART AND SHE DID NOT PROVIDE ANY FURTHER INTEL ON THIS ROGUE GROUP.
YOU CAN UNDERSTAND WHY THIS WOULD BE OF SOME CONCERN SINCE YOU YOURSELF TOLD US, AND I QUOTE, "THEY ARE A GROUP THAT EXISTS SOLELY TO INTERFERE WITH GOVERNMENT ESPIONAGE AGENCIES."

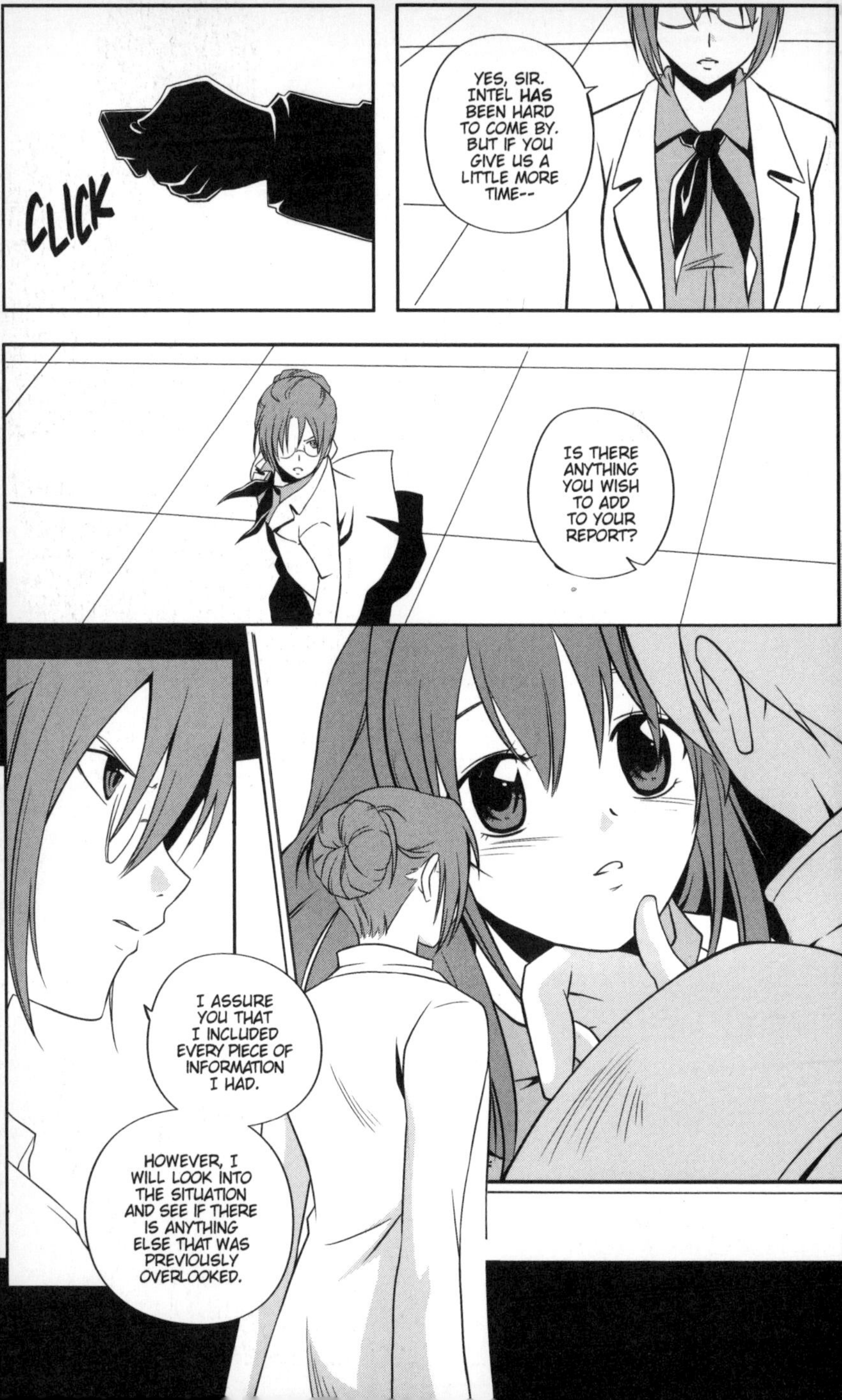
YES, SIR. INTEL HAS BEEN HARD TO COME BY. BUT IF YOU GIVE US A LITTLE MORE TIME--
CLICK
IS THERE ANYTHING YOU WISH TO ADD TO YOUR REPORT?
I ASSURE YOU THAT I INCLUDED EVERY PIECE OF INFORMATION I HAD.
HOWEVER, I WILL LOOK INTO THE SITUATION AND SEE IF THERE IS ANYTHING ELSE THAT WAS PREVIOUSLY OVERLOOKED.

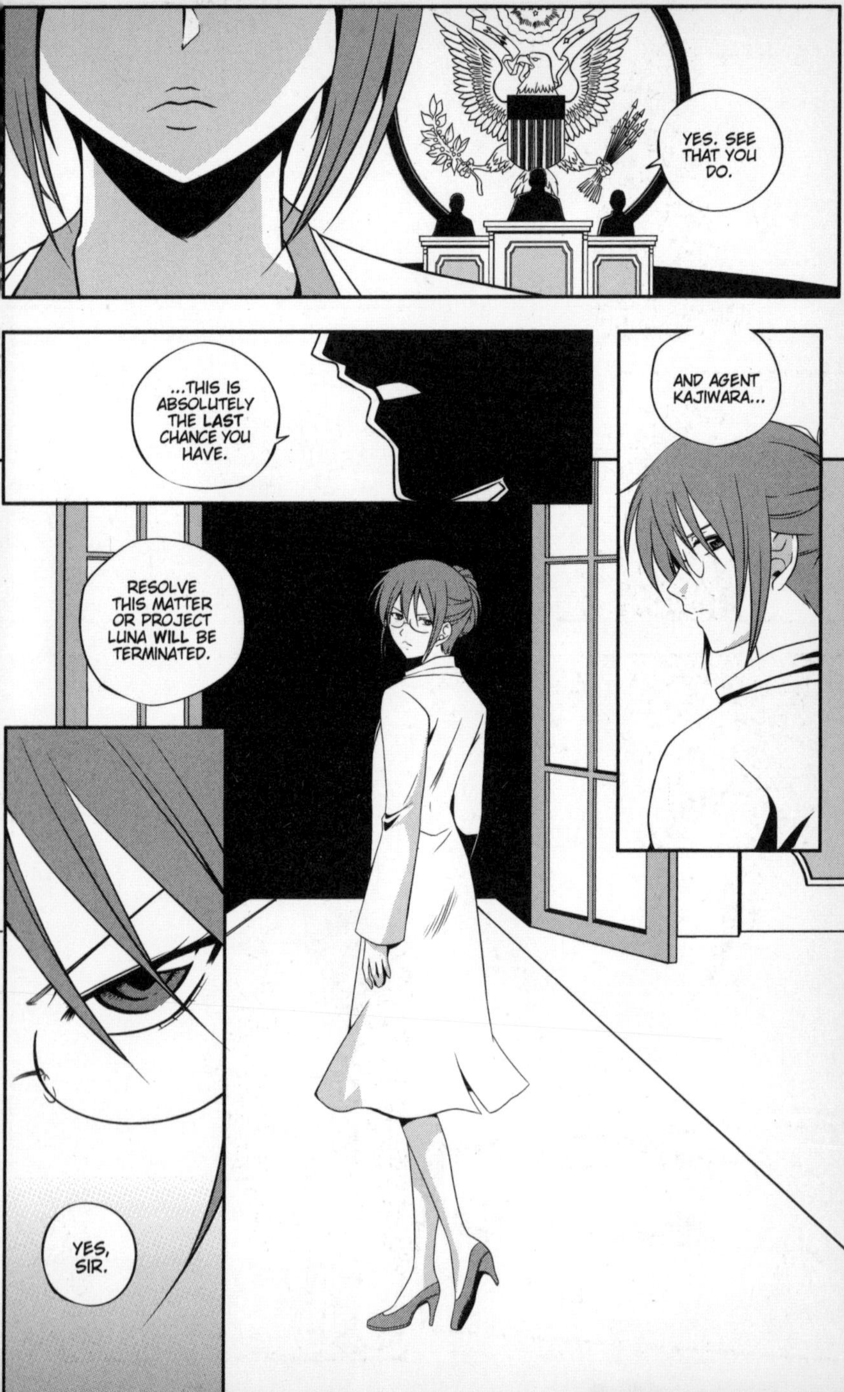
YES. SEE THAT YOU DO.
AND AGENT KAJIWARA...
...THIS IS ABSOLUTELY THE LAST CHANCE YOU HAVE.
RESOLVE THIS MATTER OR PROJECT LUNA WILL BE TERMINATED.
YES, SIR.

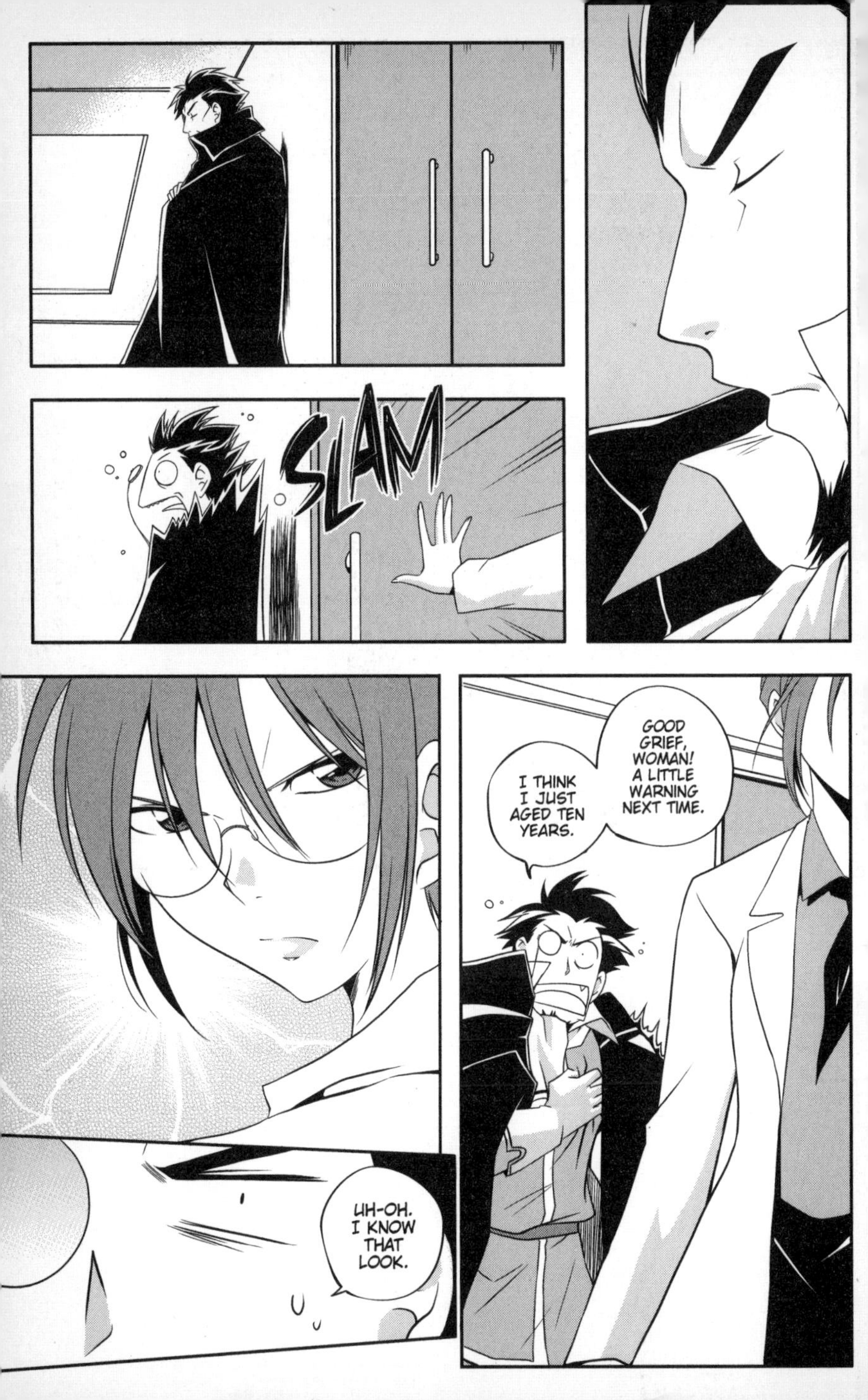
SLAM
GOOD GRIEF, WOMAN! A LITTLE WARNING NEXT TIME.
I THINK I JUST AGED TEN YEARS.
UH-OH. I KNOW THAT LOOK.

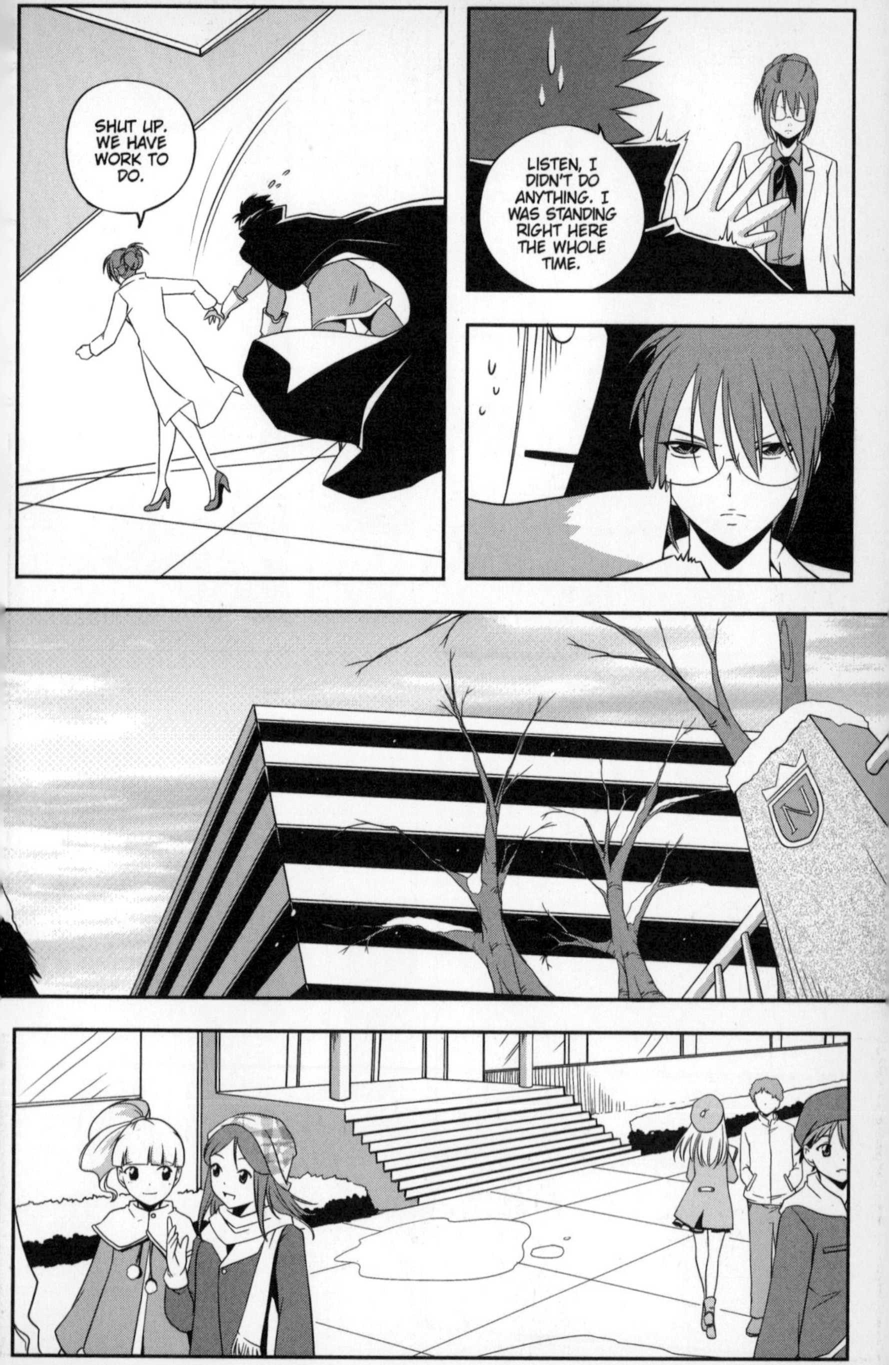
LISTEN, I DIDN'T DO ANYTHING. I WAS STANDING RIGHT HERE THE WHOLE TIME.
SHUT UP. WE HAVE WORK TO DO.

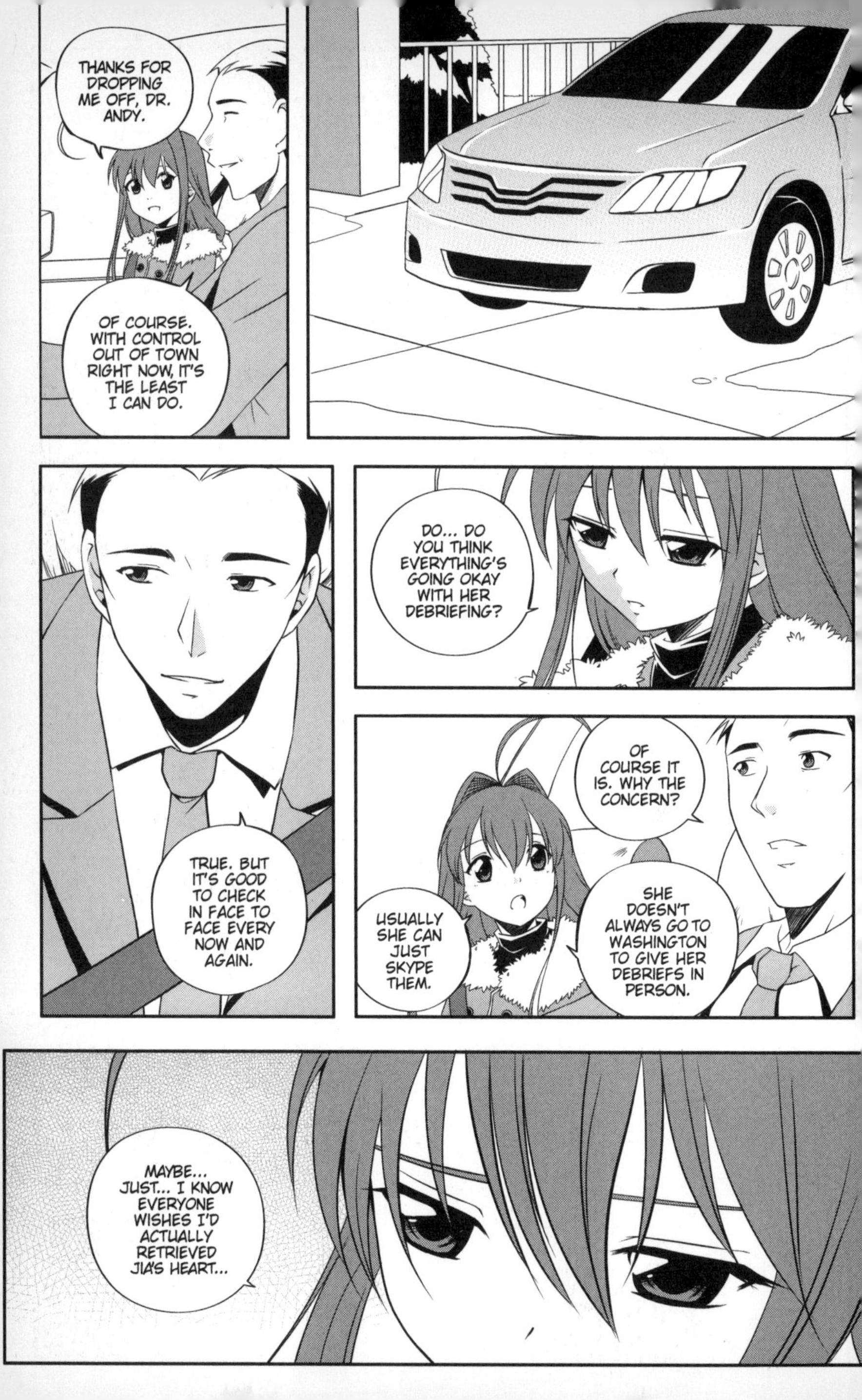
THANKS FOR DROPPING ME OFF, DR. ANDY.
OF COURSE. WITH CONTROL OUT OF TOWN RIGHT NOW, IT'S THE LEAST I CAN DO.
DO... DO YOU THINK EVERYTHING'S GOING OKAY WITH HER DEBRIEFING?
OF COURSE IT IS. WHY THE CONCERN?
SHE DOESN'T ALWAYS GO TO WASHINGTON TO GIVE HER DEBRIEFS IN PERSON.
USUALLY SHE CAN JUST SKYPE THEM.
TRUE. BUT IT'S GOOD TO CHECK IN FACE TO FACE EVERY NOW AND AGAIN.
MAYBE... JUST... I KNOW EVERYONE WISHES I'D ACTUALLY RETRIEVED JIA'S HEART...

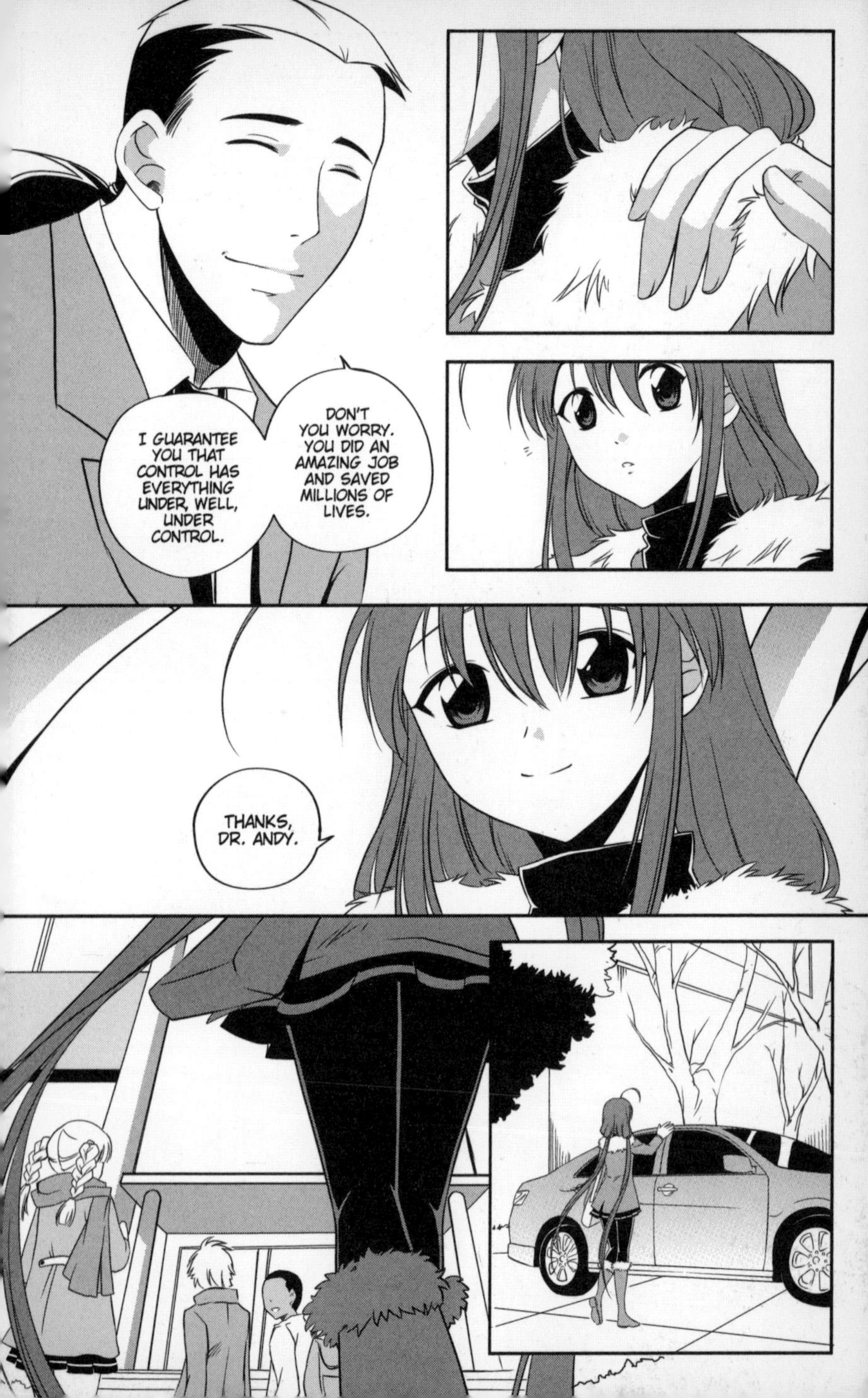
DON'T YOU WORRY. YOU DID AN AMAZING JOB AND SAVED MILLIONS OF LIVES.
I GUARANTEE YOU THAT CONTROL HAS EVERYTHING UNDER, WELL, UNDER CONTROL.
THANKS, DR. ANDY.

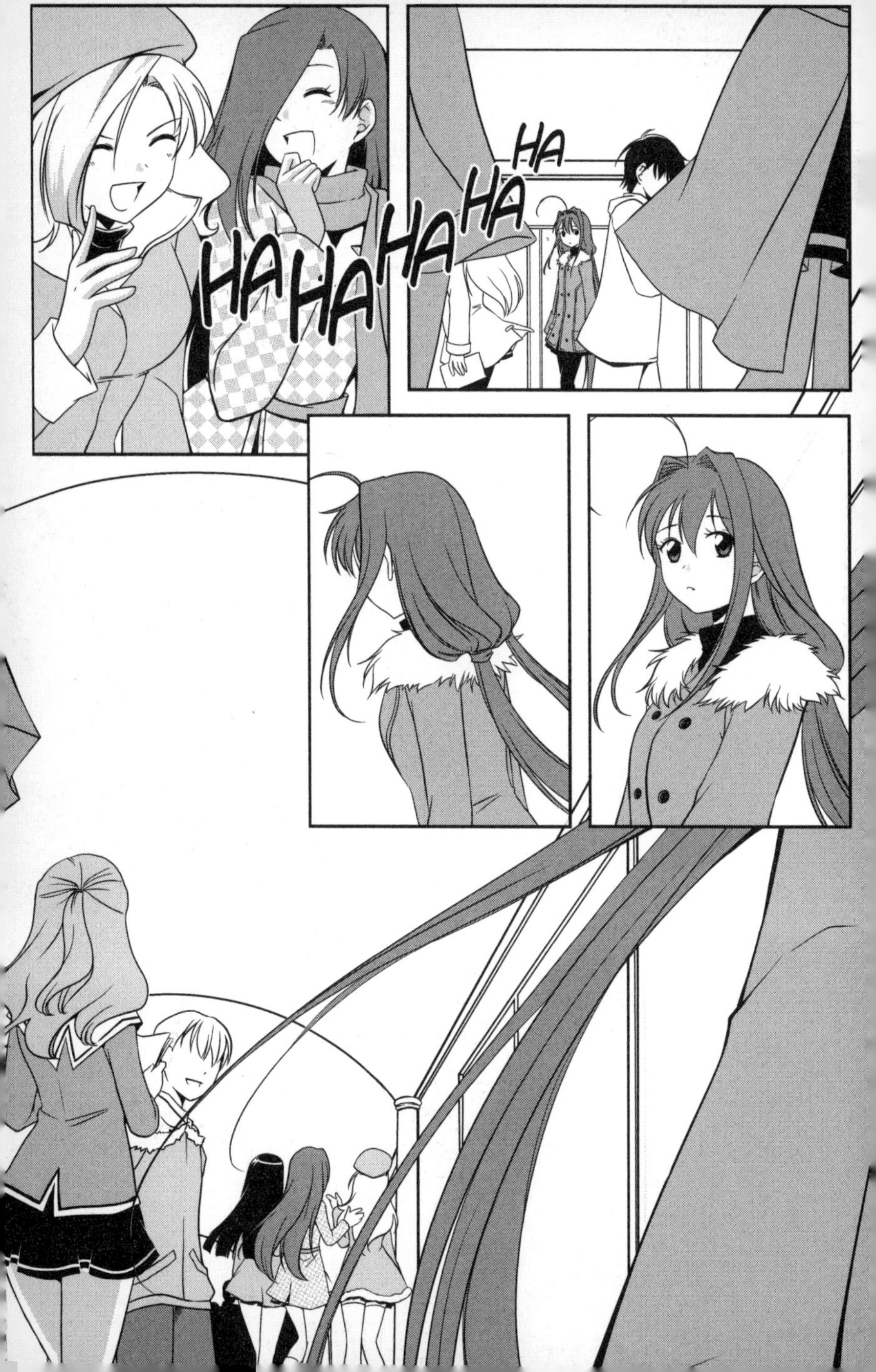
HA HA HA HA HA HA

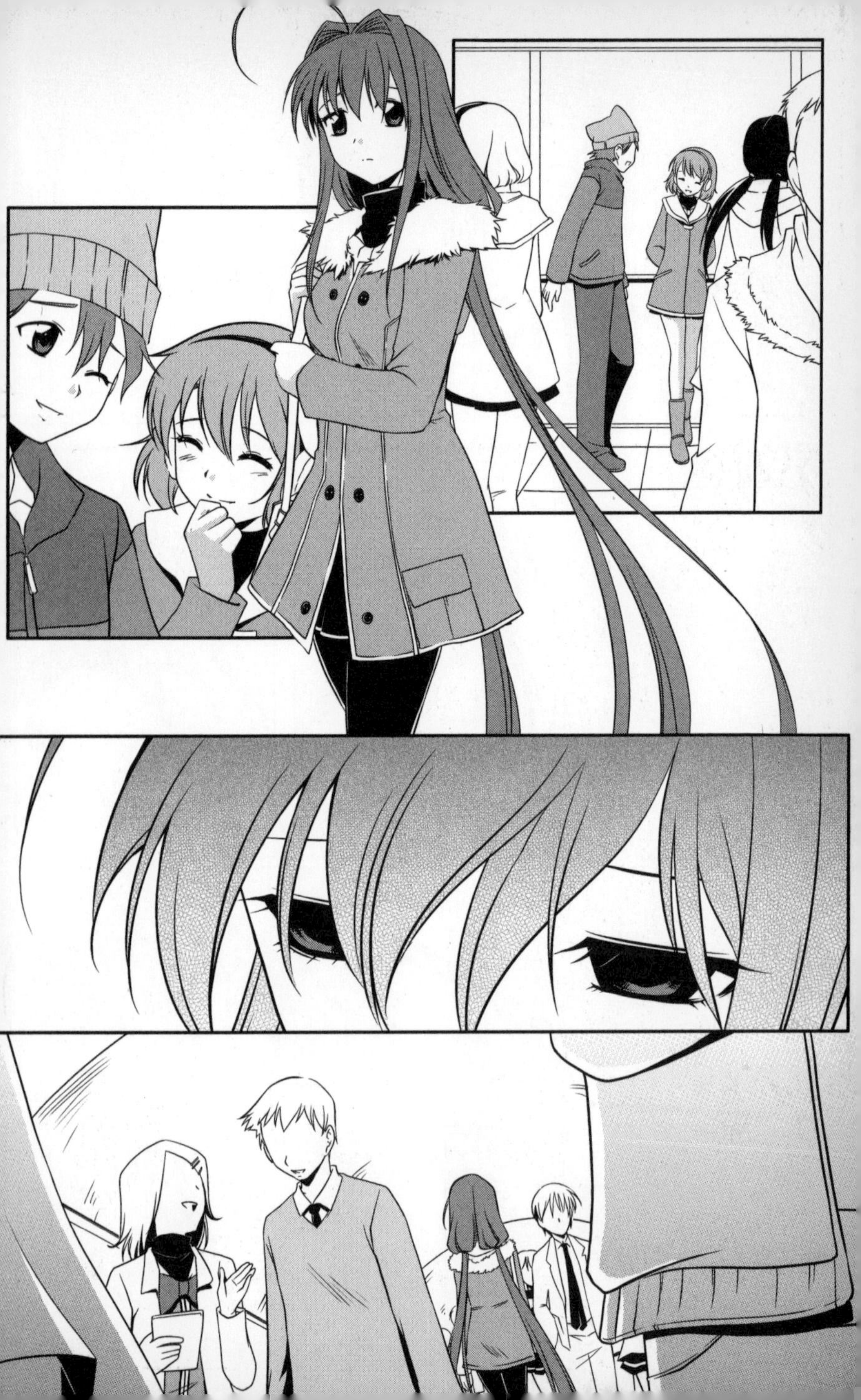

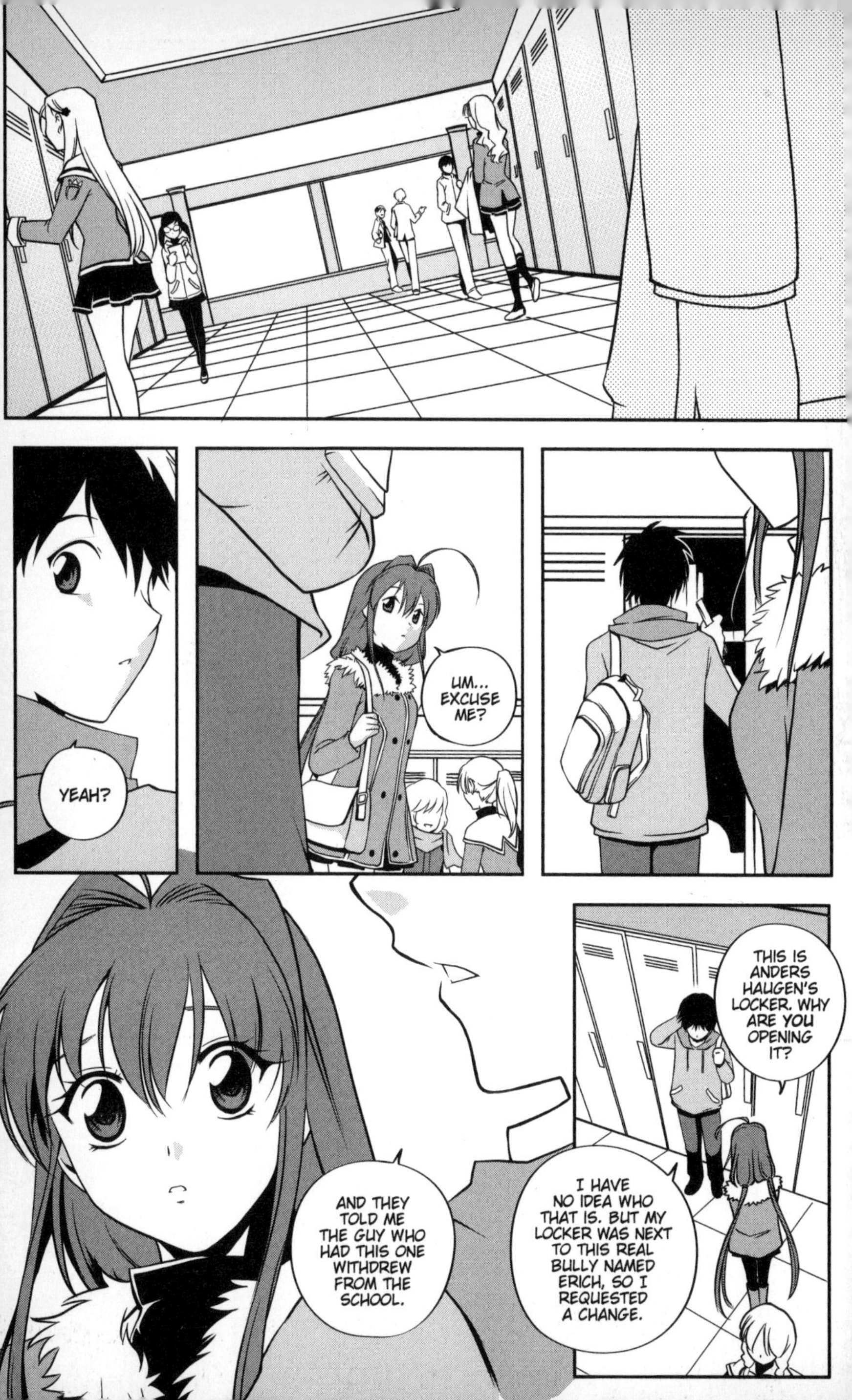
UM... EXCUSE ME?
YEAH?
THIS IS ANDERS HAUGEN'S LOCKER. WHY ARE YOU OPENING IT?
I HAVE NO IDEA WHO THAT IS. BUT MY LOCKER WAS NEXT TO THIS REAL BULLY NAMED ERICH, SO I REQUESTED A CHANGE.
AND THEY TOLD ME THE GUY WHO HAD THIS ONE WITHDREW FROM THE SCHOOL.

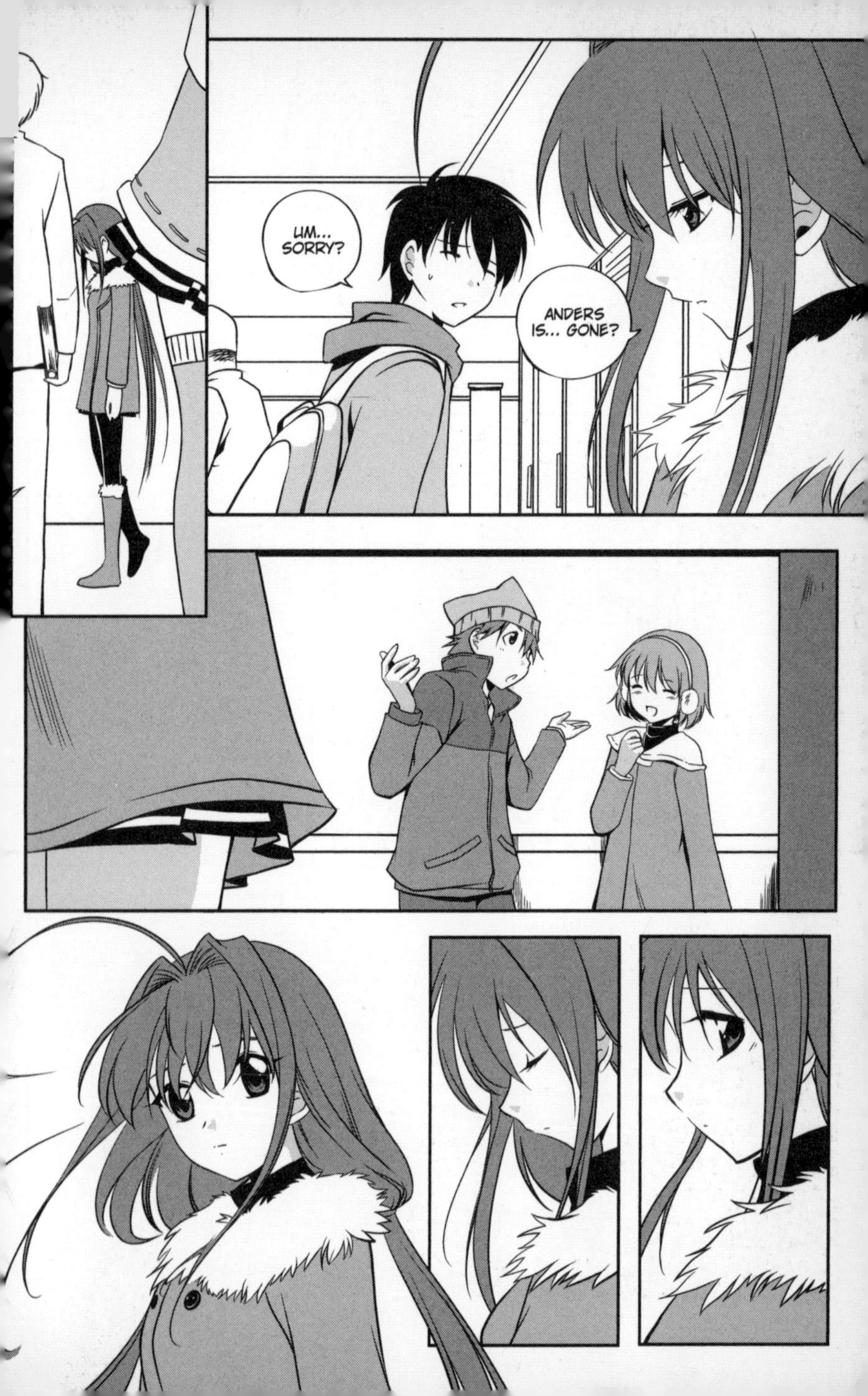
ANDERS IS... GONE?
UM... SORRY?

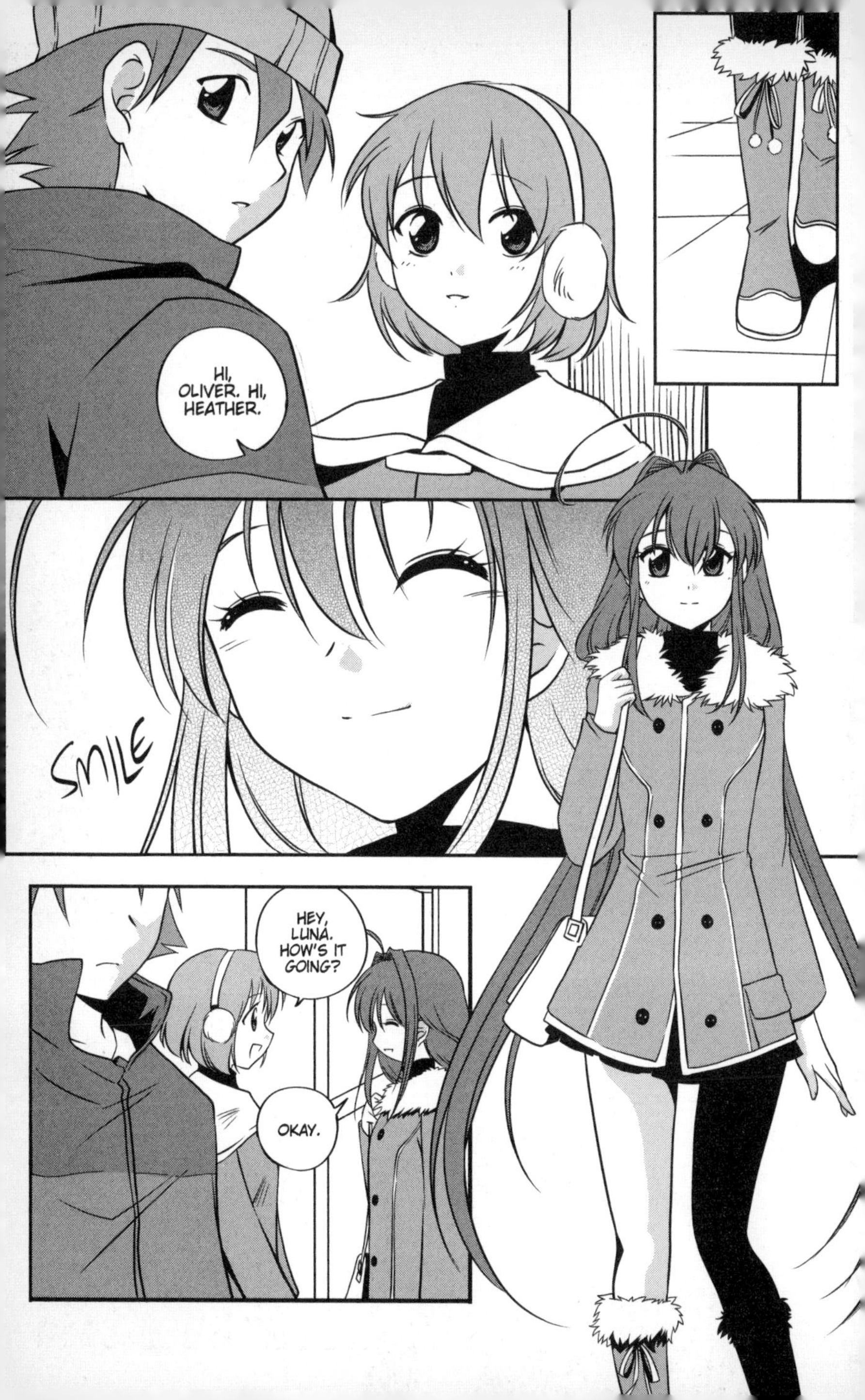
HI, OLIVER. HI, HEATHER.
SMILE
HEY, LUNA. HOW'S IT GOING?
OKAY.

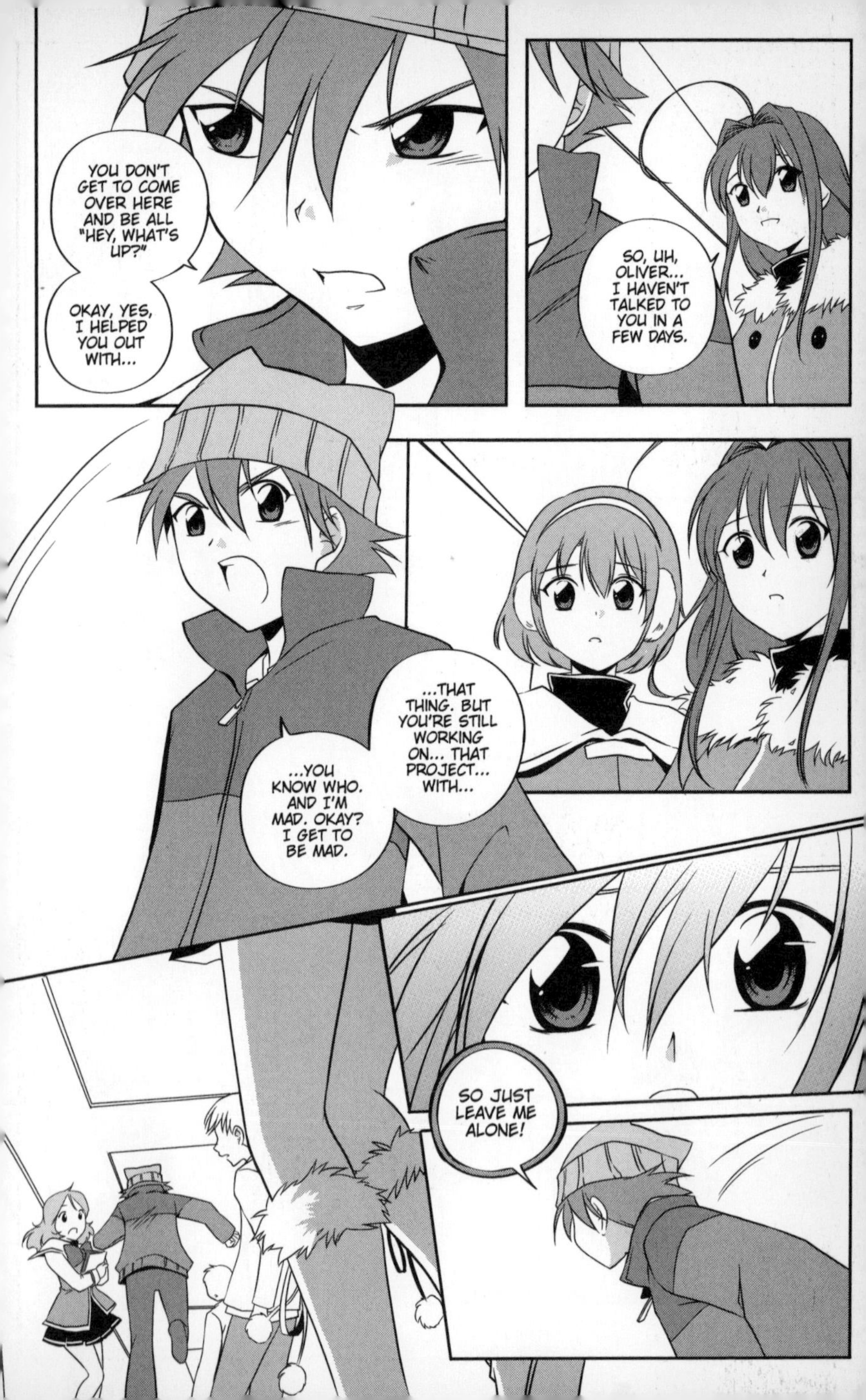
SO, UH, OLIVER... I HAVEN'T TALKED TO YOU IN A FEW DAYS.
YOU DON'T GET TO COME OVER HERE AND BE ALL "HEY, WHAT'S UP?"
OKAY, YES, I HELPED YOU OUT WITH...
...THAT THING. BUT YOU'RE STILL WORKING ON... THAT PROJECT... WITH...
...YOU KNOW WHO. AND I'M MAD. OKAY? I GET TO BE MAD.
SO JUST LEAVE ME ALONE!

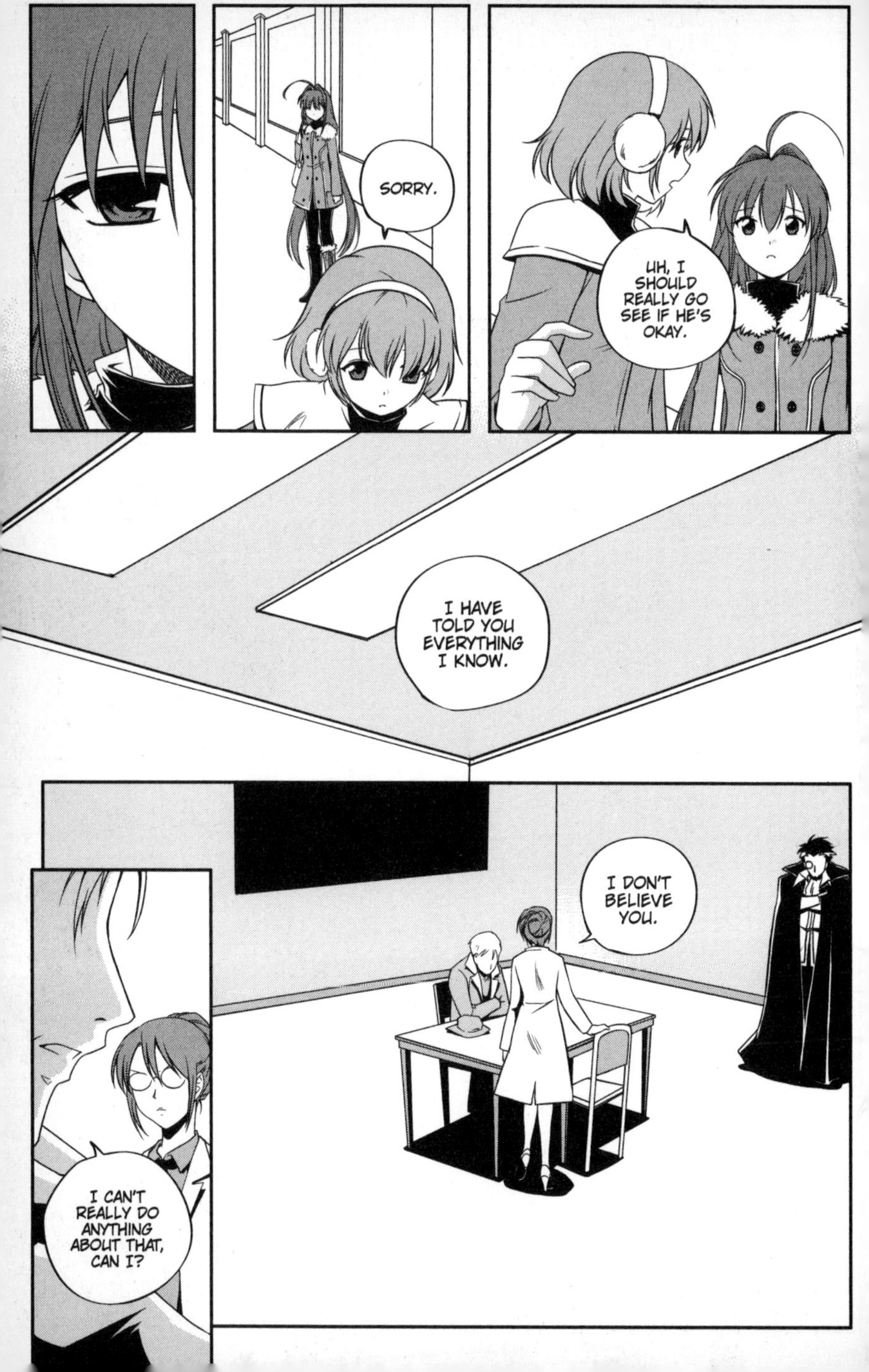
UH, I SHOULD REALLY GO SEE IF HE'S OKAY.
SORRY.
I HAVE TOLD YOU EVERYTHING I KNOW.
I DON'T BELIEVE YOU.
I CAN'T REALLY DO ANYTHING ABOUT THAT, CAN I?

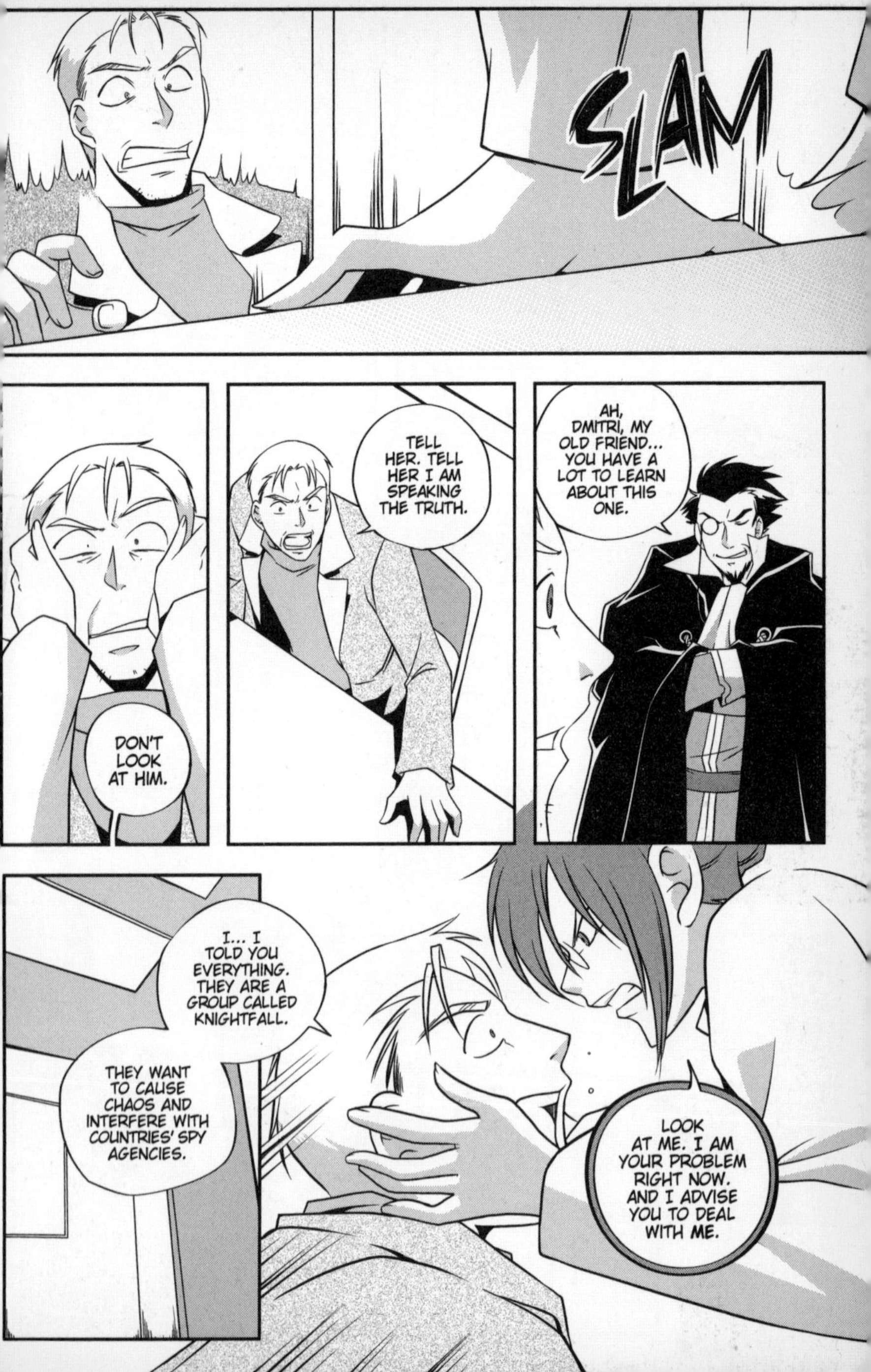
SLAM
AH, DMITRI, MY OLD FRIEND... YOU HAVE A LOT TO LEARN ABOUT THIS ONE.
TELL HER. TELL HER I AM SPEAKING THE TRUTH.
DON'T LOOK AT HIM.
I... I TOLD YOU EVERYTHING. THEY ARE A GROUP CALLED KNIGHTFALL.
THEY WANT TO CAUSE CHAOS AND INTERFERE WITH COUNTRIES' SPY AGENCIES.
LOOK AT ME. I AM YOUR PROBLEM RIGHT NOW. AND I ADVISE YOU TO DEAL WITH ME.

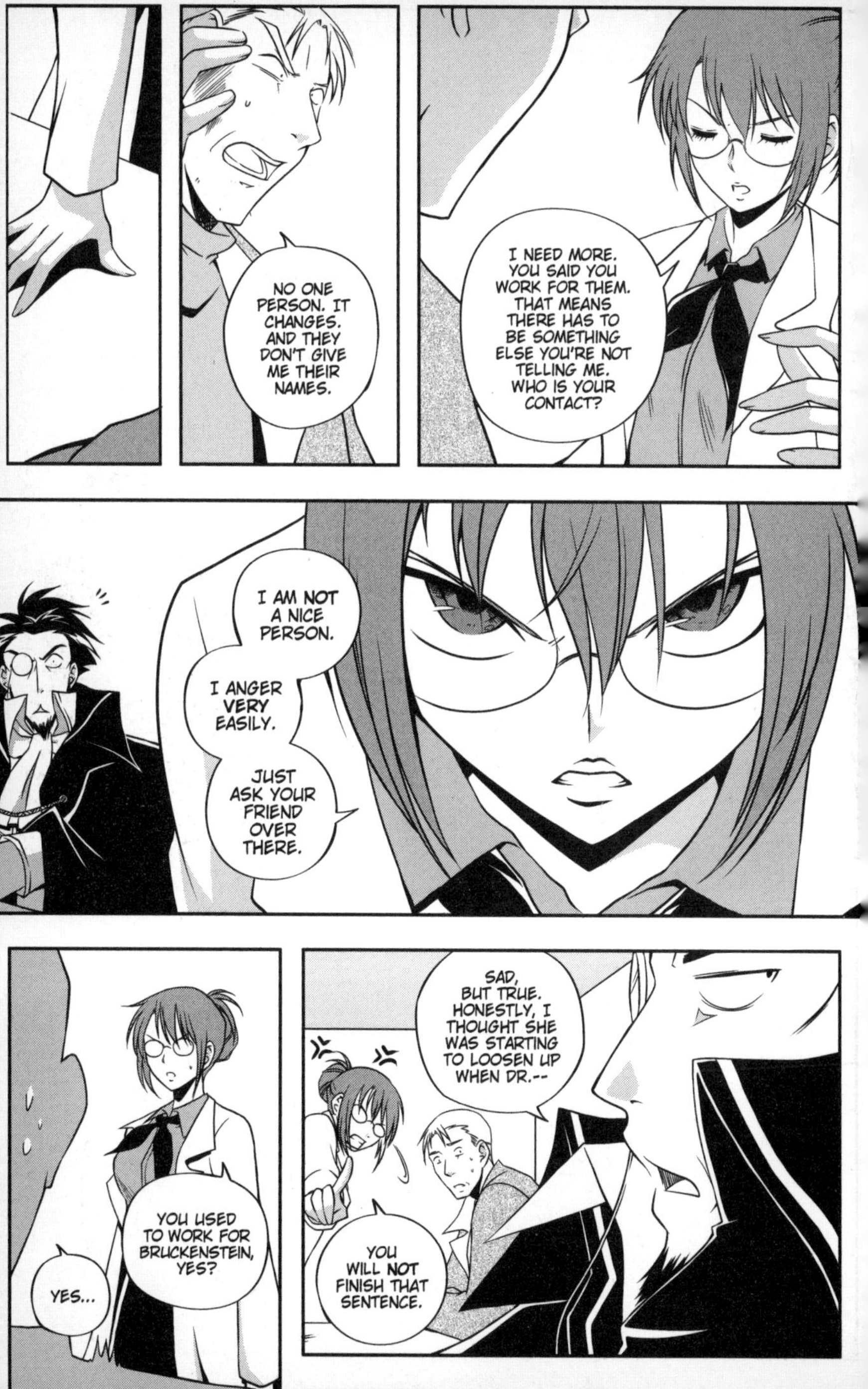
I NEED MORE. YOU SAID YOU WORK FOR THEM. THAT MEANS THERE HAS TO BE SOMETHING ELSE YOU'RE NOT TELLING ME. WHO IS YOUR CONTACT?
NO ONE PERSON. IT CHANGES. AND THEY DON'T GIVE ME THEIR NAMES.
I AM NOT A NICE PERSON.
I ANGER VERY EASILY.
JUST ASK YOUR FRIEND OVER THERE.
SAD, BUT TRUE. HONESTLY, I THOUGHT SHE WAS STARTING TO LOOSEN UP WHEN DR.--
YOU WILL NOT FINISH THAT SENTENCE.
YOU USED TO WORK FOR BRUCKENSTEIN, YES?
YES...

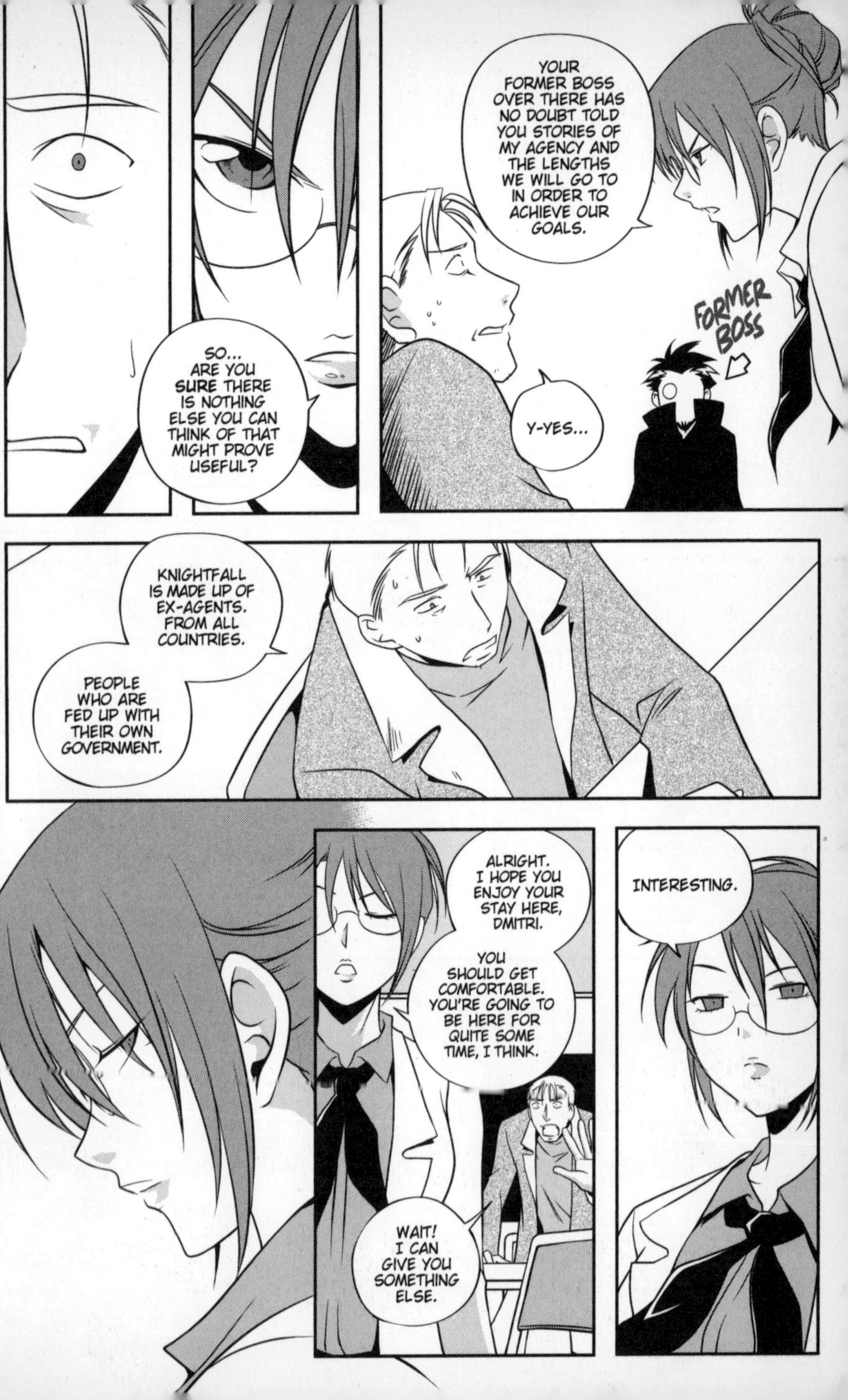
YOUR FORMER BOSS OVER THERE HAS NO DOUBT TOLD YOU STORIES OF MY AGENCY AND THE LENGTHS WE WILL GO TO IN ORDER TO ACHIEVE OUR GOALS.
FORMER BOSS
Y-YES...
SO... ARE YOU SURE THERE IS NOTHING ELSE YOU CAN THINK OF THAT MIGHT PROVE USEFUL?
KNIGHTFALL IS MADE UP OF EX-AGENTS. FROM ALL COUNTRIES.
PEOPLE WHO ARE FED UP WITH THEIR OWN GOVERNMENT.
INTERESTING.
ALRIGHT. I HOPE YOU ENJOY YOUR STAY HERE, DMITRI.
YOU SHOULD GET COMFORTABLE. YOU'RE GOING TO BE HERE FOR QUITE SOME TIME, I THINK.
WAIT! I CAN GIVE YOU SOMETHING ELSE.

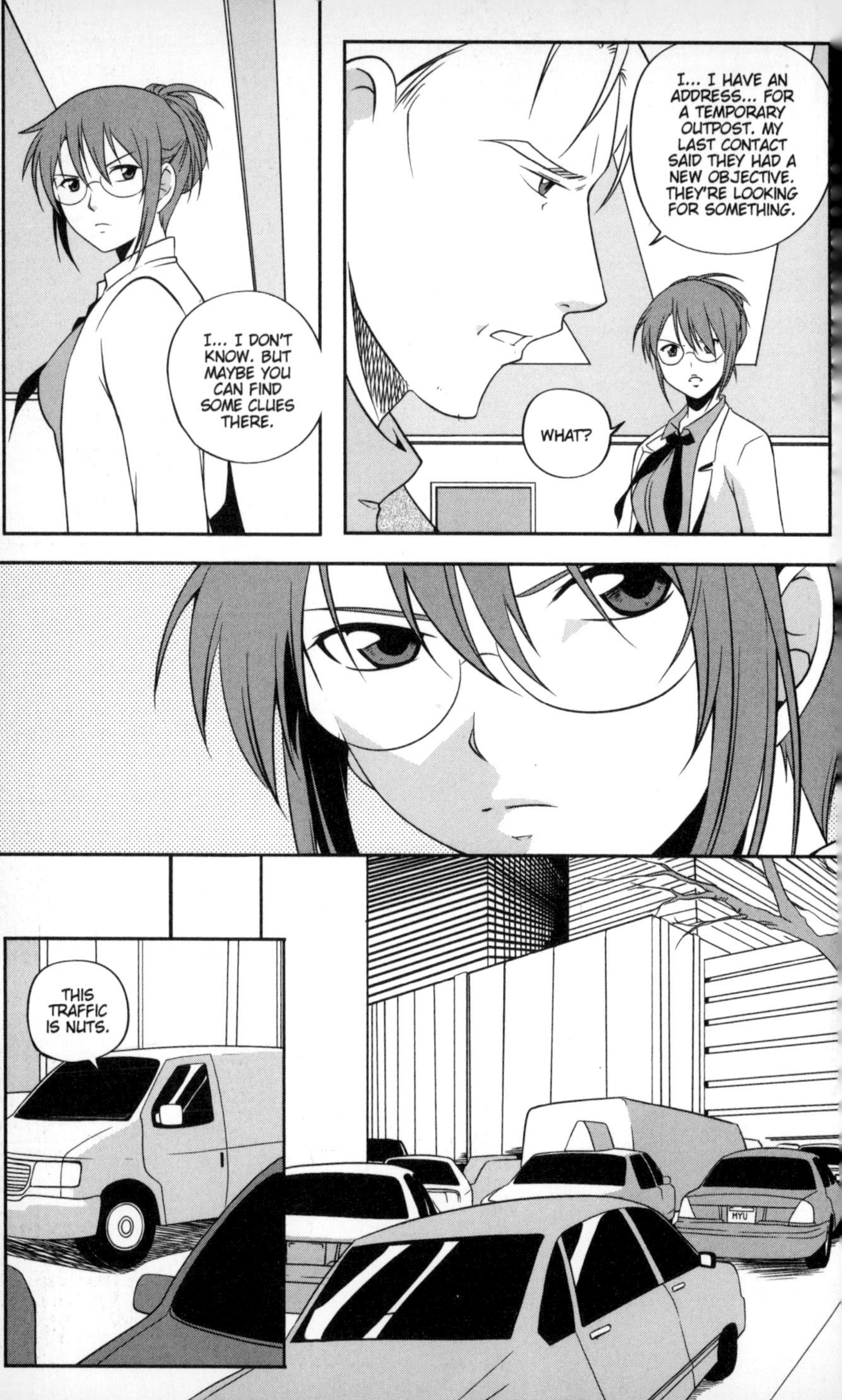
I... I HAVE AN ADDRESS... FOR A TEMPORARY OUTPOST. MY LAST CONTACT SAID THEY HAD A NEW OBJECTIVE. THEY'RE LOOKING FOR SOMETHING.
WHAT?
I... I DON'T KNOW. BUT MAYBE YOU CAN FIND SOME CLUES THERE.
MYU
THIS TRAFFIC IS NUTS.

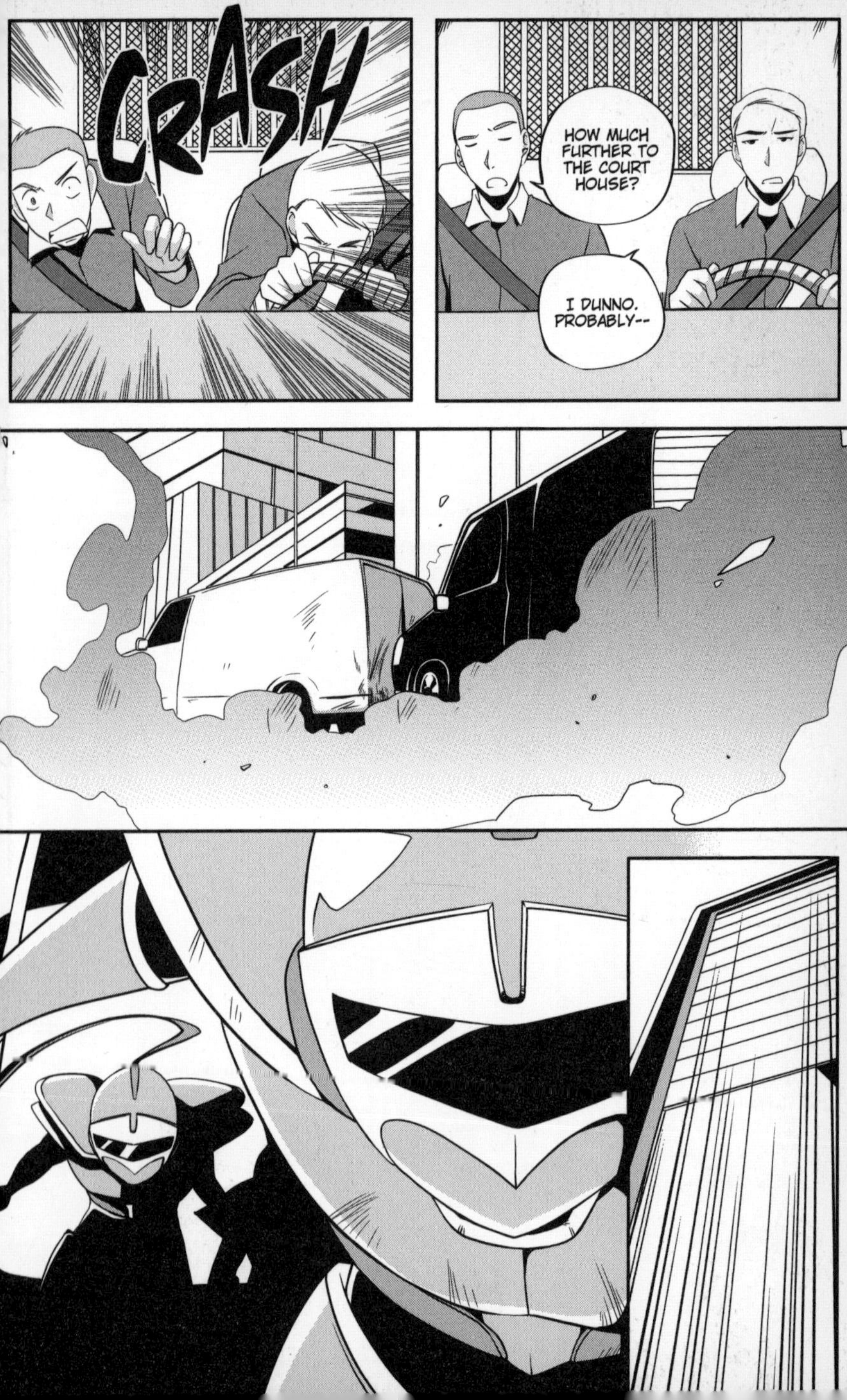
HOW MUCH FURTHER TO THE COURT HOUSE?
I DUNNO. PROBABLY--
CRASH

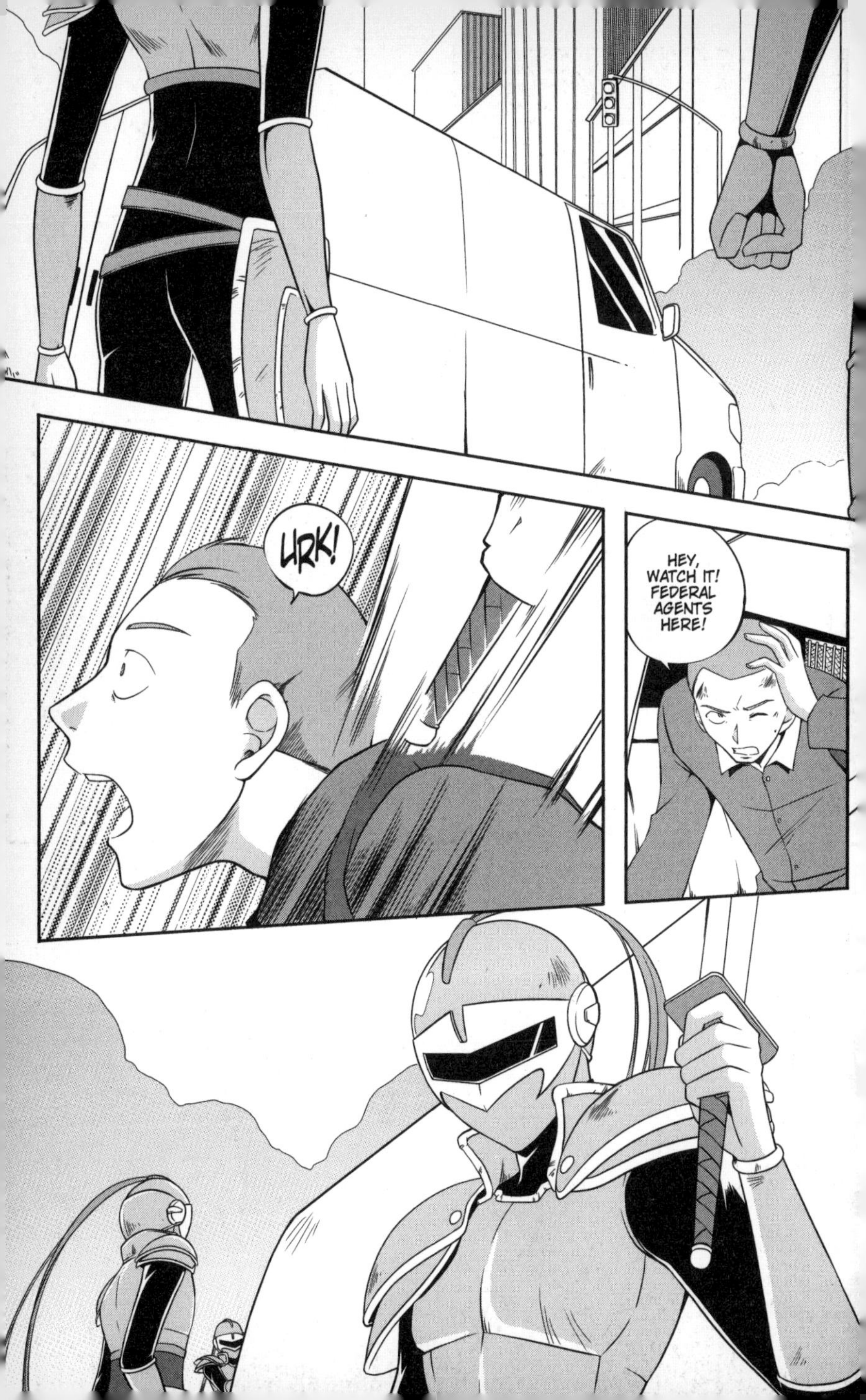
HEY, WATCH IT! FEDERAL AGENTS HERE!
URK!

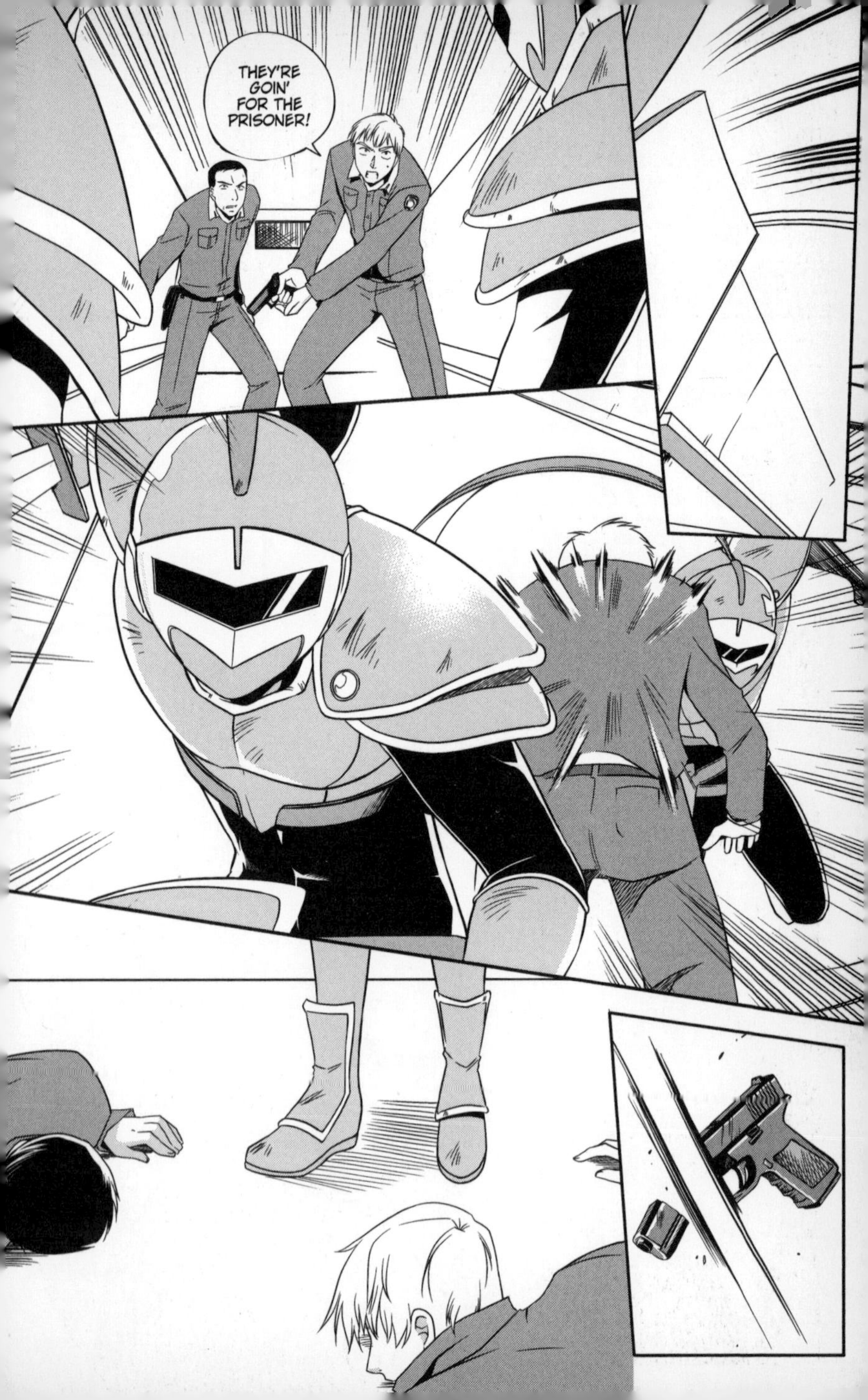
THEY'RE GOIN' FOR THE PRISONER!

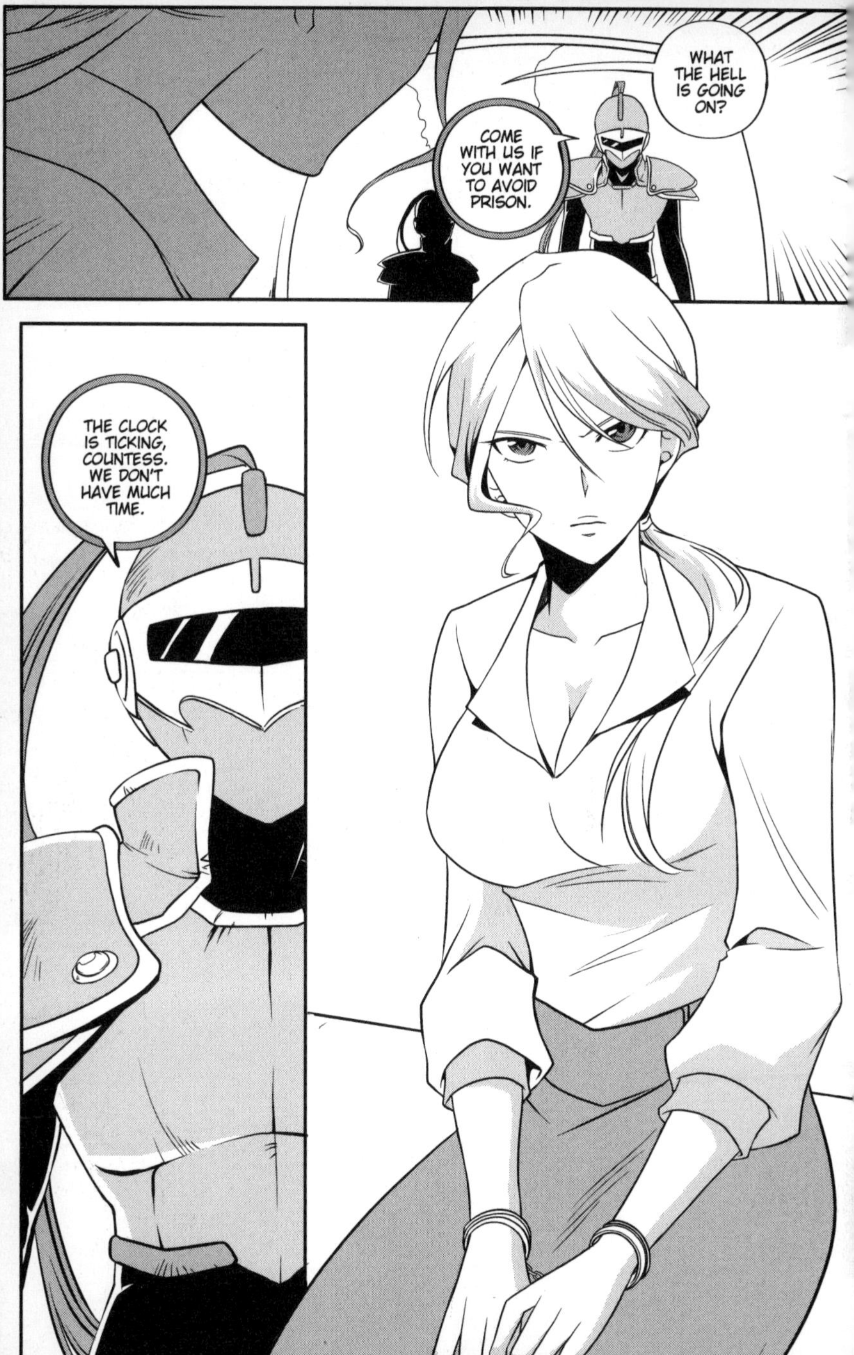
WHAT THE HELL IS GOING ON?
COME WITH US IF YOU WANT TO AVOID PRISON.
THE CLOCK IS TICKING, COUNTESS. WE DON'T HAVE MUCH TIME.

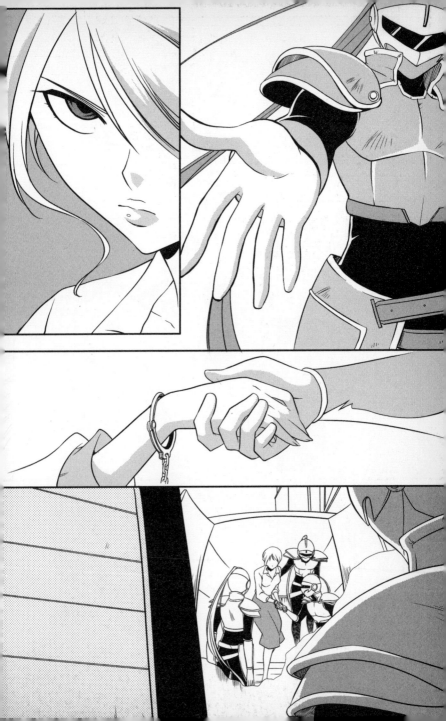

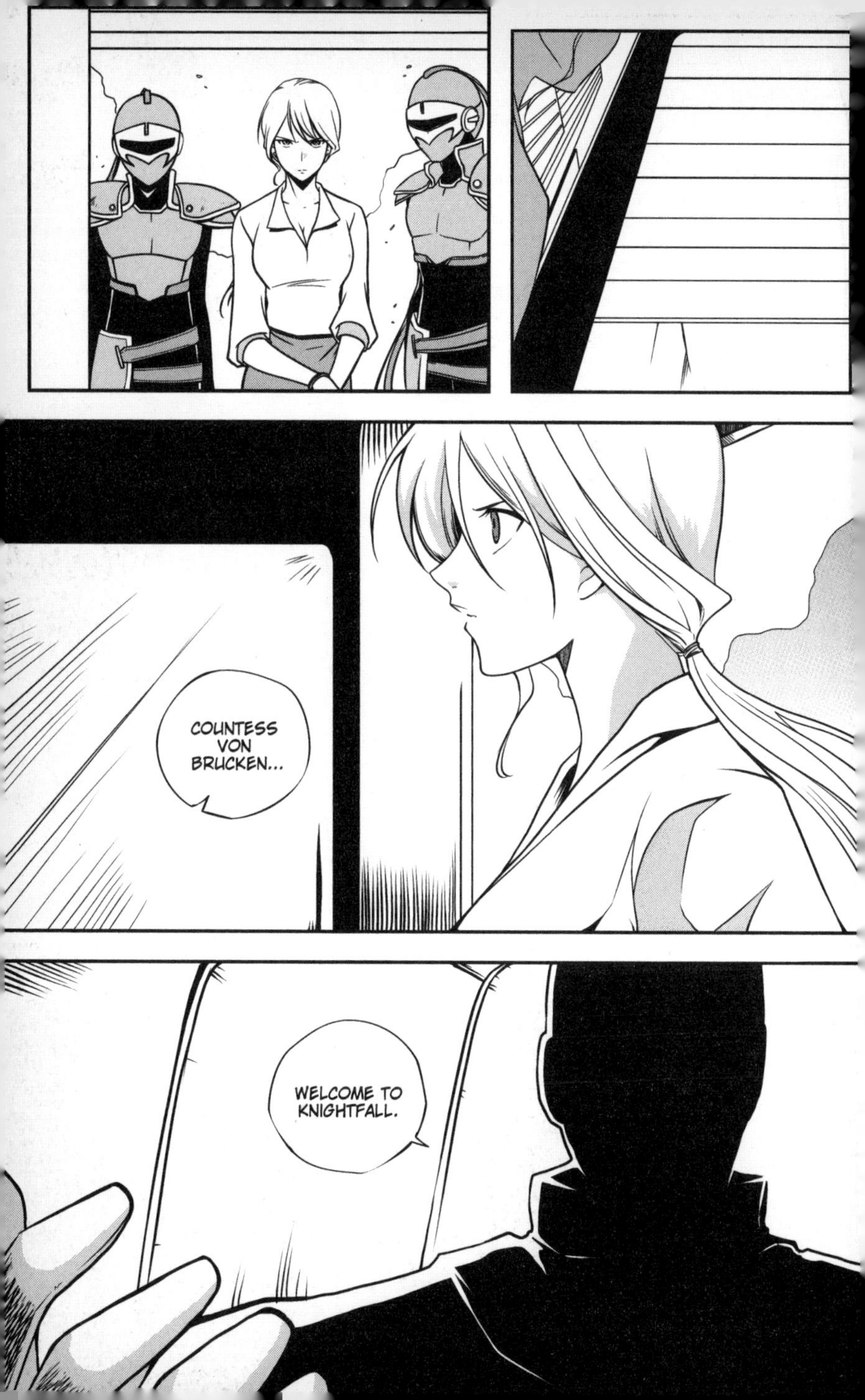
COUNTESS VON BRUCKEN...
WELCOME TO KNIGHTFALL.

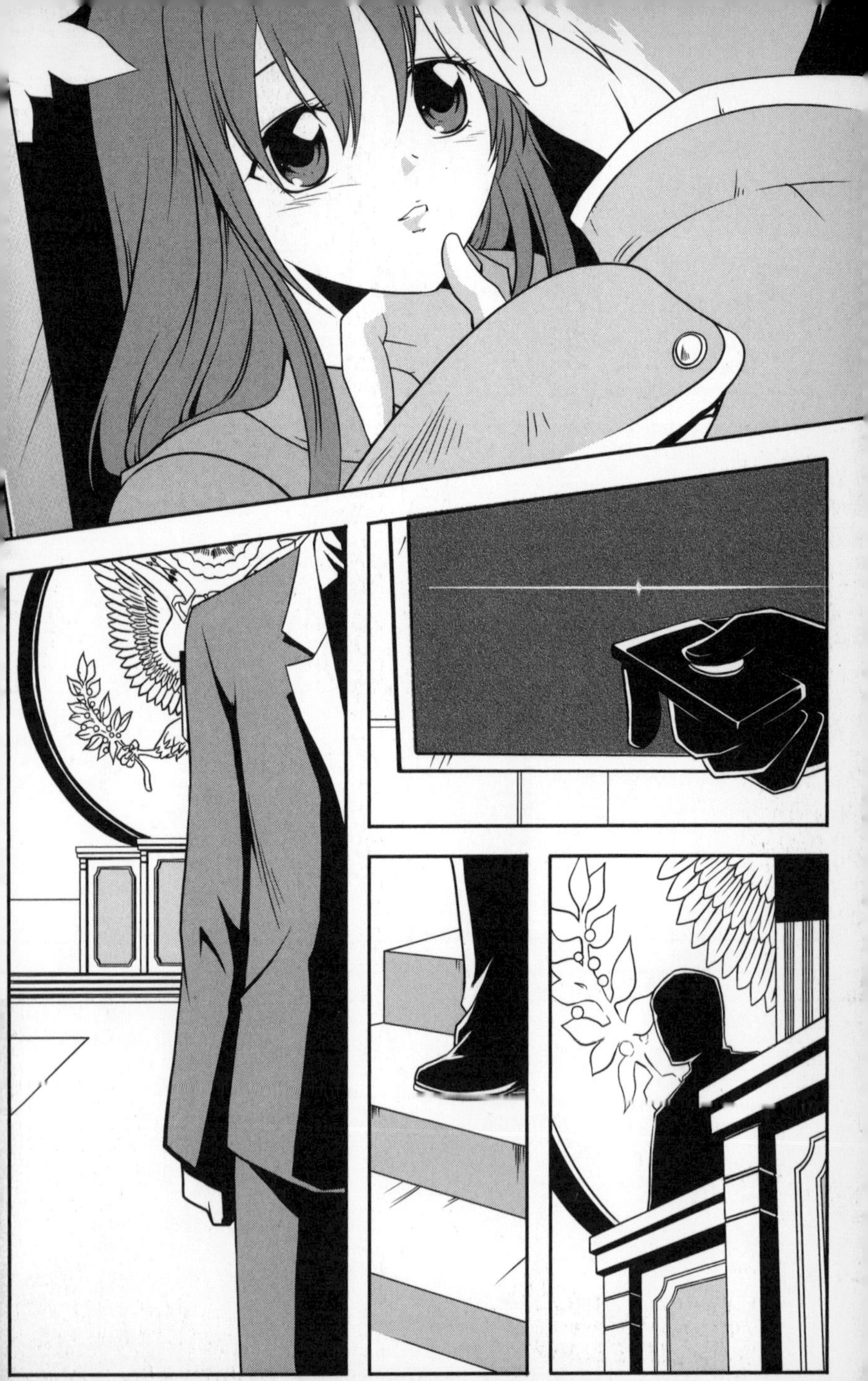

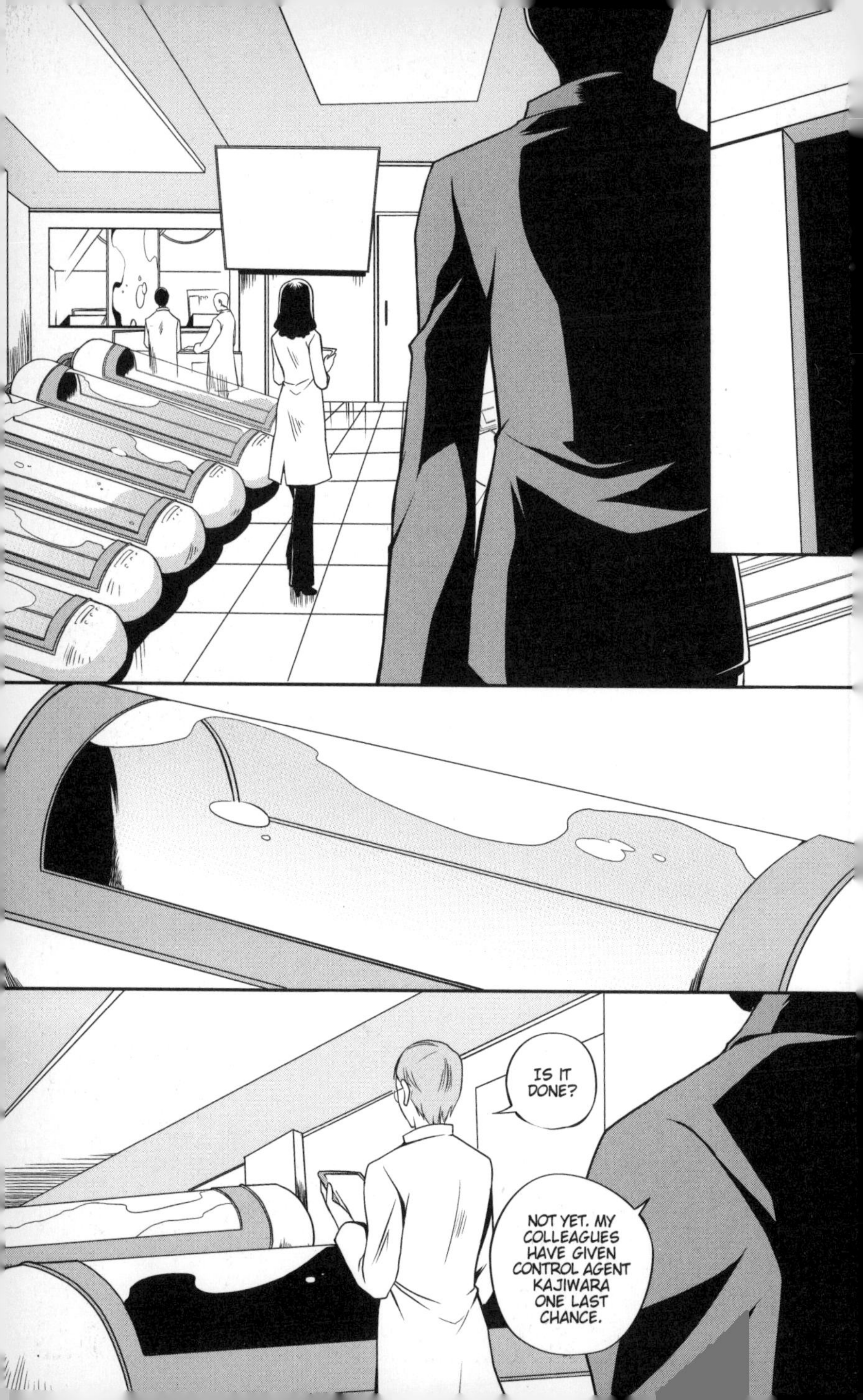
IS IT DONE?
NOT YET. MY COLLEAGUES HAVE GIVEN CONTROL AGENT KAJIWARA ONE LAST CHANCE.

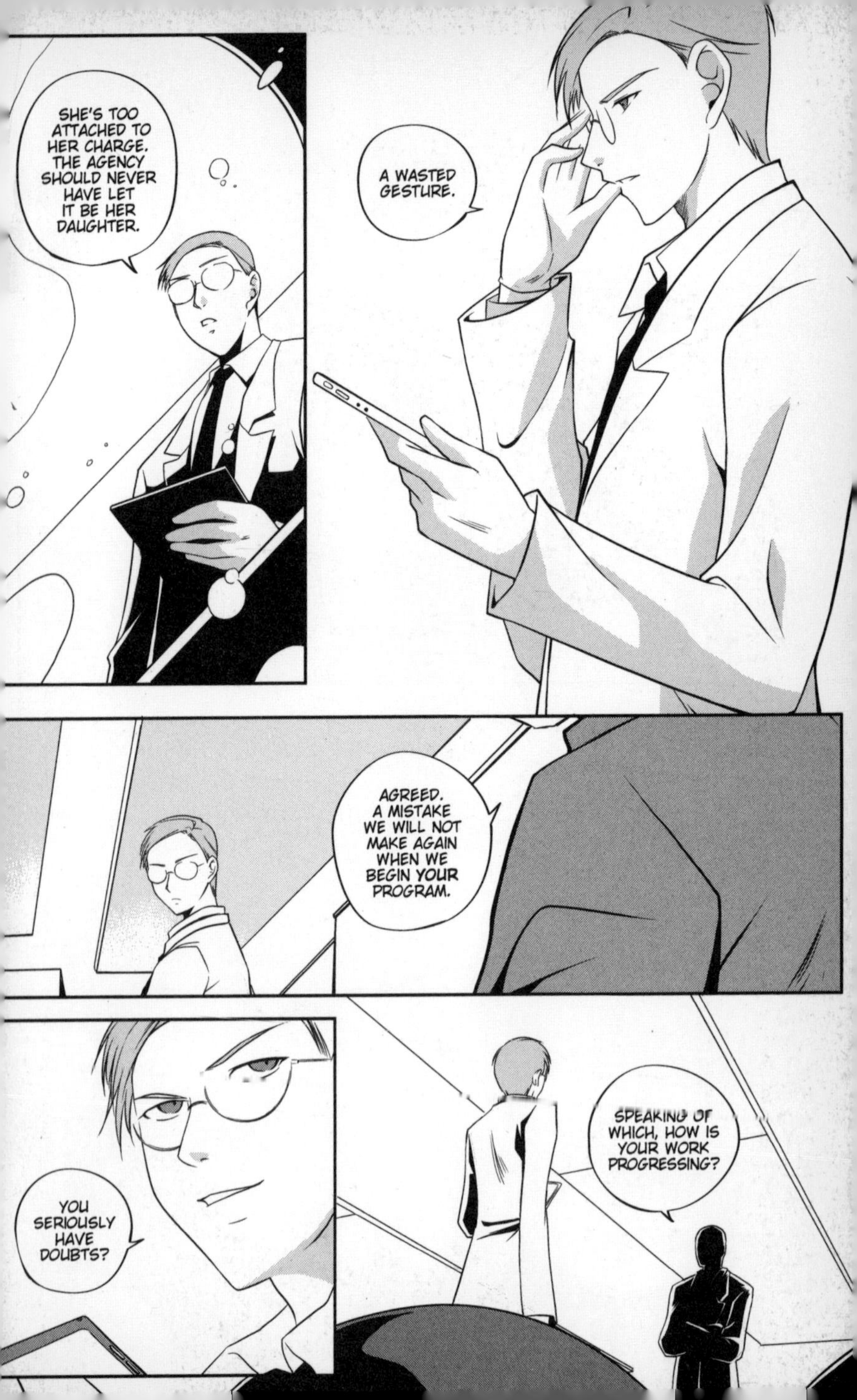
A WASTED GESTURE.
SHE'S TOO ATTACHED TO HER CHARGE. THE AGENCY SHOULD NEVER HAVE LET IT BE HER DAUGHTER.
AGREED. A MISTAKE WE WILL NOT MAKE AGAIN WHEN WE BEGIN YOUR PROGRAM.
SPEAKING OF WHICH, HOW IS YOUR WORK PROGRESSING?
YOU SERIOUSLY HAVE DOUBTS?

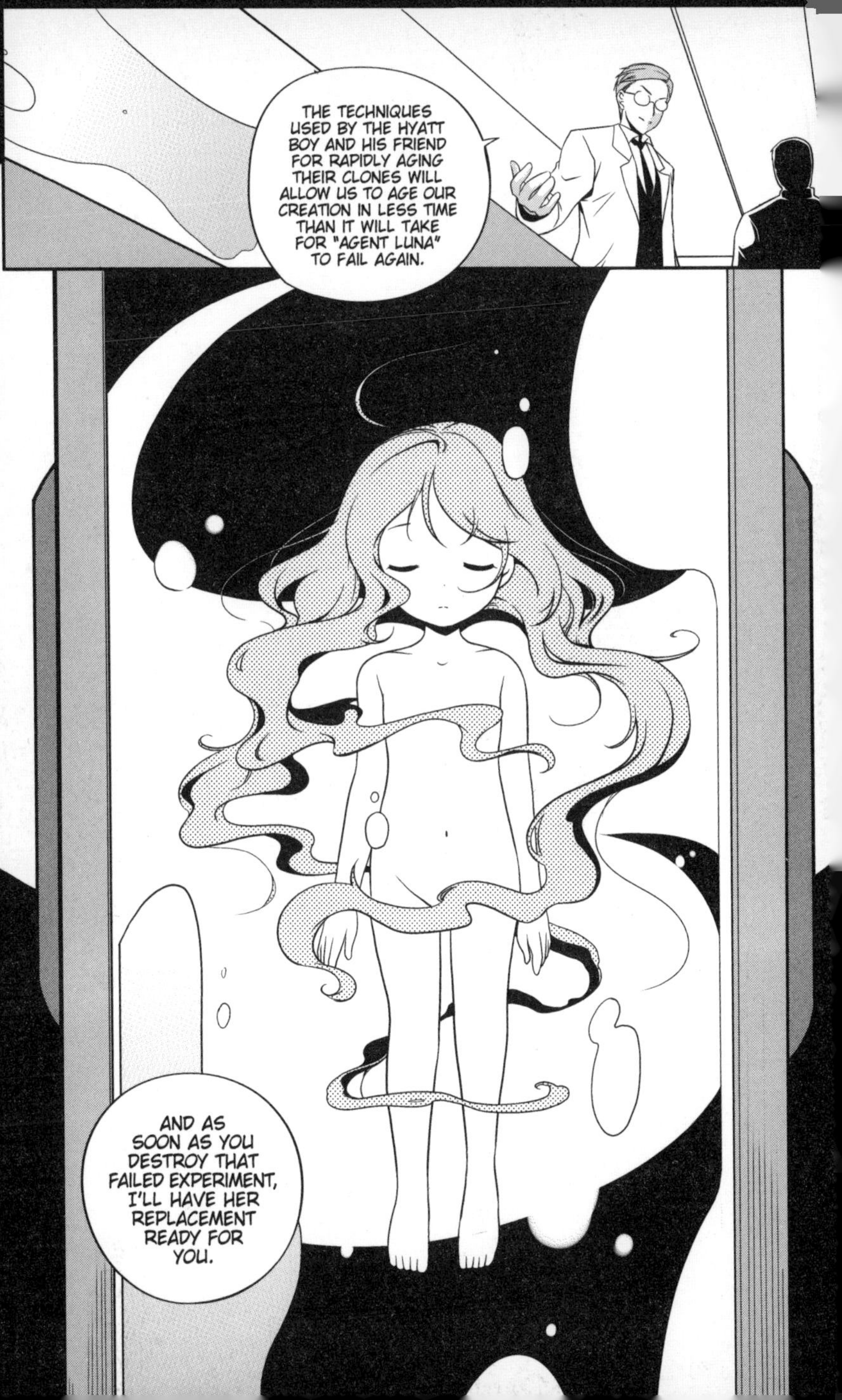
THE TECHNIQUES USED BY THE HYATT BOY AND HIS FRIEND FOR RAPIDLY AGING THEIR CLONES WILL ALLOW US TO AGE OUR CREATION IN LESS TIME THAN IT WILL TAKE FOR "AGENT LUNA" TO FAIL AGAIN.
AND AS SOON AS YOU DESTROY THAT FAILED EXPERIMENT, I'LL HAVE HER REPLACEMENT READY FOR YOU.

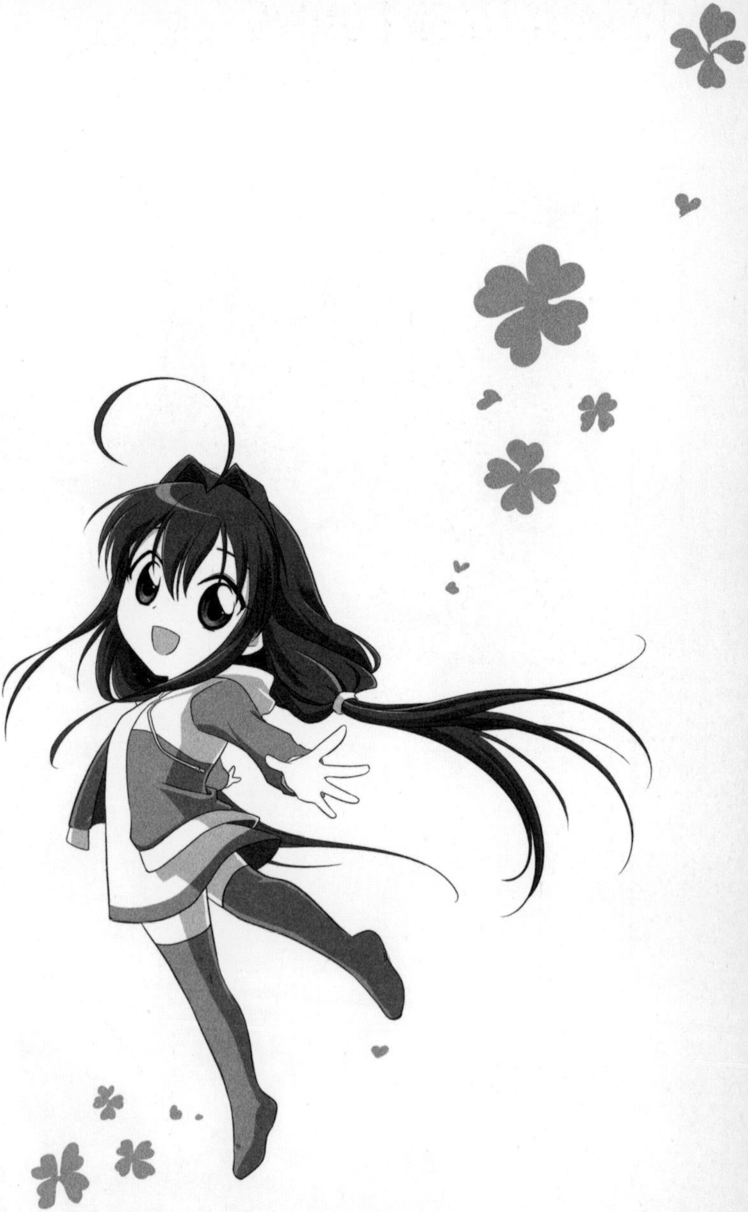

File 41
RECRUITMENT DRIVE

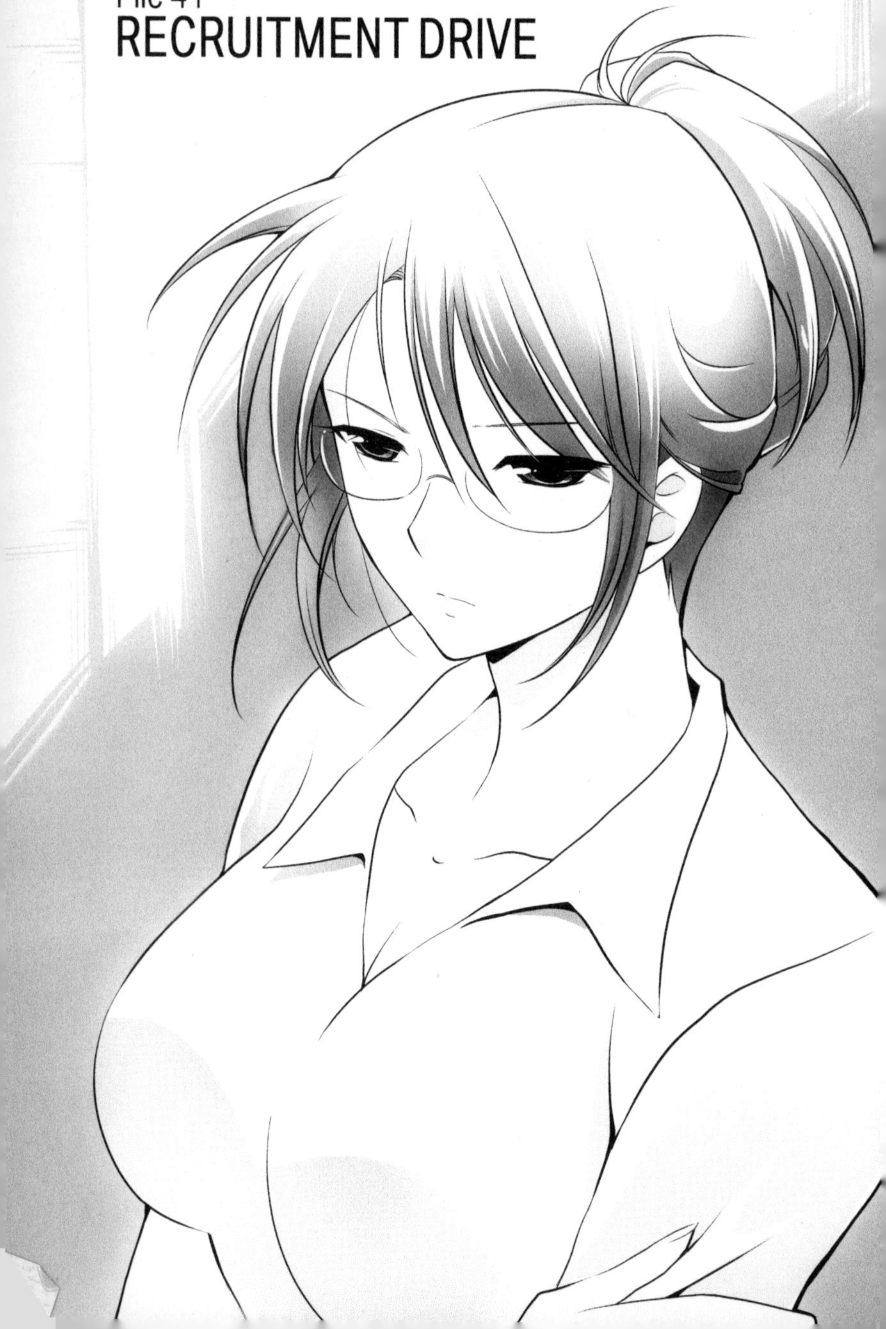

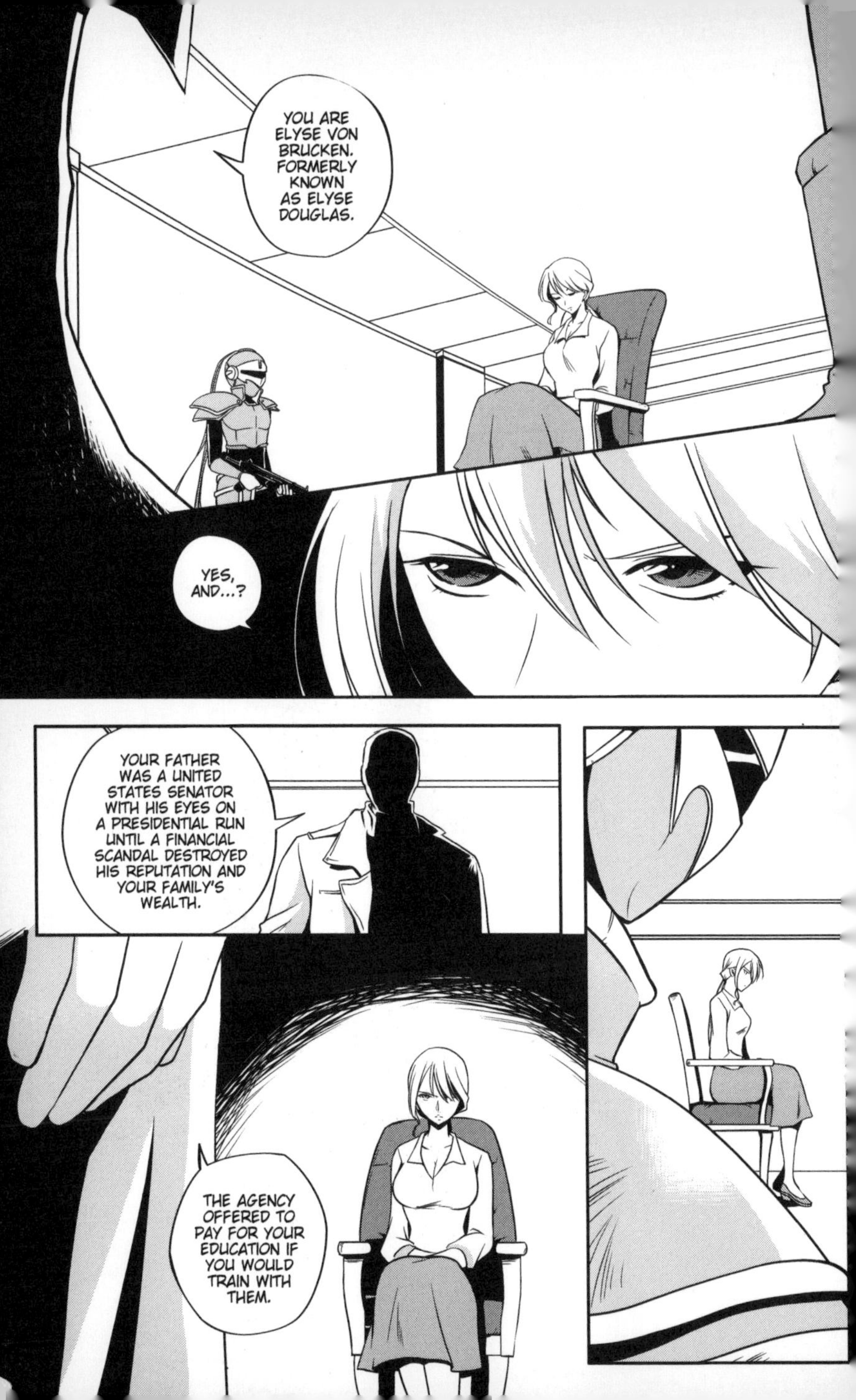
YOU ARE ELYSE VON BRUCKEN. FORMERLY KNOWN AS ELYSE DOUGLAS.
YES, AND...?
YOUR FATHER WAS A UNITED STATES SENATOR WITH HIS EYES ON A PRESIDENTIAL RUN UNTIL A FINANCIAL SCANDAL DESTROYED HIS REPUTATION AND YOUR FAMILY'S WEALTH.
THE AGENCY OFFERED TO PAY FOR YOUR EDUCATION IF YOU WOULD TRAIN WITH THEM.

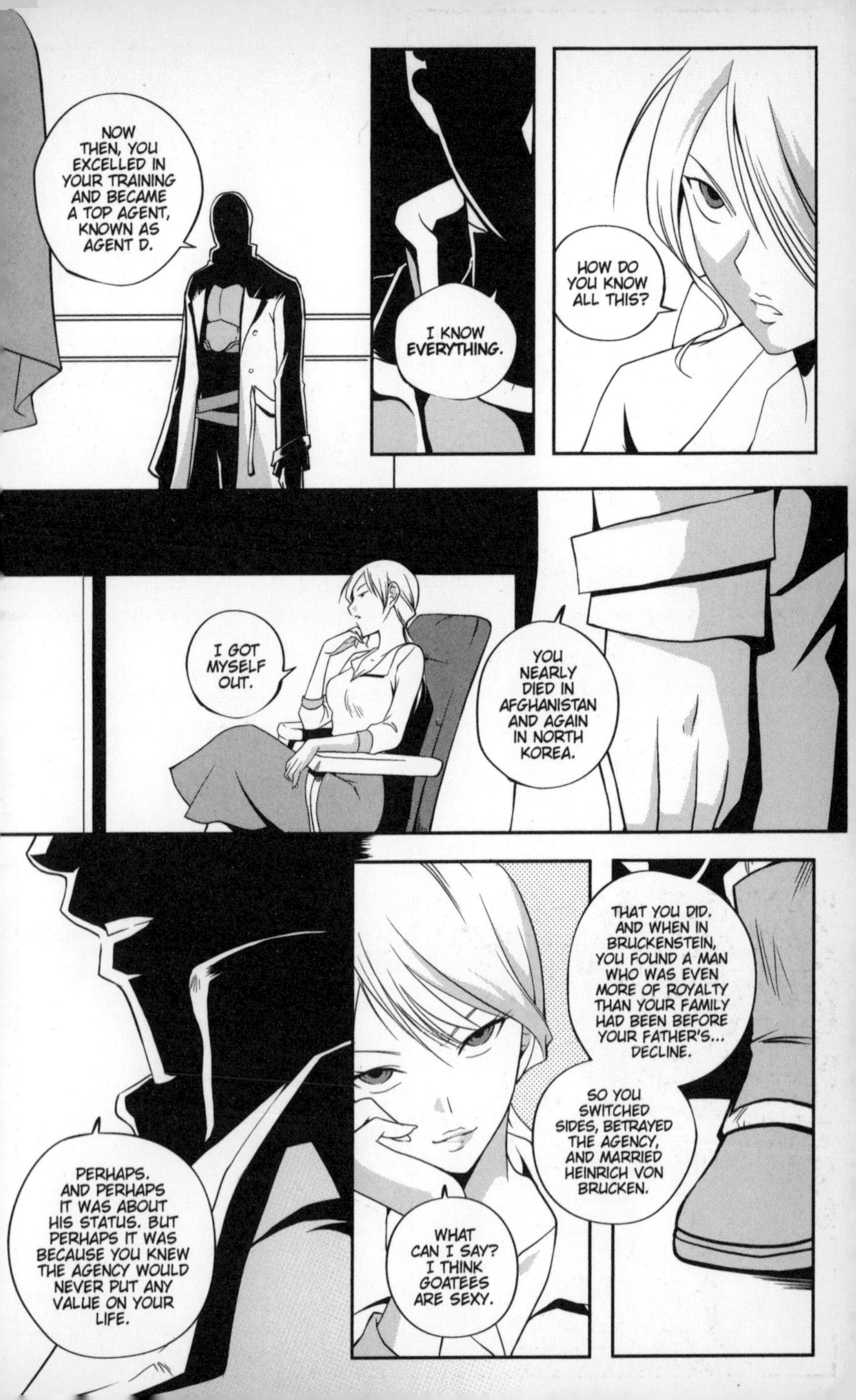
HOW DO YOU KNOW ALL THIS?
I KNOW EVERYTHING.
NOW THEN, YOU EXCELLED IN YOUR TRAINING AND BECAME A TOP AGENT, KNOWN AS AGENT D.
YOU NEARLY DIED IN AFGHANISTAN AND AGAIN IN NORTH KOREA.
I GOT MYSELF OUT.
THAT YOU DID. AND WHEN IN BRUCKENSTEIN, YOU FOUND A MAN WHO WAS EVEN MORE OF ROYALTY THAN YOUR FAMILY HAD BEEN BEFORE YOUR FATHER'S... DECLINE.
SO YOU SWITCHED SIDES, BETRAYED THE AGENCY, AND MARRIED HEINRICH VON BRUCKEN.
WHAT CAN I SAY? I THINK GOATEES ARE SEXY.
PERHAPS. AND PERHAPS IT WAS ABOUT HIS STATUS. BUT PERHAPS IT WAS BECAUSE YOU KNEW THE AGENCY WOULD NEVER PUT ANY VALUE ON YOUR LIFE.

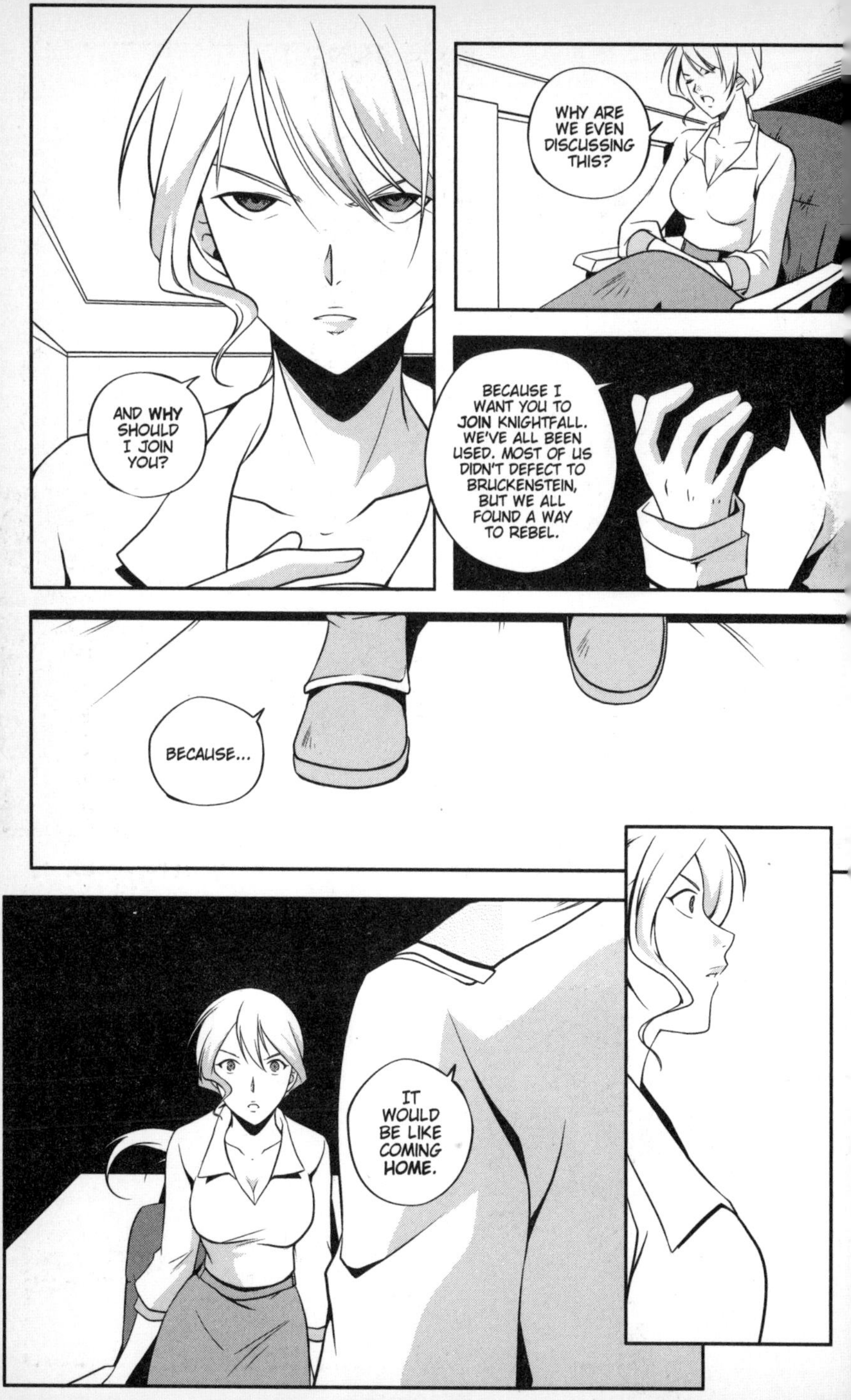
WHY ARE WE EVEN DISCUSSING THIS?
BECAUSE I WANT YOU TO JOIN KNIGHTFALL. WE'VE ALL BEEN USED. MOST OF US DIDN'T DEFECT TO BRUCKENSTEIN, BUT WE ALL FOUND A WAY TO REBEL.
AND WHY SHOULD I JOIN YOU?
BECAUSE...
IT WOULD BE LIKE COMING HOME.

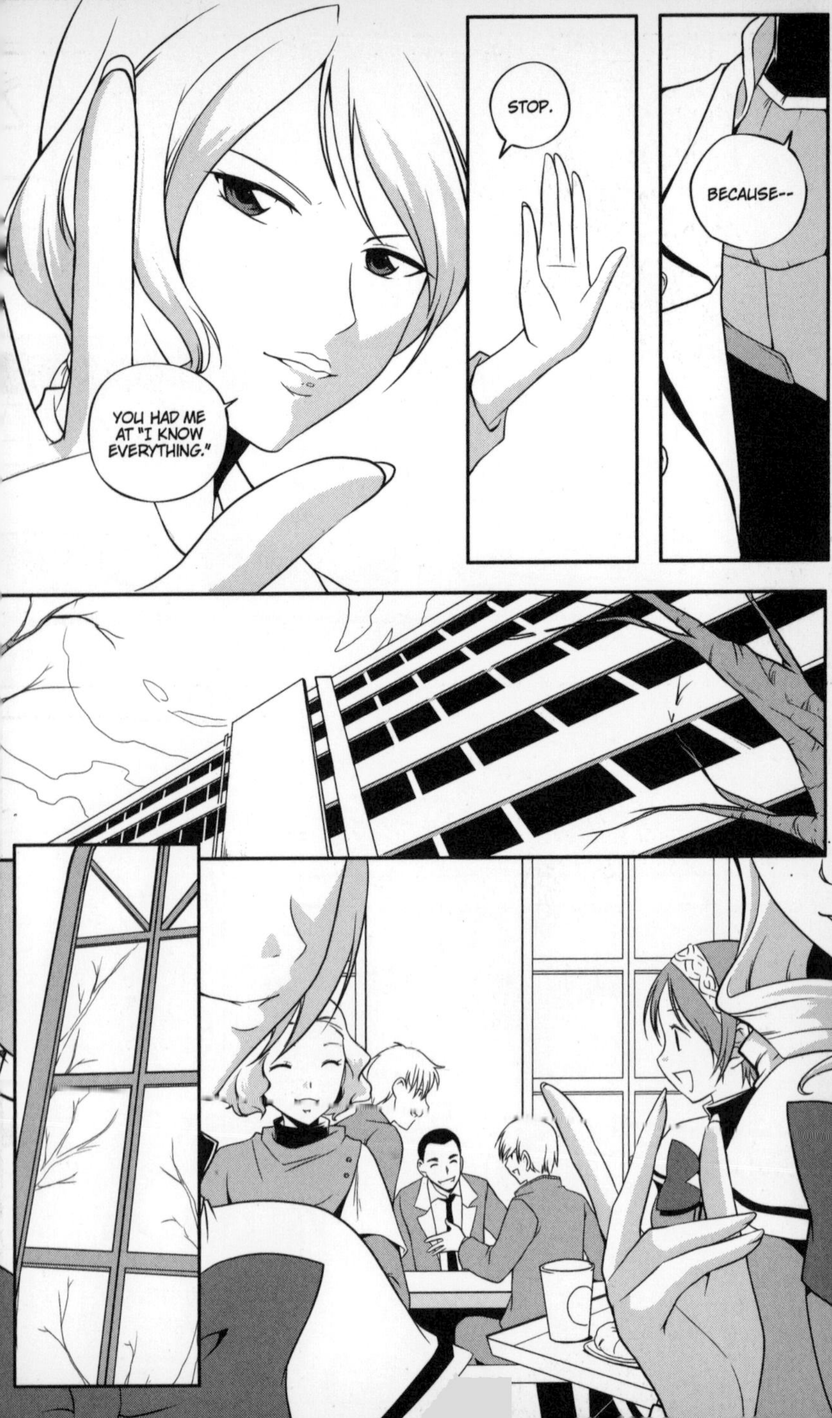
BECAUSE--
STOP.
YOU HAD ME AT "I KNOW EVERYTHING."

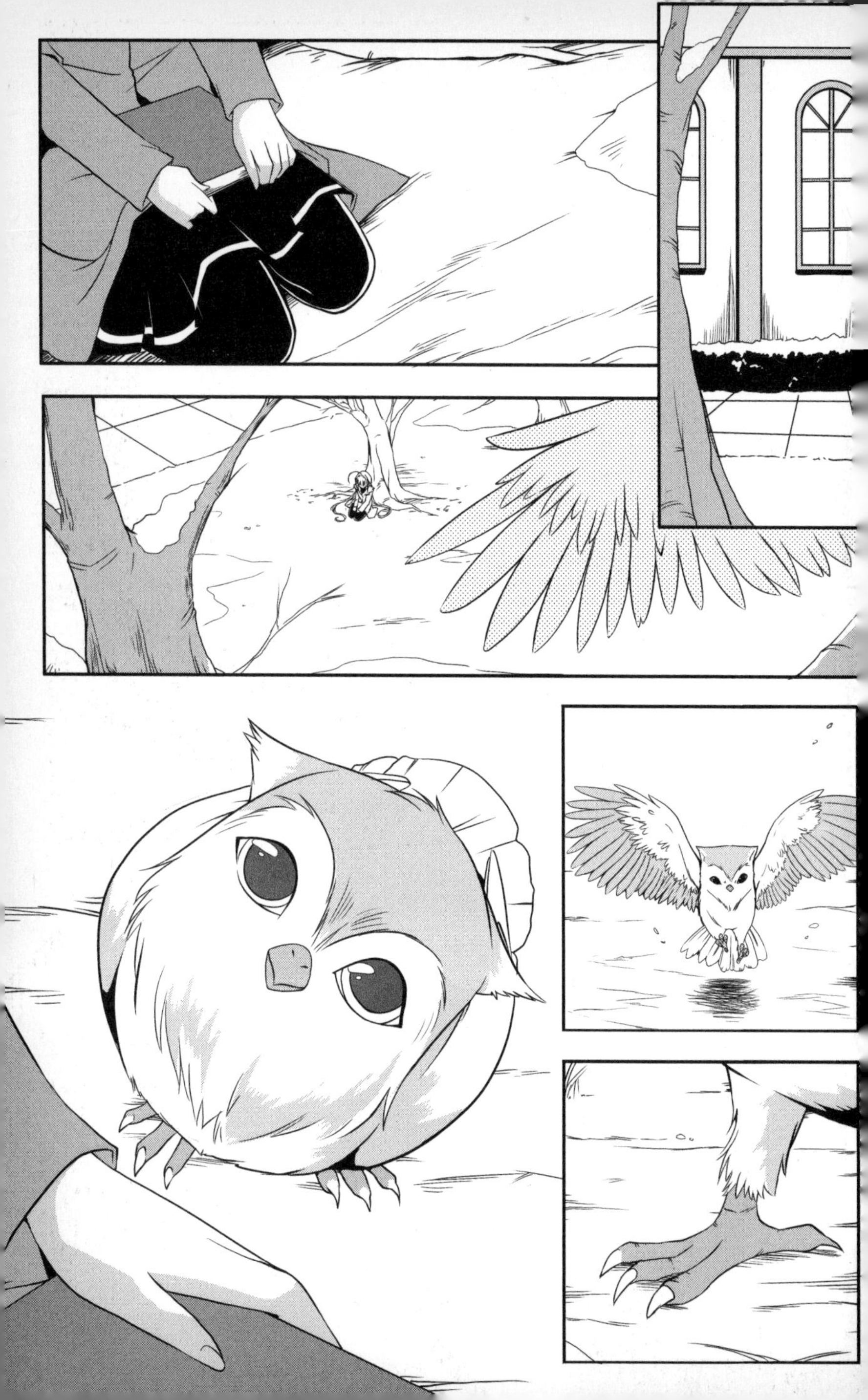

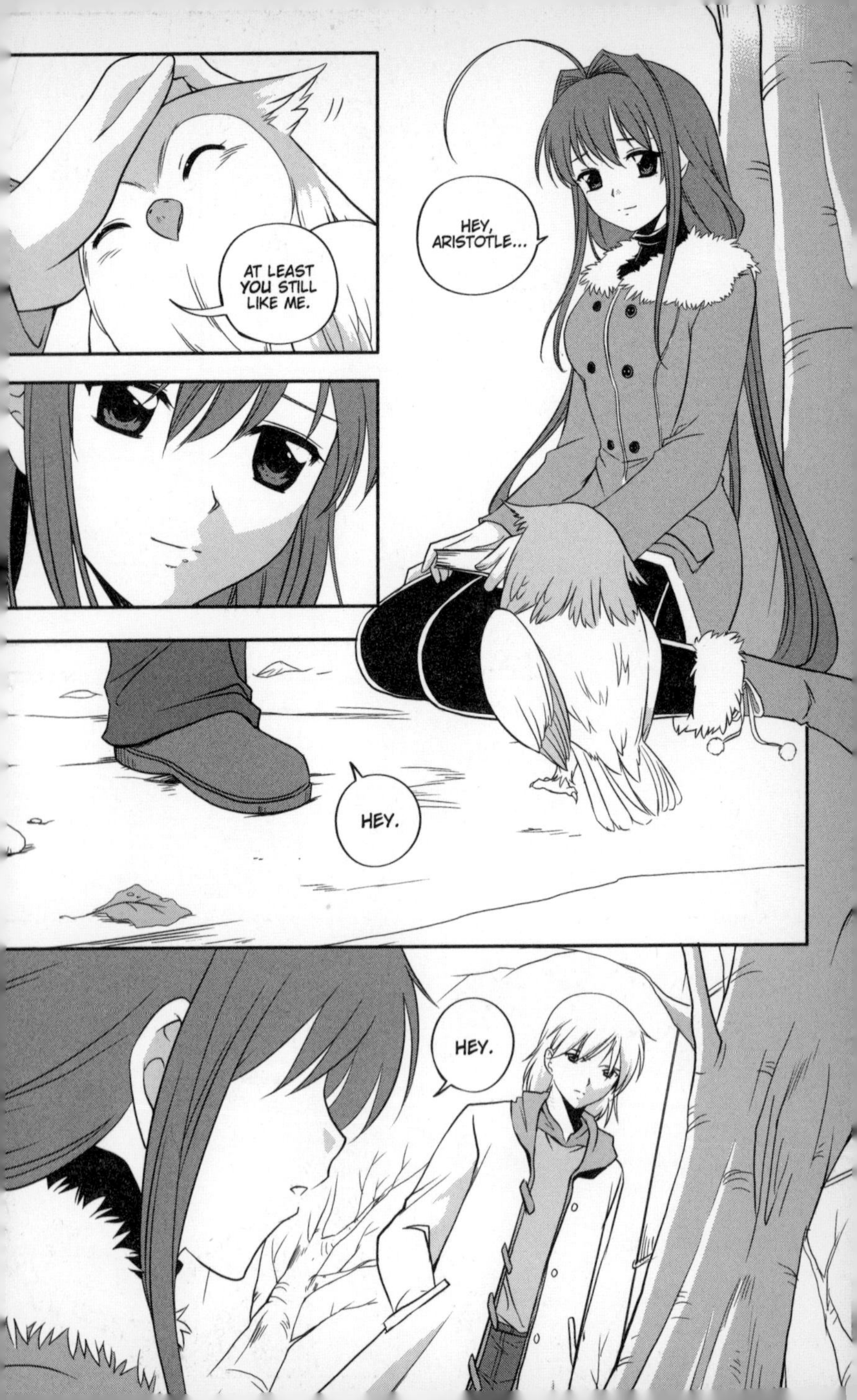
HEY, ARISTOTLE...
AT LEAST YOU STILL LIKE ME.
HEY.
HEY.

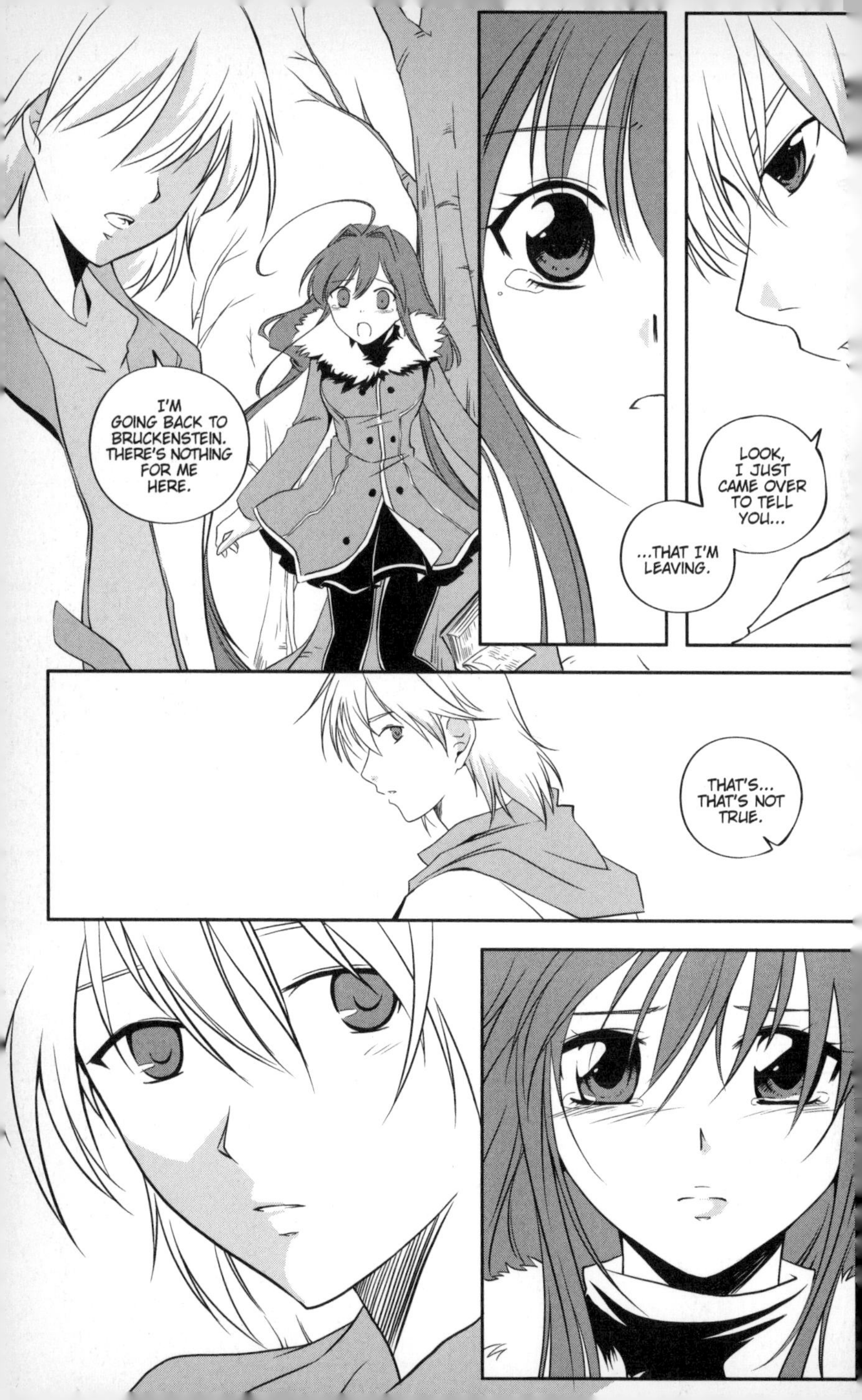
LOOK, I JUST CAME OVER TO TELL YOU...
...THAT I'M LEAVING.
I'M GOING BACK TO BRUCKENSTEIN. THERE'S NOTHING FOR ME HERE.
THAT'S... THAT'S NOT TRUE.

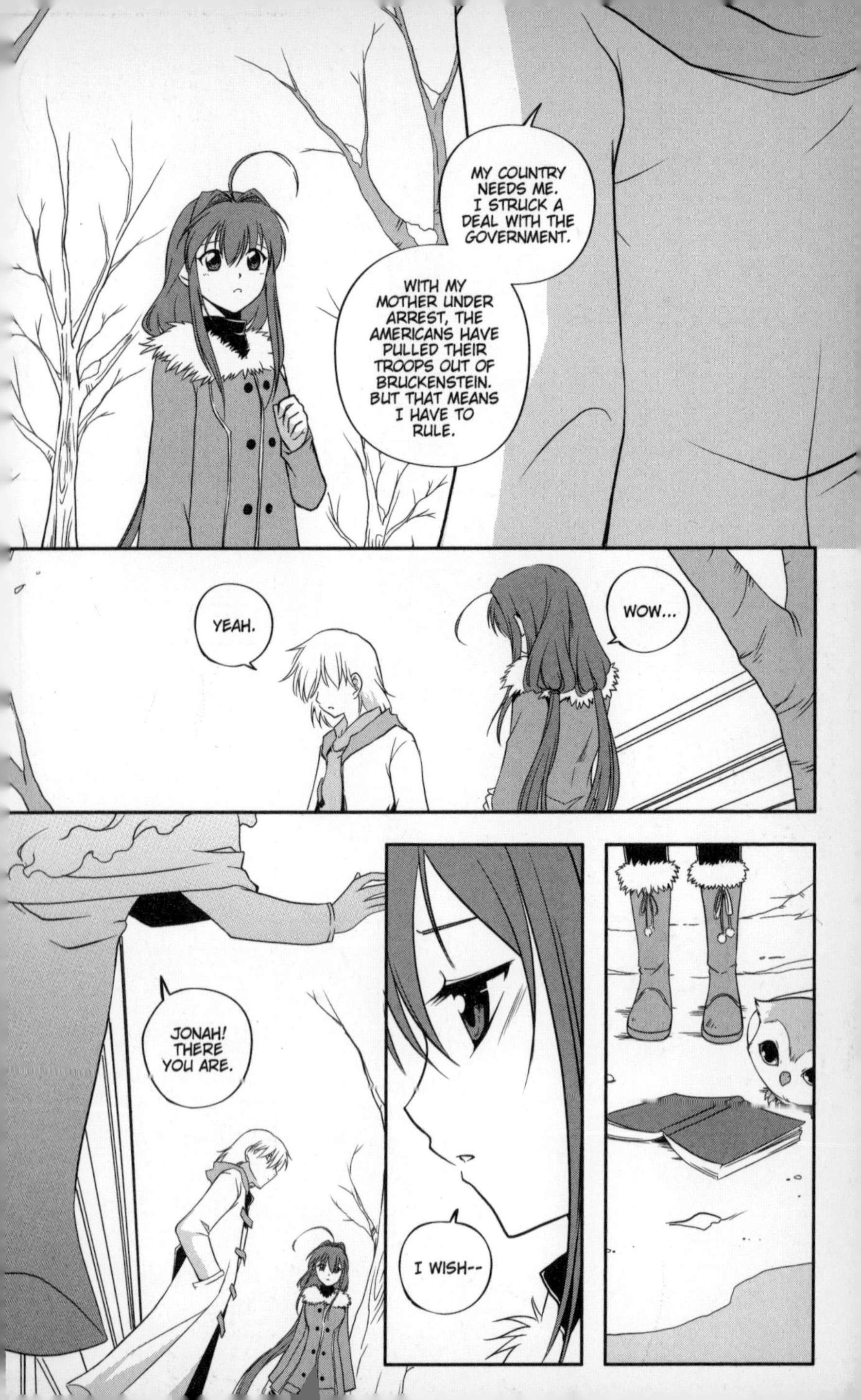
MY COUNTRY NEEDS ME. I STRUCK A DEAL WITH THE GOVERNMENT.
WITH MY MOTHER UNDER ARREST, THE AMERICANS HAVE PULLED THEIR TROOPS OUT OF BRUCKENSTEIN. BUT THAT MEANS I HAVE TO RULE.
WOW...
YEAH.
I WISH--
JONAH! THERE YOU ARE.

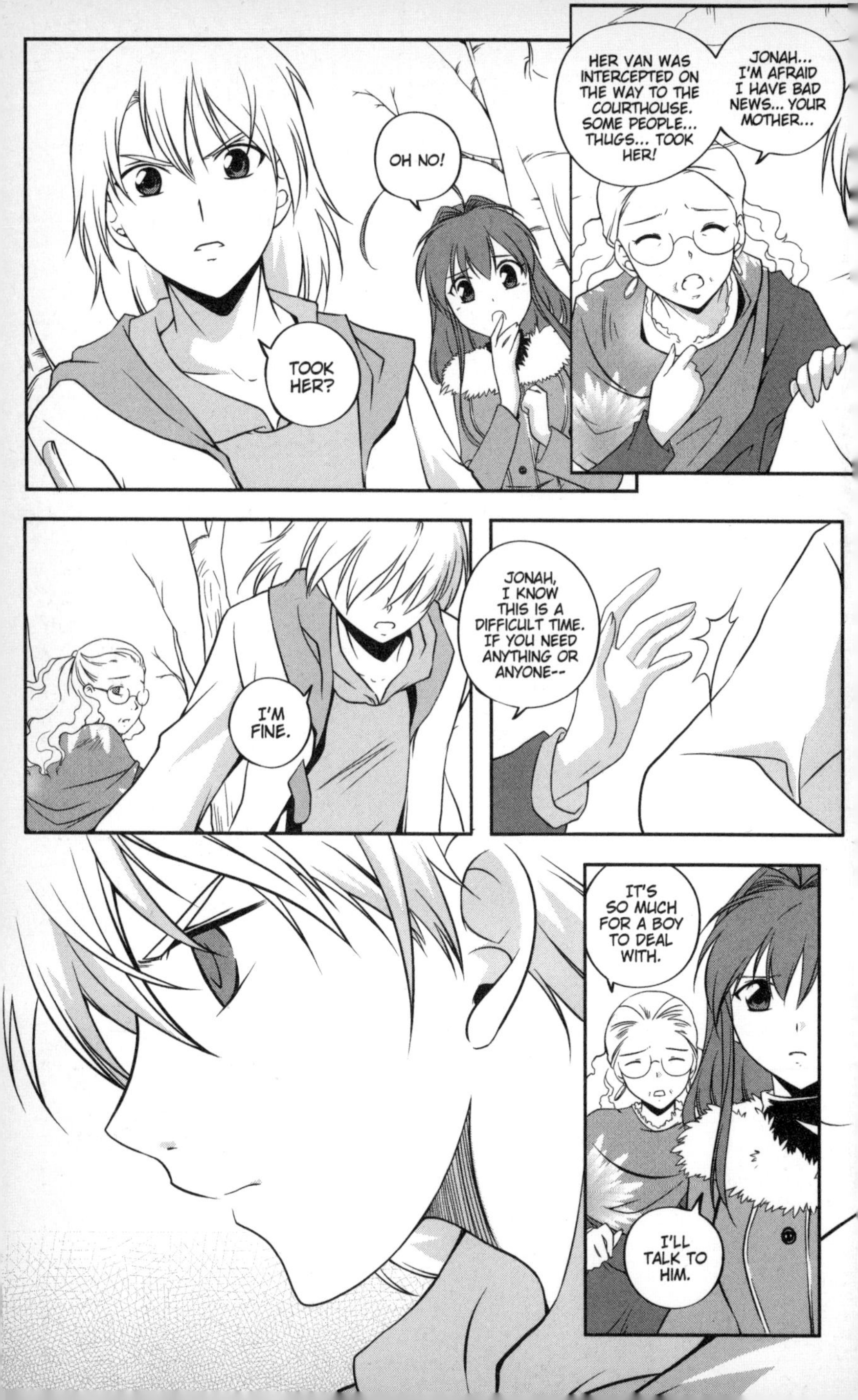
JONAH... I'M AFRAID I HAVE BAD NEWS... YOUR MOTHER...
HER VAN WAS INTERCEPTED ON THE WAY TO THE COURTHOUSE. SOME PEOPLE... THUGS... TOOK HER!
OH NO!
TOOK HER?
JONAH, I KNOW THIS IS A DIFFICULT TIME. IF YOU NEED ANYTHING OR ANYONE--
I'M FINE.
IT'S SO MUCH FOR A BOY TO DEAL WITH.
I'LL TALK TO HIM.

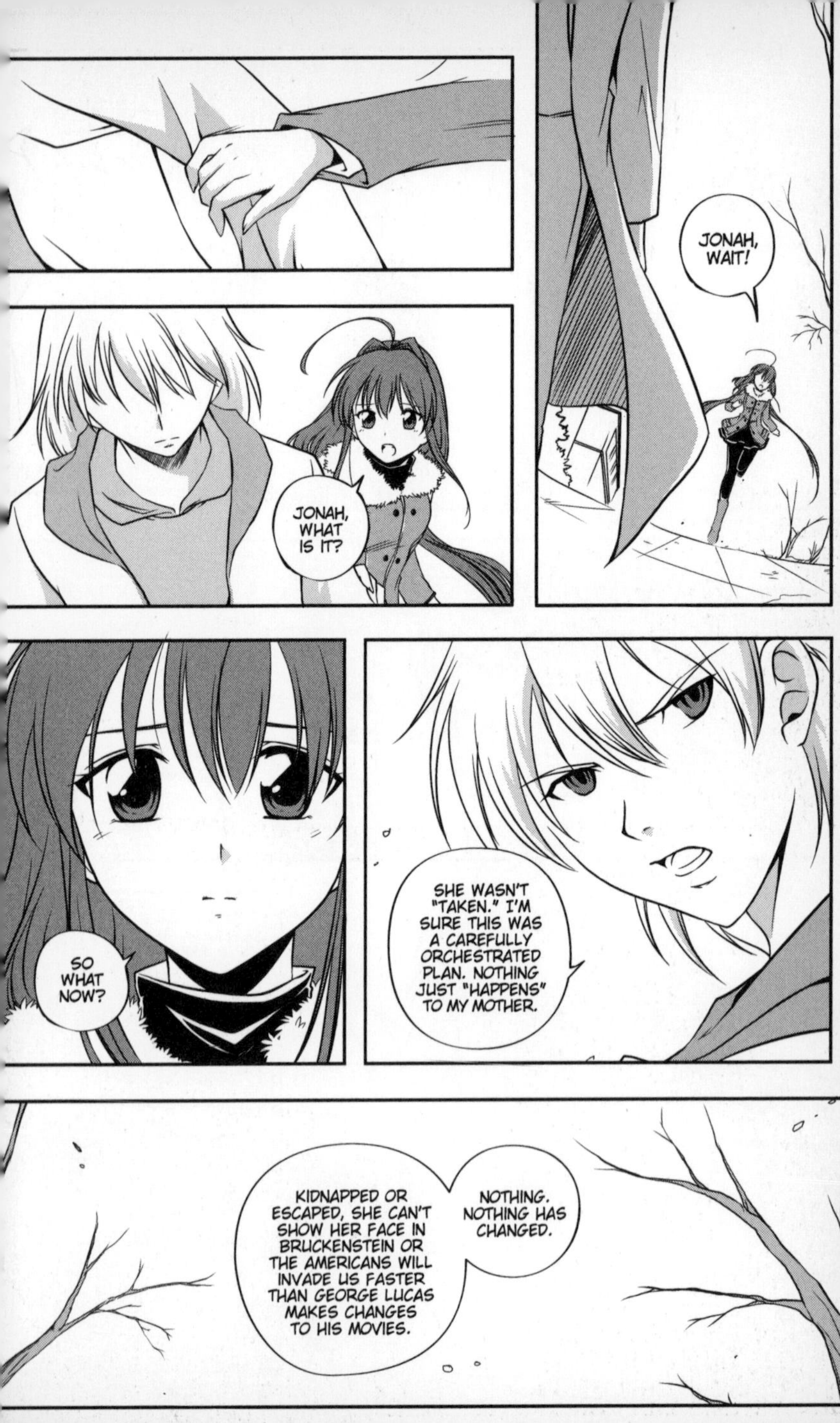
JONAH, WAIT!
JONAH, WHAT IS IT?
SHE WASN'T "TAKEN." I'M SURE THIS WAS A CAREFULLY ORCHESTRATED PLAN. NOTHING JUST "HAPPENS" TO MY MOTHER.
SO WHAT NOW?
NOTHING. NOTHING HAS CHANGED.
KIDNAPPED OR ESCAPED, SHE CAN'T SHOW HER FACE IN BRUCKENSTEIN OR THE AMERICANS WILL INVADE US FASTER THAN GEORGE LUCAS MAKES CHANGES TO HIS MOVIES.

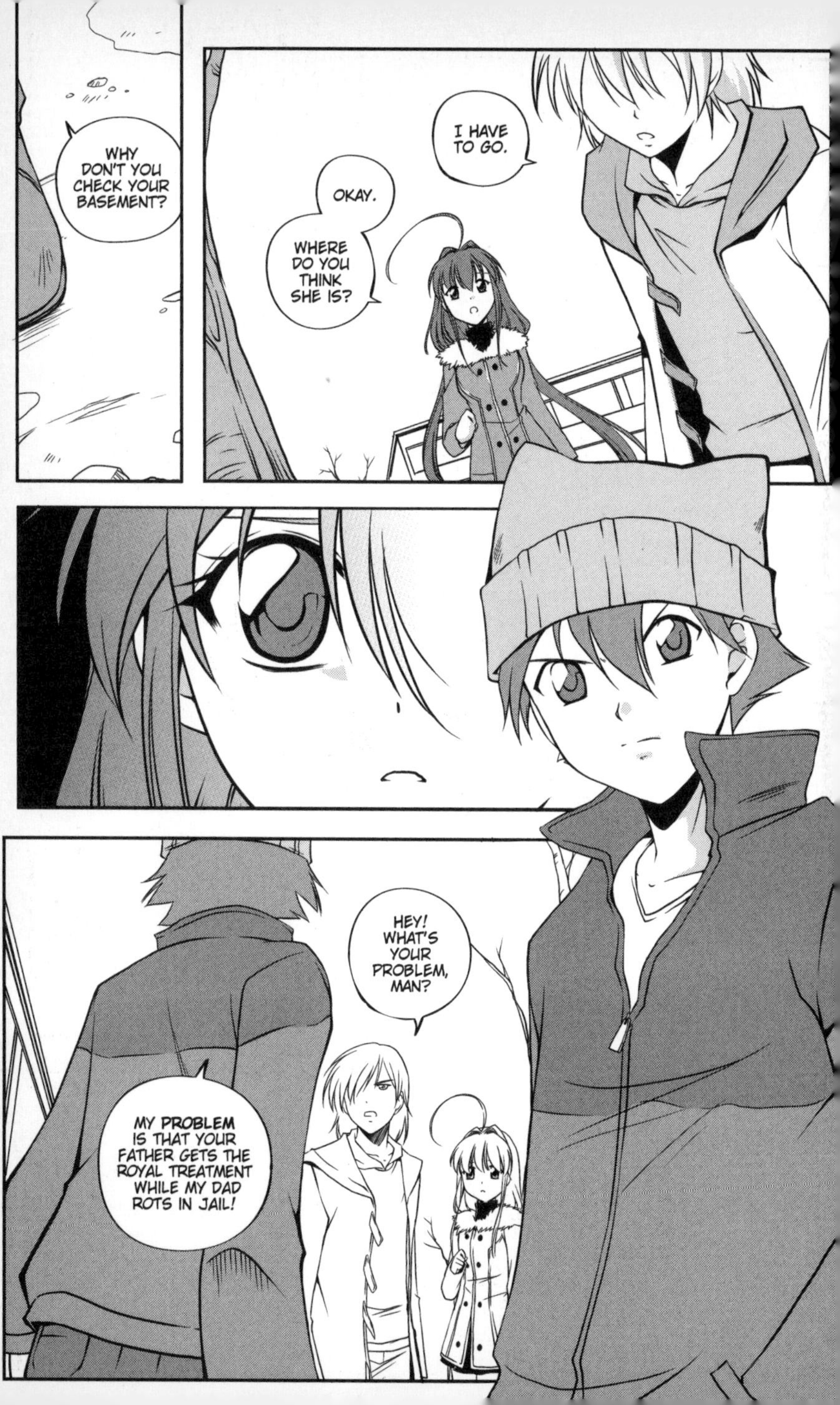
I HAVE TO GO.
OKAY.
WHERE DO YOU THINK SHE IS?
WHY DON'T YOU CHECK YOUR BASEMENT?
HEY! WHAT'S YOUR PROBLEM, MAN?
MY PROBLEM IS THAT YOUR FATHER GETS THE ROYAL TREATMENT WHILE MY DAD ROTS IN JAIL!

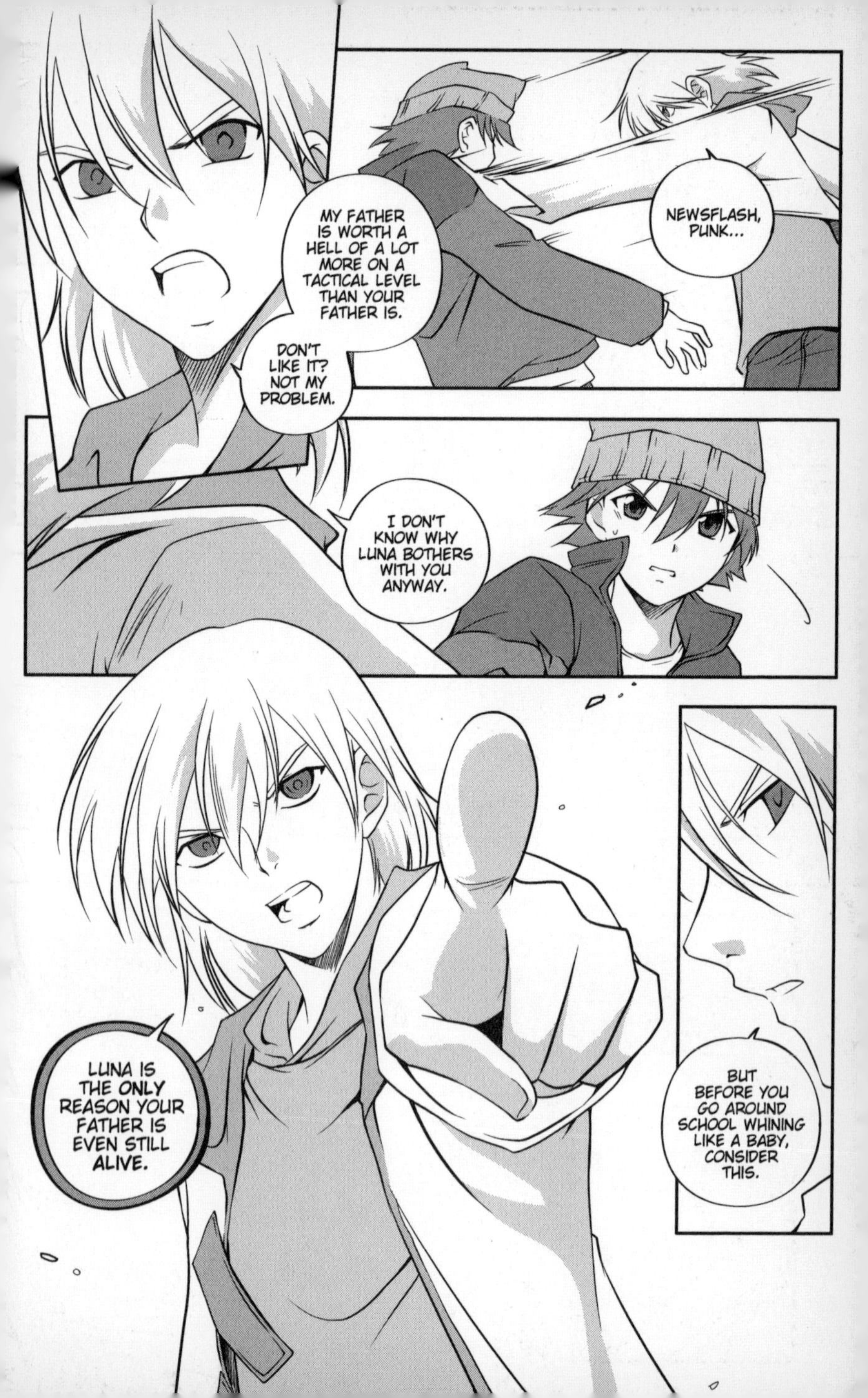
NEWSFLASH, PUNK...
MY FATHER IS WORTH A HELL OF A LOT MORE ON A TACTICAL LEVEL THAN YOUR FATHER IS.
DON'T LIKE IT? NOT MY PROBLEM.
I DON'T KNOW WHY LUNA BOTHERS WITH YOU ANYWAY.
BUT BEFORE YOU GO AROUND SCHOOL WHINING LIKE A BABY, CONSIDER THIS.
LUNA IS THE ONLY REASON YOUR FATHER IS EVEN STILL ALIVE.

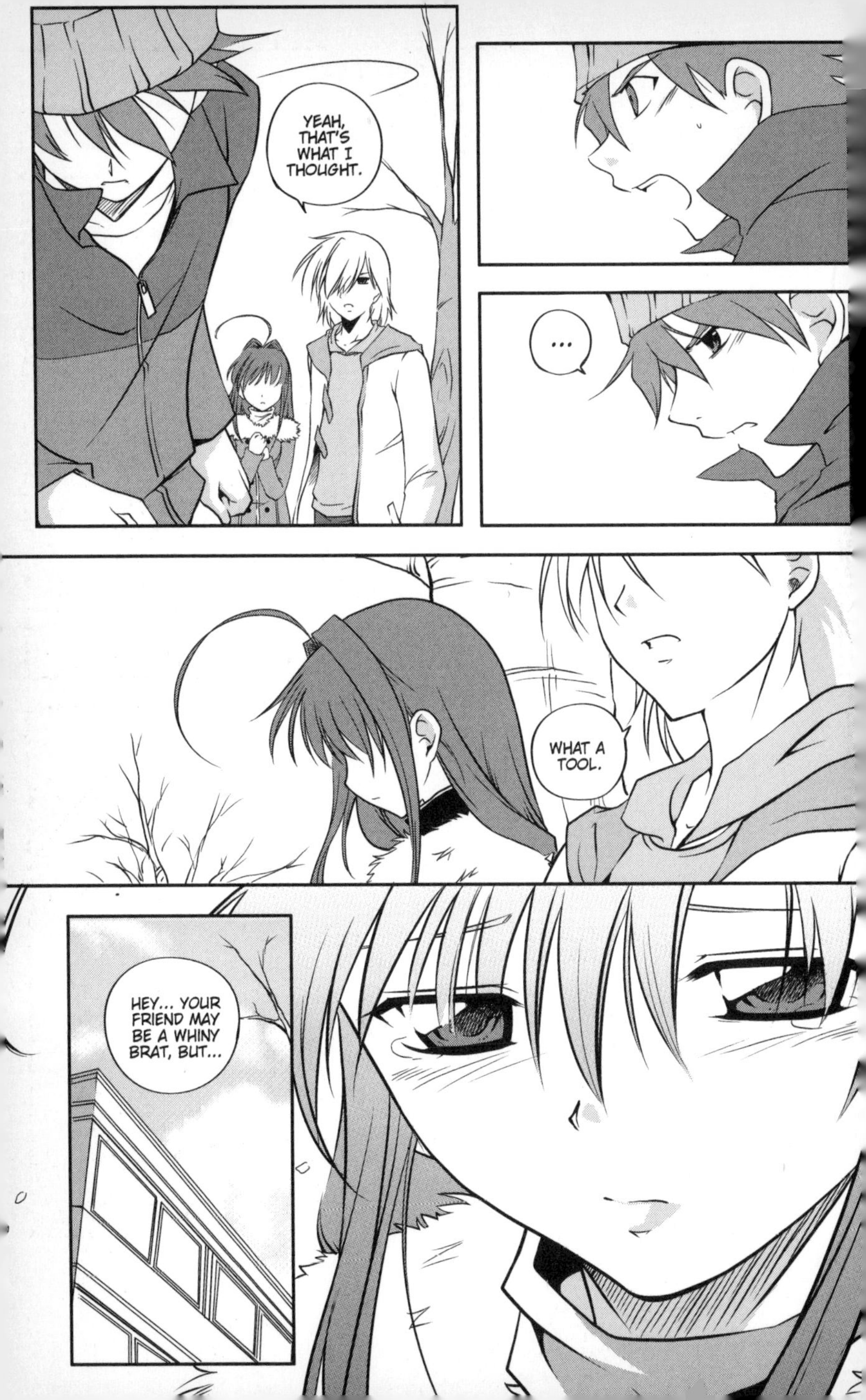
...
YEAH, THAT'S WHAT I THOUGHT.
WHAT A TOOL.
HEY... YOUR FRIEND MAY BE A WHINY BRAT, BUT...

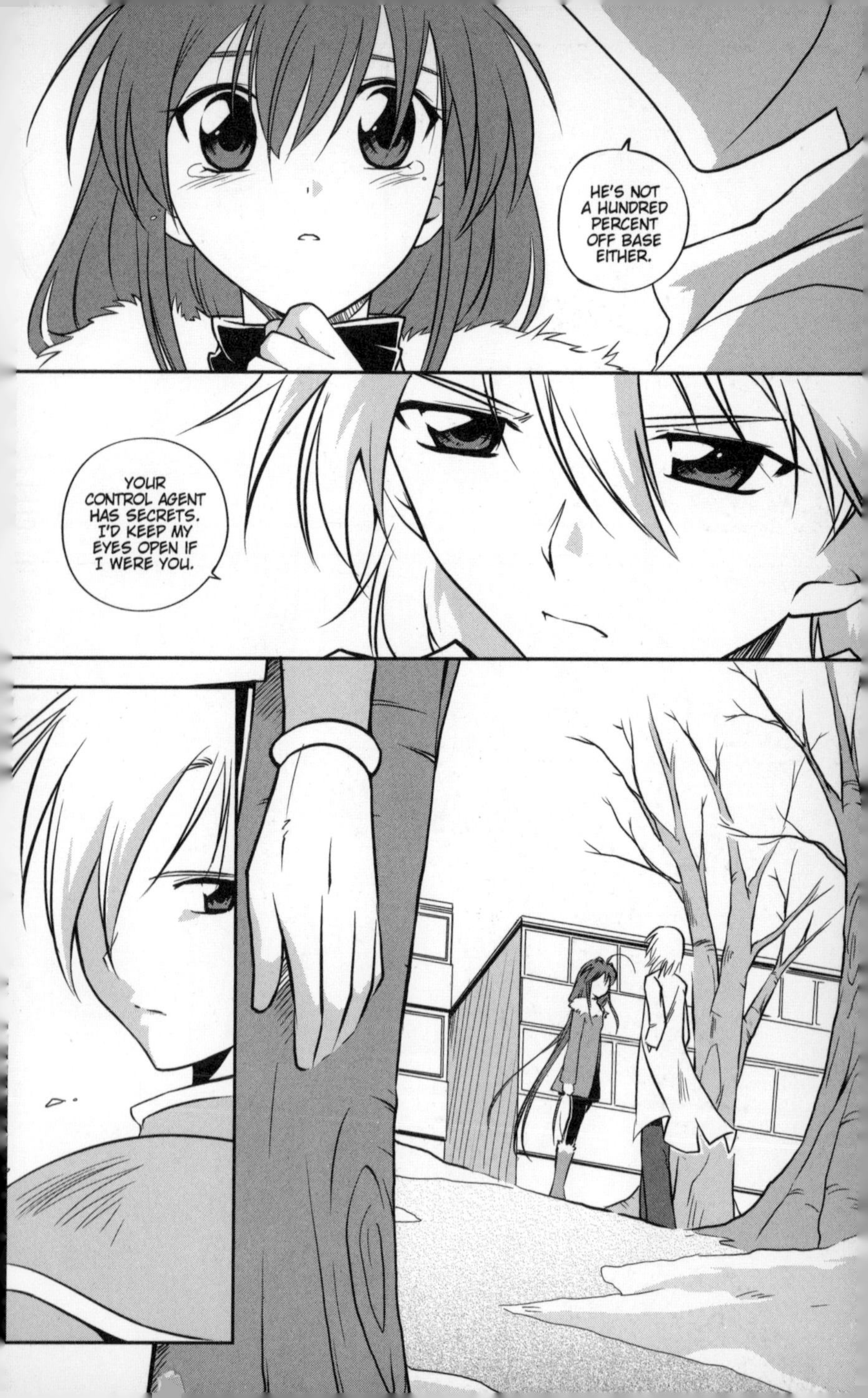
HE'S NOT A HUNDRED PERCENT OFF BASE EITHER.
YOUR CONTROL AGENT HAS SECRETS. I'D KEEP MY EYES OPEN IF I WERE YOU.

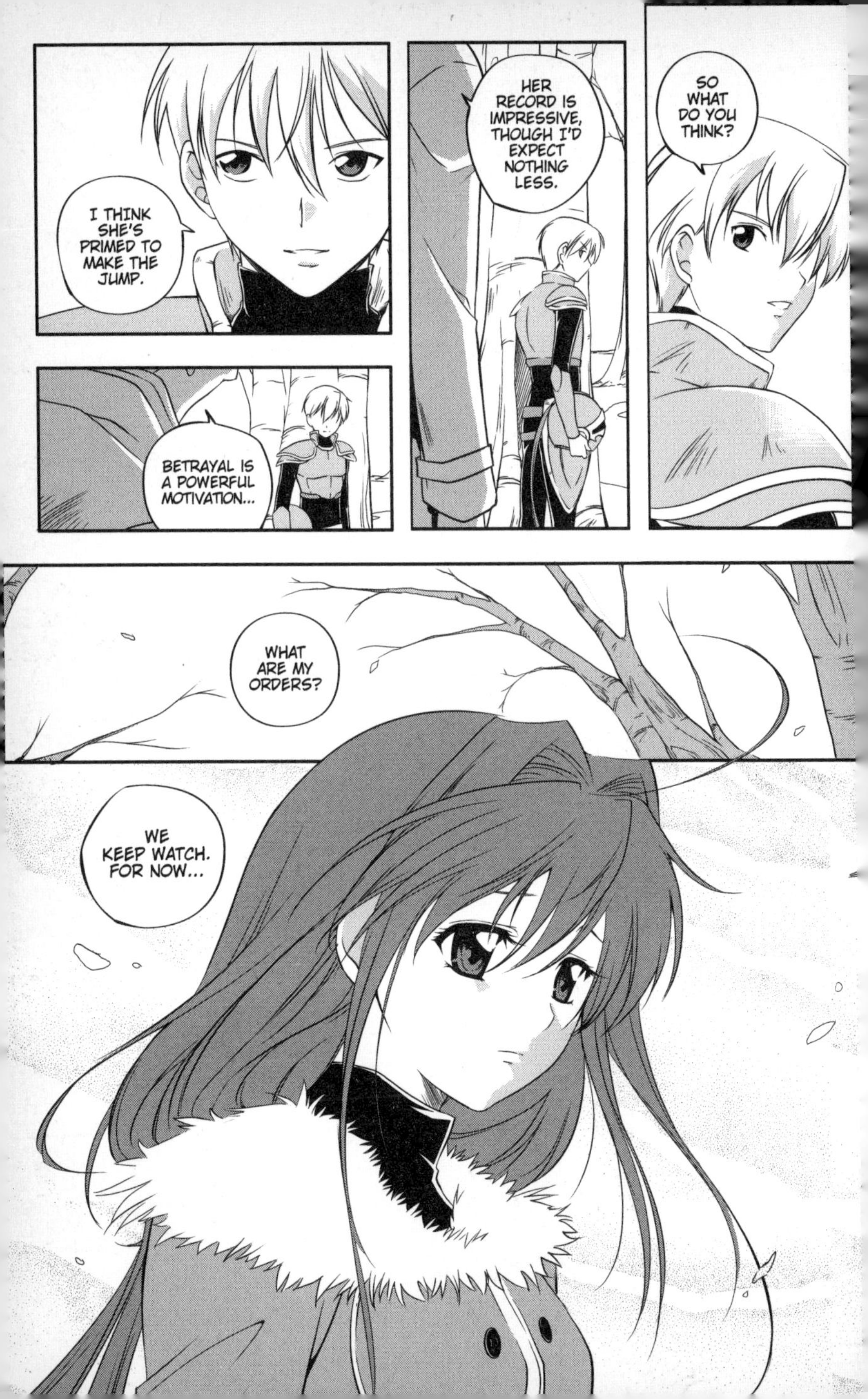
SO WHAT DO YOU THINK?
HER RECORD IS IMPRESSIVE, THOUGH I'D EXPECT NOTHING LESS.
I THINK SHE'S PRIMED TO MAKE THE JUMP.
BETRAYAL IS A POWERFUL MOTIVATION...
WHAT ARE MY ORDERS?
WE KEEP WATCH. FOR NOW...

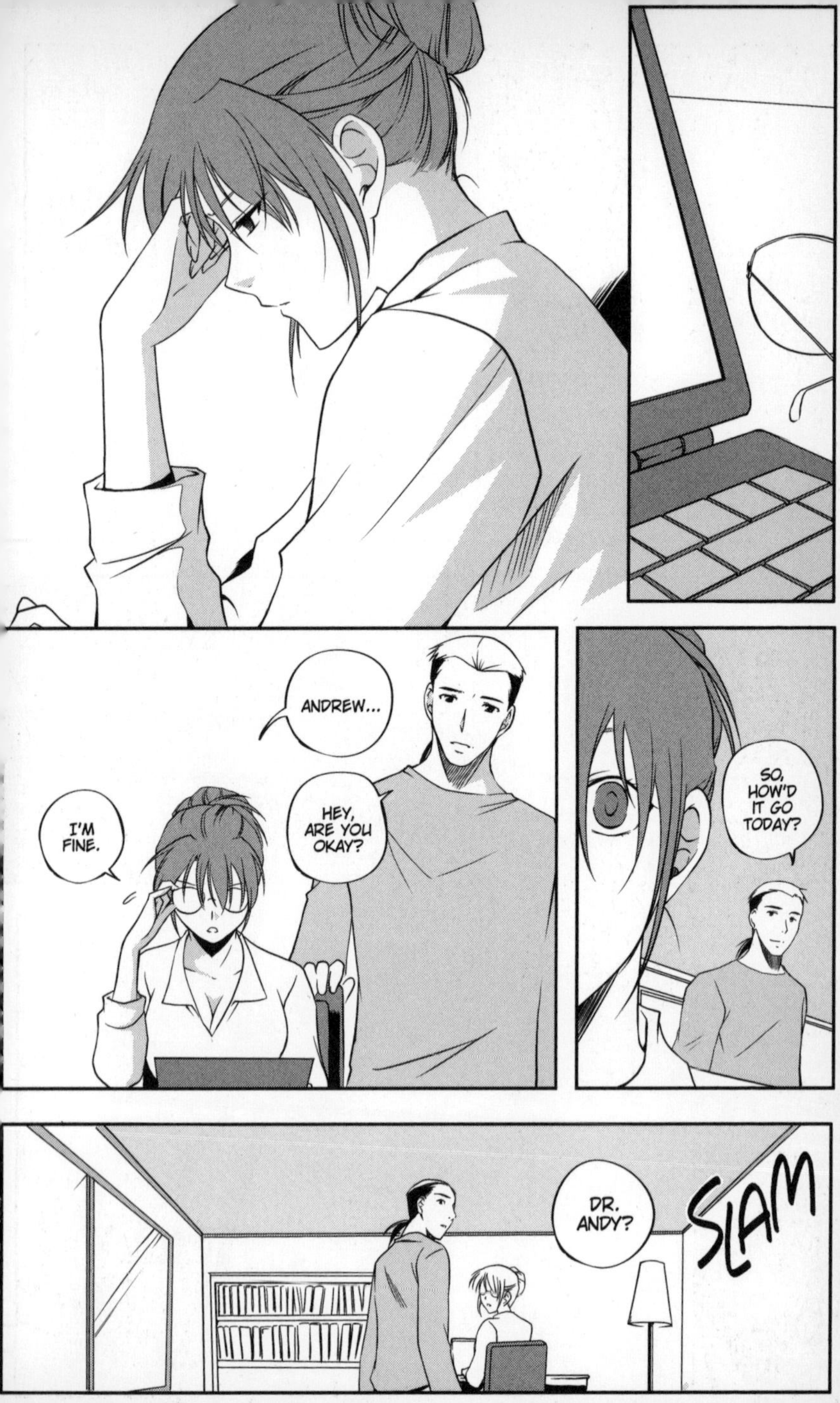
SO, HOW'D IT GO TODAY?
ANDREW...
HEY, ARE YOU OKAY?
I'M FINE.
SLAM
DR. ANDY?

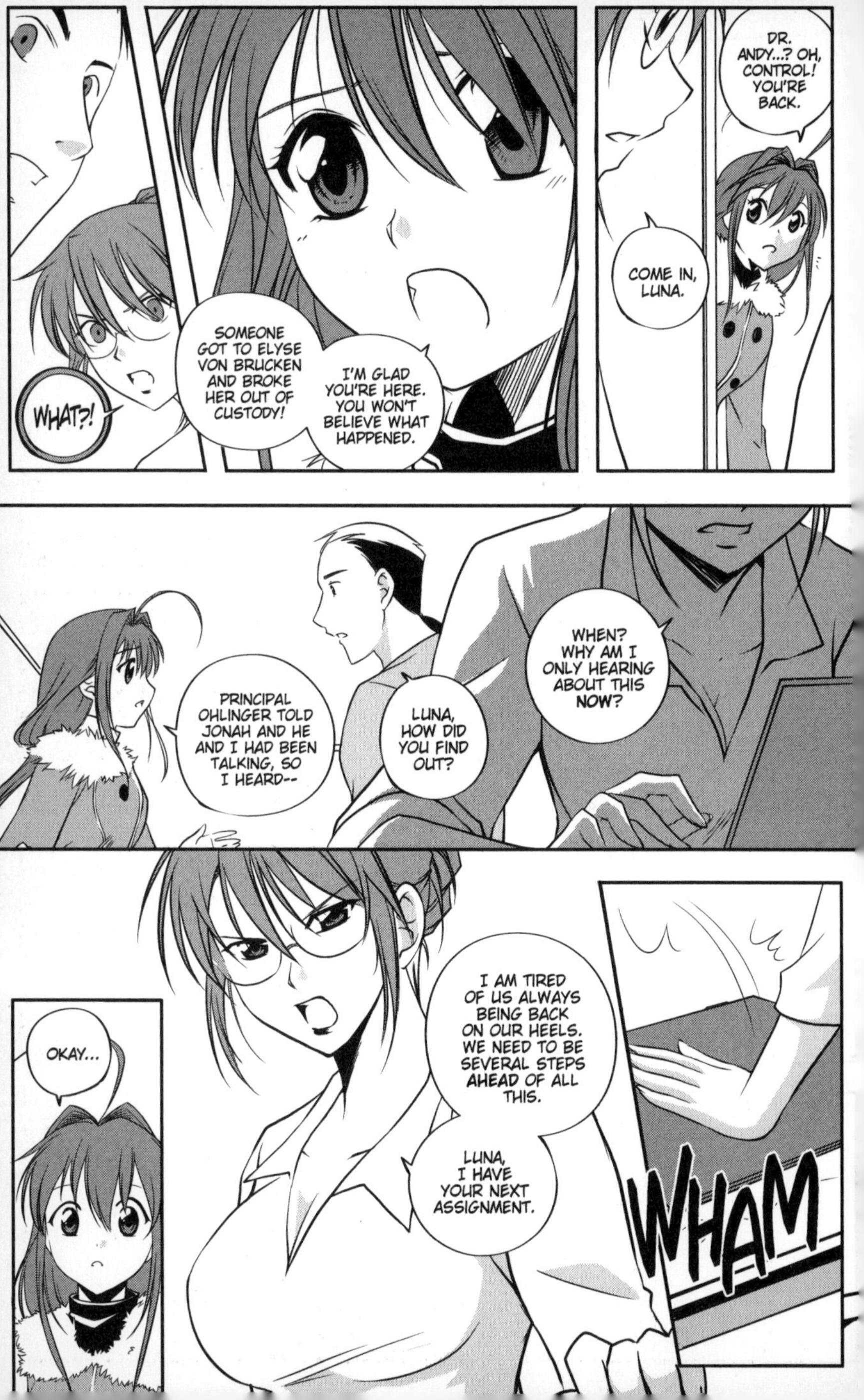
DR. ANDY...? OH, CONTROL! YOU'RE BACK.
COME IN, LUNA.
I'M GLAD YOU'RE HERE. YOU WON'T BELIEVE WHAT HAPPENED.
SOMEONE GOT TO ELYSE VON BRUCKEN AND BROKE HER OUT OF CUSTODY!
WHAT?!
WHEN? WHY AM I ONLY HEARING ABOUT THIS NOW?
LUNA, HOW DID YOU FIND OUT?
PRINCIPAL OHLINGER TOLD JONAH AND HE AND I HAD BEEN TALKING, SO I HEARD--
WHAM
I AM TIRED OF US ALWAYS BEING BACK ON OUR HEELS. WE NEED TO BE SEVERAL STEPS AHEAD OF ALL THIS.
LUNA, I HAVE YOUR NEXT ASSIGNMENT.
OKAY...

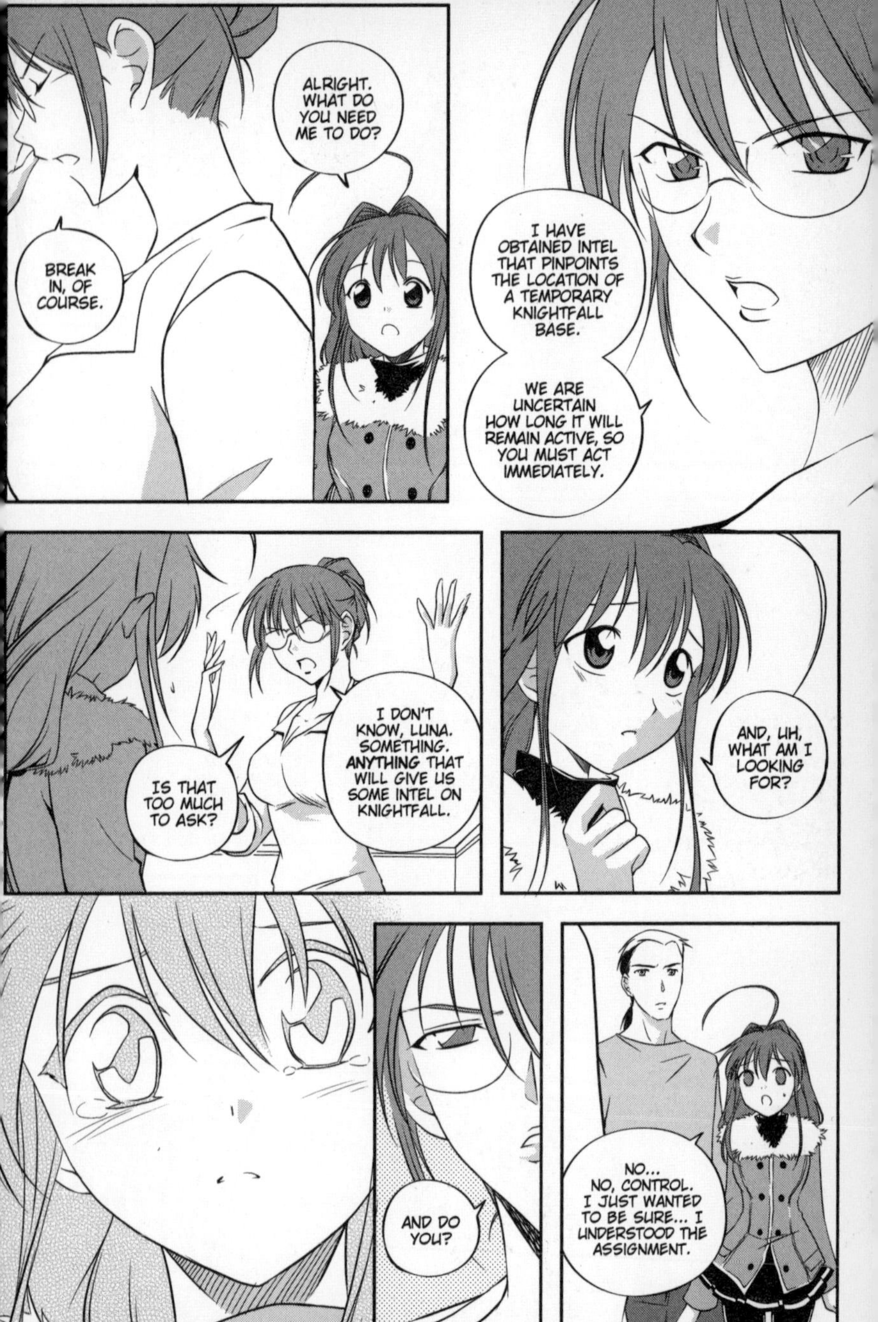
I HAVE OBTAINED INTEL THAT PINPOINTS THE LOCATION OF A TEMPORARY KNIGHTFALL BASE.
WE ARE UNCERTAIN HOW LONG IT WILL REMAIN ACTIVE, SO YOU MUST ACT IMMEDIATELY.
ALRIGHT. WHAT DO YOU NEED ME TO DO?
BREAK IN, OF COURSE.
AND, UH, WHAT AM I LOOKING FOR?
I DON'T KNOW, LUNA. SOMETHING. ANYTHING THAT WILL GIVE US SOME INTEL ON KNIGHTFALL.
IS THAT TOO MUCH TO ASK?
NO... NO, CONTROL. I JUST WANTED TO BE SURE... I UNDERSTOOD THE ASSIGNMENT.
AND DO YOU?

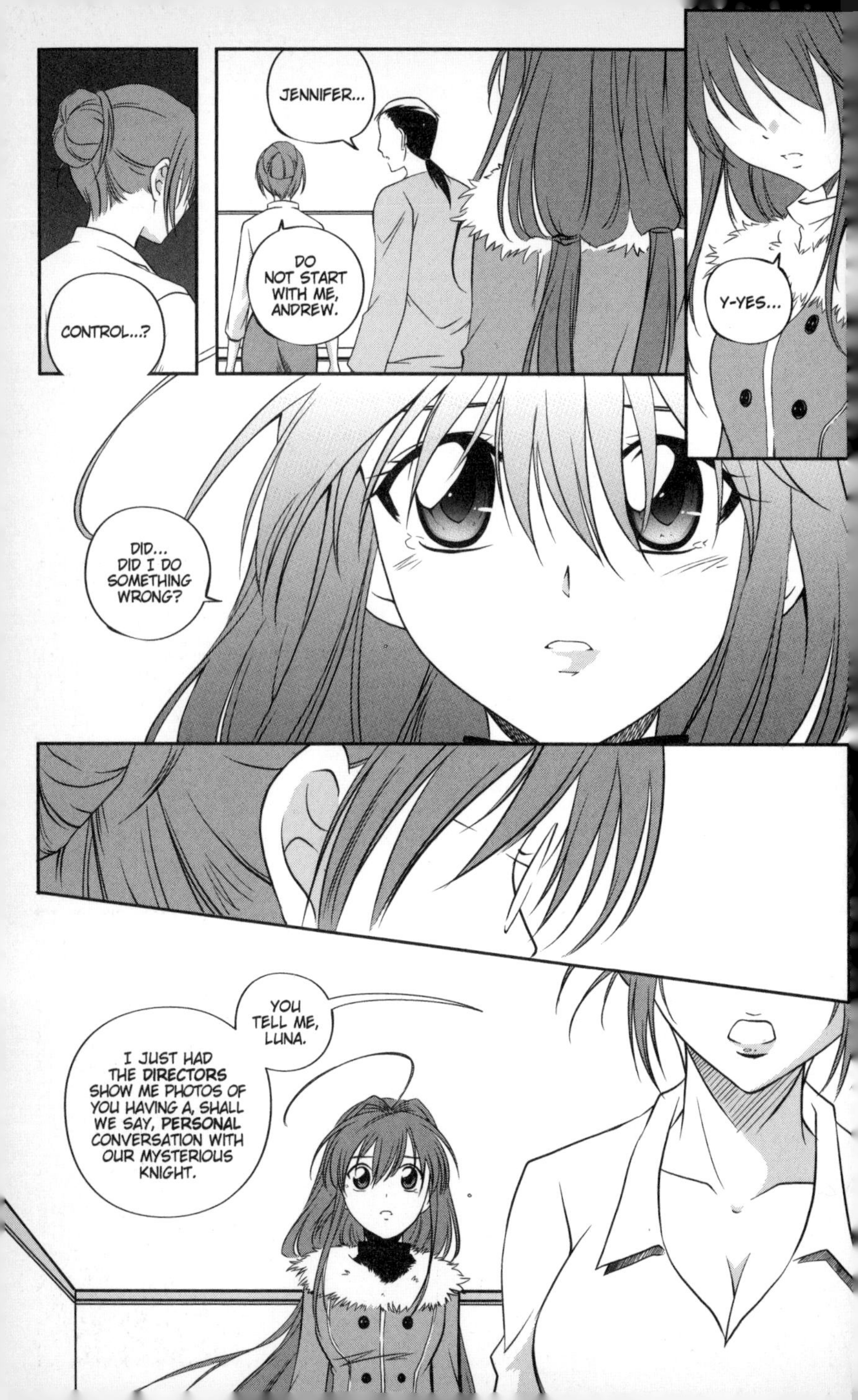
Y-YES...
JENNIFER...
DO NOT START WITH ME, ANDREW.
CONTROL...?
DID... DID I DO SOMETHING WRONG?
YOU TELL ME, LUNA.
I JUST HAD THE **DIRECTORS** SHOW ME PHOTOS OF YOU HAVING A, SHALL WE SAY, **PERSONAL** CONVERSATION WITH OUR MYSTERIOUS KNIGHT.

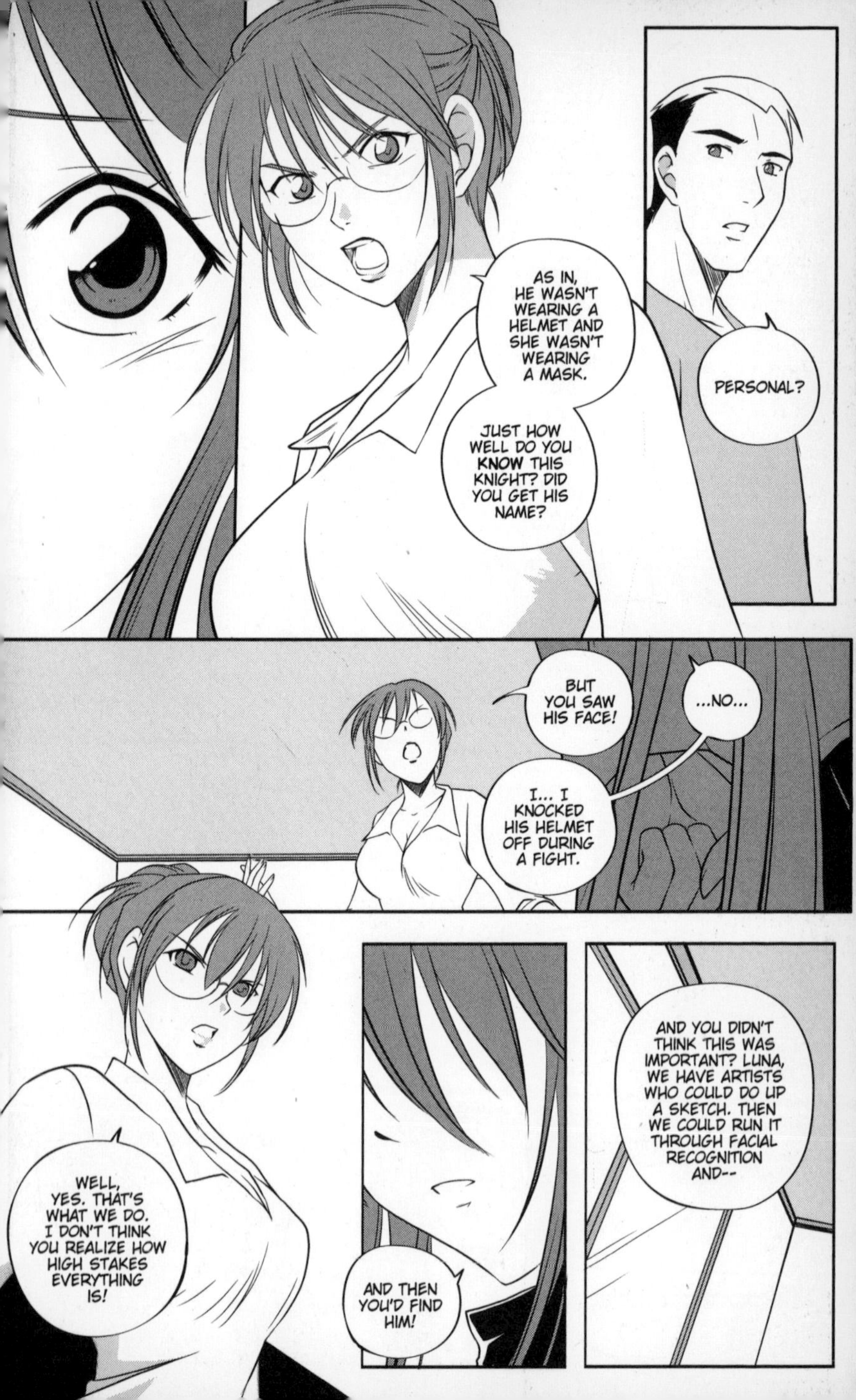
PERSONAL?
AS IN, HE WASN'T WEARING A HELMET AND SHE WASN'T WEARING A MASK.
JUST HOW WELL DO YOU KNOW THIS KNIGHT? DID YOU GET HIS NAME?
...NO...
BUT YOU SAW HIS FACE!
I... I KNOCKED HIS HELMET OFF DURING A FIGHT.
AND YOU DIDN'T THINK THIS WAS IMPORTANT? LUNA, WE HAVE ARTISTS WHO COULD DO UP A SKETCH. THEN WE COULD RUN IT THROUGH FACIAL RECOGNITION AND--
AND THEN YOU'D FIND HIM!
WELL, YES. THAT'S WHAT WE DO. I DON'T THINK YOU REALIZE HOW HIGH STAKES EVERYTHING IS!

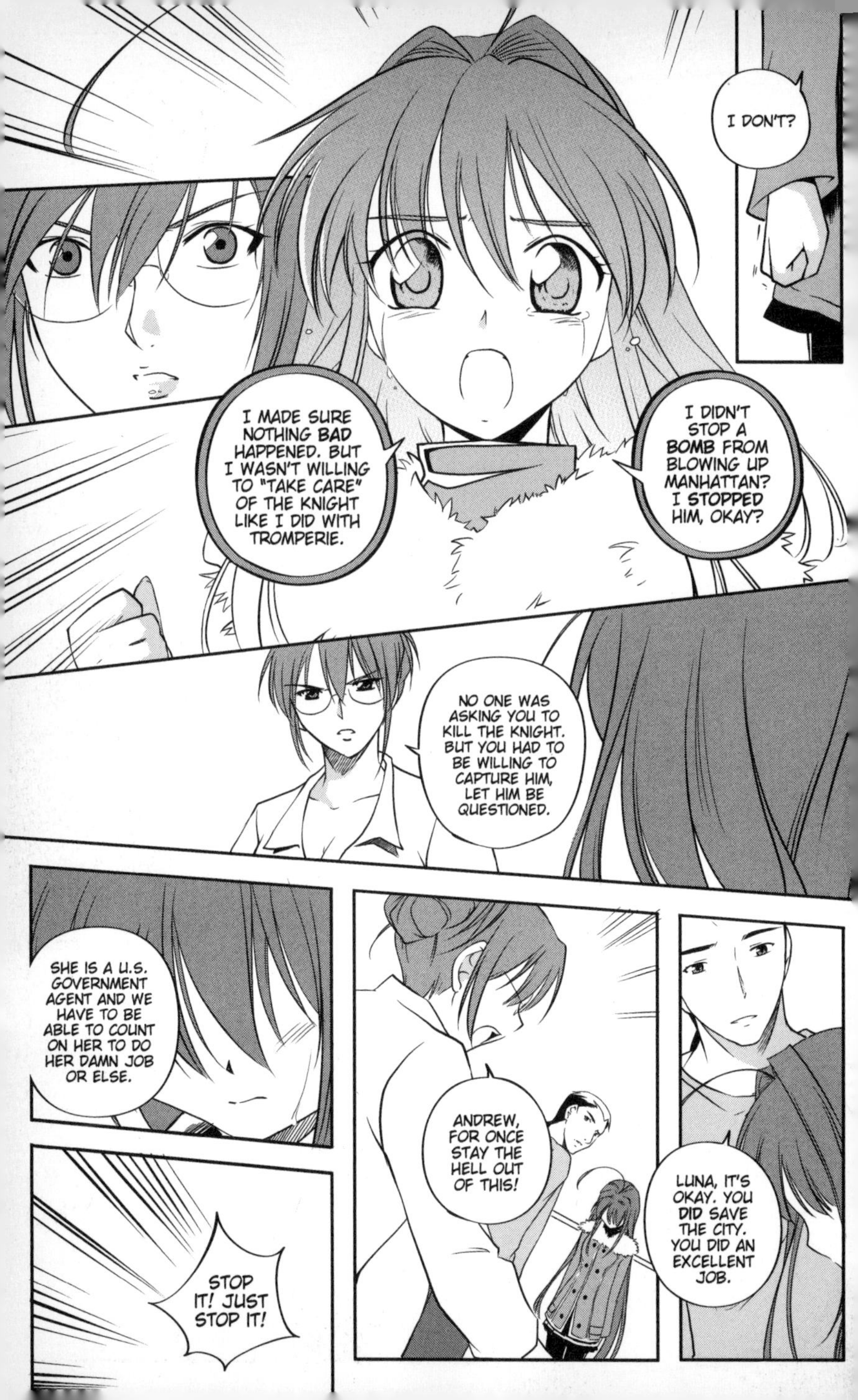
I DON'T?
I DIDN'T STOP A BOMB FROM BLOWING UP MANHATTAN? I STOPPED HIM, OKAY?
I MADE SURE NOTHING BAD HAPPENED. BUT I WASN'T WILLING TO "TAKE CARE" OF THE KNIGHT LIKE I DID WITH TROMPERIE.
NO ONE WAS ASKING YOU TO KILL THE KNIGHT. BUT YOU HAD TO BE WILLING TO CAPTURE HIM, LET HIM BE QUESTIONED.
LUNA, IT'S OKAY. YOU DID SAVE THE CITY. YOU DID AN EXCELLENT JOB.
ANDREW, FOR ONCE STAY THE HELL OUT OF THIS!
SHE IS A U.S. GOVERNMENT AGENT AND WE HAVE TO BE ABLE TO COUNT ON HER TO DO HER DAMN JOB OR ELSE.
STOP IT! JUST STOP IT!

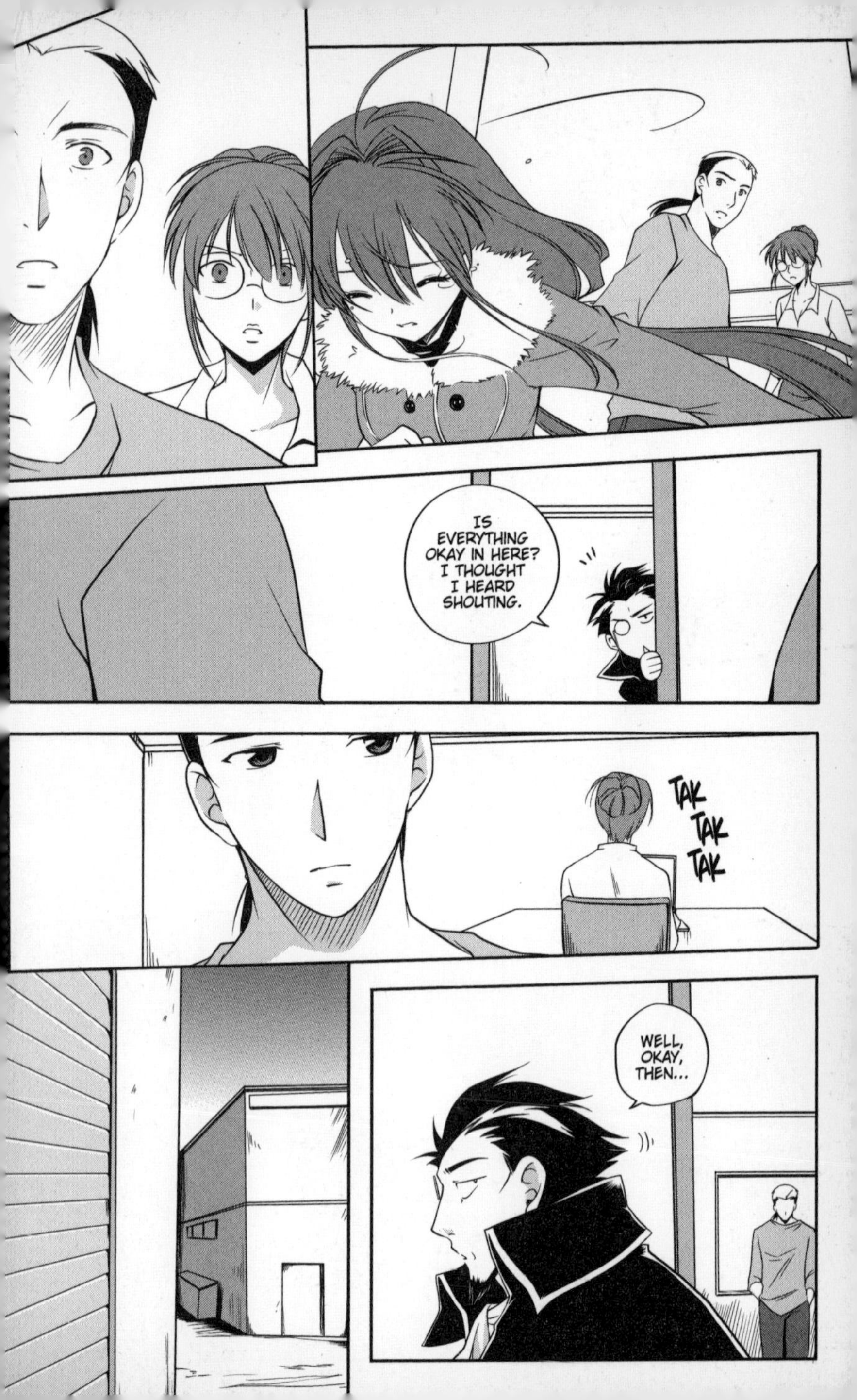
IS EVERYTHING OKAY IN HERE? I THOUGHT I HEARD SHOUTING.
TAK TAK TAK
WELL, OKAY, THEN...

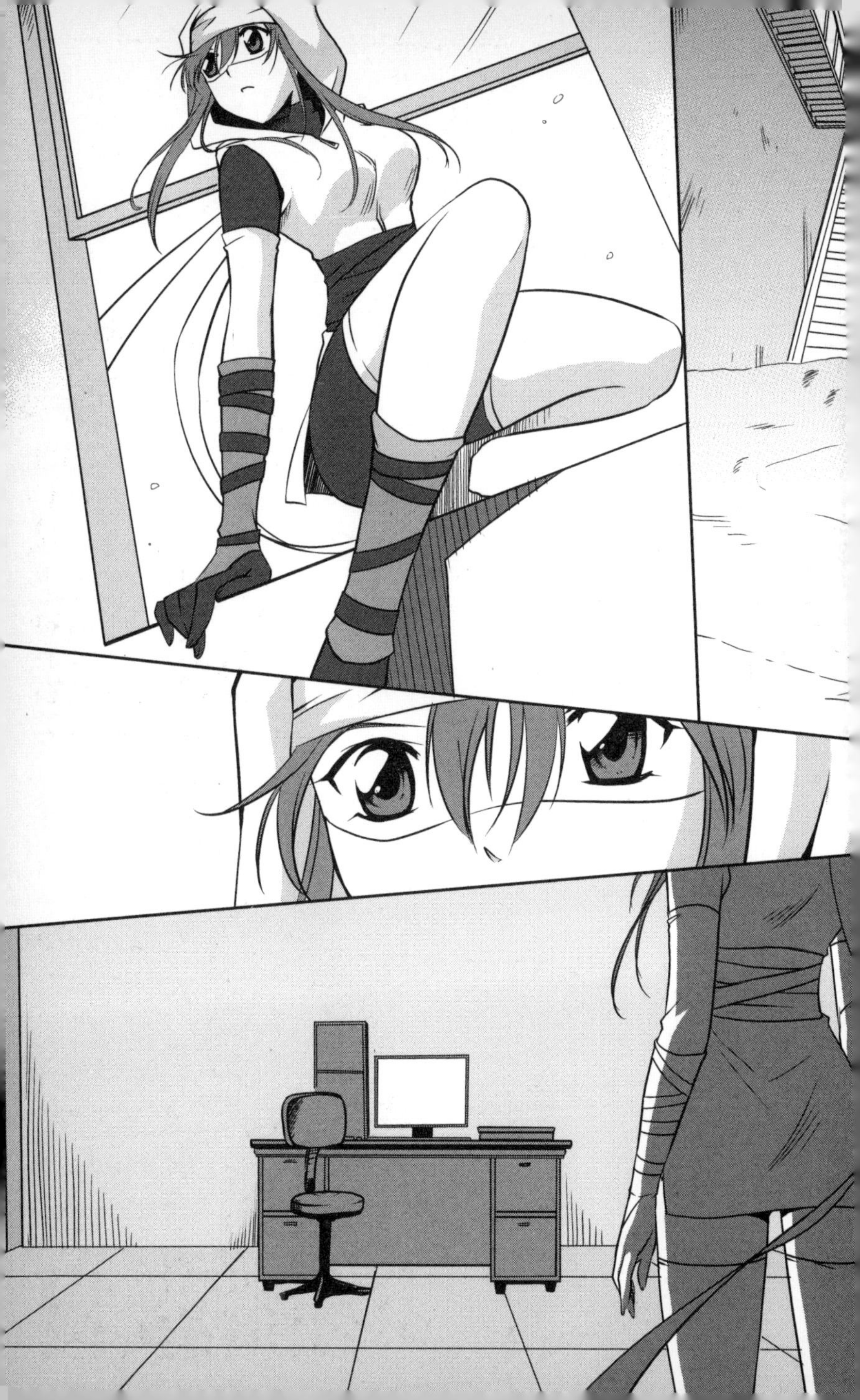

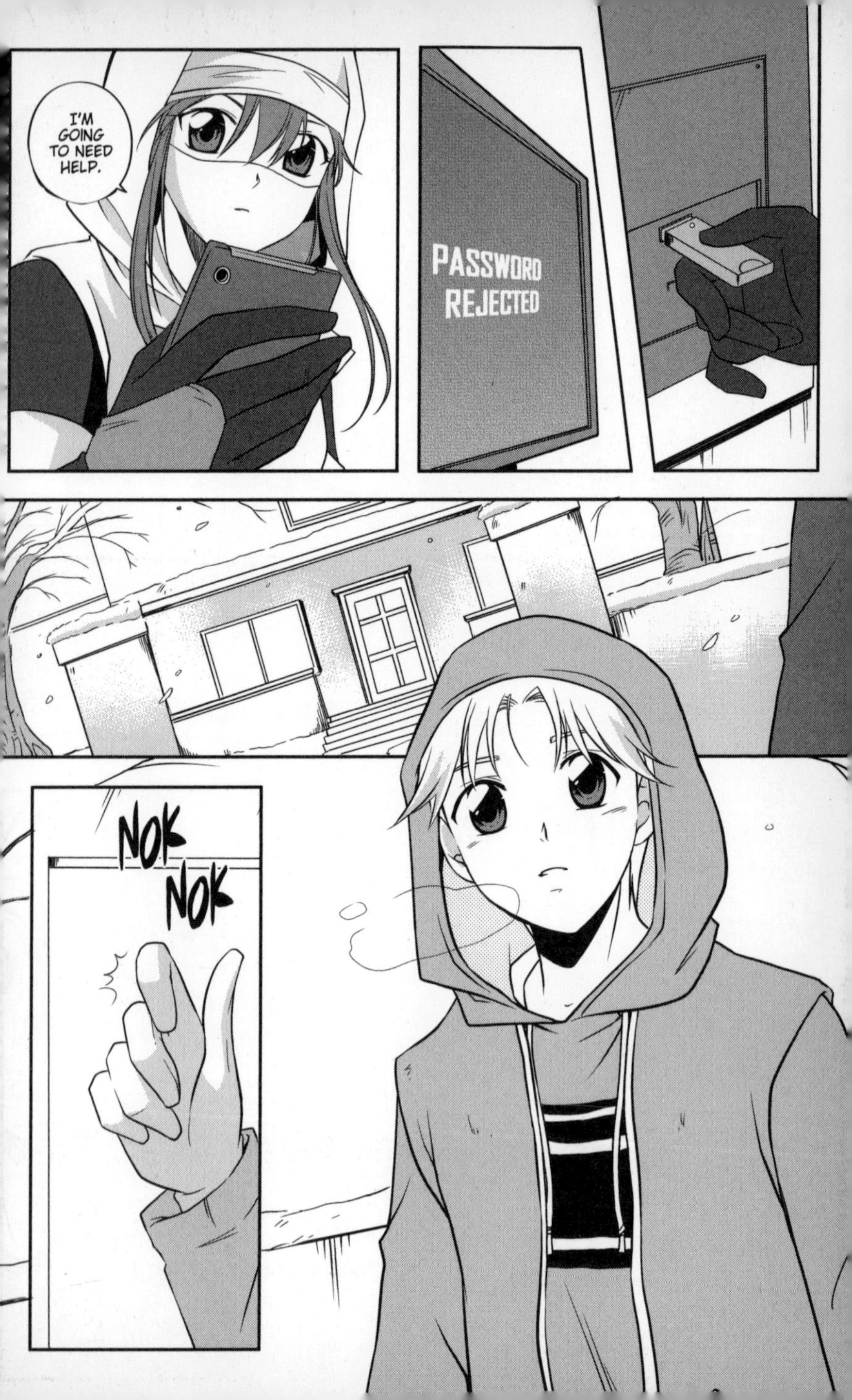
PASSWORD REJECTED
I'M GOING TO NEED HELP.
NOK NOK

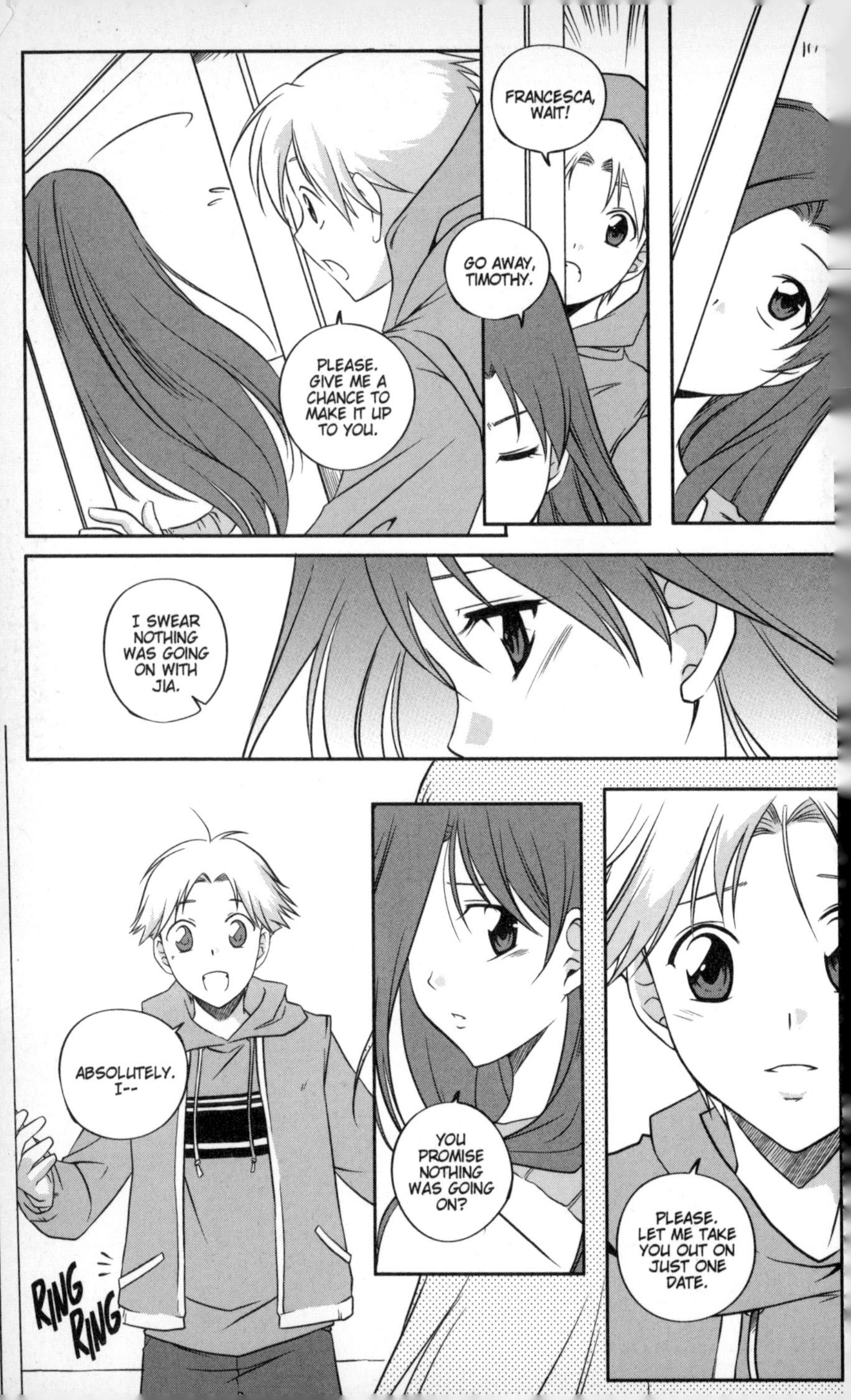
FRANCESCA, WAIT!
GO AWAY, TIMOTHY.
PLEASE. GIVE ME A CHANCE TO MAKE IT UP TO YOU.
I SWEAR NOTHING WAS GOING ON WITH JIA.
PLEASE. LET ME TAKE YOU OUT ON JUST ONE DATE.
YOU PROMISE NOTHING WAS GOING ON?
ABSOLUTELY. I--
RING RING

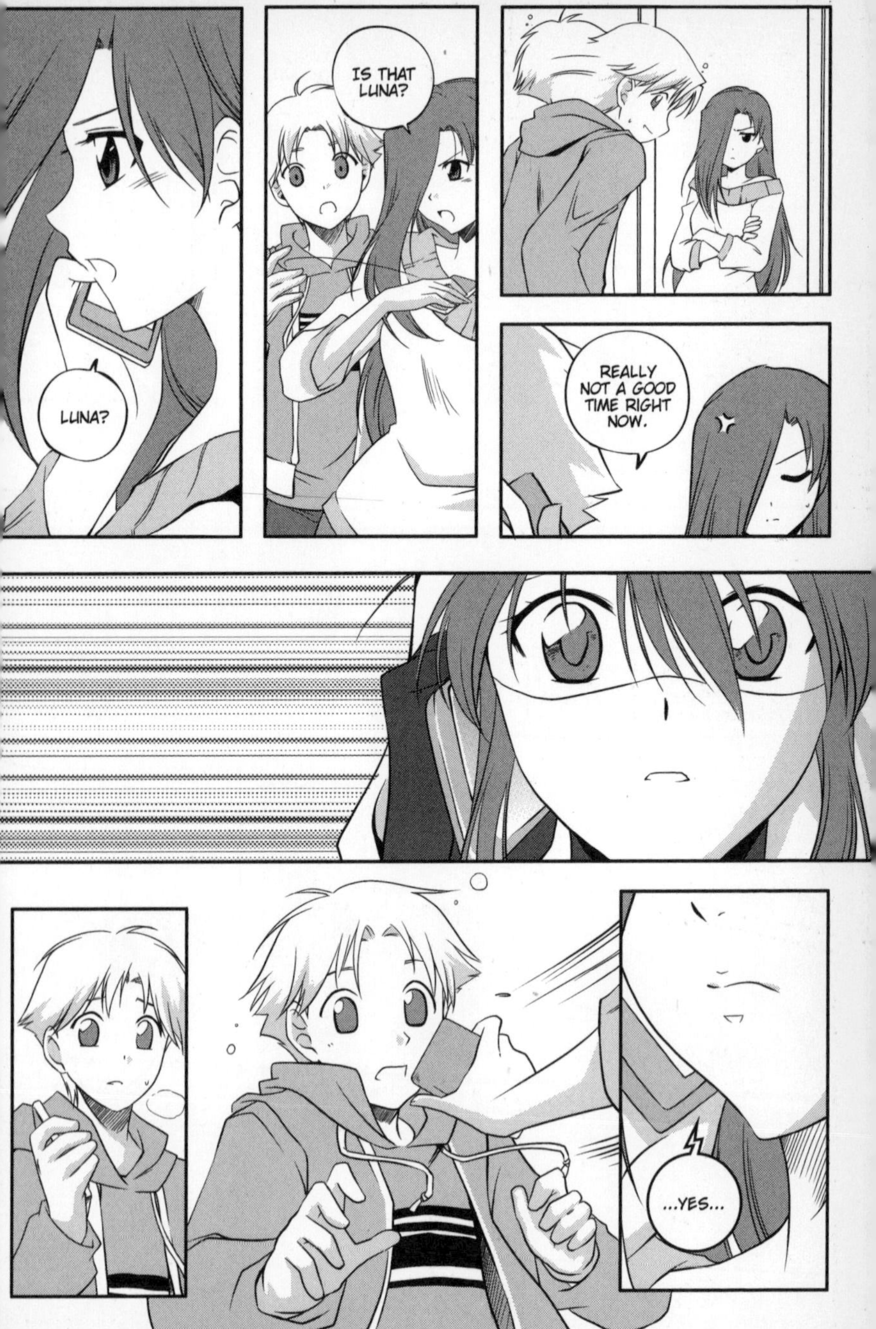
REALLY NOT A GOOD TIME RIGHT NOW.
IS THAT LUNA?
LUNA?
...YES...

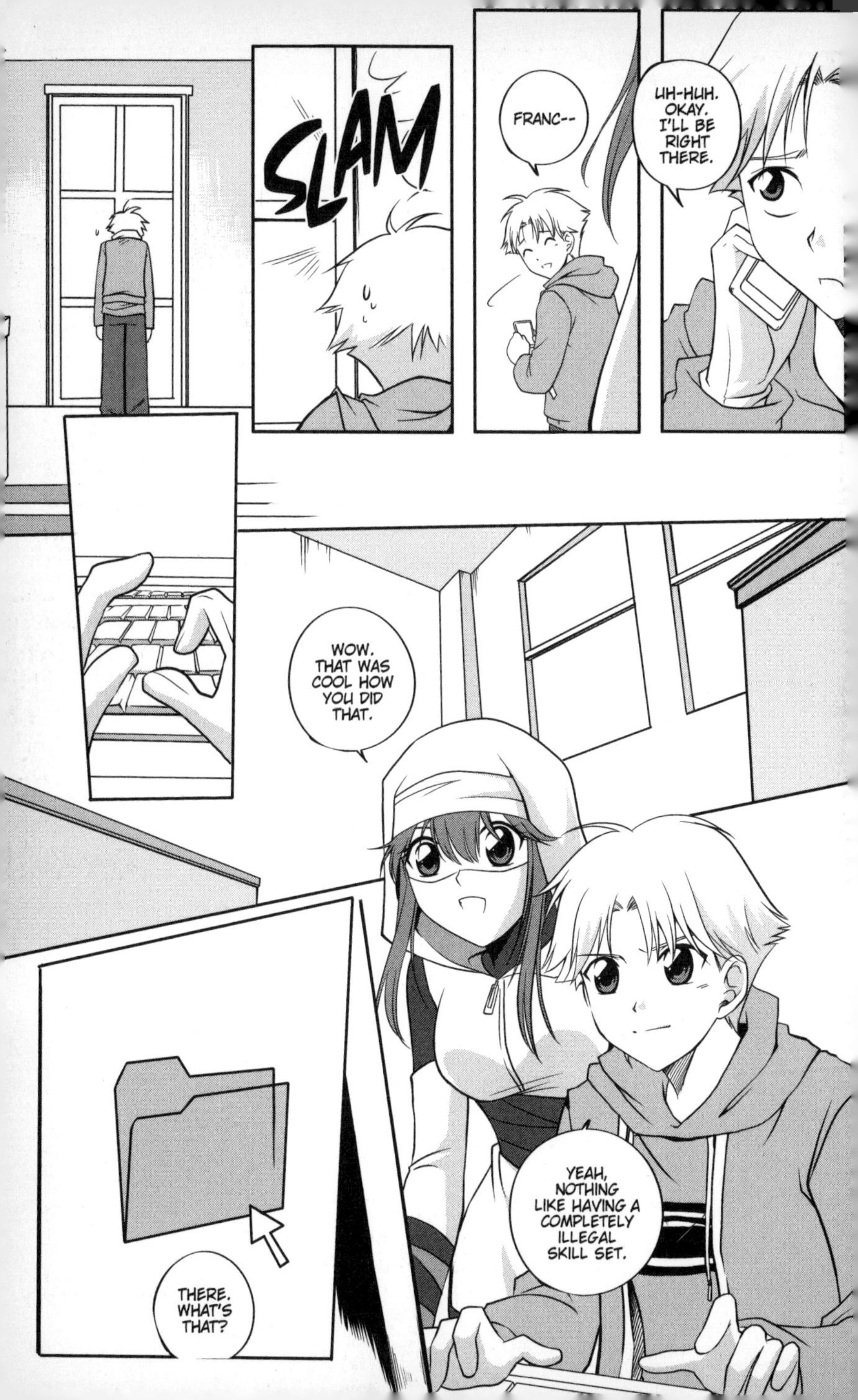
UH-HUH. OKAY. I'LL BE RIGHT THERE.
FRANC--
SLAM
WOW. THAT WAS COOL HOW YOU DID THAT.
YEAH, NOTHING LIKE HAVING A COMPLETELY ILLEGAL SKILL SET.
THERE. WHAT'S THAT?

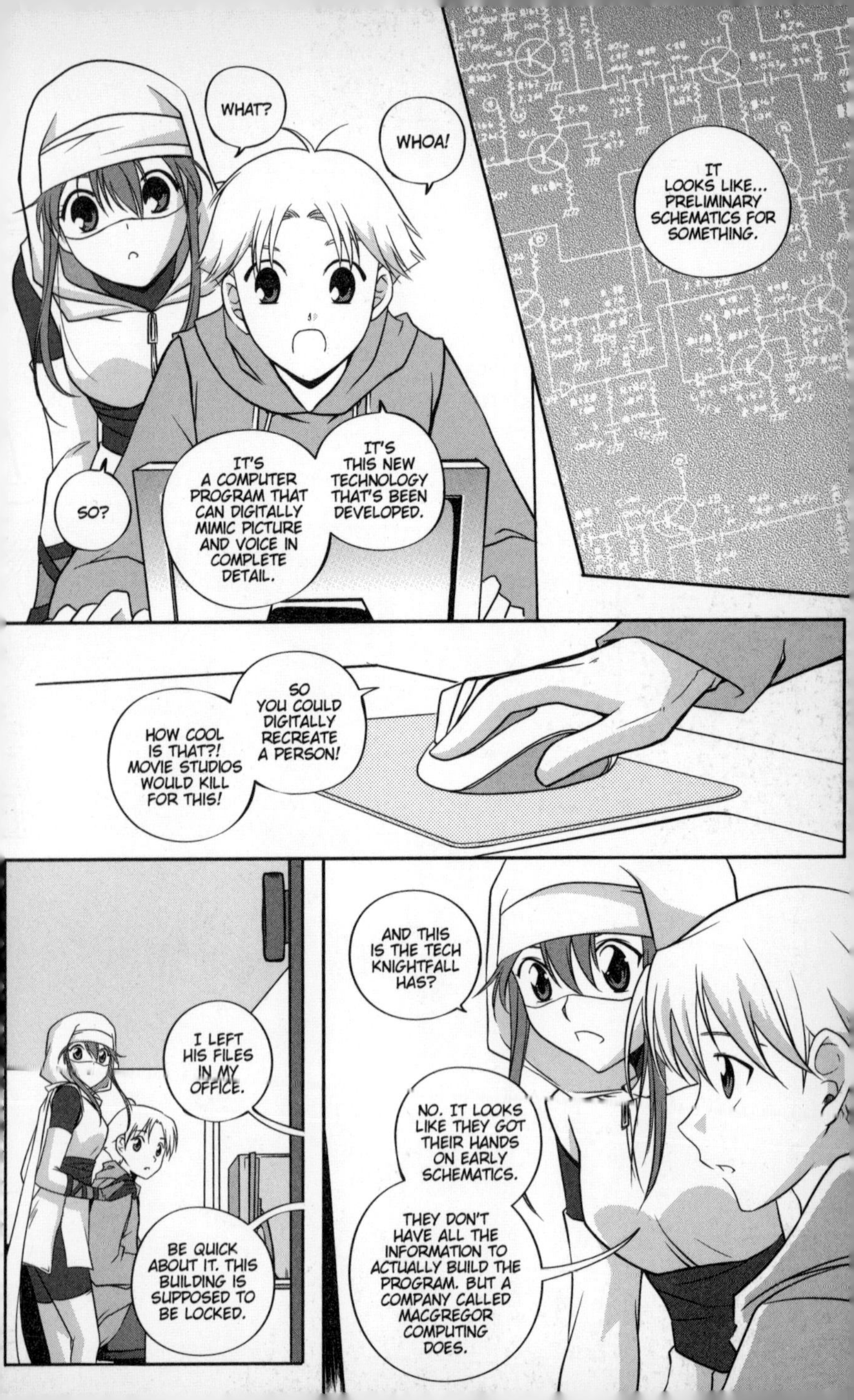
IT LOOKS LIKE... PRELIMINARY SCHEMATICS FOR SOMETHING.
WHOA!
WHAT?
IT'S THIS NEW TECHNOLOGY THAT'S BEEN DEVELOPED.
IT'S A COMPUTER PROGRAM THAT CAN DIGITALLY MIMIC PICTURE AND VOICE IN COMPLETE DETAIL.
SO?
SO YOU COULD DIGITALLY RECREATE A PERSON!
HOW COOL IS THAT?! MOVIE STUDIOS WOULD KILL FOR THIS!
AND THIS IS THE TECH KNIGHTFALL HAS?
NO. IT LOOKS LIKE THEY GOT THEIR HANDS ON EARLY SCHEMATICS.
THEY DON'T HAVE ALL THE INFORMATION TO ACTUALLY BUILD THE PROGRAM. BUT A COMPANY CALLED MACGREGOR COMPUTING DOES.
I LEFT HIS FILES IN MY OFFICE.
BE QUICK ABOUT IT. THIS BUILDING IS SUPPOSED TO BE LOCKED.

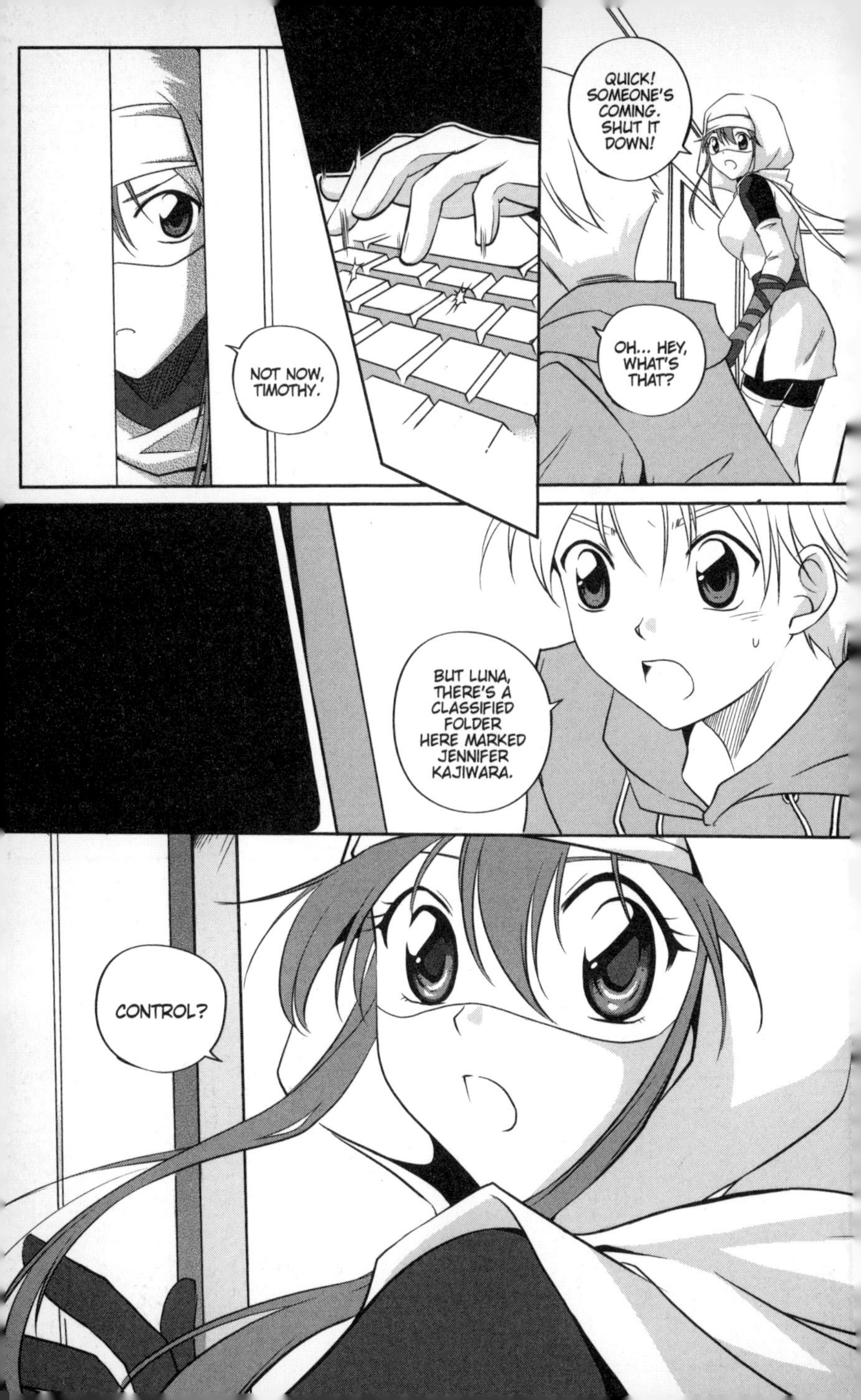
QUICK! SOMEONE'S COMING. SHUT IT DOWN!
OH... HEY, WHAT'S THAT?
NOT NOW, TIMOTHY.
BUT LUNA, THERE'S A CLASSIFIED FOLDER HERE MARKED JENNIFER KAJIWARA.
CONTROL?

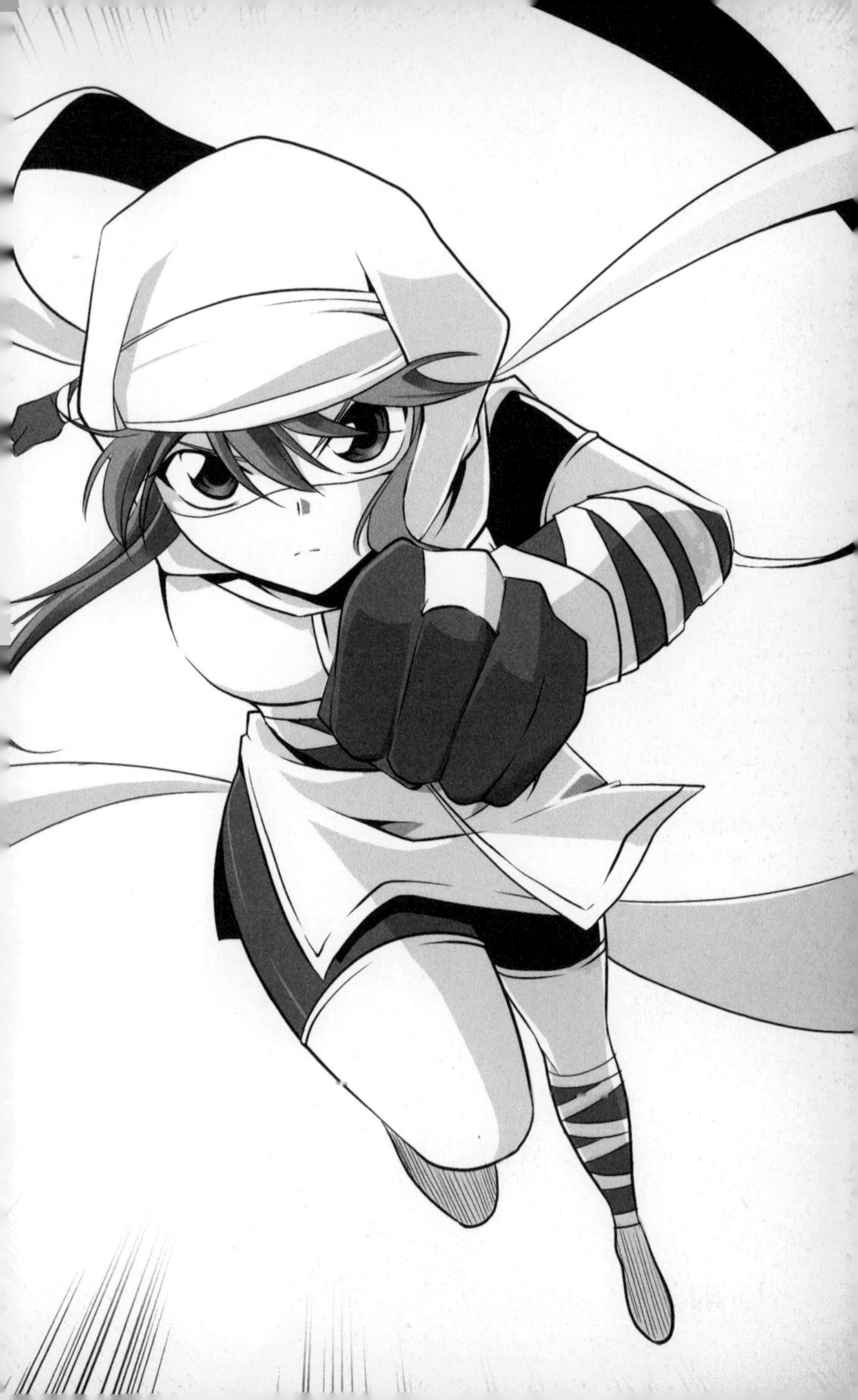

File 42
FISTICUFFS

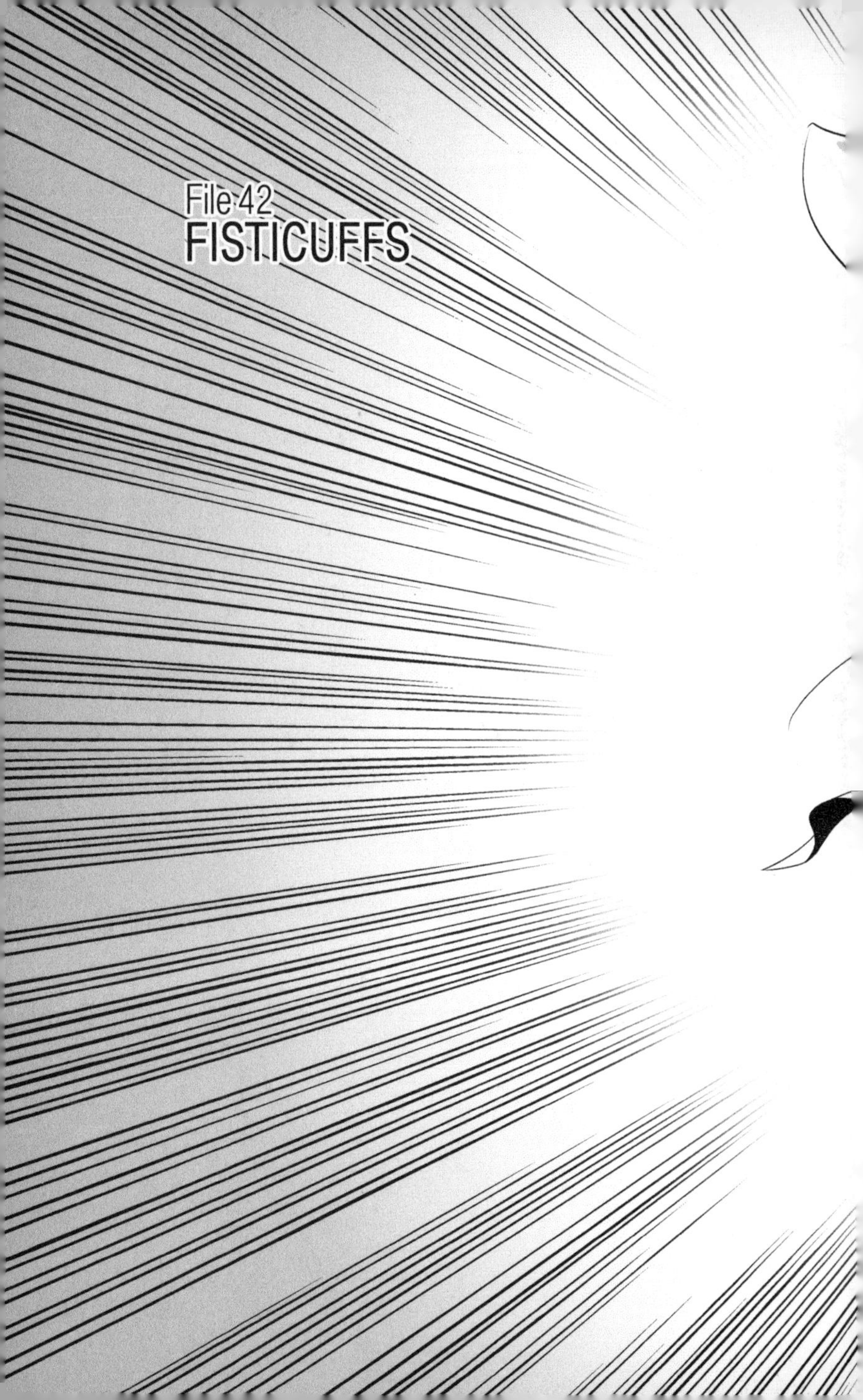

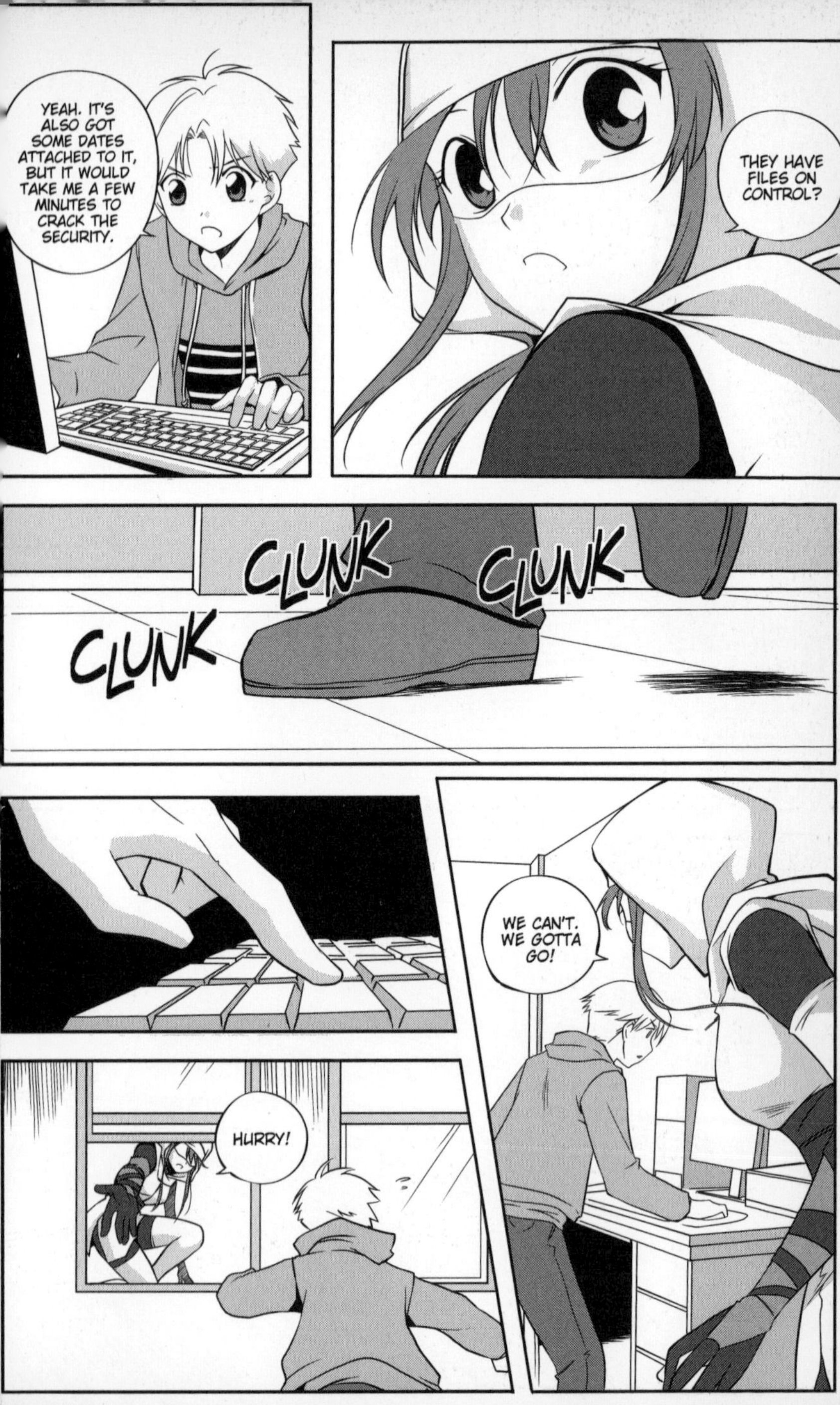
THEY HAVE FILES ON CONTROL?
YEAH. IT'S ALSO GOT SOME DATES ATTACHED TO IT, BUT IT WOULD TAKE ME A FEW MINUTES TO CRACK THE SECURITY.
CLUNK
CLUNK
CLUNK
WE CAN'T. WE GOTTA GO!
HURRY!

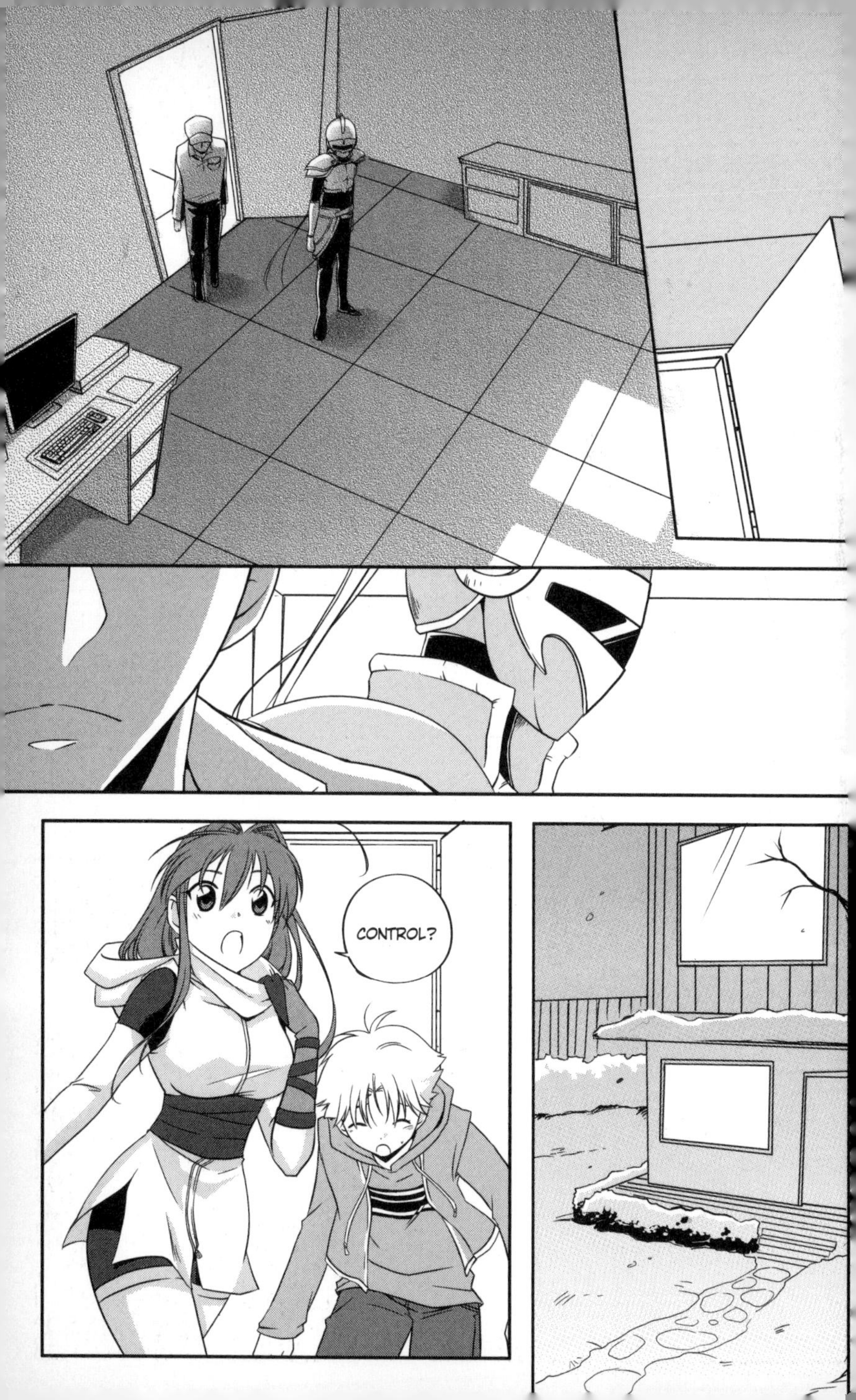
CONTROL?

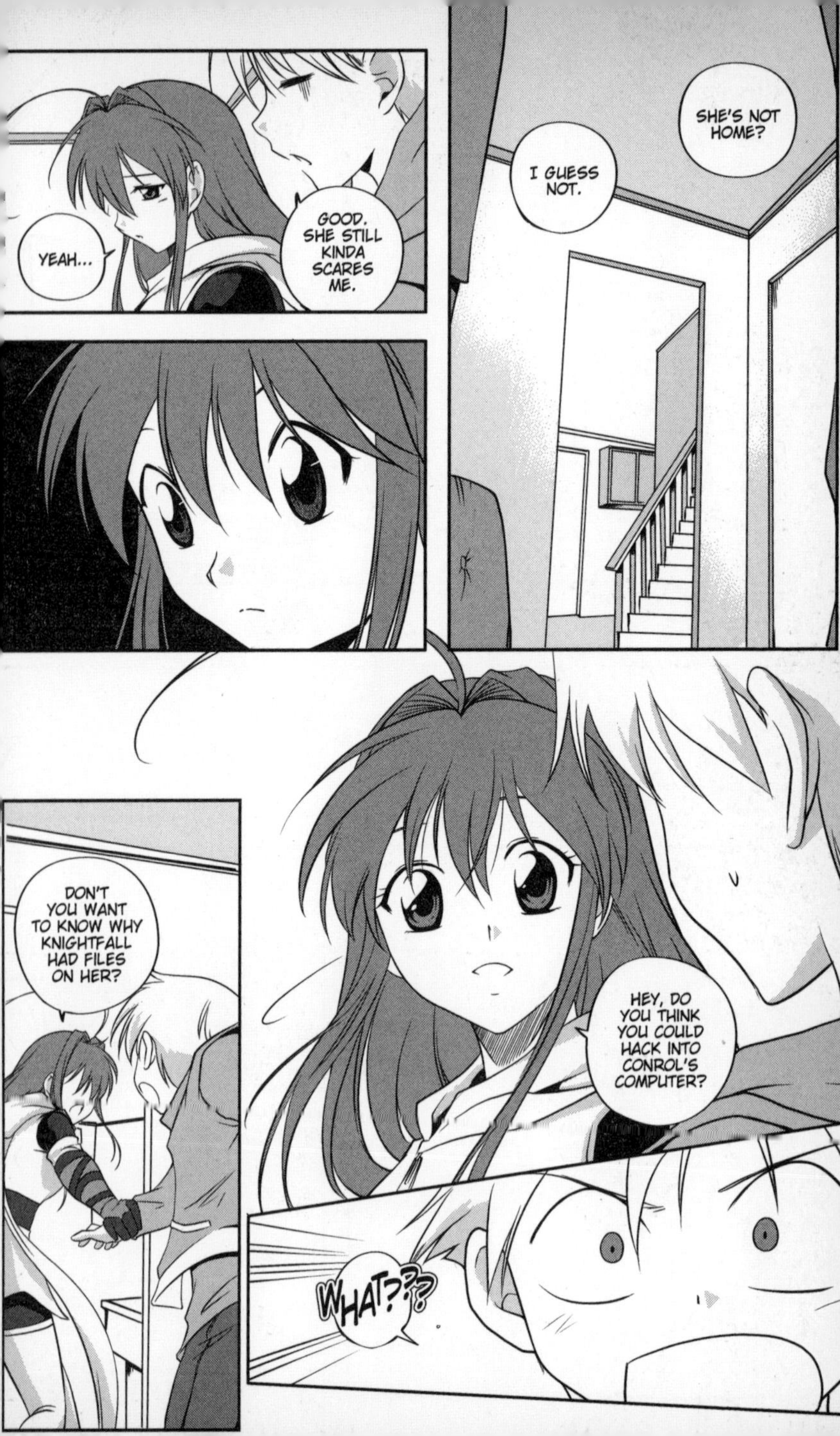
SHE'S NOT HOME?
I GUESS NOT.
GOOD. SHE STILL KINDA SCARES ME.
YEAH...
HEY, DO YOU THINK YOU COULD HACK INTO CONROL'S COMPUTER?
WHAT?!?
DON'T YOU WANT TO KNOW WHY KNIGHTFALL HAD FILES ON HER?

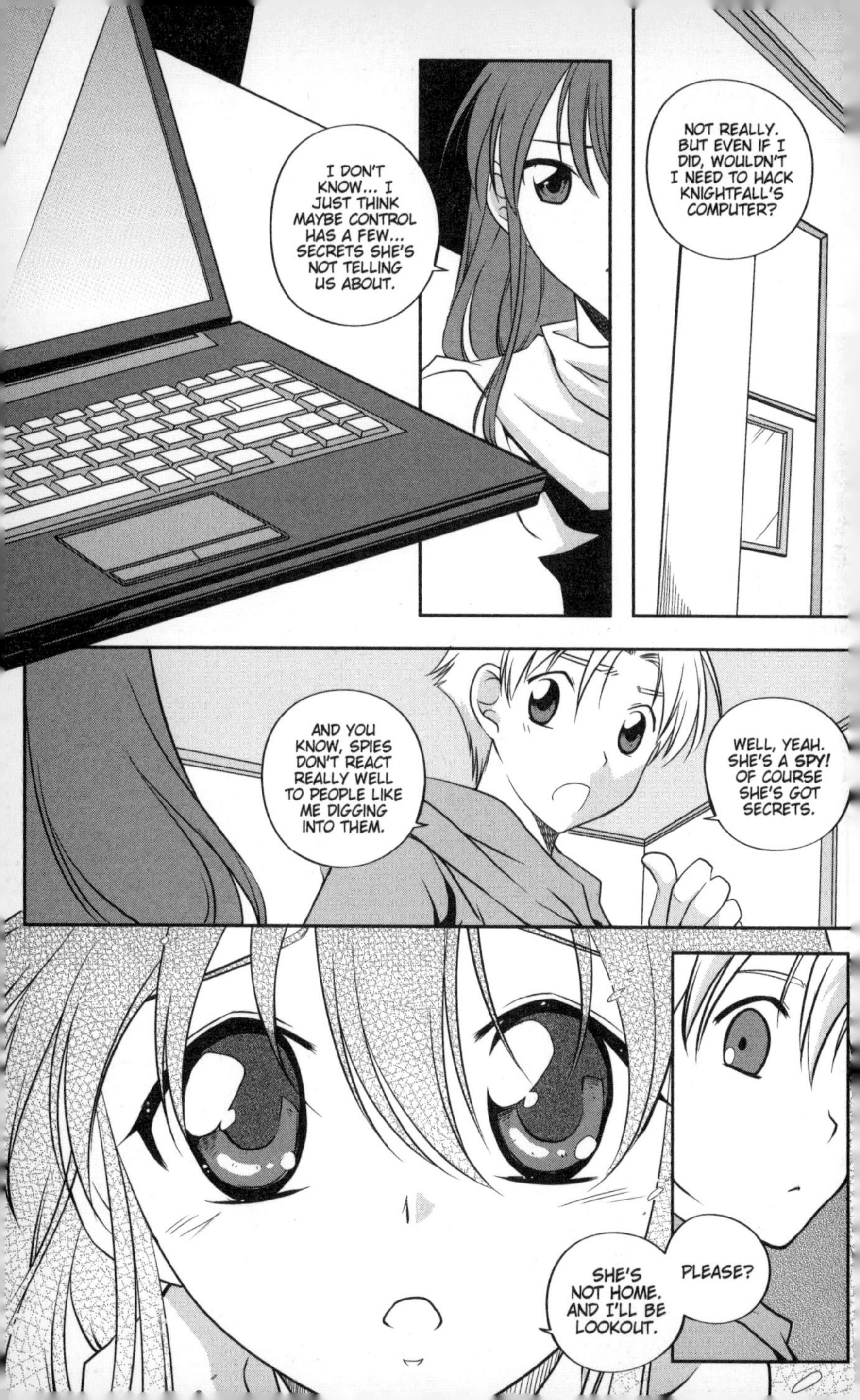
NOT REALLY. BUT EVEN IF I DID, WOULDN'T I NEED TO HACK KNIGHTFALL'S COMPUTER?
I DON'T KNOW... I JUST THINK MAYBE CONTROL HAS A FEW... SECRETS SHE'S NOT TELLING US ABOUT.
WELL, YEAH. SHE'S A **SPY!** OF COURSE SHE'S GOT SECRETS.
AND YOU KNOW, SPIES DON'T REACT REALLY WELL TO PEOPLE LIKE ME DIGGING INTO THEM.
PLEASE?
SHE'S NOT HOME. AND I'LL BE LOOKOUT.

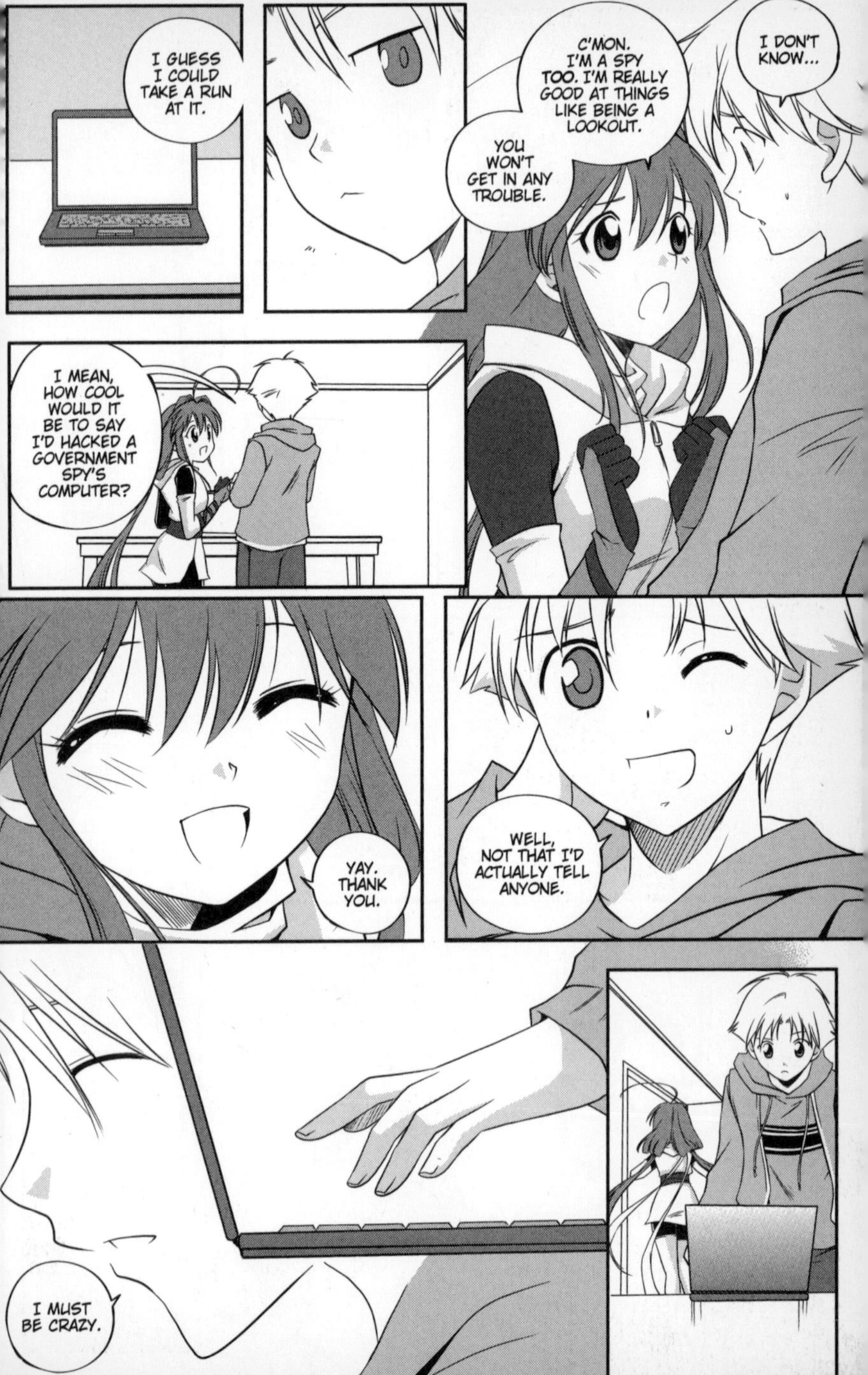
I DON'T KNOW...
C'MON. I'M A SPY TOO. I'M REALLY GOOD AT THINGS LIKE BEING A LOOKOUT.
YOU WON'T GET IN ANY TROUBLE.
I GUESS I COULD TAKE A RUN AT IT.
I MEAN, HOW COOL WOULD IT BE TO SAY I'D HACKED A GOVERNMENT SPY'S COMPUTER?
WELL, NOT THAT I'D ACTUALLY TELL ANYONE.
YAY. THANK YOU.
I MUST BE CRAZY.

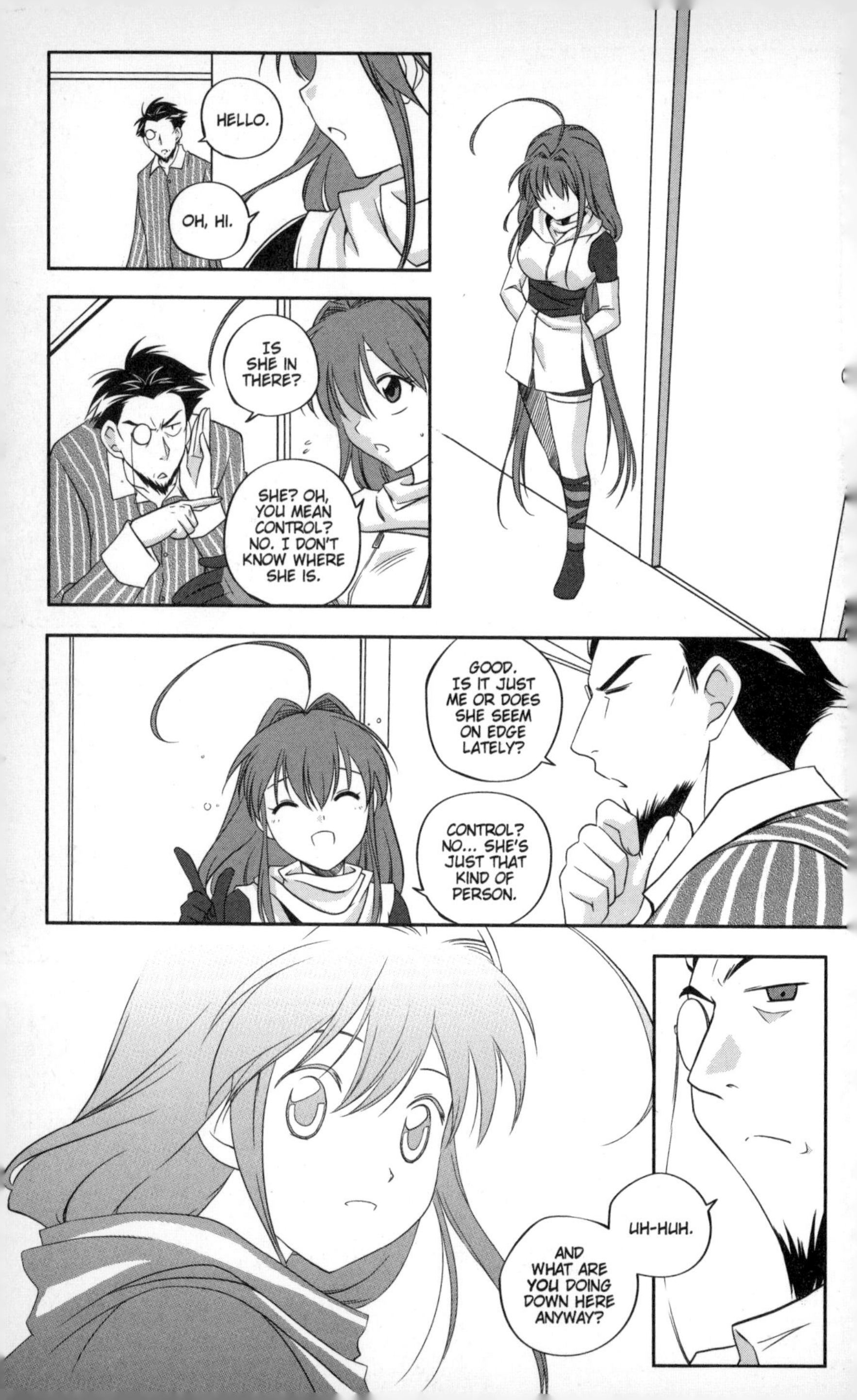

HELLO.
OH, HI.
IS SHE IN THERE?
SHE? OH, YOU MEAN CONTROL? NO. I DON'T KNOW WHERE SHE IS.
GOOD. IS IT JUST ME OR DOES SHE SEEM ON EDGE LATELY?
CONTROL? NO... SHE'S JUST THAT KIND OF PERSON.
UH-HUH.
AND WHAT ARE YOU DOING DOWN HERE ANYWAY?

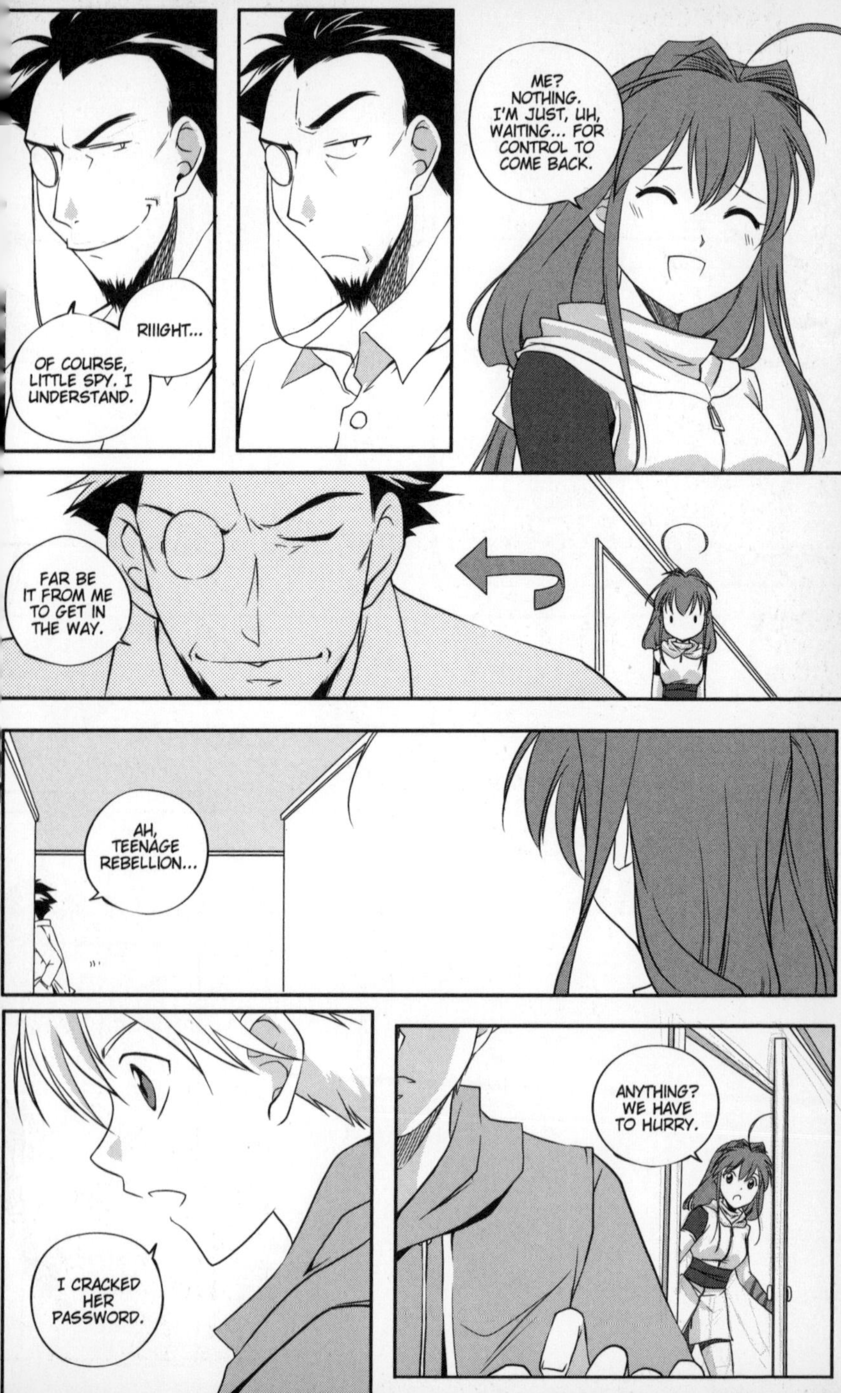
ME? NOTHING. I'M JUST, UH, WAITING... FOR CONTROL TO COME BACK.
RIIIGHT...
OF COURSE, LITTLE SPY. I UNDERSTAND.
FAR BE IT FROM ME TO GET IN THE WAY.
AH, TEENAGE REBELLION...
ANYTHING? WE HAVE TO HURRY.
I CRACKED HER PASSWORD.

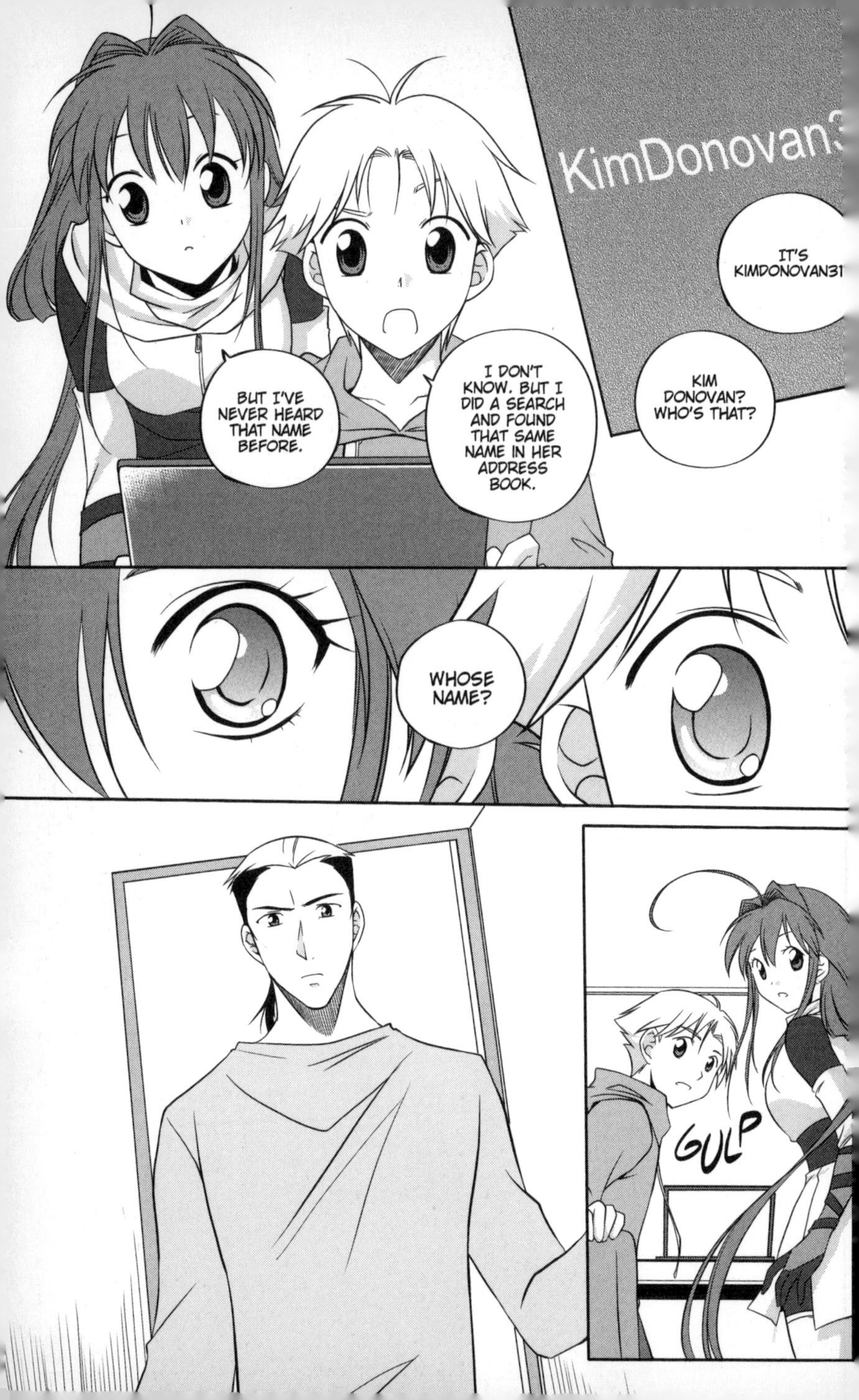
KimDonovan3
IT'S KIMDONOVAN31
KIM DONOVAN? WHO'S THAT?
I DON'T KNOW. BUT I DID A SEARCH AND FOUND THAT SAME NAME IN HER ADDRESS BOOK.
BUT I'VE NEVER HEARD THAT NAME BEFORE.
WHOSE NAME?
GULP

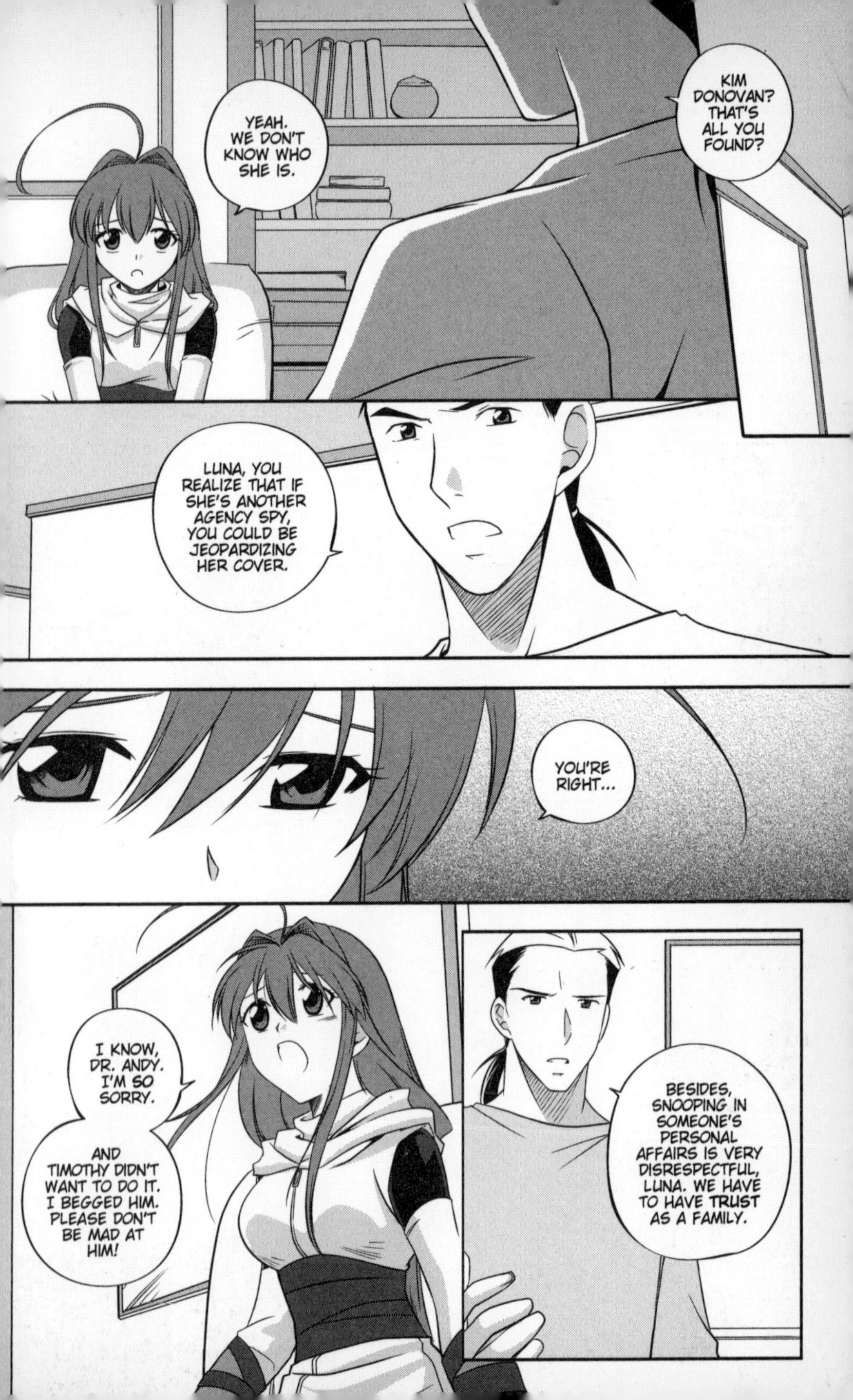
KIM DONOVAN? THAT'S ALL YOU FOUND?
YEAH. WE DON'T KNOW WHO SHE IS.
LUNA, YOU REALIZE THAT IF SHE'S ANOTHER AGENCY SPY, YOU COULD BE JEOPARDIZING HER COVER.
YOU'RE RIGHT...
BESIDES, SNOOPING IN SOMEONE'S PERSONAL AFFAIRS IS VERY DISRESPECTFUL, LUNA. WE HAVE TO HAVE TRUST AS A FAMILY.
I KNOW, DR. ANDY. I'M SO SORRY.
AND TIMOTHY DIDN'T WANT TO DO IT. I BEGGED HIM. PLEASE DON'T BE MAD AT HIM!

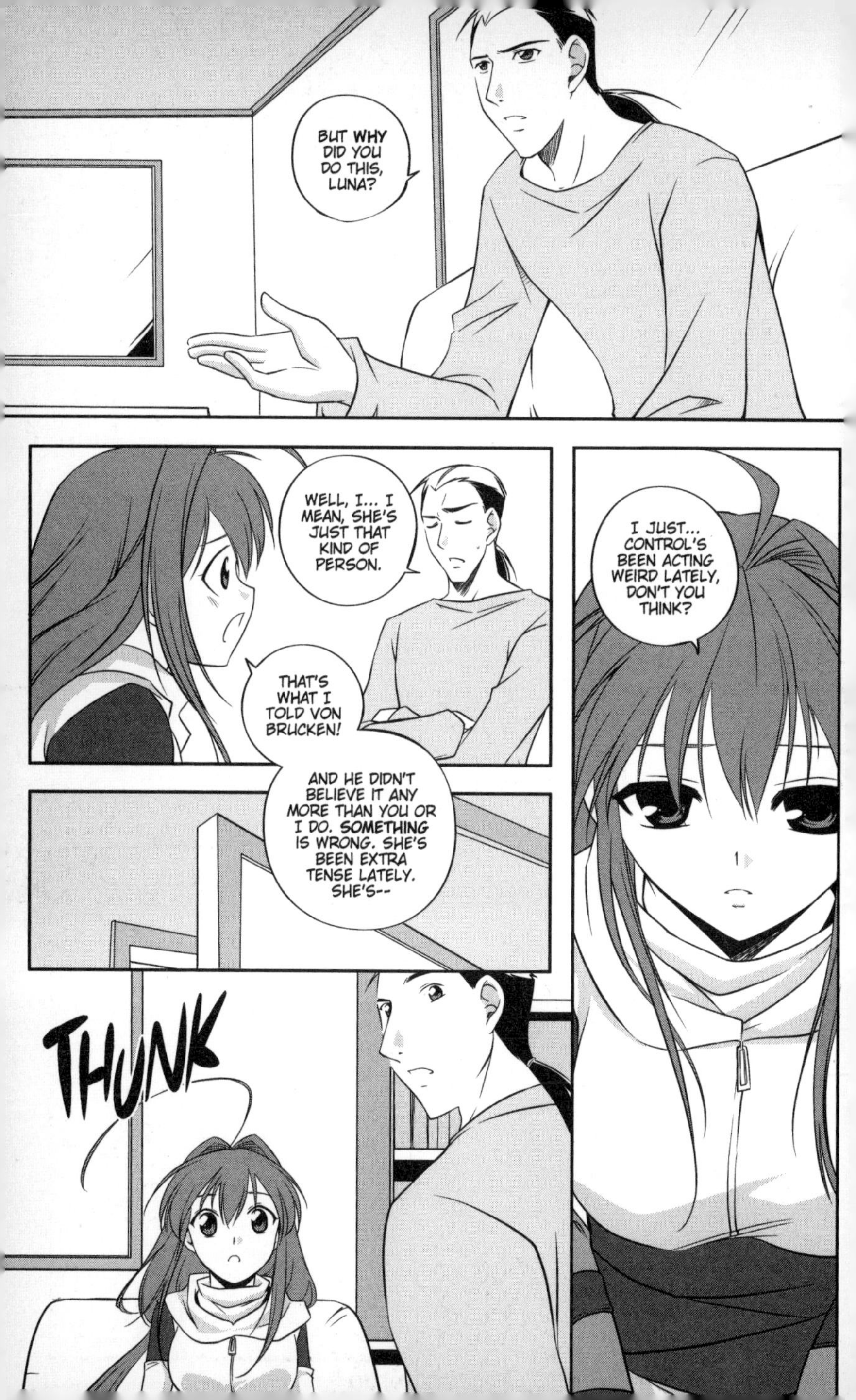
BUT WHY DID YOU DO THIS, LUNA?
I JUST... CONTROL'S BEEN ACTING WEIRD LATELY, DON'T YOU THINK?
WELL, I... I MEAN, SHE'S JUST THAT KIND OF PERSON.
THAT'S WHAT I TOLD VON BRUCKEN!
AND HE DIDN'T BELIEVE IT ANY MORE THAN YOU OR I DO. SOMETHING IS WRONG. SHE'S BEEN EXTRA TENSE LATELY. SHE'S--
THUNK

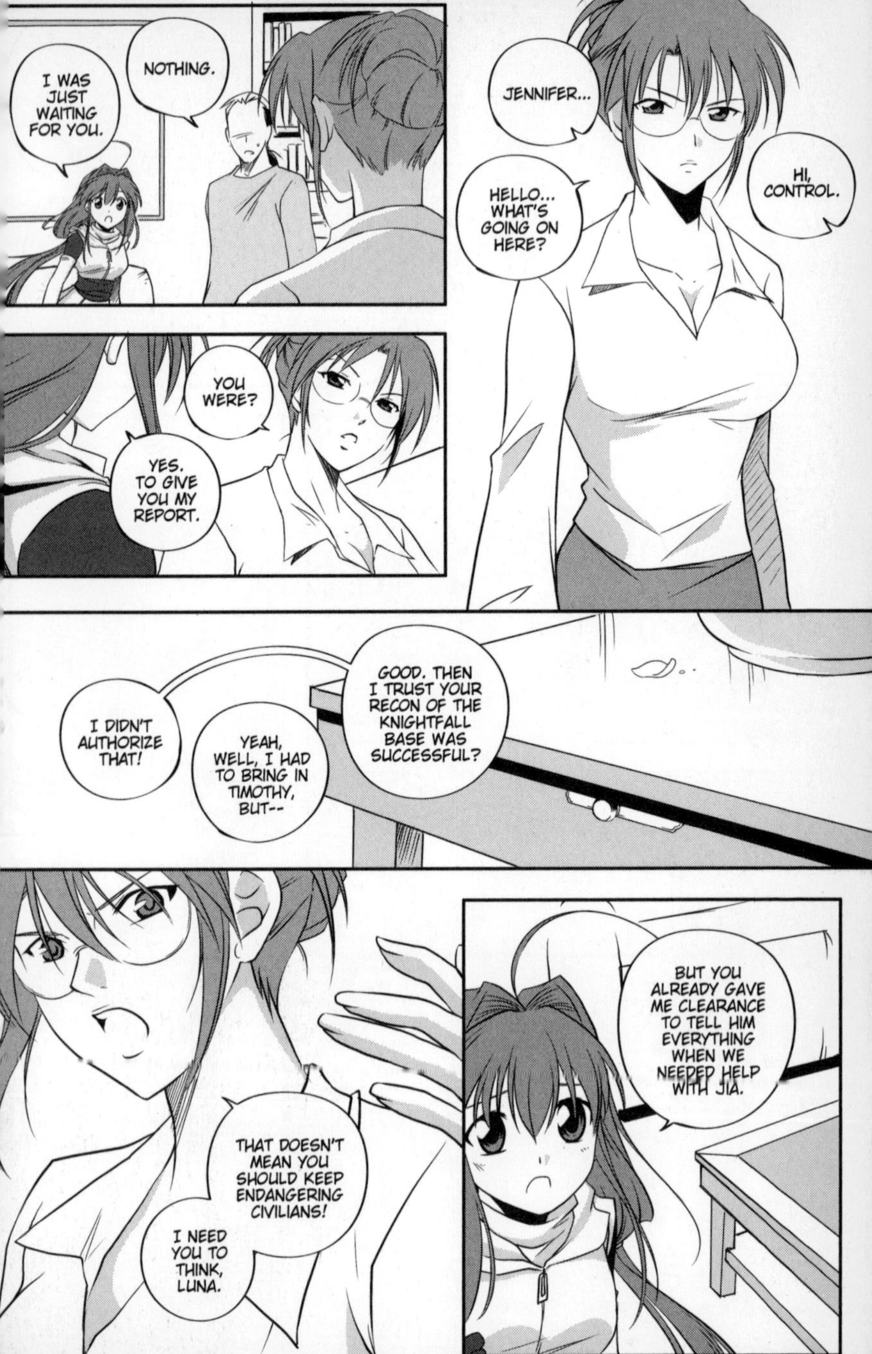
JENNIFER...
HI, CONTROL.
HELLO... WHAT'S GOING ON HERE?
NOTHING.
I WAS JUST WAITING FOR YOU.
YOU WERE?
YES. TO GIVE YOU MY REPORT.
GOOD. THEN I TRUST YOUR RECON OF THE KNIGHTFALL BASE WAS SUCCESSFUL?
YEAH, WELL, I HAD TO BRING IN TIMOTHY, BUT--
I DIDN'T AUTHORIZE THAT!
BUT YOU ALREADY GAVE ME CLEARANCE TO TELL HIM EVERYTHING WHEN WE NEEDED HELP WITH JIA.
THAT DOESN'T MEAN YOU SHOULD KEEP ENDANGERING CIVILIANS!
I NEED YOU TO THINK, LUNA.

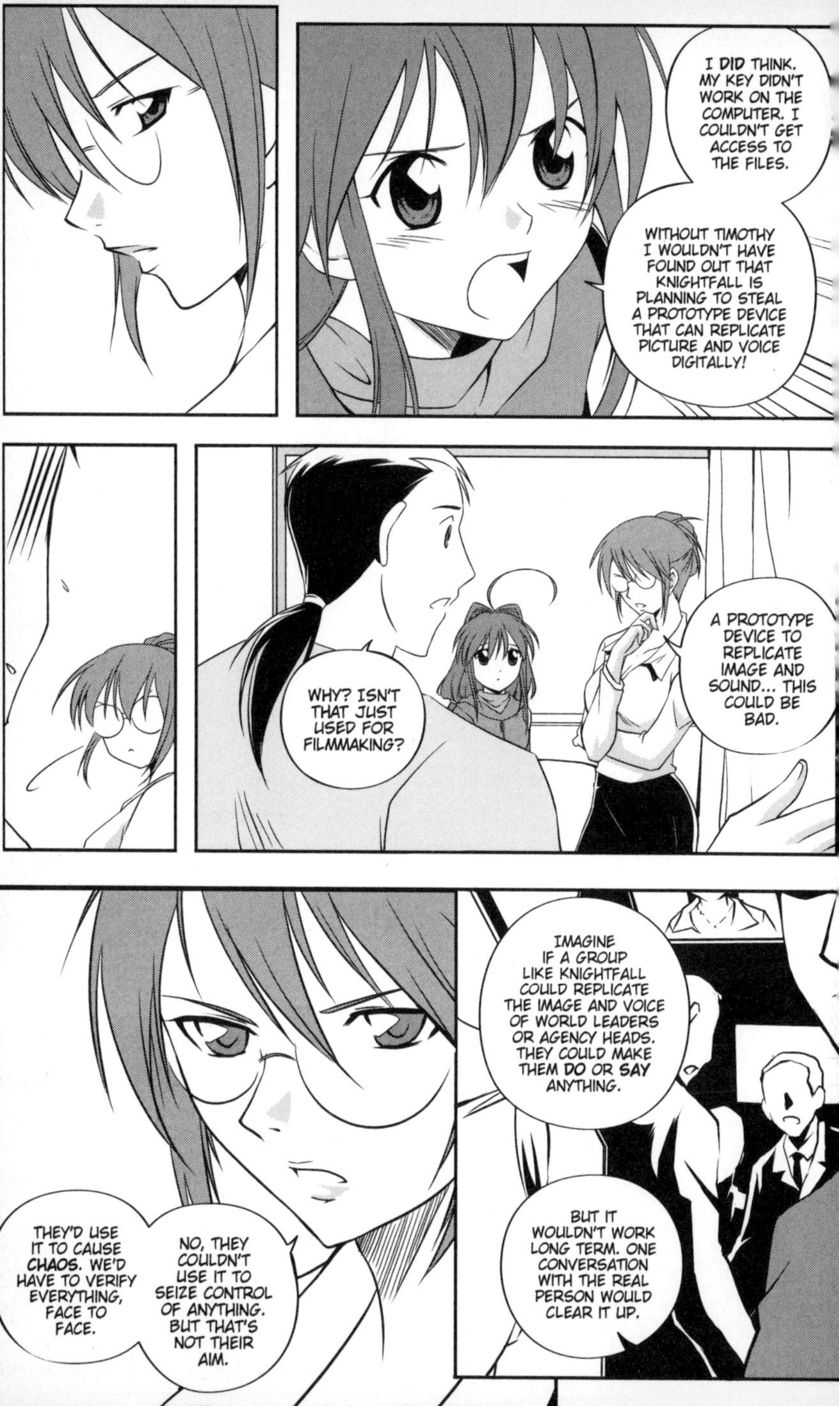
I **DID** THINK. MY KEY DIDN'T WORK ON THE COMPUTER. I COULDN'T GET ACCESS TO THE FILES.
WITHOUT TIMOTHY I WOULDN'T HAVE FOUND OUT THAT KNIGHTFALL IS PLANNING TO STEAL A PROTOTYPE DEVICE THAT CAN REPLICATE PICTURE AND VOICE DIGITALLY!
A PROTOTYPE DEVICE TO REPLICATE IMAGE AND SOUND... THIS COULD BE BAD.
WHY? ISN'T THAT JUST USED FOR FILMMAKING?
IMAGINE IF A GROUP LIKE KNIGHTFALL COULD REPLICATE THE IMAGE AND VOICE OF WORLD LEADERS OR AGENCY HEADS. THEY COULD MAKE THEM **DO** OR **SAY** ANYTHING.
BUT IT WOULDN'T WORK LONG TERM. ONE CONVERSATION WITH THE REAL PERSON WOULD CLEAR IT UP.
NO, THEY COULDN'T USE IT TO SEIZE CONTROL OF ANYTHING. BUT THAT'S NOT THEIR AIM.
THEY'D USE IT TO CAUSE **CHAOS**. WE'D HAVE TO VERIFY EVERYTHING, FACE TO FACE.

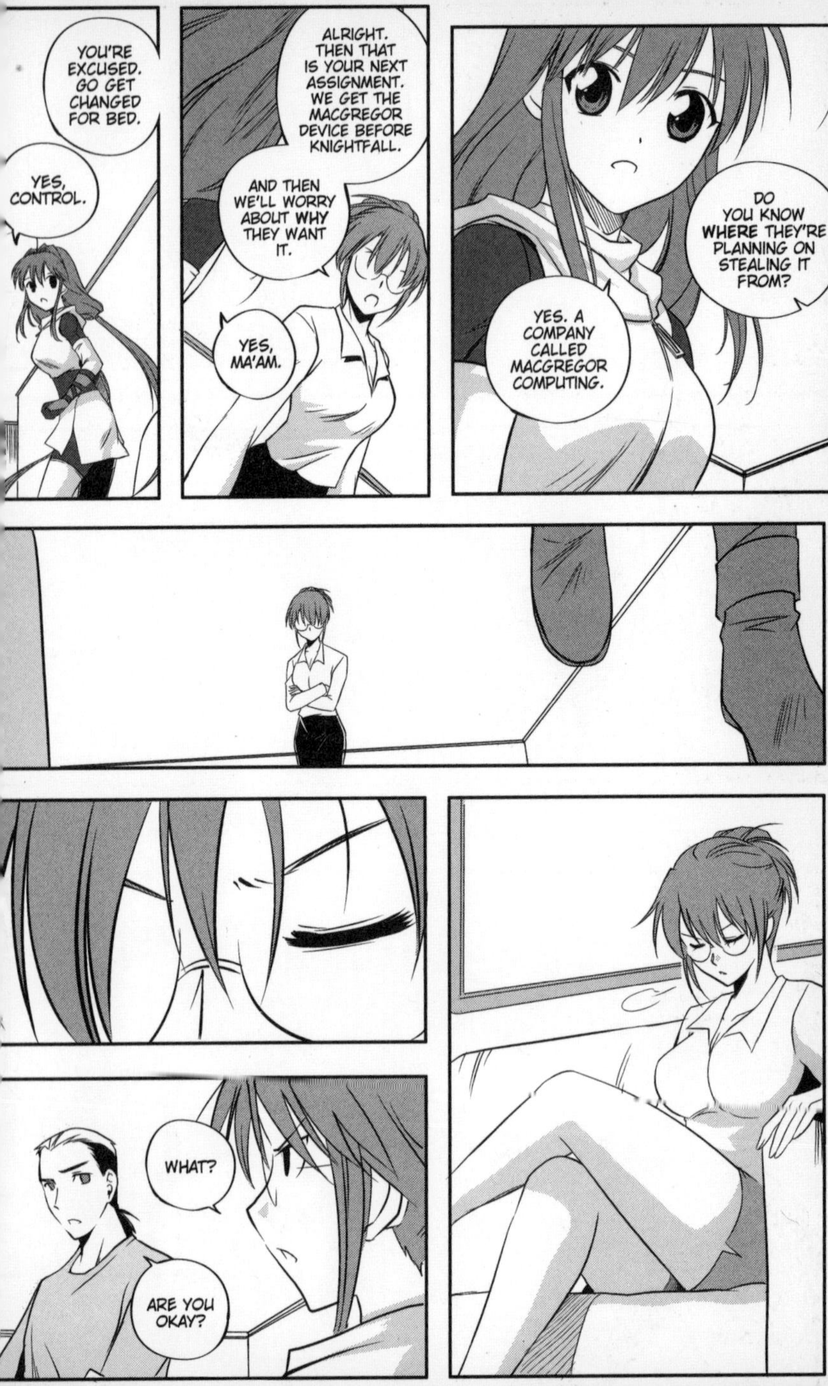
DO YOU KNOW WHERE THEY'RE PLANNING ON STEALING IT FROM?
YES. A COMPANY CALLED MACGREGOR COMPUTING.
ALRIGHT. THEN THAT IS YOUR NEXT ASSIGNMENT. WE GET THE MACGREGOR DEVICE BEFORE KNIGHTFALL.
AND THEN WE'LL WORRY ABOUT WHY THEY WANT IT.
YES, MA'AM.
YOU'RE EXCUSED. GO GET CHANGED FOR BED.
YES, CONTROL.
WHAT?
ARE YOU OKAY?

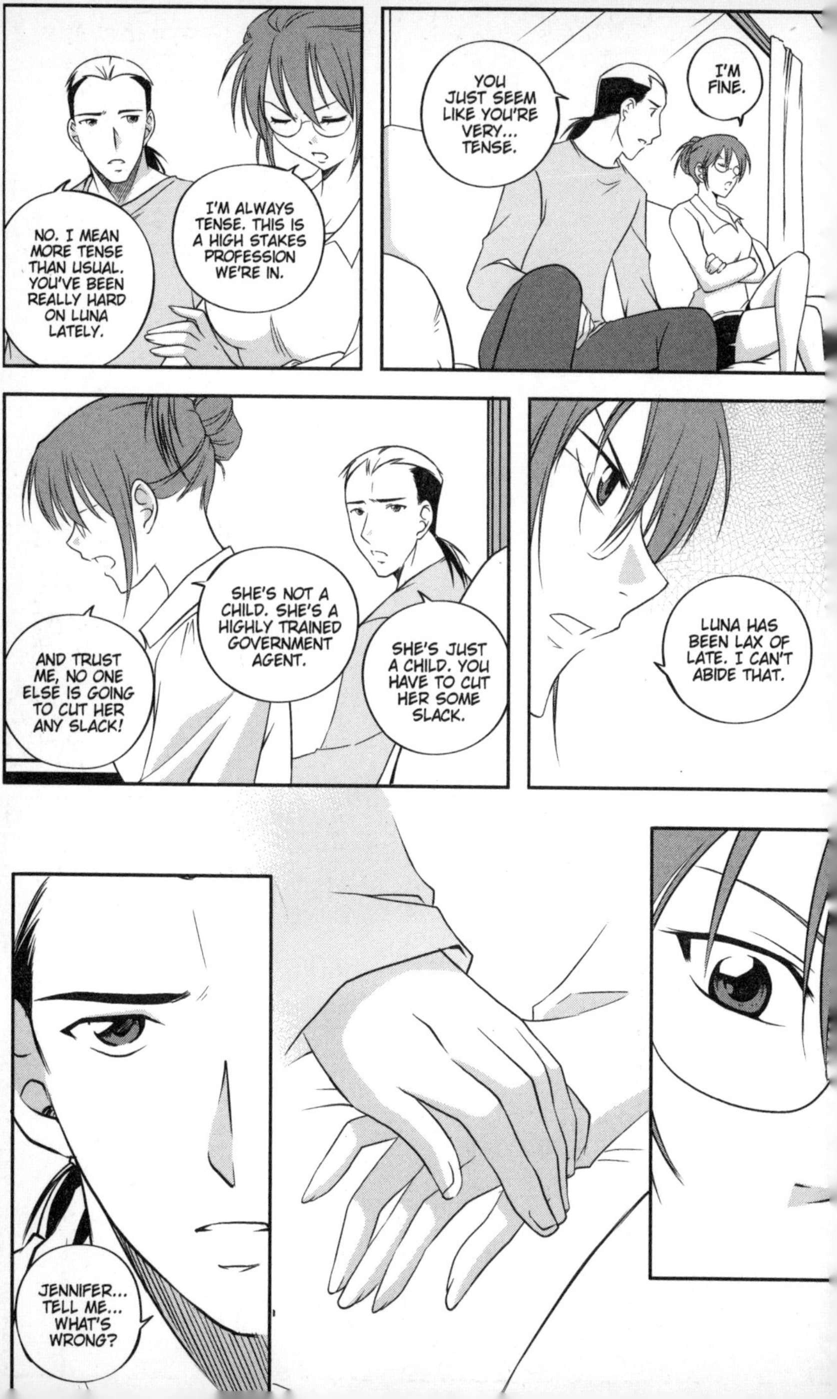
I'M FINE.
YOU JUST SEEM LIKE YOU'RE VERY... TENSE.
I'M ALWAYS TENSE. THIS IS A HIGH STAKES PROFESSION WE'RE IN.
NO. I MEAN MORE TENSE THAN USUAL. YOU'VE BEEN REALLY HARD ON LUNA LATELY.
LUNA HAS BEEN LAX OF LATE. I CAN'T ABIDE THAT.
SHE'S JUST A CHILD. YOU HAVE TO CUT HER SOME SLACK.
SHE'S NOT A CHILD. SHE'S A HIGHLY TRAINED GOVERNMENT AGENT.
AND TRUST ME, NO ONE ELSE IS GOING TO CUT HER ANY SLACK!
JENNIFER... TELL ME... WHAT'S WRONG?

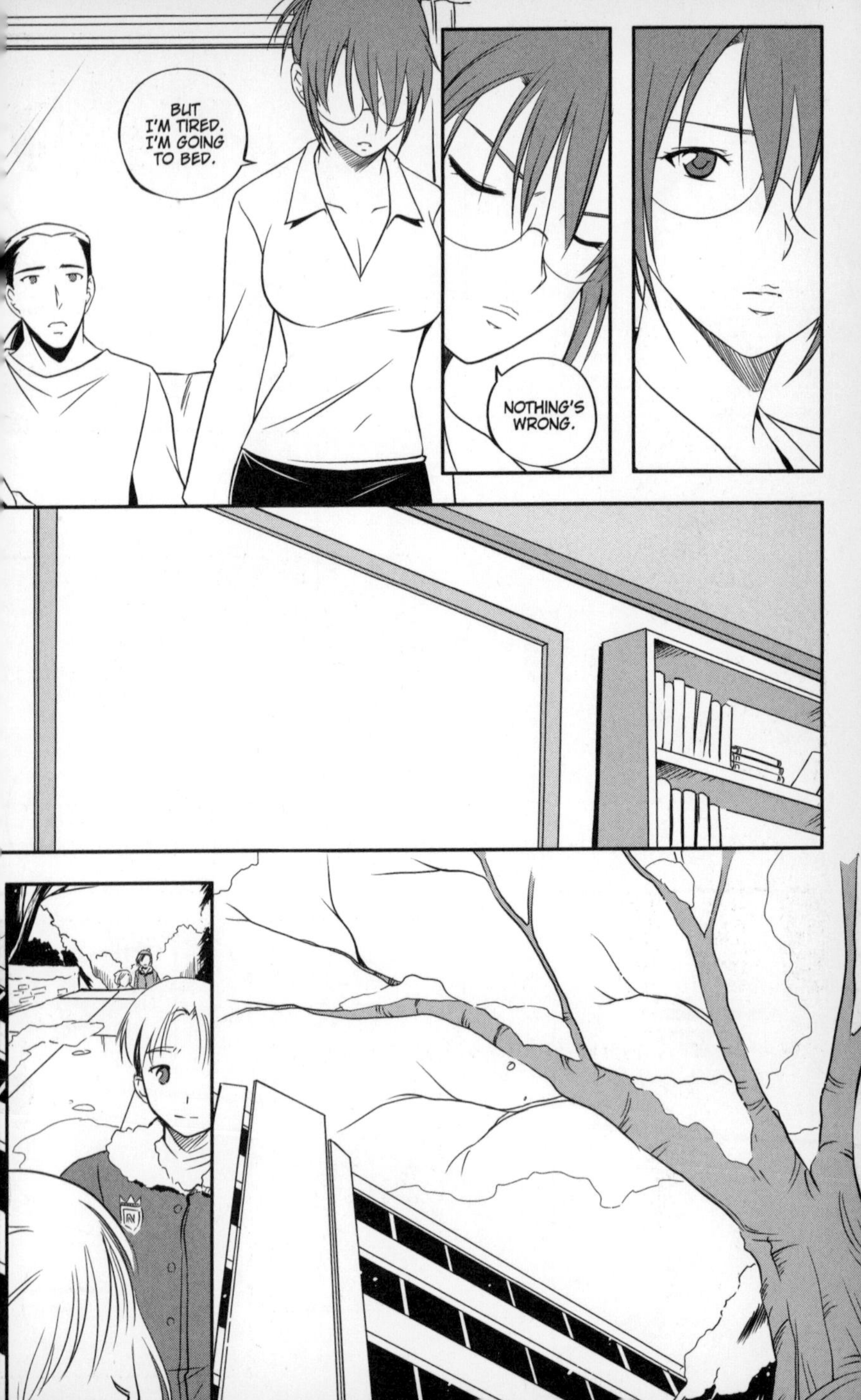
NOTHING'S WRONG.
BUT I'M TIRED. I'M GOING TO BED.

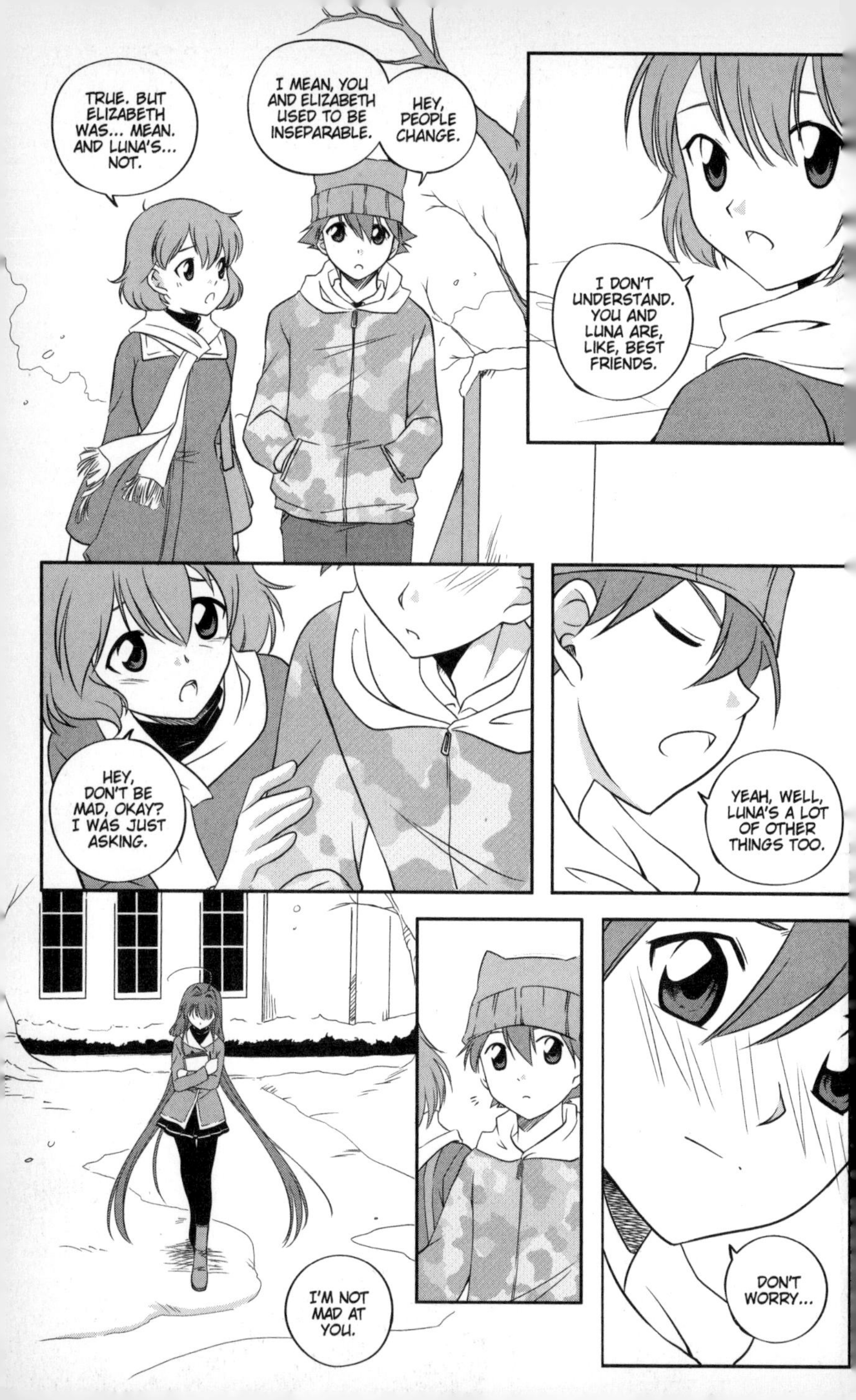
I DON'T UNDERSTAND. YOU AND LUNA ARE, LIKE, BEST FRIENDS.
HEY, PEOPLE CHANGE.
I MEAN, YOU AND ELIZABETH USED TO BE INSEPARABLE.
TRUE. BUT ELIZABETH WAS... MEAN. AND LUNA'S... NOT.
YEAH, WELL, LUNA'S A LOT OF OTHER THINGS TOO.
HEY, DON'T BE MAD, OKAY? I WAS JUST ASKING.
DON'T WORRY...
I'M NOT MAD AT YOU.

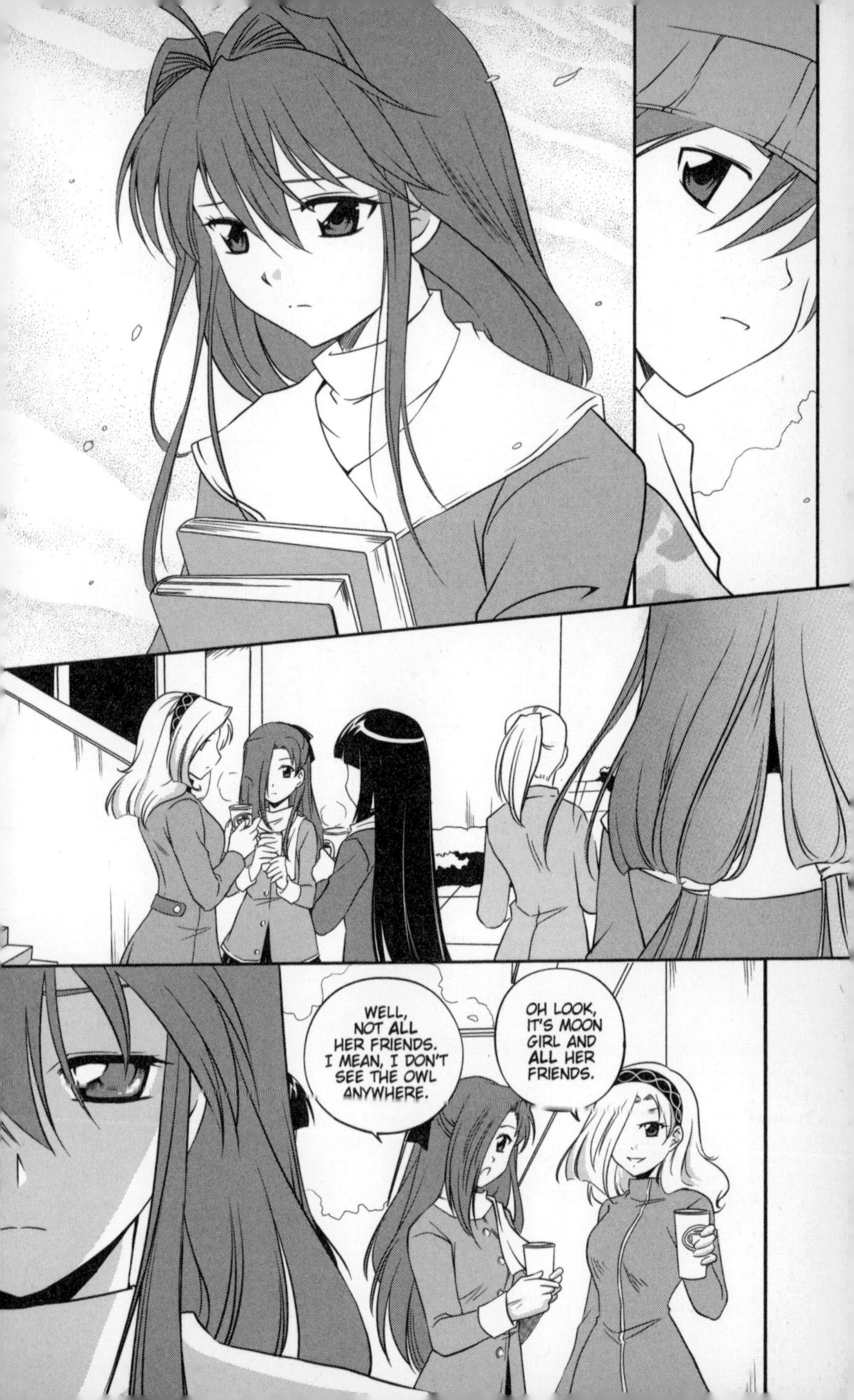
OH LOOK, IT'S MOON GIRL AND ALL HER FRIENDS.
WELL, NOT ALL HER FRIENDS. I MEAN, I DON'T SEE THE OWL ANYWHERE.

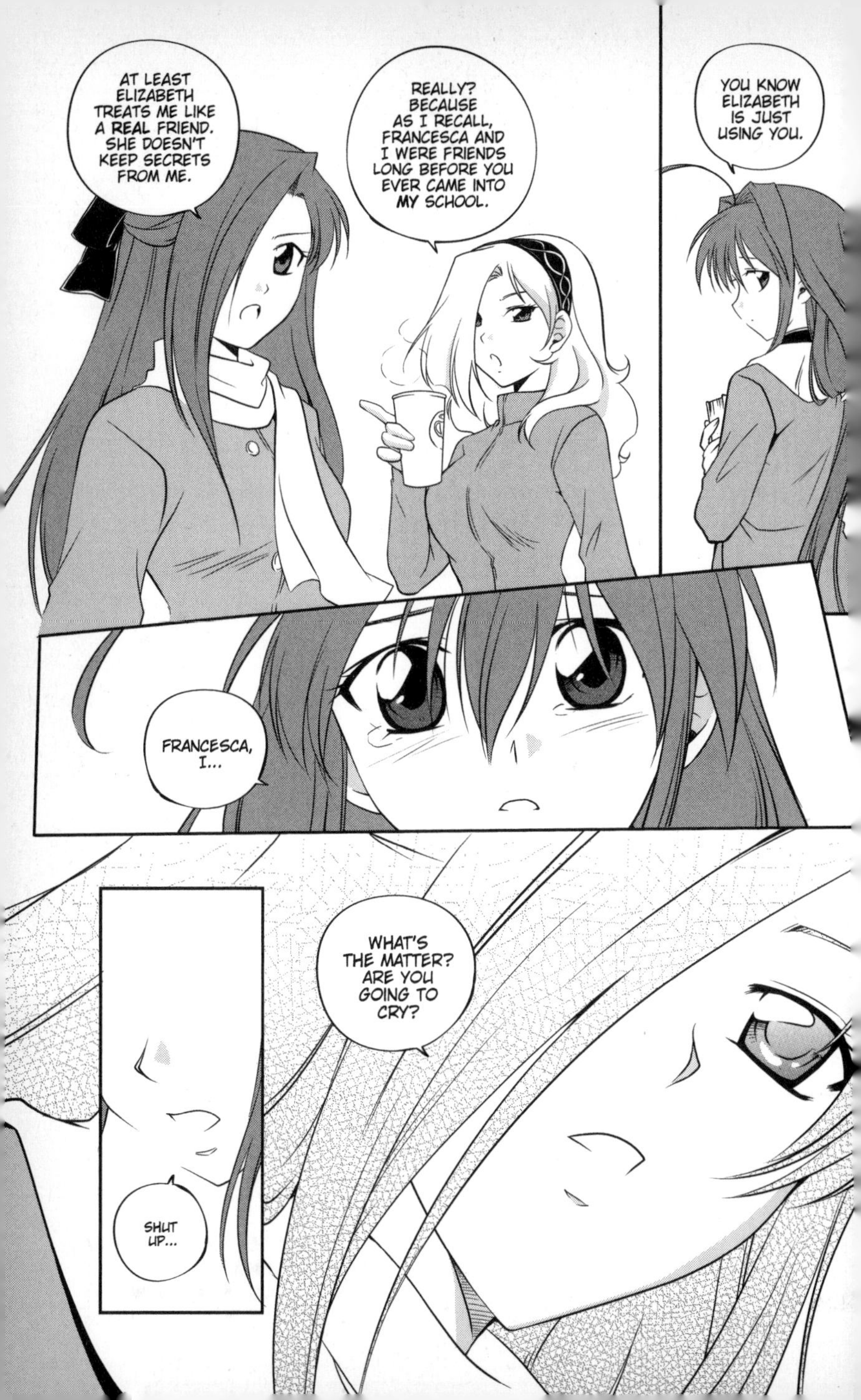
YOU KNOW ELIZABETH IS JUST USING YOU.
AT LEAST ELIZABETH TREATS ME LIKE A REAL FRIEND. SHE DOESN'T KEEP SECRETS FROM ME.
REALLY? BECAUSE AS I RECALL, FRANCESCA AND I WERE FRIENDS LONG BEFORE YOU EVER CAME INTO MY SCHOOL.
FRANCESCA, I...
WHAT'S THE MATTER? ARE YOU GOING TO CRY?
SHUT UP...

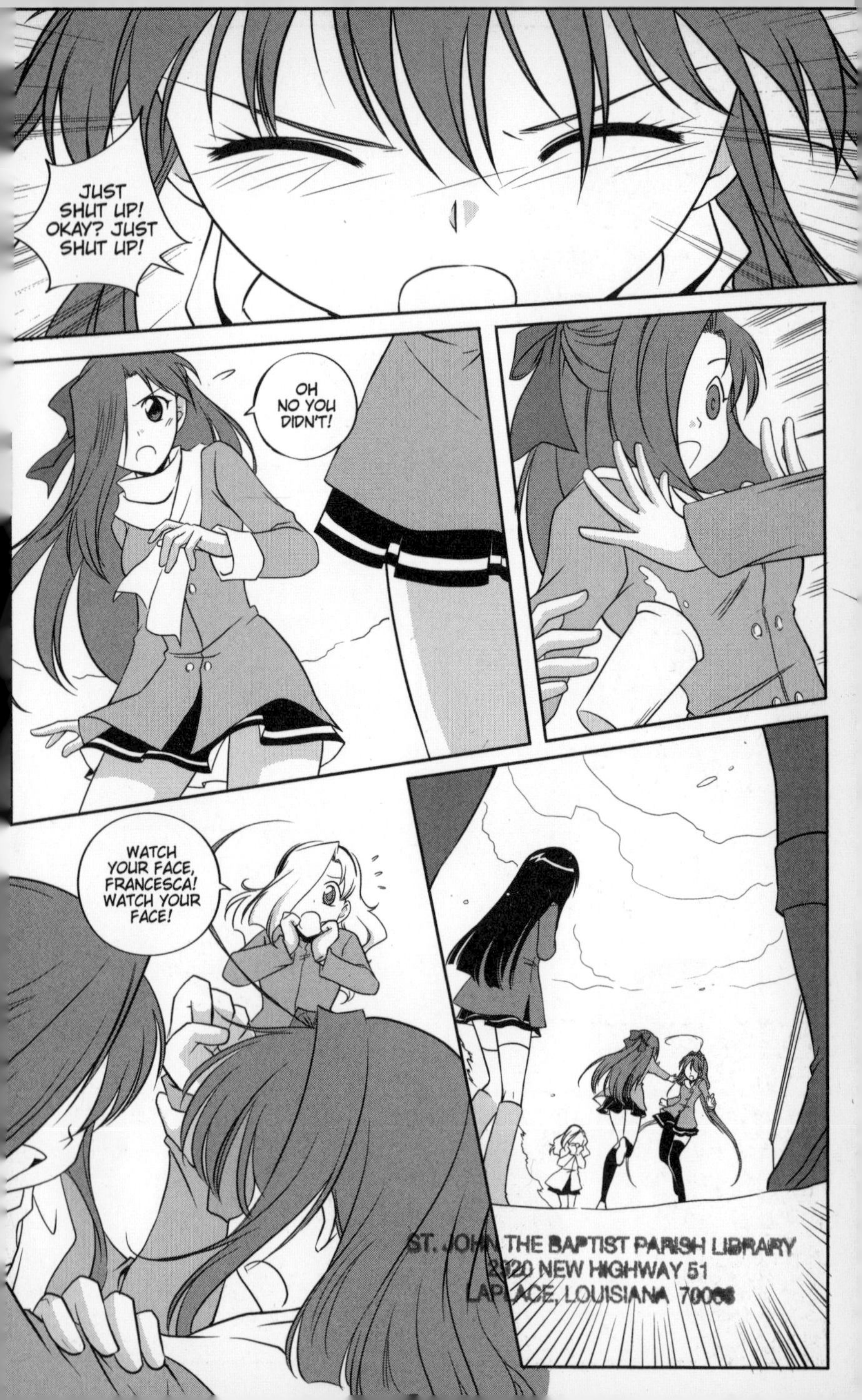
JUST SHUT UP! OKAY? JUST SHUT UP!
OH NO YOU DIDN'T!
WATCH YOUR FACE, FRANCESCA! WATCH YOUR FACE!

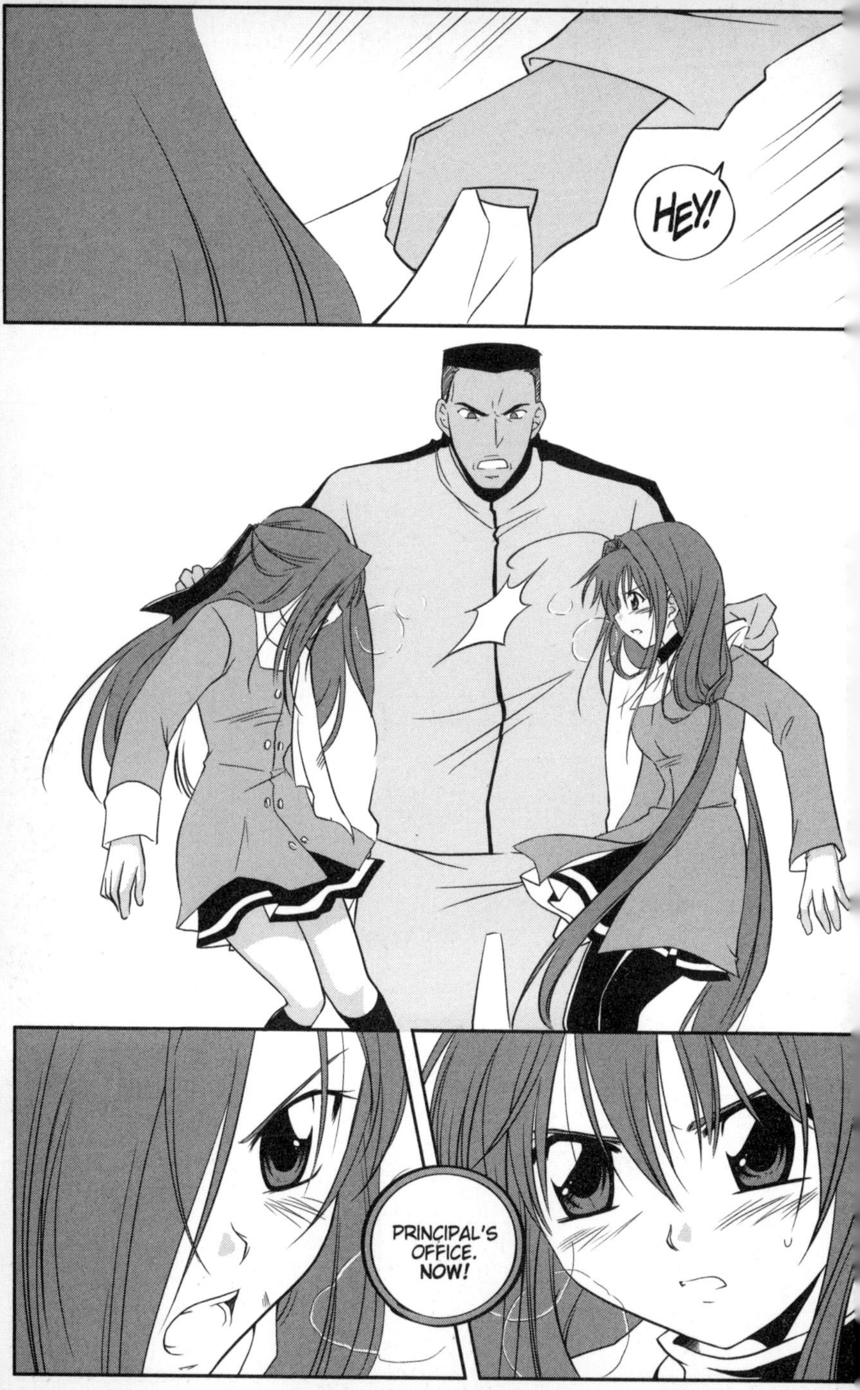
HEY!
PRINCIPAL'S OFFICE. NOW!

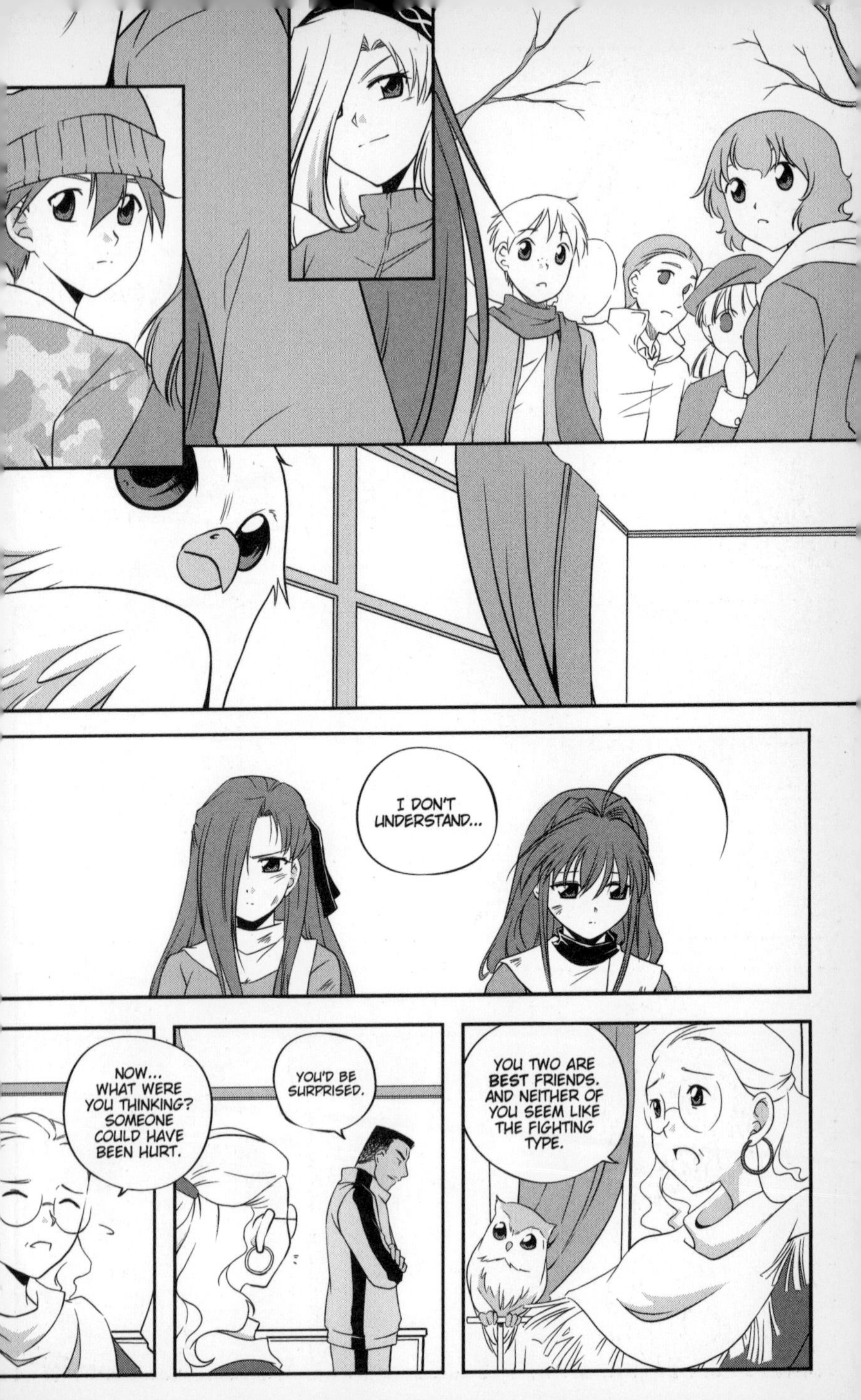
I DON'T UNDERSTAND...
YOU TWO ARE BEST FRIENDS. AND NEITHER OF YOU SEEM LIKE THE FIGHTING TYPE.
YOU'D BE SURPRISED.
NOW... WHAT WERE YOU THINKING? SOMEONE COULD HAVE BEEN HURT.

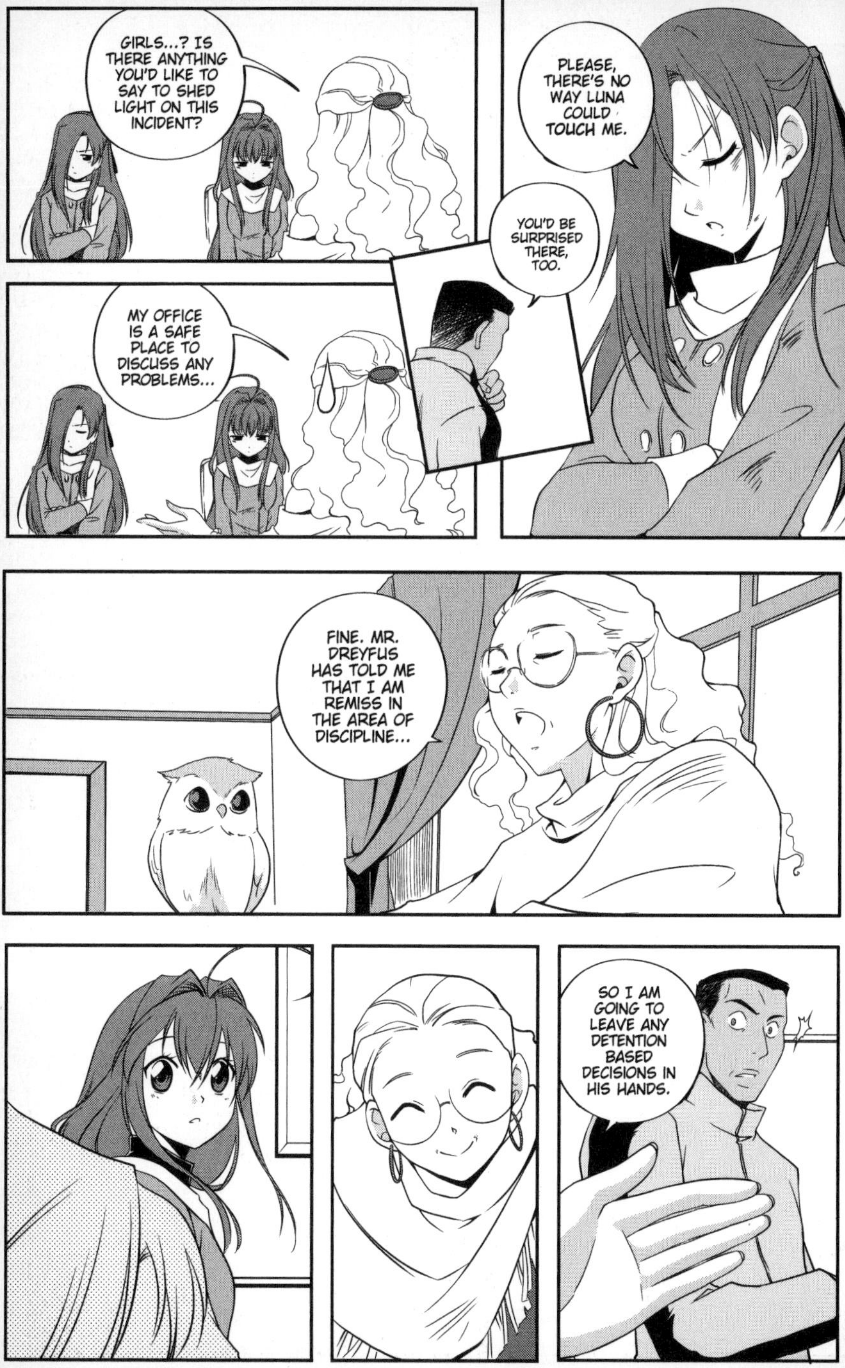
PLEASE, THERE'S NO WAY LUNA COULD TOUCH ME.
YOU'D BE SURPRISED THERE, TOO.
GIRLS...? IS THERE ANYTHING YOU'D LIKE TO SAY TO SHED LIGHT ON THIS INCIDENT?
MY OFFICE IS A SAFE PLACE TO DISCUSS ANY PROBLEMS...
FINE. MR. DREYFUS HAS TOLD ME THAT I AM REMISS IN THE AREA OF DISCIPLINE...
SO I AM GOING TO LEAVE ANY DETENTION BASED DECISIONS IN HIS HANDS.

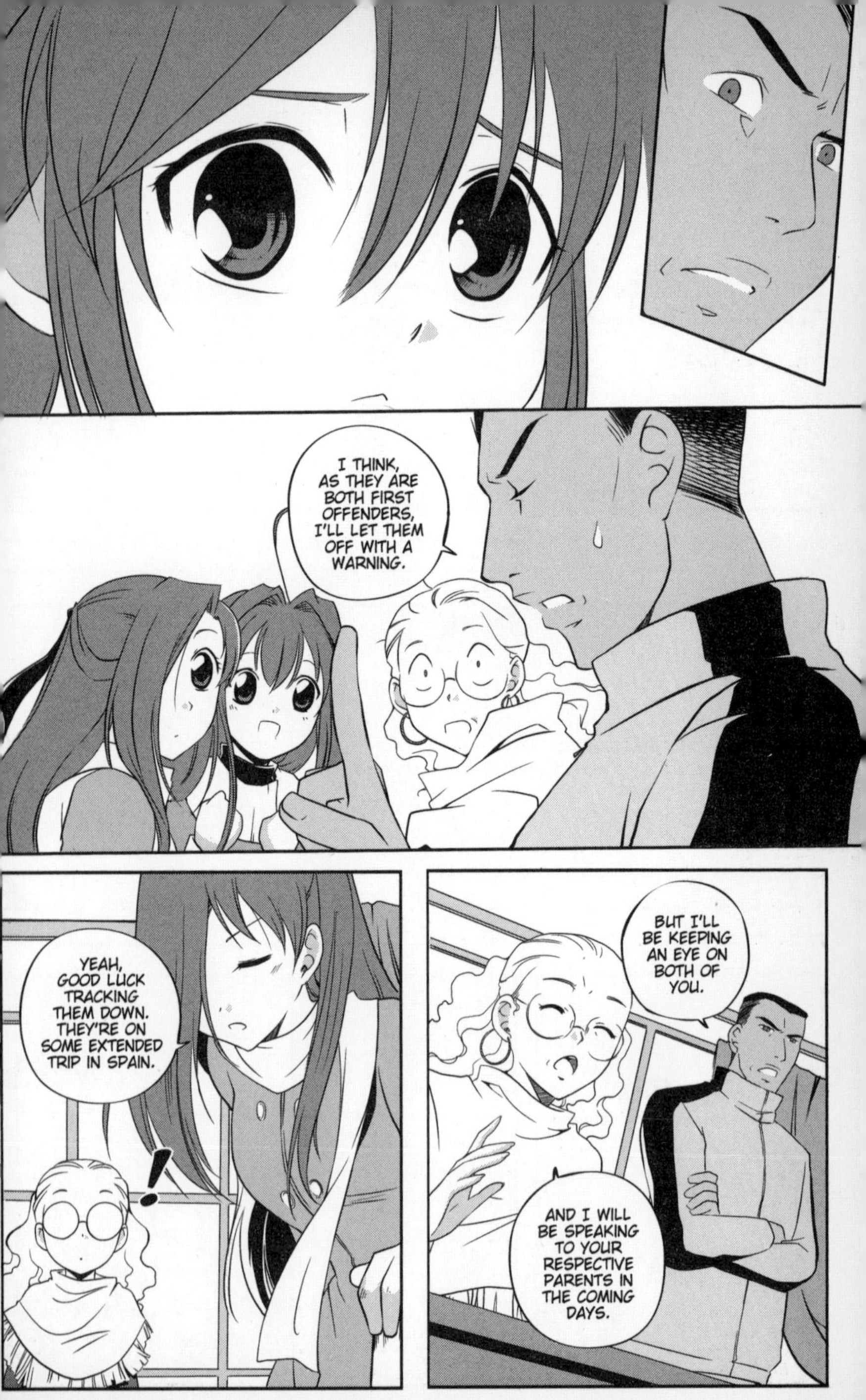
I THINK, AS THEY ARE BOTH FIRST OFFENDERS, I'LL LET THEM OFF WITH A WARNING.
BUT I'LL BE KEEPING AN EYE ON BOTH OF YOU.
AND I WILL BE SPEAKING TO YOUR RESPECTIVE PARENTS IN THE COMING DAYS.
YEAH, GOOD LUCK TRACKING THEM DOWN. THEY'RE ON SOME EXTENDED TRIP IN SPAIN.
!

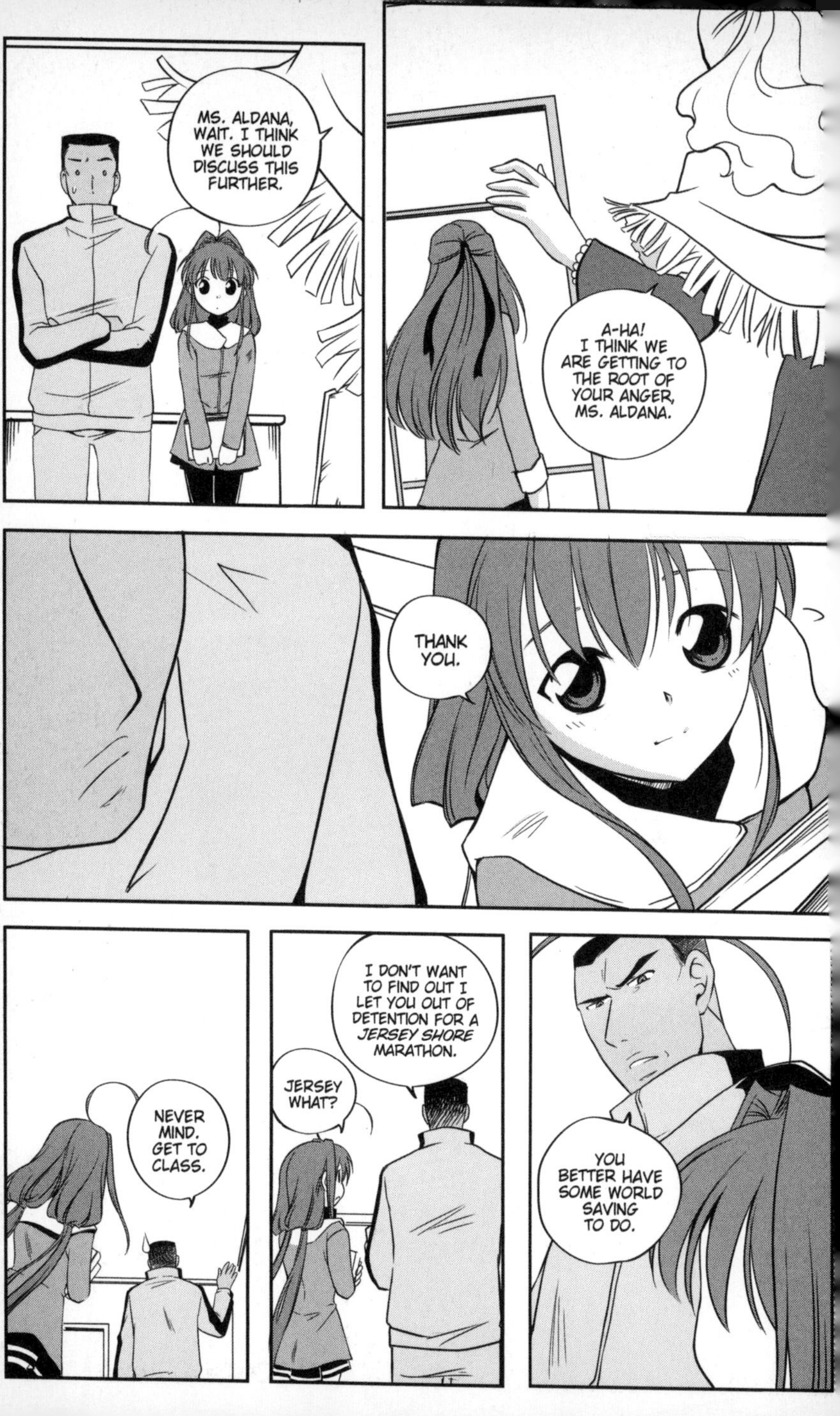
A-HA! I THINK WE ARE GETTING TO THE ROOT OF YOUR ANGER, MS. ALDANA.
MS. ALDANA, WAIT. I THINK WE SHOULD DISCUSS THIS FURTHER.
THANK YOU.
YOU BETTER HAVE SOME WORLD SAVING TO DO.
I DON'T WANT TO FIND OUT I LET YOU OUT OF DETENTION FOR A *JERSEY SHORE* MARATHON.
JERSEY WHAT?
NEVER MIND. GET TO CLASS.

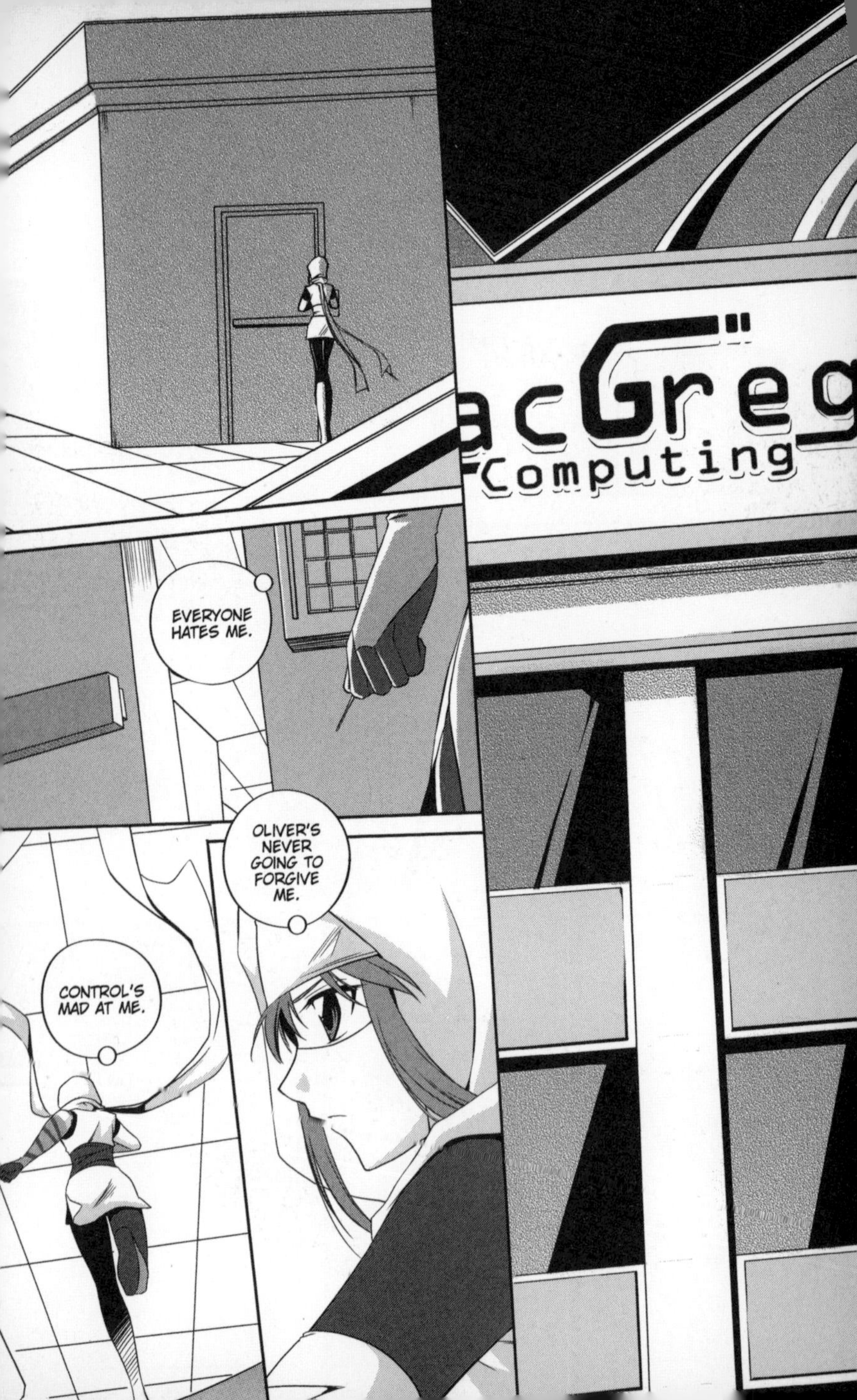
acGreg
Computing
EVERYONE HATES ME.
OLIVER'S NEVER GOING TO FORGIVE ME.
CONTROL'S MAD AT ME.

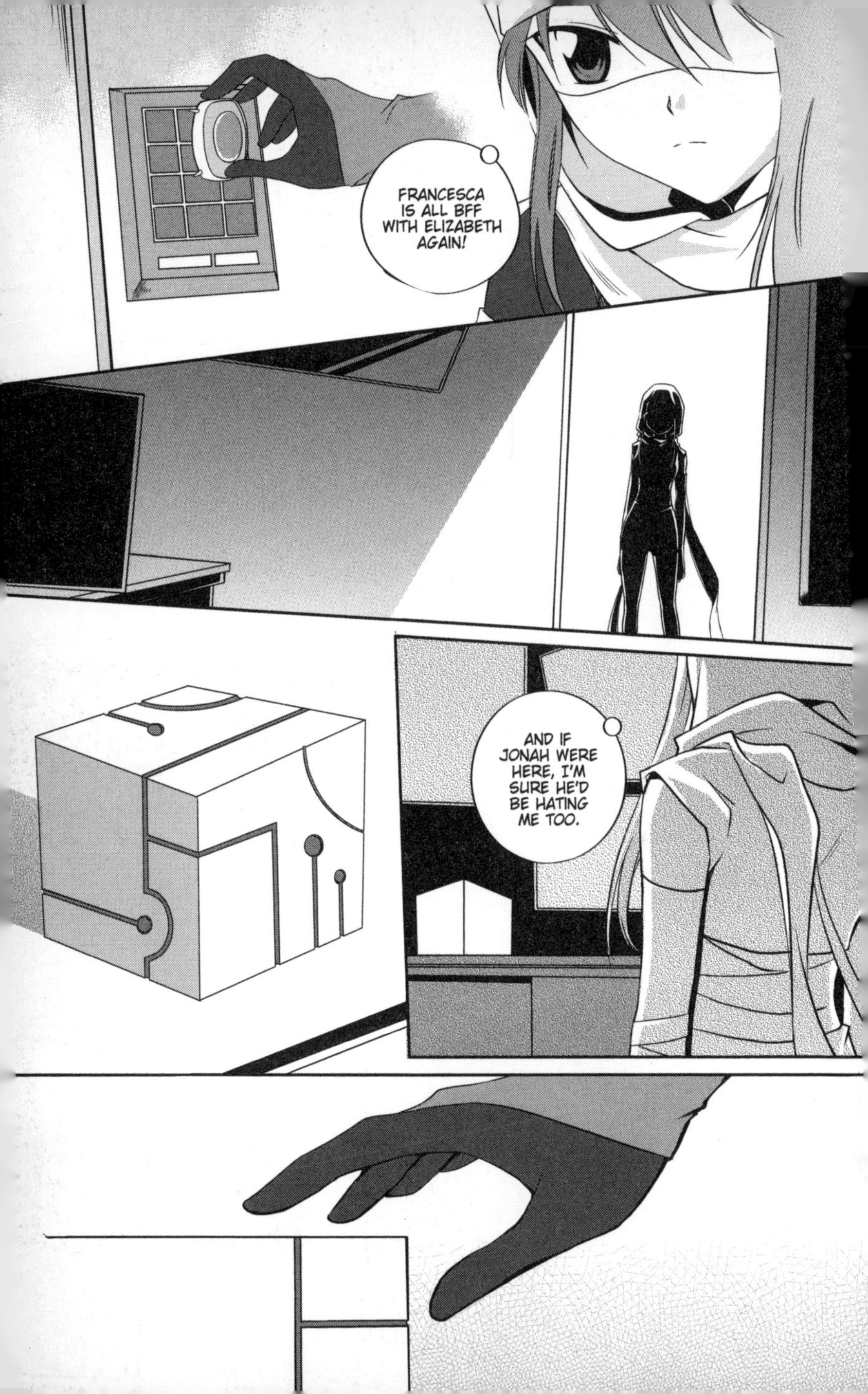
FRANCESCA IS ALL BFF WITH ELIZABETH AGAIN!
AND IF JONAH WERE HERE, I'M SURE HE'D BE HATING ME TOO.

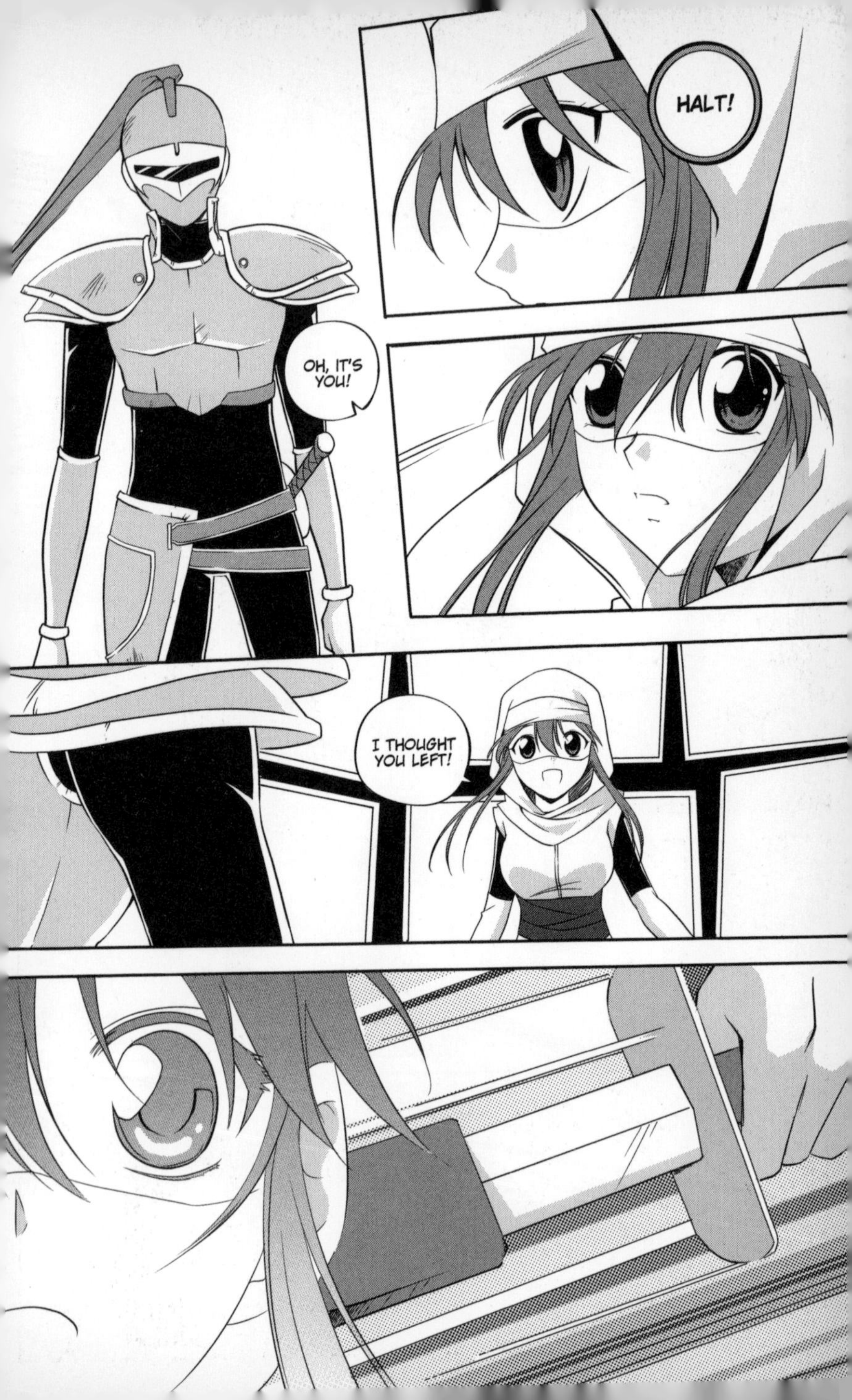
HALT!
OH, IT'S YOU!
I THOUGHT YOU LEFT!

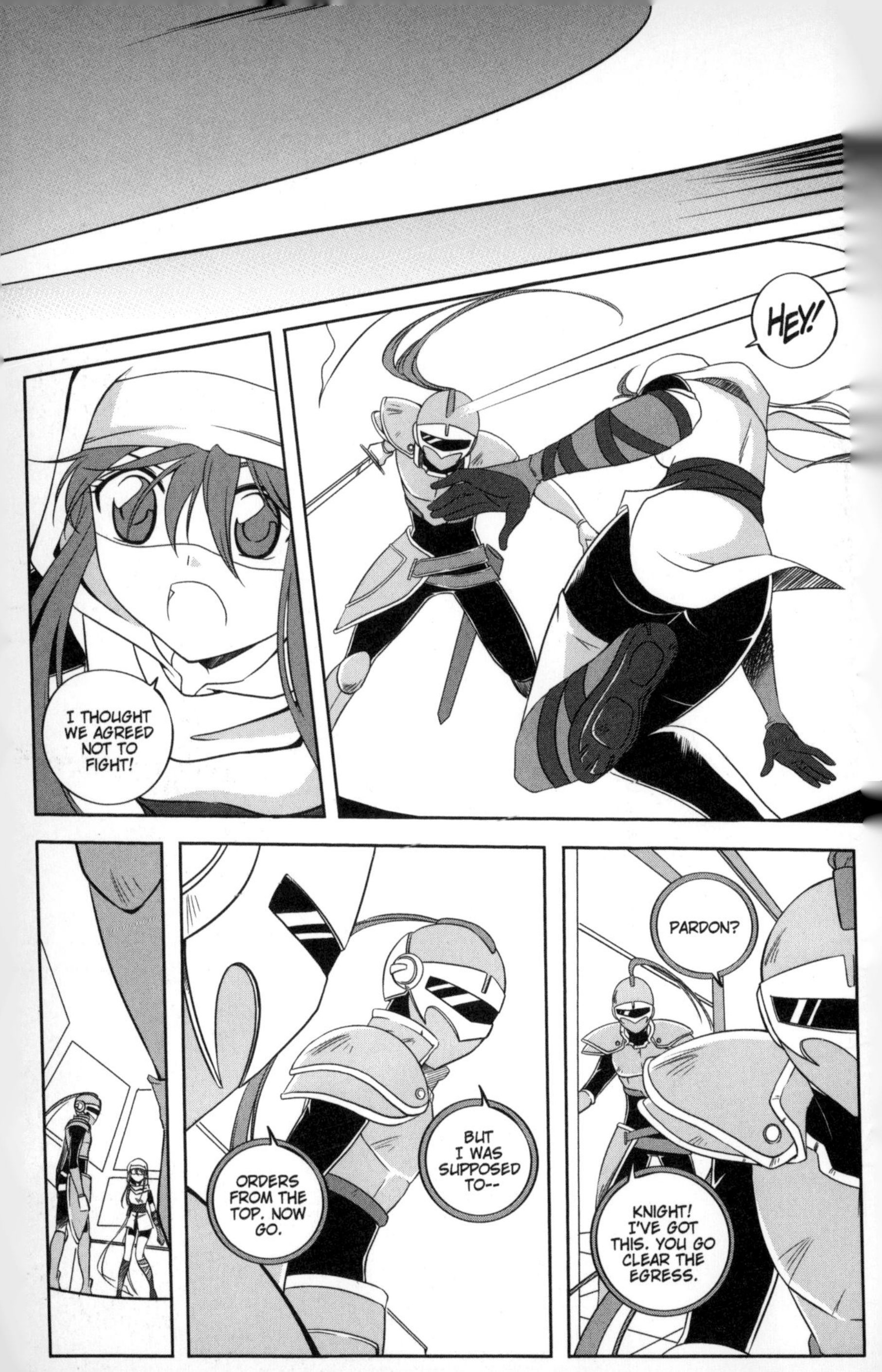
HEY!
I THOUGHT WE AGREED NOT TO FIGHT!
PARDON?
KNIGHT! I'VE GOT THIS. YOU GO CLEAR THE EGRESS.
BUT I WAS SUPPOSED TO--
ORDERS FROM THE TOP. NOW GO.

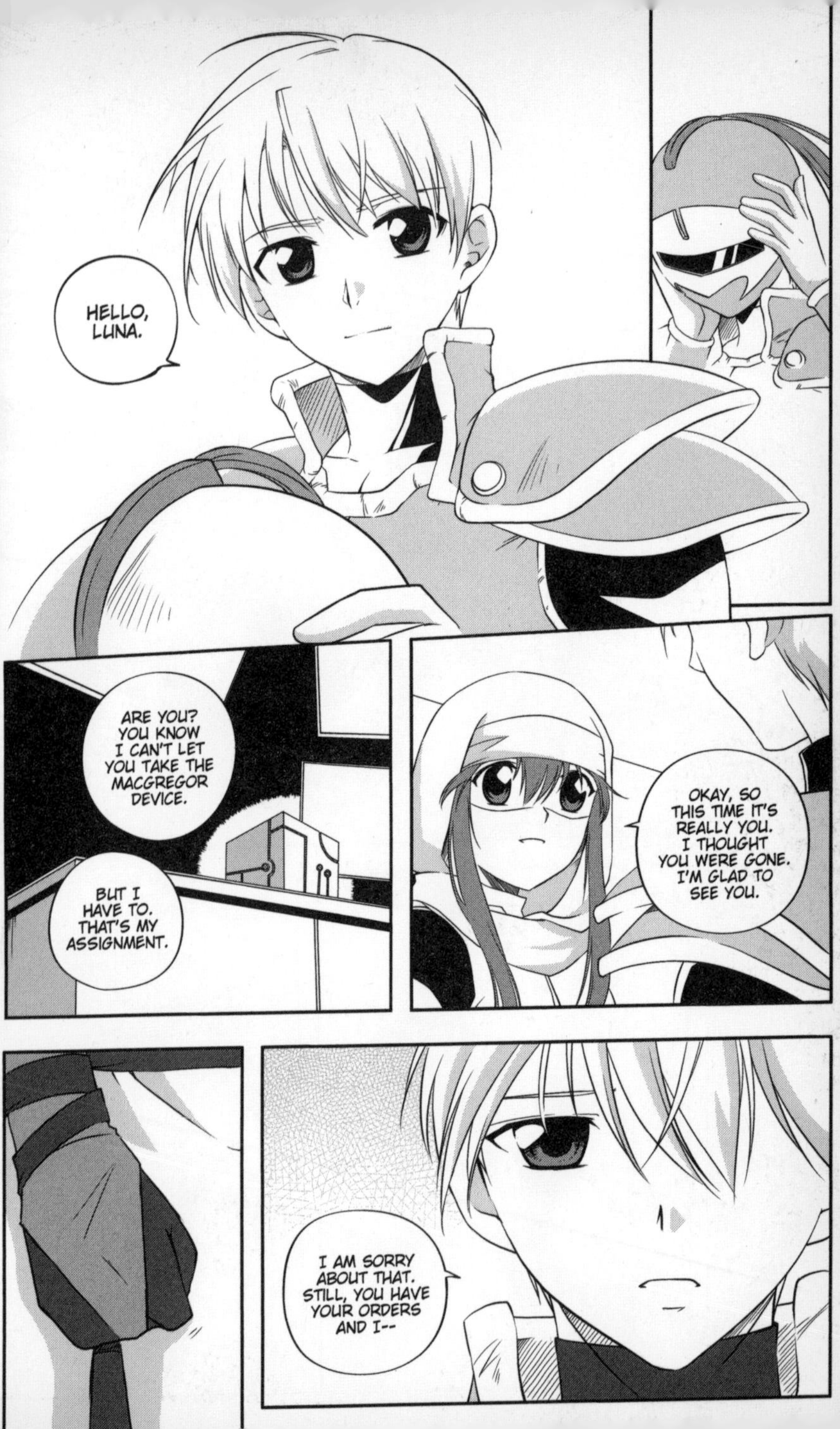
HELLO, LUNA.
OKAY, SO THIS TIME IT'S REALLY YOU. I THOUGHT YOU WERE GONE. I'M GLAD TO SEE YOU.
ARE YOU? YOU KNOW I CAN'T LET YOU TAKE THE MACGREGOR DEVICE.
BUT I HAVE TO. THAT'S MY ASSIGNMENT.
I AM SORRY ABOUT THAT. STILL, YOU HAVE YOUR ORDERS AND I--

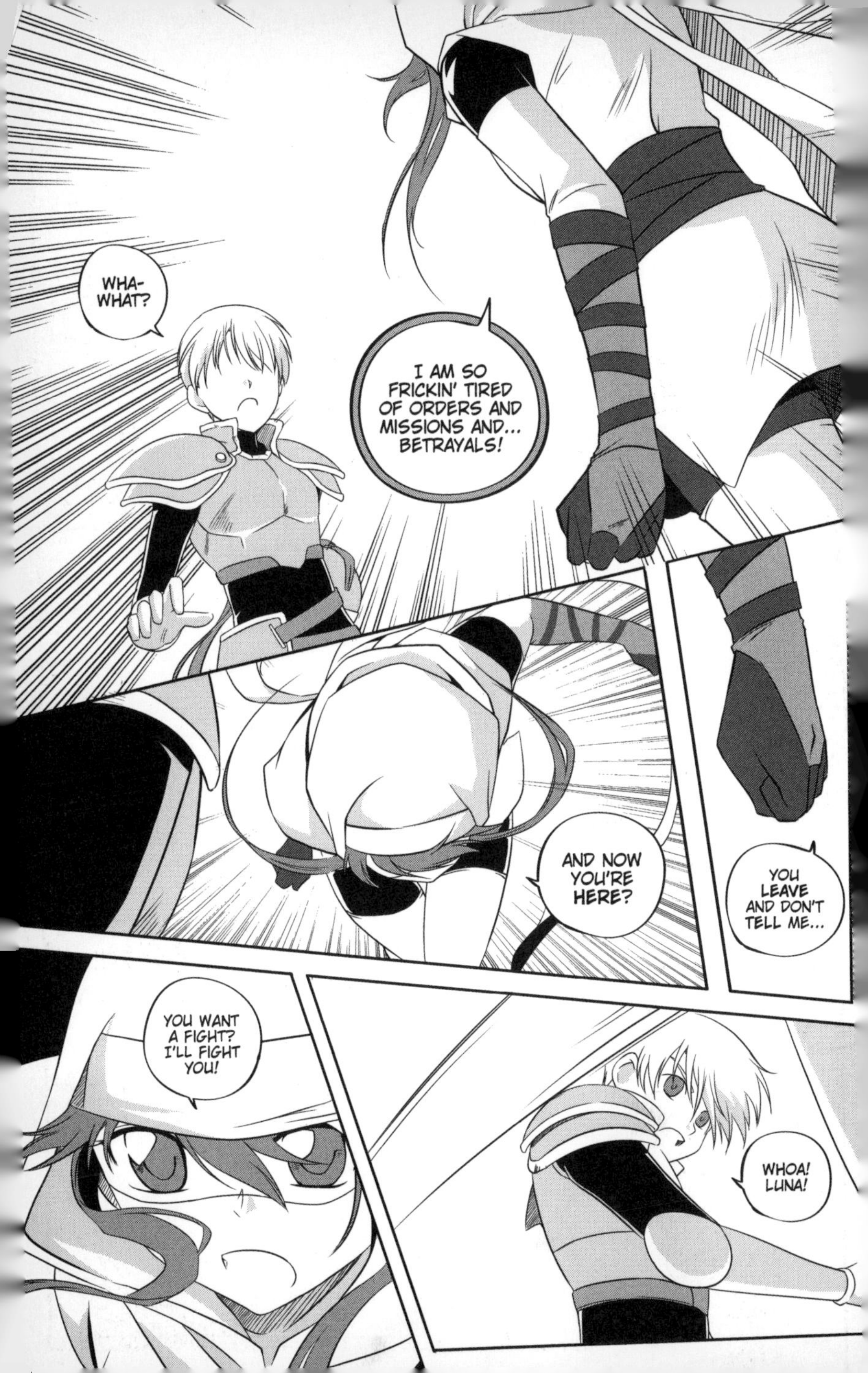
WHA-WHAT?
I AM SO FRICKIN' TIRED OF ORDERS AND MISSIONS AND... BETRAYALS!
YOU LEAVE AND DON'T TELL ME...
AND NOW YOU'RE HERE?
WHOA! LUNA!
YOU WANT A FIGHT? I'LL FIGHT YOU!

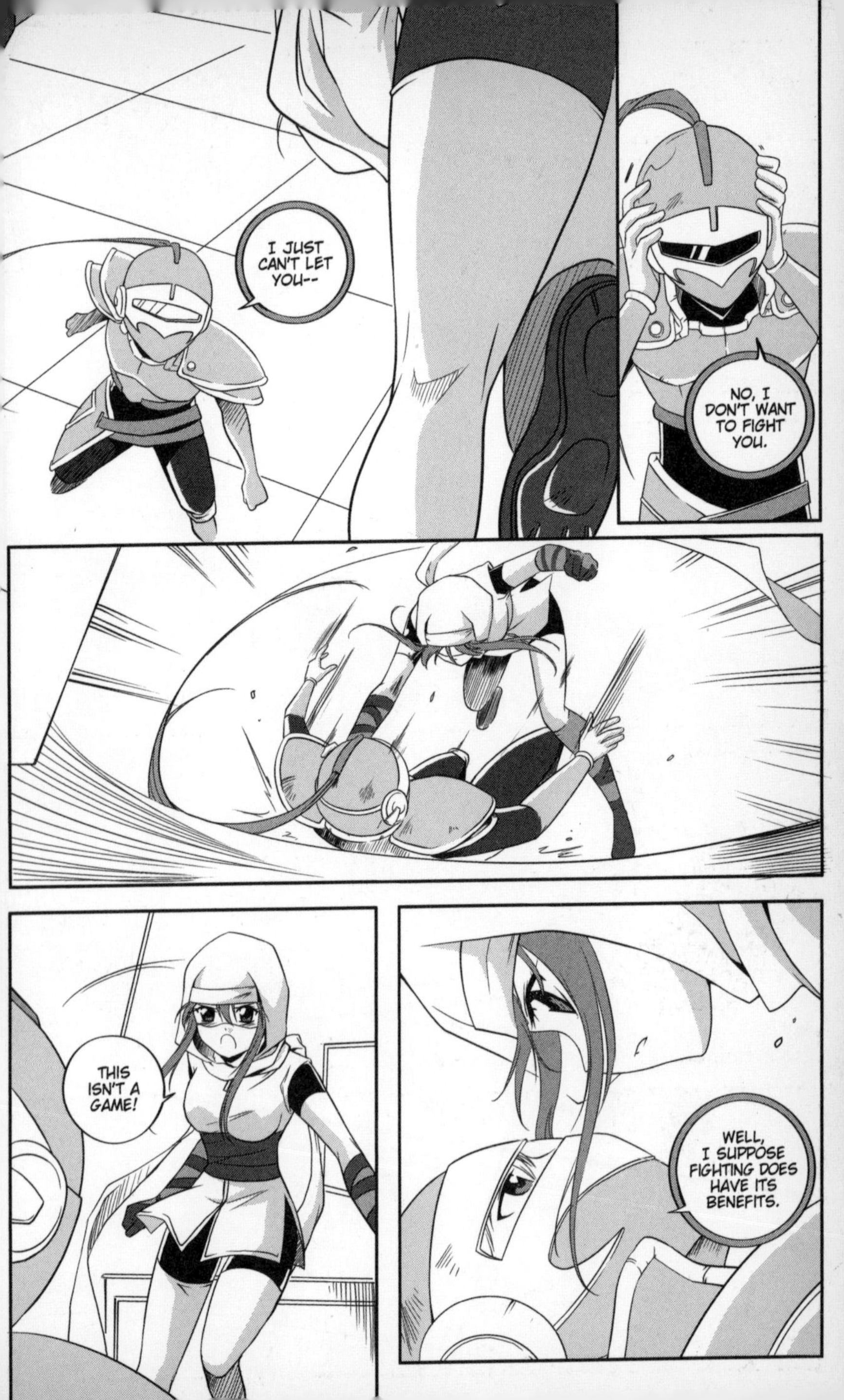
NO, I DON'T WANT TO FIGHT YOU.
I JUST CAN'T LET YOU--
WELL, I SUPPOSE FIGHTING DOES HAVE ITS BENEFITS.
THIS ISN'T A GAME!

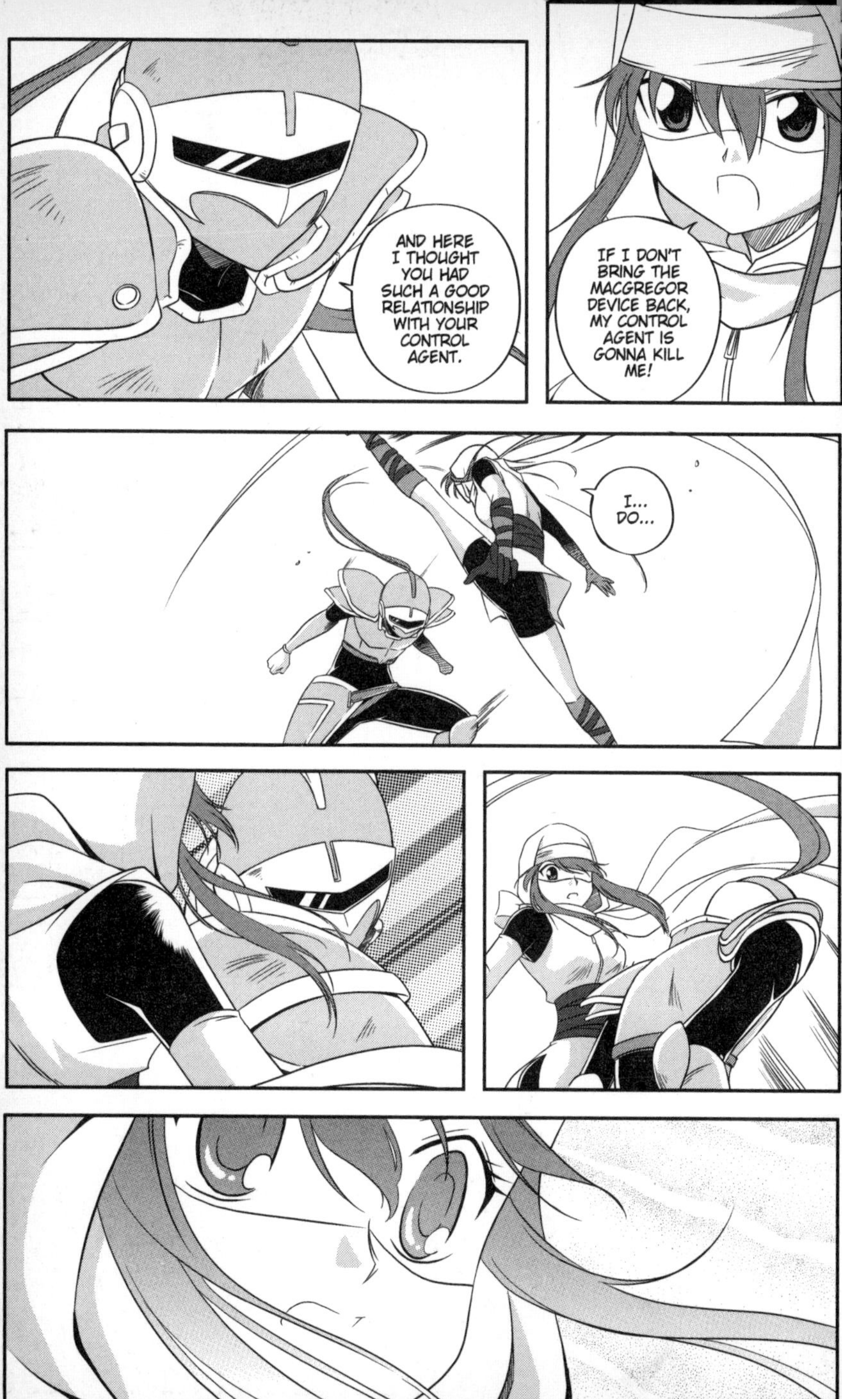
IF I DON'T BRING THE MACGREGOR DEVICE BACK, MY CONTROL AGENT IS GONNA KILL ME!
AND HERE I THOUGHT YOU HAD SUCH A GOOD RELATIONSHIP WITH YOUR CONTROL AGENT.
I... DO...

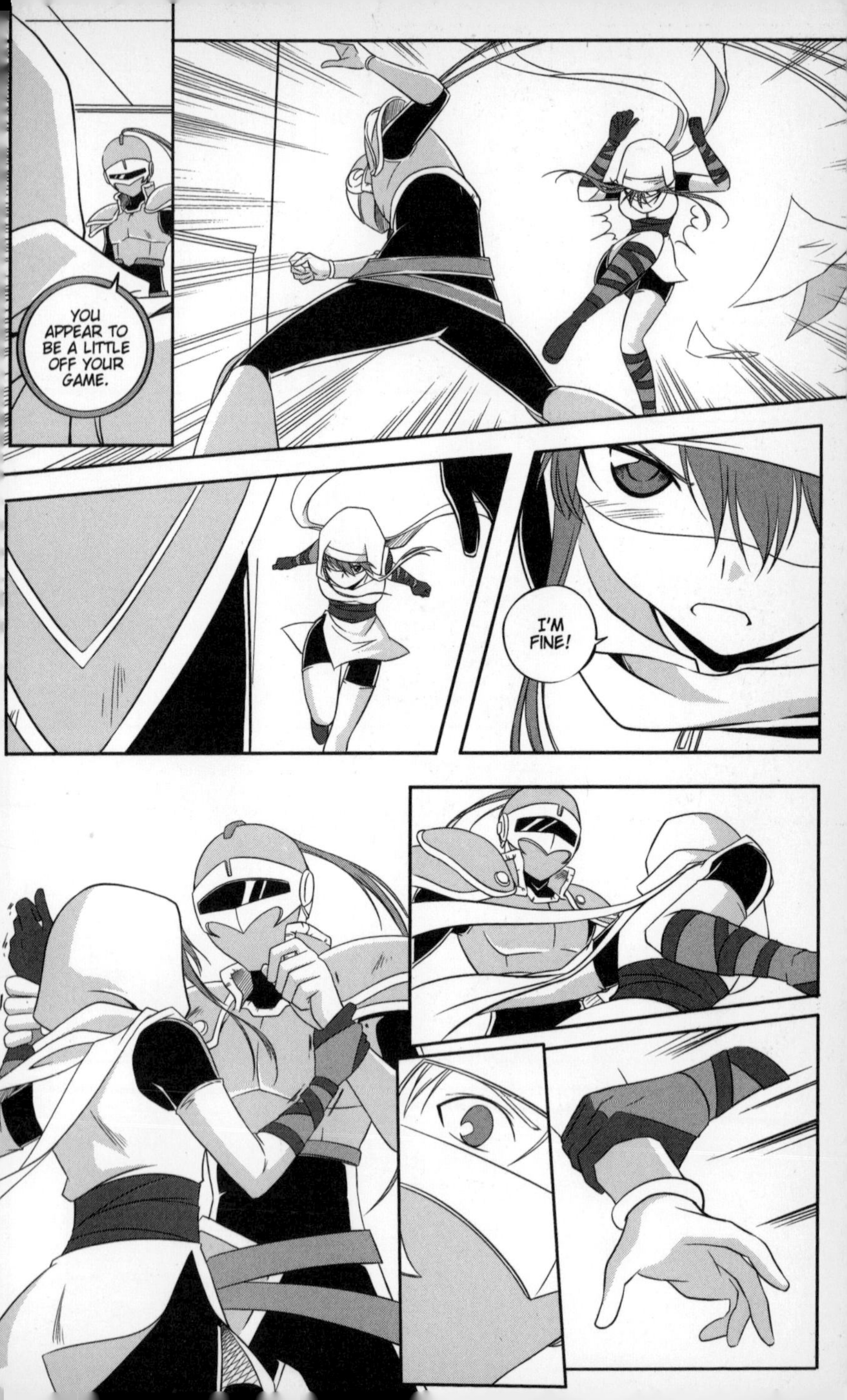
YOU APPEAR TO BE A LITTLE OFF YOUR GAME.
I'M FINE!

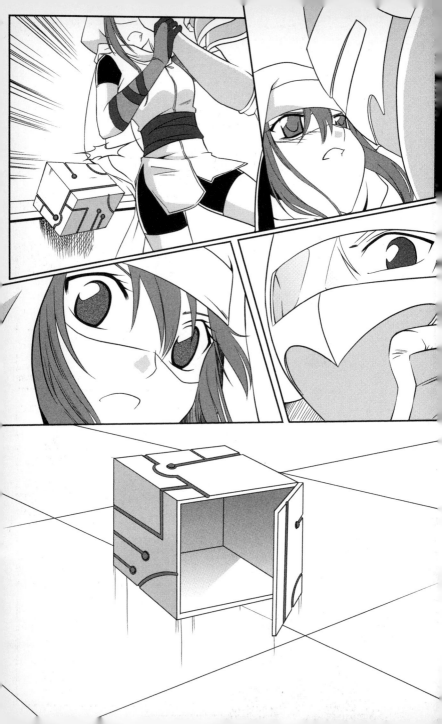

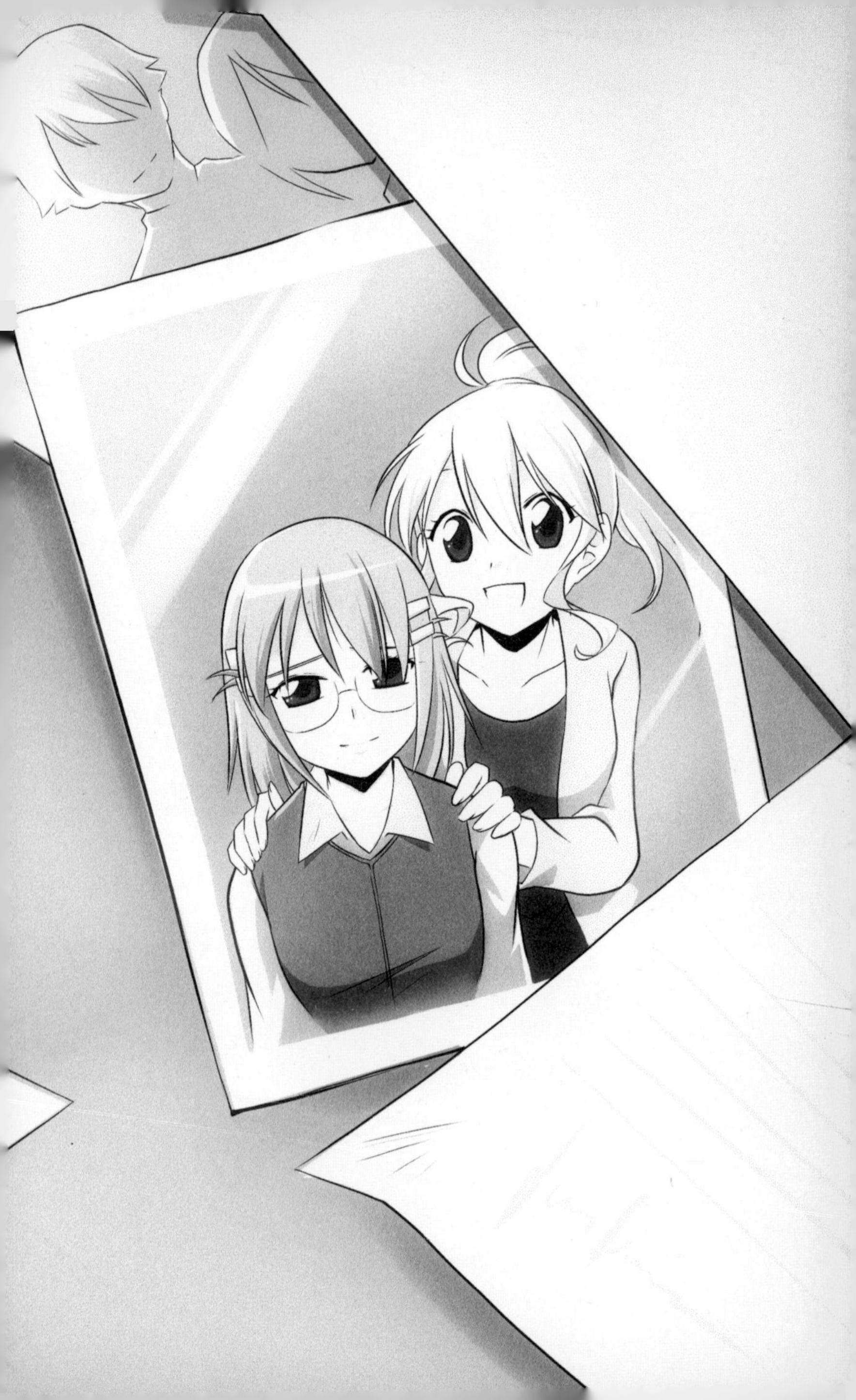

File 43
SECRETS & LIES

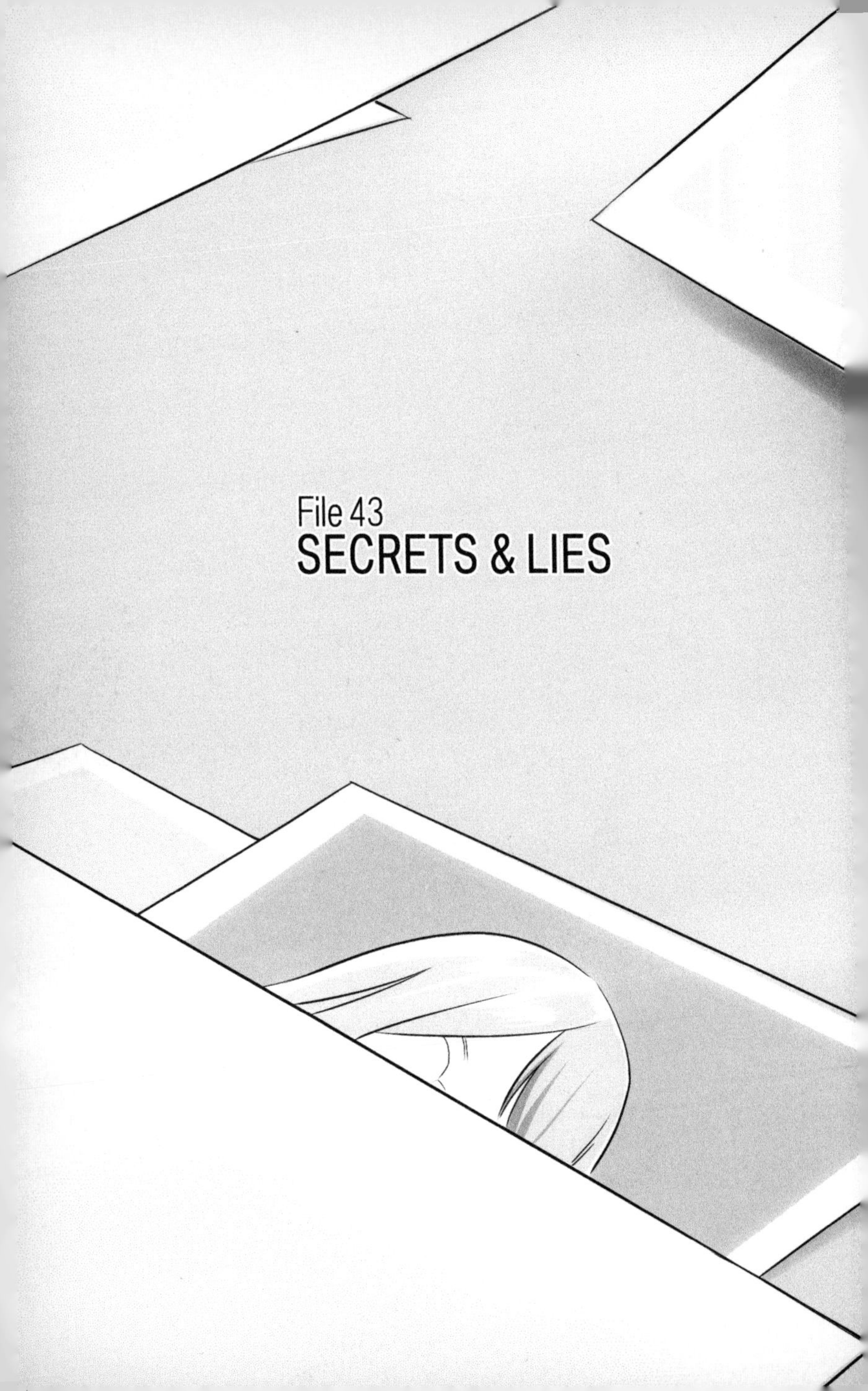

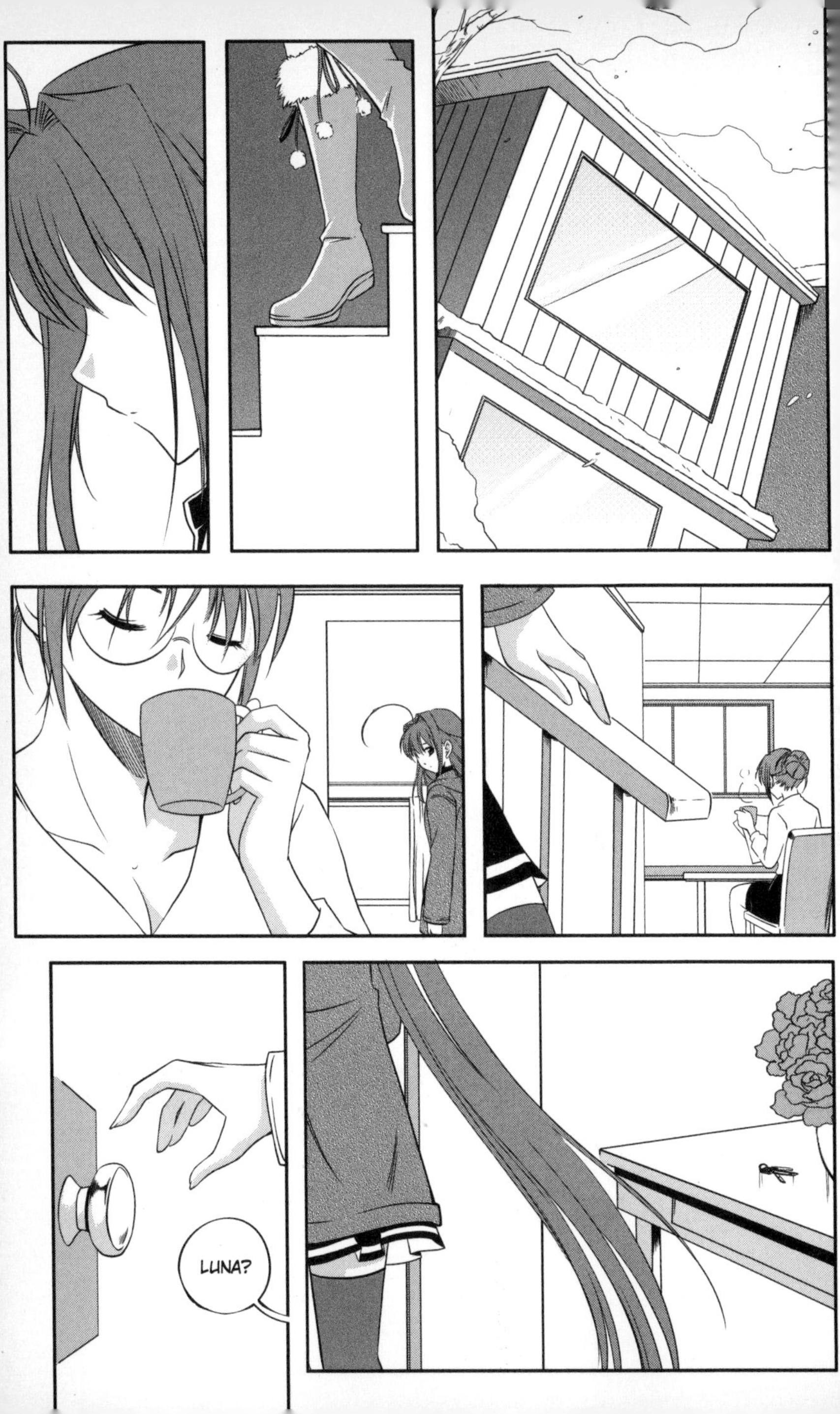
LUNA?

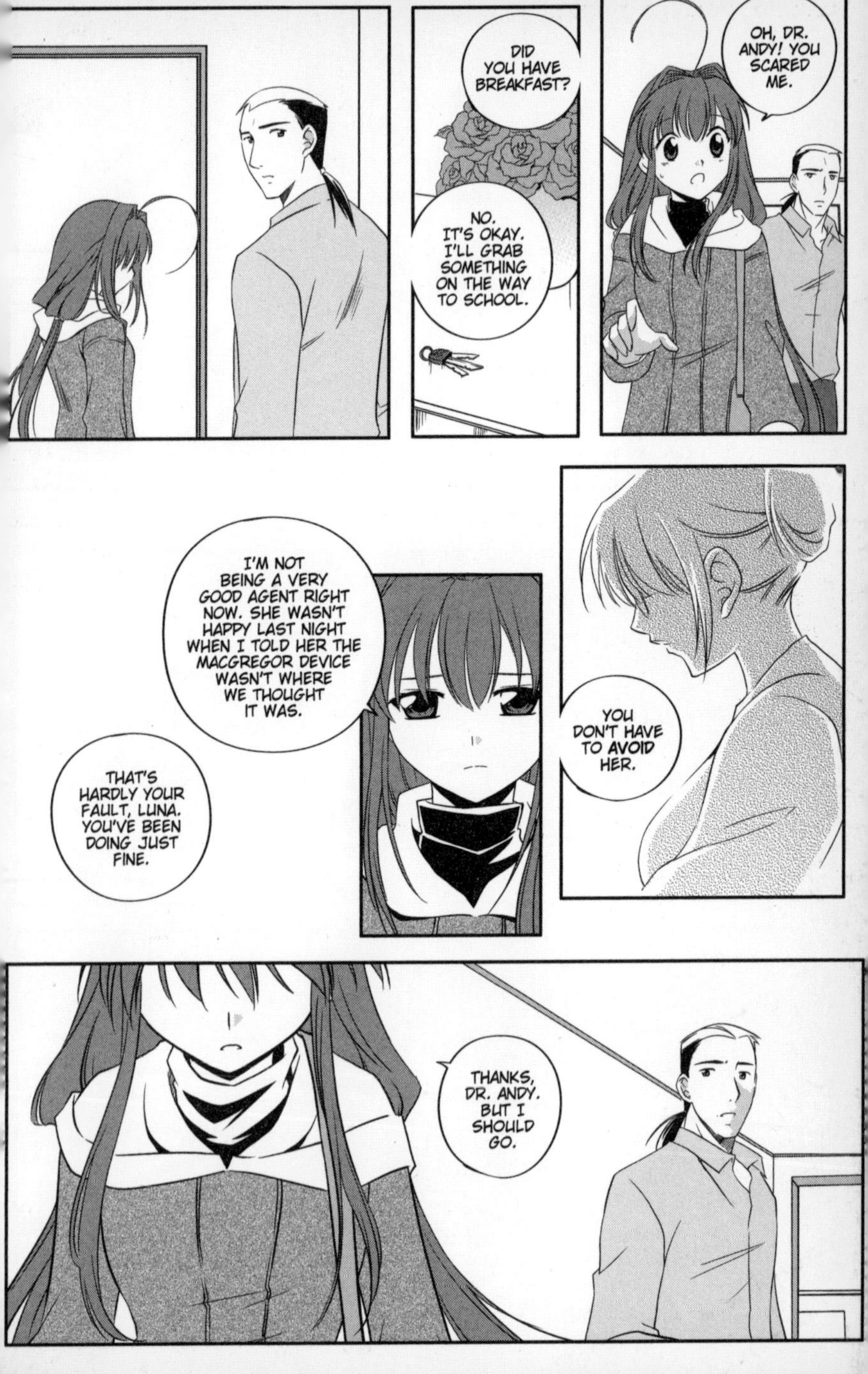
OH, DR. ANDY! YOU SCARED ME.
DID YOU HAVE BREAKFAST?
NO. IT'S OKAY. I'LL GRAB SOMETHING ON THE WAY TO SCHOOL.
YOU DON'T HAVE TO AVOID HER.
I'M NOT BEING A VERY GOOD AGENT RIGHT NOW. SHE WASN'T HAPPY LAST NIGHT WHEN I TOLD HER THE MACGREGOR DEVICE WASN'T WHERE WE THOUGHT IT WAS.
THAT'S HARDLY YOUR FAULT, LUNA. YOU'VE BEEN DOING JUST FINE.
THANKS, DR. ANDY. BUT I SHOULD GO.

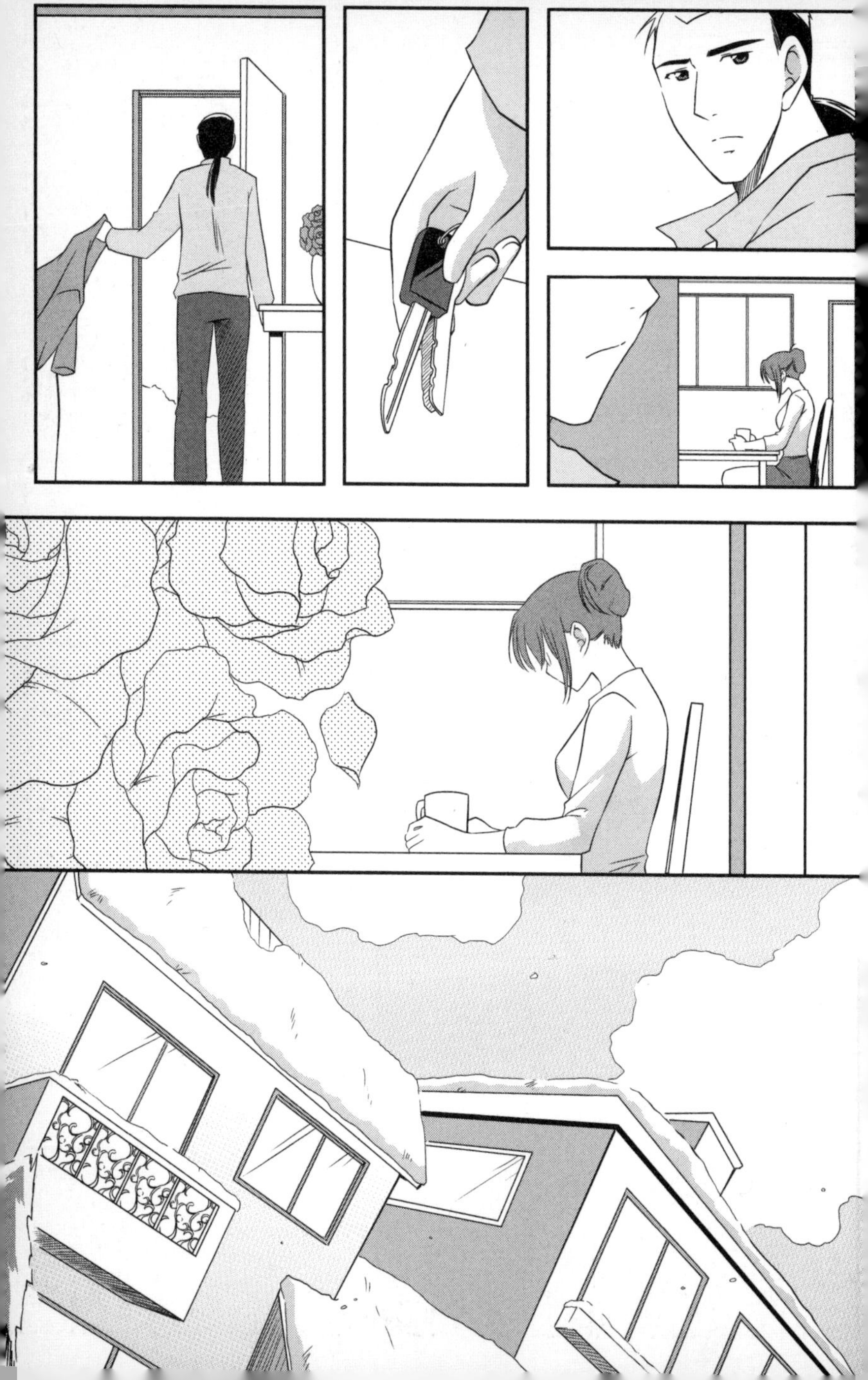

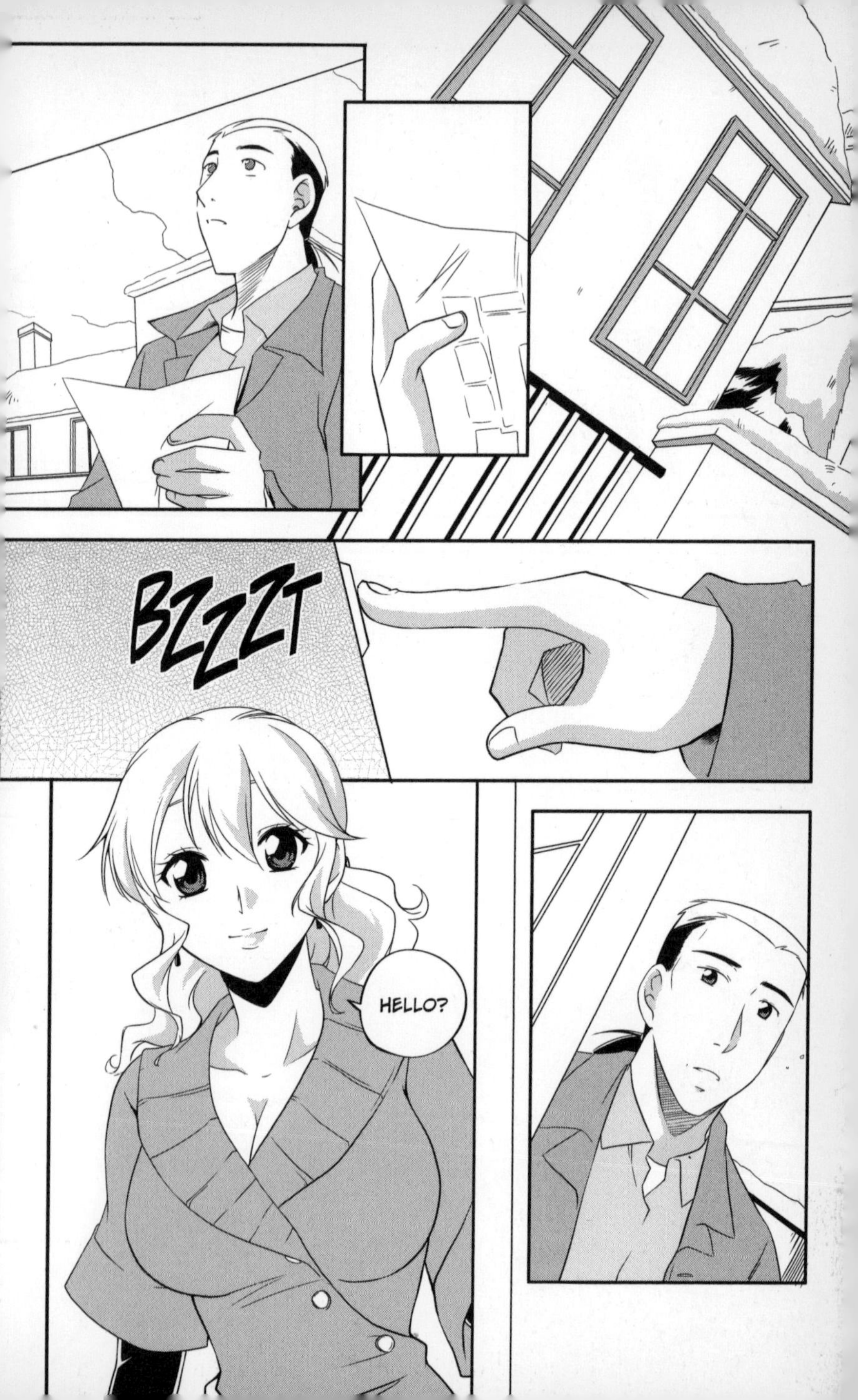
BZZZT
HELLO?

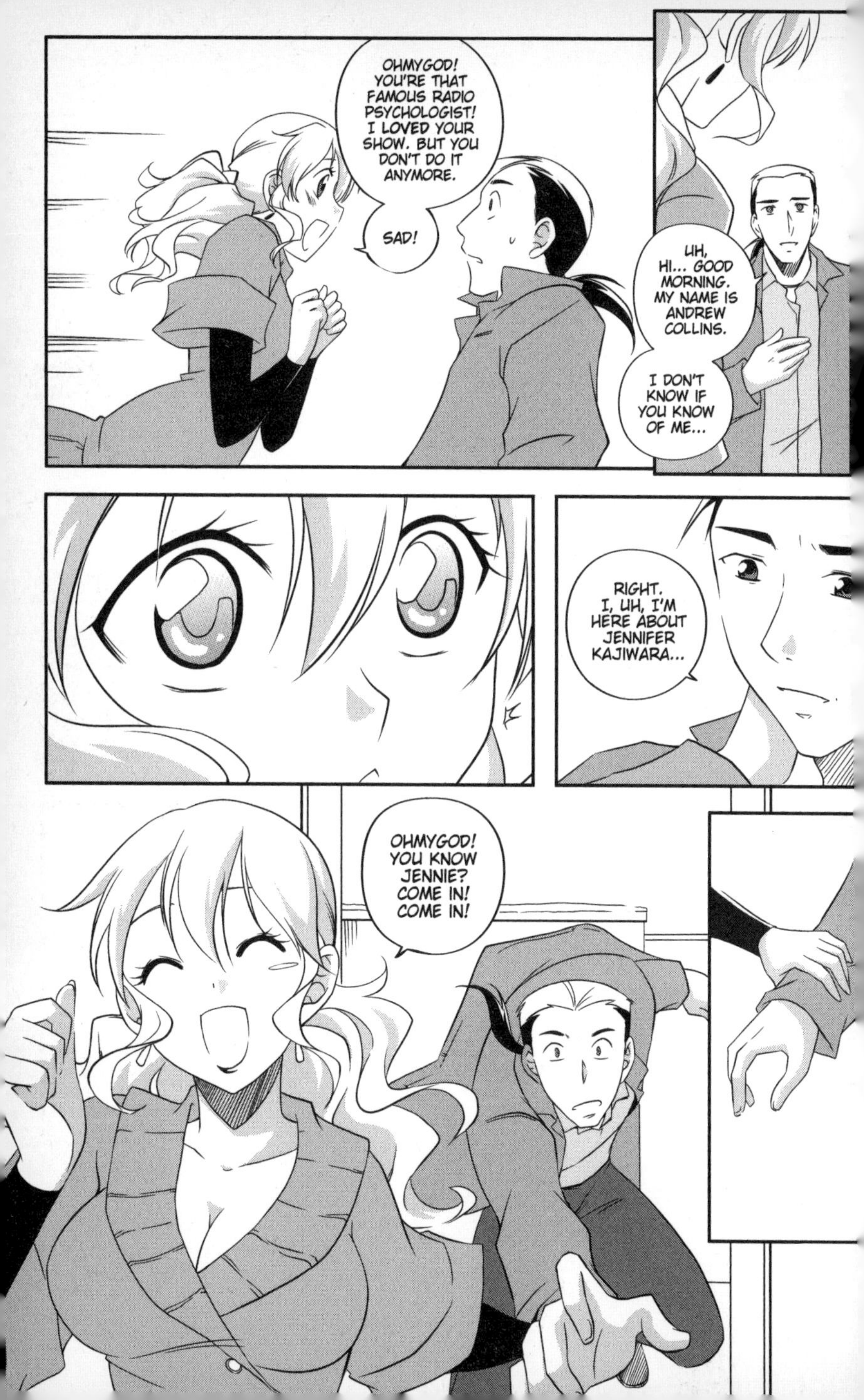
UH, HI... GOOD MORNING. MY NAME IS ANDREW COLLINS.
I DON'T KNOW IF YOU KNOW OF ME...
OHMYGOD! YOU'RE THAT FAMOUS RADIO PSYCHOLOGIST! I LOVED YOUR SHOW. BUT YOU DON'T DO IT ANYMORE.
SAD!
RIGHT. I, UH, I'M HERE ABOUT JENNIFER KAJIWARA...
OHMYGOD! YOU KNOW JENNIE? COME IN! COME IN!

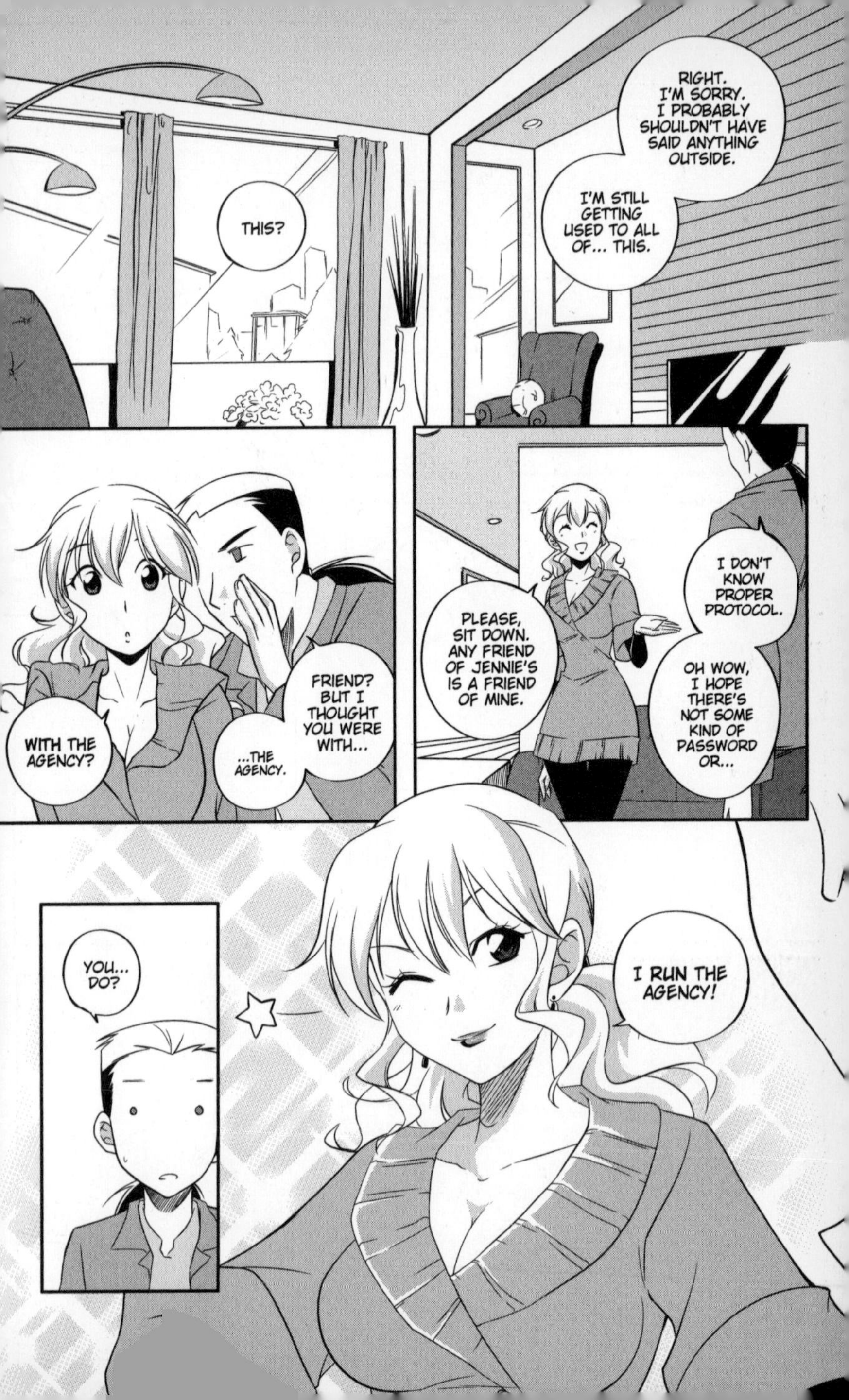
RIGHT. I'M SORRY. I PROBABLY SHOULDN'T HAVE SAID ANYTHING OUTSIDE.
I'M STILL GETTING USED TO ALL OF... THIS.
THIS?
I DON'T KNOW PROPER PROTOCOL.
OH WOW, I HOPE THERE'S NOT SOME KIND OF PASSWORD OR...
PLEASE, SIT DOWN. ANY FRIEND OF JENNIE'S IS A FRIEND OF MINE.
FRIEND? BUT I THOUGHT YOU WERE WITH...
...THE AGENCY.
WITH THE AGENCY?
I RUN THE AGENCY!
YOU... DO?

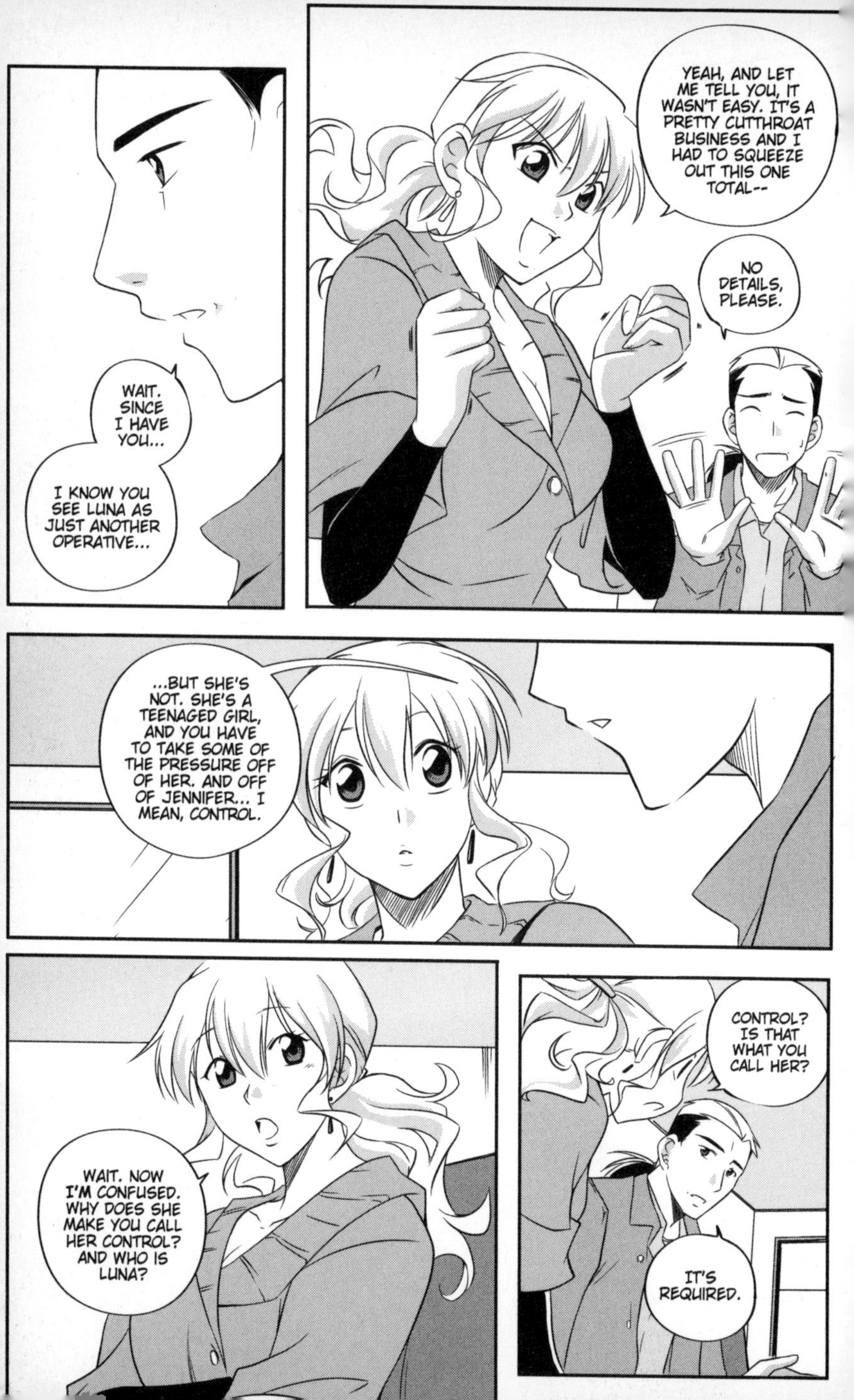
YEAH, AND LET ME TELL YOU, IT WASN'T EASY. IT'S A PRETTY CUTTHROAT BUSINESS AND I HAD TO SQUEEZE OUT THIS ONE TOTAL--
NO DETAILS, PLEASE.
WAIT. SINCE I HAVE YOU...
I KNOW YOU SEE LUNA AS JUST ANOTHER OPERATIVE...
...BUT SHE'S NOT. SHE'S A TEENAGED GIRL, AND YOU HAVE TO TAKE SOME OF THE PRESSURE OFF OF HER. AND OFF OF JENNIFER... I MEAN, CONTROL.
CONTROL? IS THAT WHAT YOU CALL HER?
IT'S REQUIRED.
WAIT. NOW I'M CONFUSED. WHY DOES SHE MAKE YOU CALL HER CONTROL? AND WHO IS LUNA?

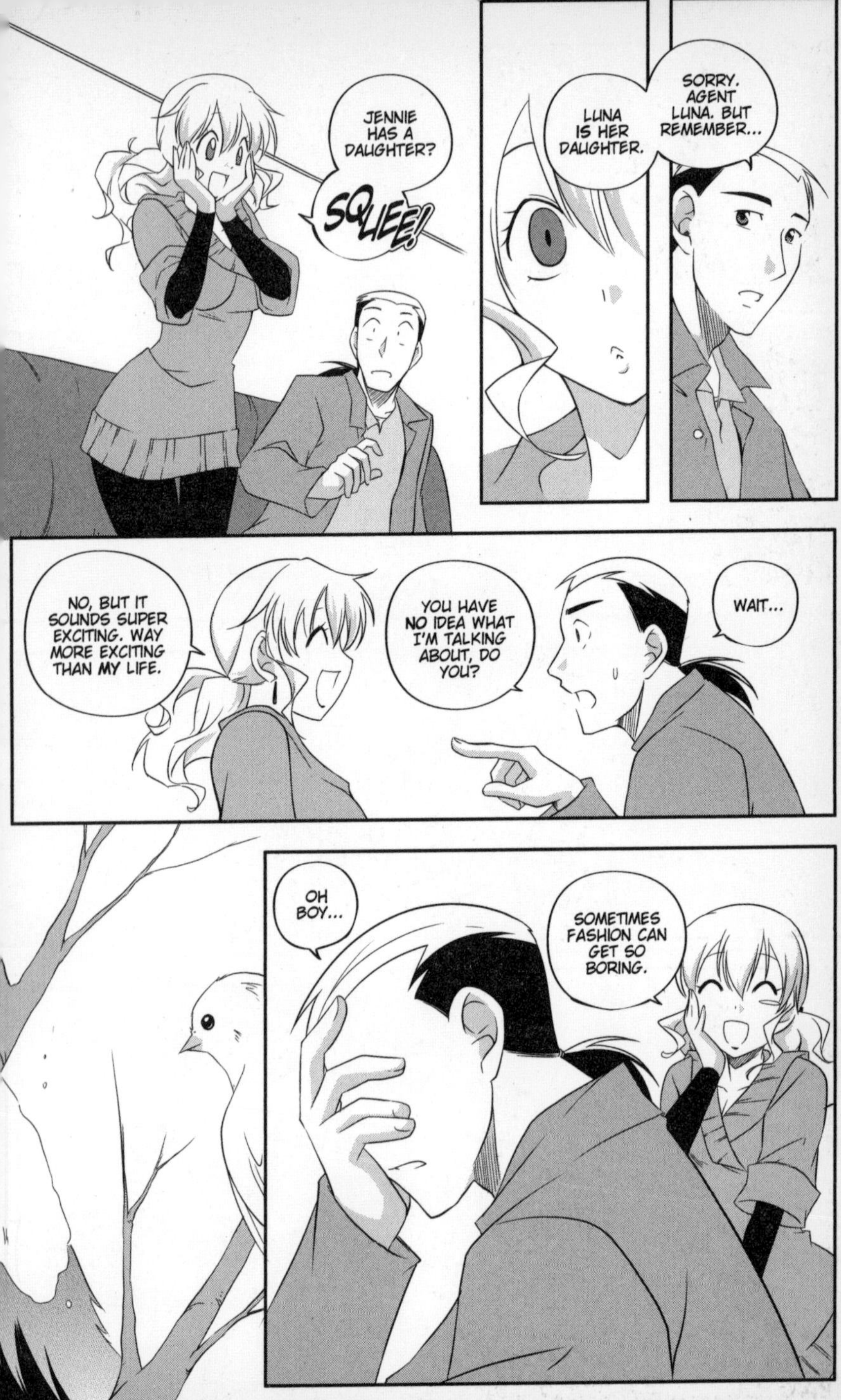
SORRY. AGENT LUNA. BUT REMEMBER...
LUNA IS HER DAUGHTER.
JENNIE HAS A DAUGHTER?
SQUEE!
WAIT...
YOU HAVE NO IDEA WHAT I'M TALKING ABOUT, DO YOU?
NO, BUT IT SOUNDS SUPER EXCITING. WAY MORE EXCITING THAN MY LIFE.
SOMETIMES FASHION CAN GET SO BORING.
OH BOY...

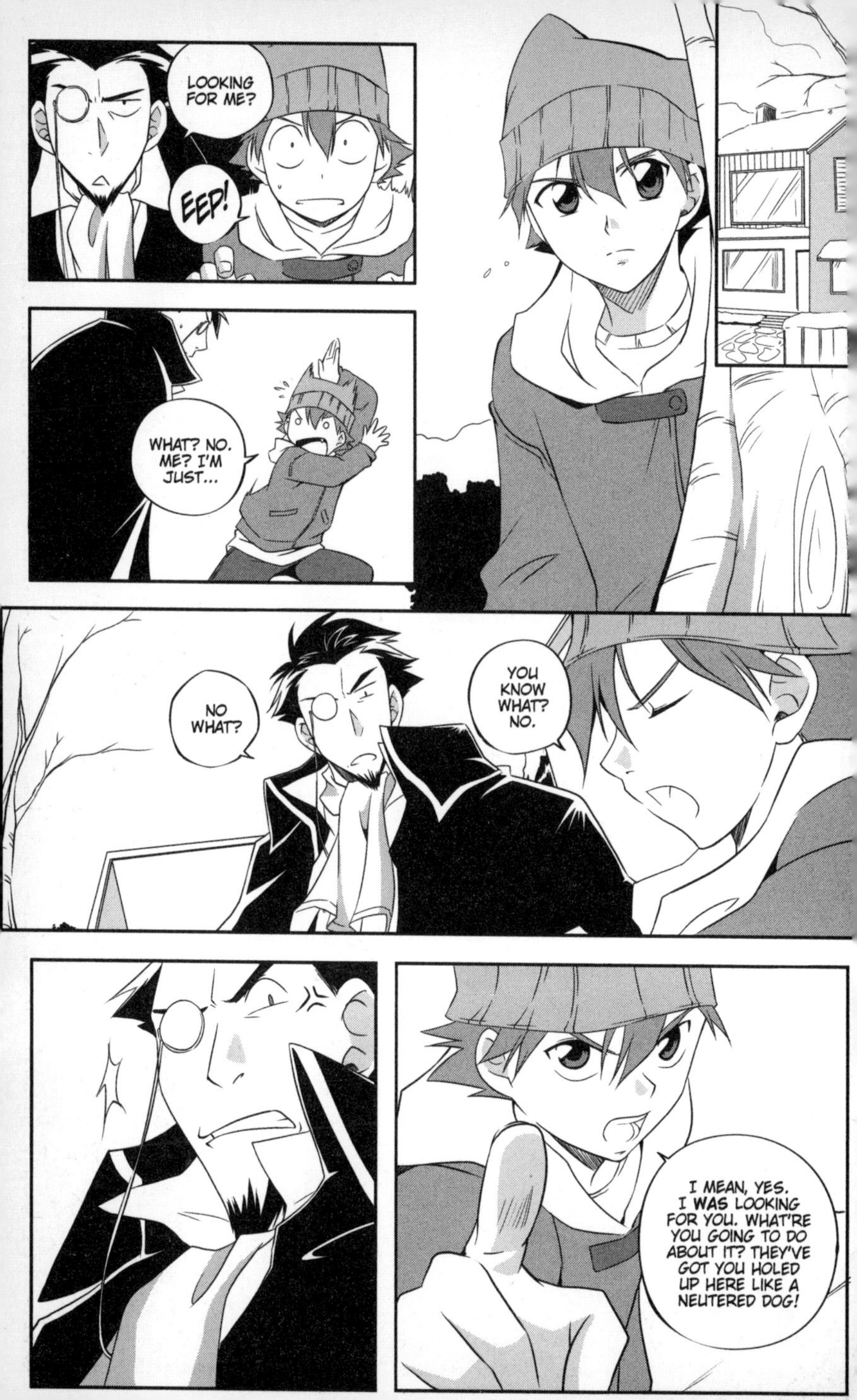
LOOKING FOR ME?
EEP!
WHAT? NO. ME? I'M JUST...
YOU KNOW WHAT? NO.
NO WHAT?
I MEAN, YES. I WAS LOOKING FOR YOU. WHAT'RE YOU GOING TO DO ABOUT IT? THEY'VE GOT YOU HOLED UP HERE LIKE A NEUTERED DOG!

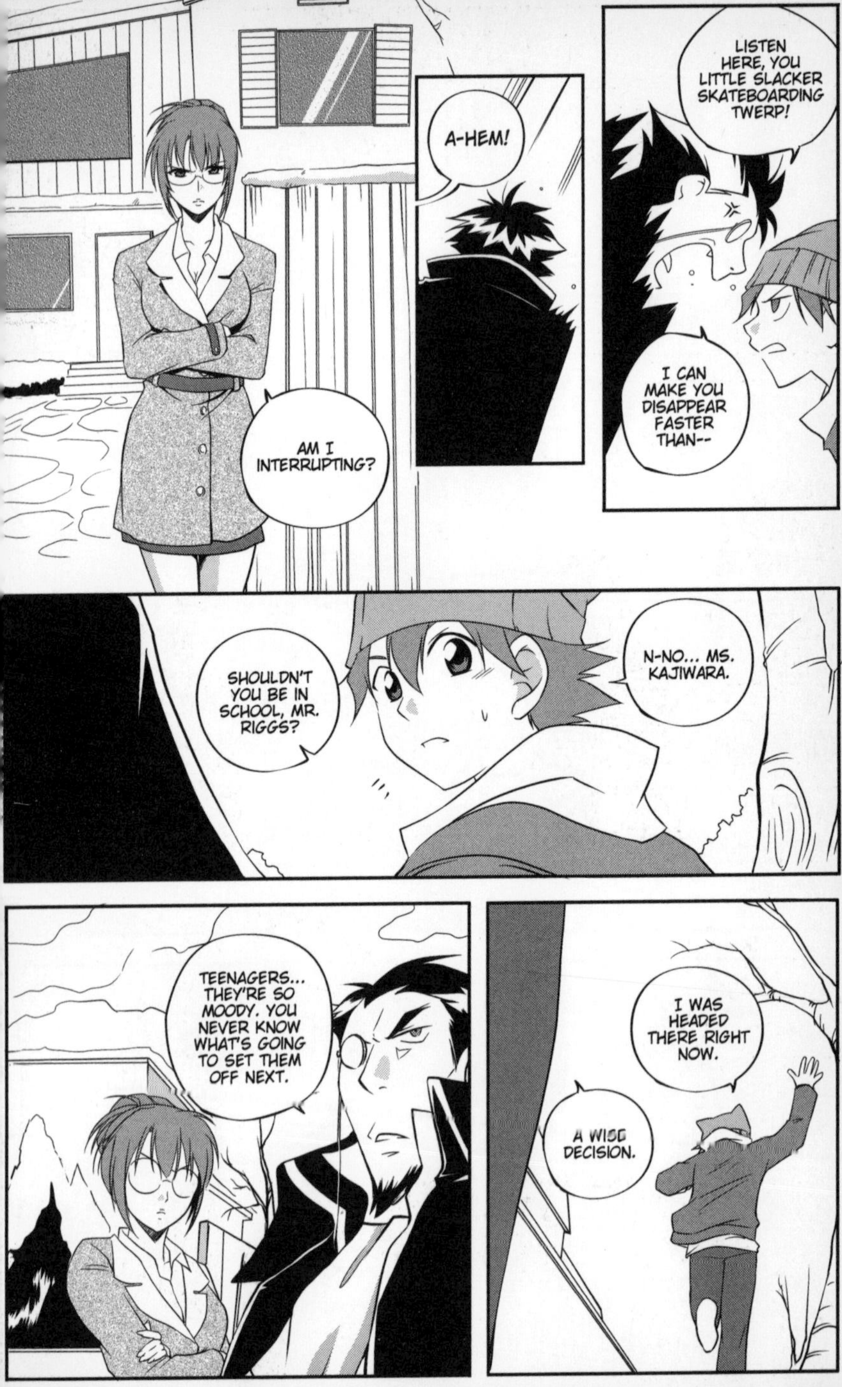
LISTEN HERE, YOU LITTLE SLACKER SKATEBOARDING TWERP!
I CAN MAKE YOU DISAPPEAR FASTER THAN--
A-HEM!
AM I INTERRUPTING?
N-NO... MS. KAJIWARA.
SHOULDN'T YOU BE IN SCHOOL, MR. RIGGS?
I WAS HEADED THERE RIGHT NOW.
A WISE DECISION.
TEENAGERS... THEY'RE SO MOODY. YOU NEVER KNOW WHAT'S GOING TO SET THEM OFF NEXT.

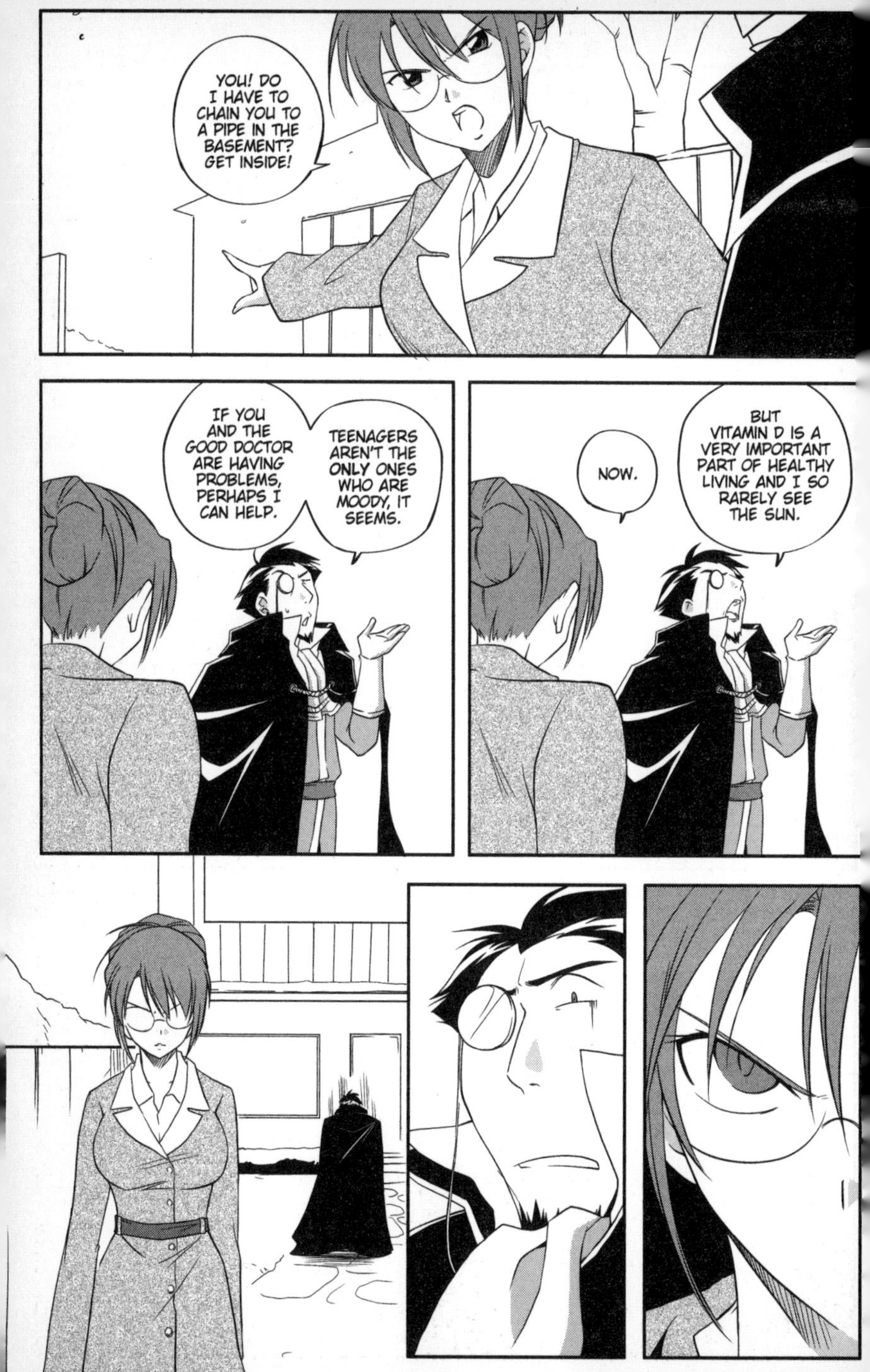
YOU! DO I HAVE TO CHAIN YOU TO A PIPE IN THE BASEMENT? GET INSIDE!
BUT VITAMIN D IS A VERY IMPORTANT PART OF HEALTHY LIVING AND I SO RARELY SEE THE SUN.
NOW.
TEENAGERS AREN'T THE ONLY ONES WHO ARE MOODY, IT SEEMS.
IF YOU AND THE GOOD DOCTOR ARE HAVING PROBLEMS, PERHAPS I CAN HELP.

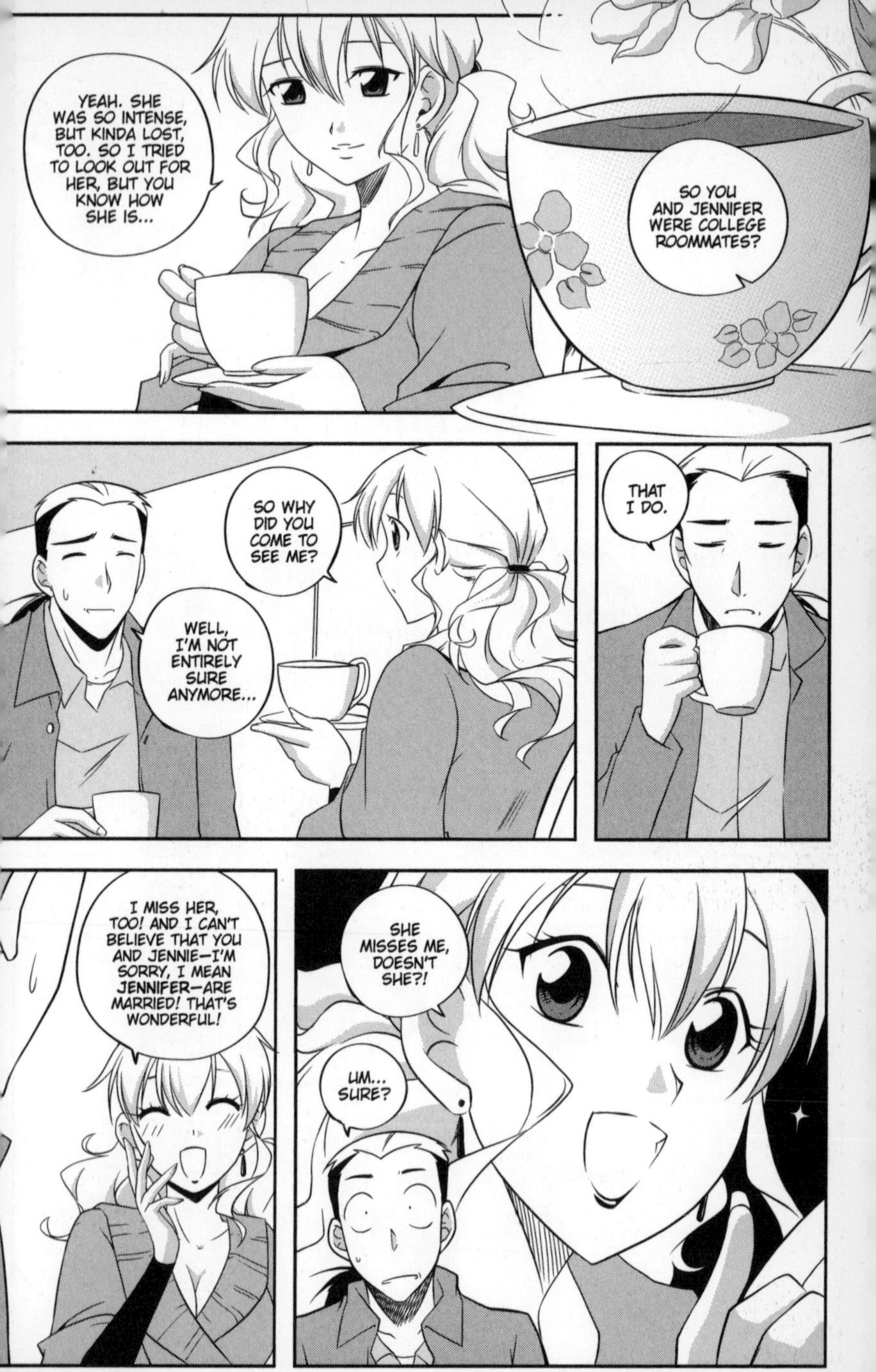
SO YOU AND JENNIFER WERE COLLEGE ROOMMATES?
YEAH. SHE WAS SO INTENSE, BUT KINDA LOST, TOO. SO I TRIED TO LOOK OUT FOR HER, BUT YOU KNOW HOW SHE IS...
THAT I DO.
SO WHY DID YOU COME TO SEE ME?
WELL, I'M NOT ENTIRELY SURE ANYMORE...
SHE MISSES ME, DOESN'T SHE?!
UM... SURE?
I MISS HER, TOO! AND I CAN'T BELIEVE THAT YOU AND JENNIE—I'M SORRY, I MEAN JENNIFER—ARE MARRIED! THAT'S WONDERFUL!

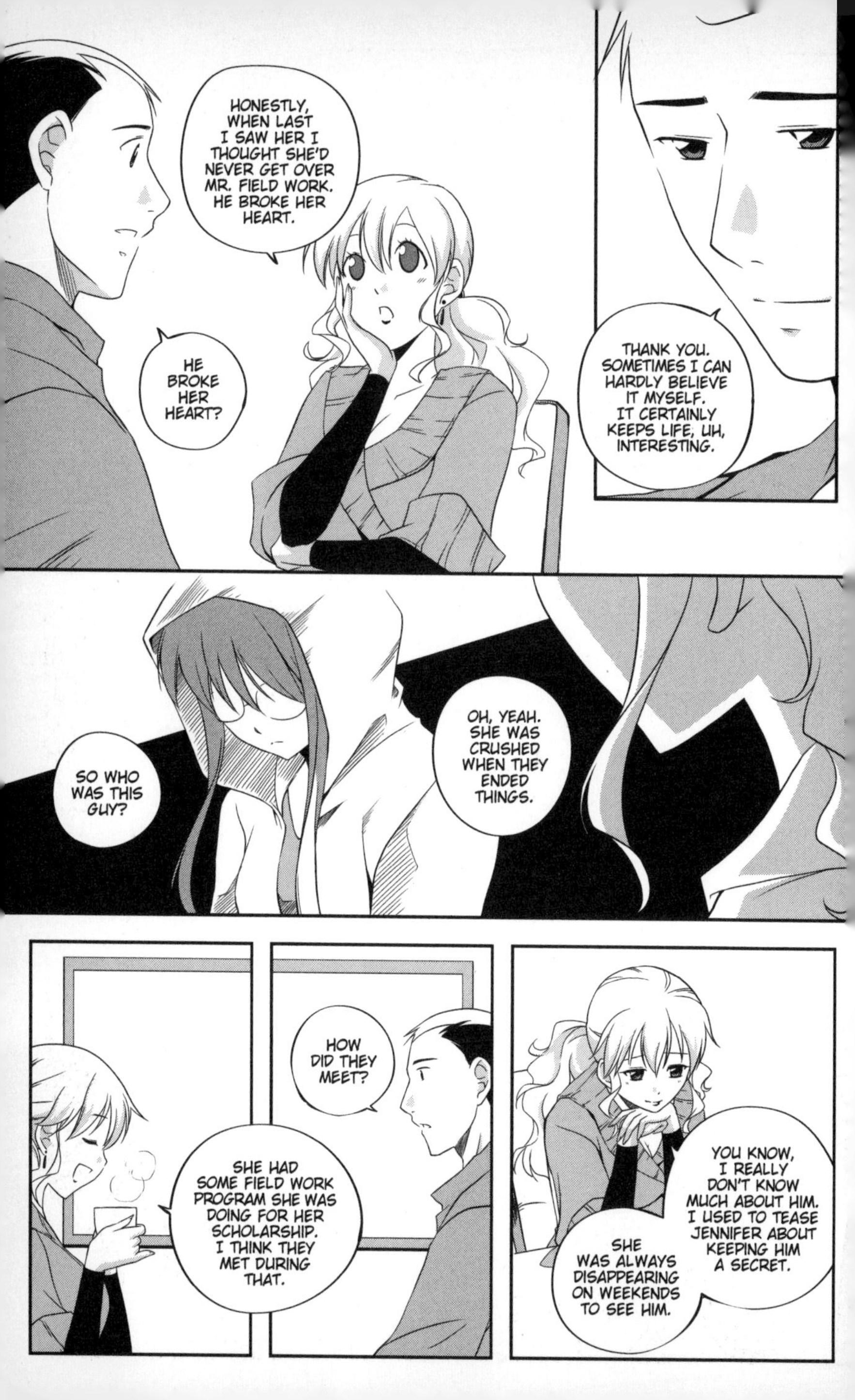
THANK YOU. SOMETIMES I CAN HARDLY BELIEVE IT MYSELF. IT CERTAINLY KEEPS LIFE, UH, INTERESTING.
HONESTLY, WHEN LAST I SAW HER I THOUGHT SHE'D NEVER GET OVER MR. FIELD WORK. HE BROKE HER HEART.
HE BROKE HER HEART?
OH, YEAH. SHE WAS CRUSHED WHEN THEY ENDED THINGS.
SO WHO WAS THIS GUY?
YOU KNOW, I REALLY DON'T KNOW MUCH ABOUT HIM. I USED TO TEASE JENNIFER ABOUT KEEPING HIM A SECRET.
SHE WAS ALWAYS DISAPPEARING ON WEEKENDS TO SEE HIM.
HOW DID THEY MEET?
SHE HAD SOME FIELD WORK PROGRAM SHE WAS DOING FOR HER SCHOLARSHIP. I THINK THEY MET DURING THAT.

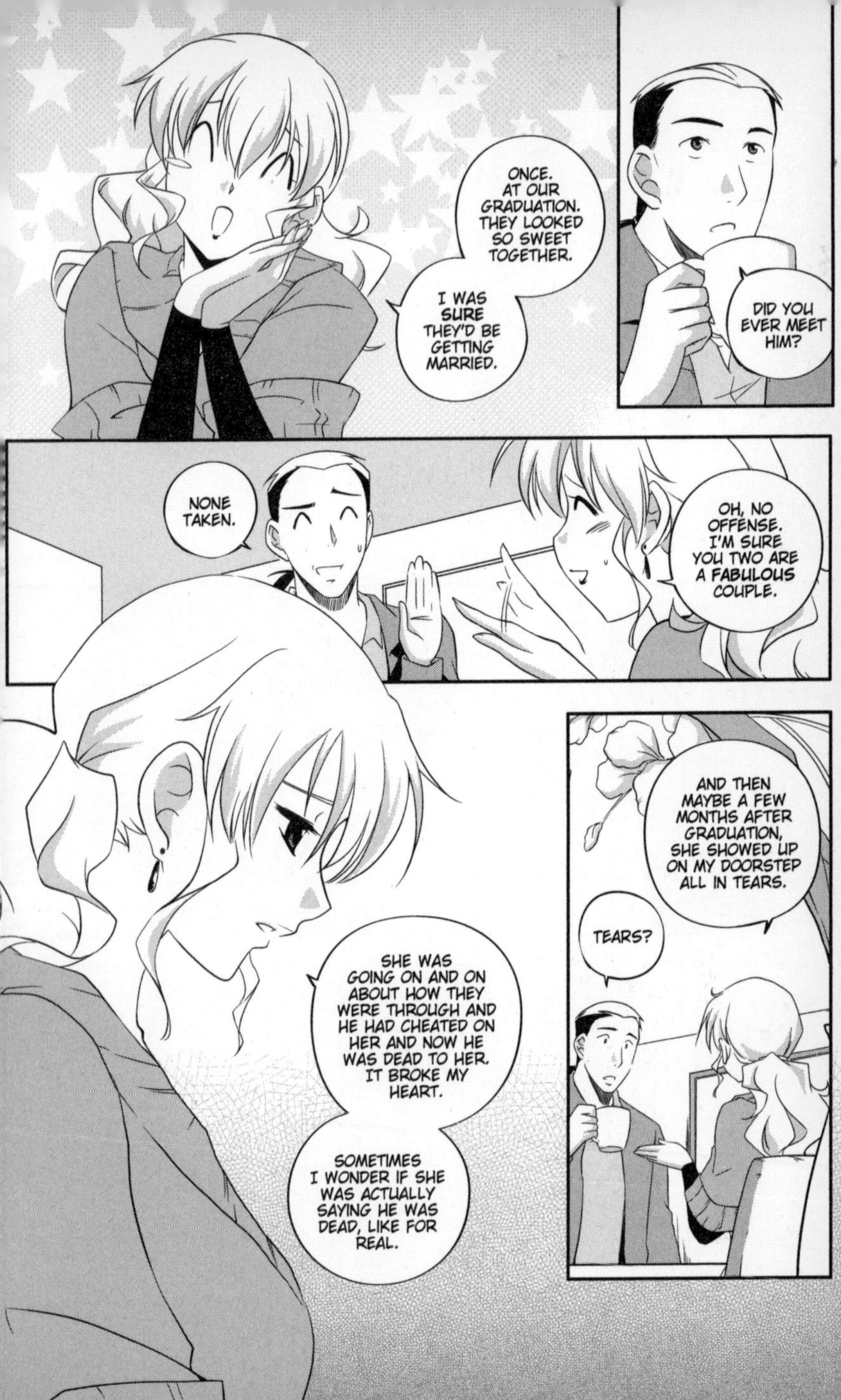
DID YOU EVER MEET HIM?
ONCE. AT OUR GRADUATION. THEY LOOKED SO SWEET TOGETHER.
I WAS **SURE** THEY'D BE GETTING MARRIED.
OH, NO OFFENSE. I'M SURE YOU TWO ARE A **FABULOUS** COUPLE.
NONE TAKEN.
AND THEN MAYBE A FEW MONTHS AFTER GRADUATION, SHE SHOWED UP ON MY DOORSTEP ALL IN TEARS.
TEARS?
SHE WAS GOING ON AND ON ABOUT HOW THEY WERE THROUGH AND HE HAD CHEATED ON HER AND NOW HE WAS DEAD TO HER. IT BROKE MY HEART.
SOMETIMES I WONDER IF SHE WAS ACTUALLY SAYING HE WAS DEAD, LIKE FOR REAL.

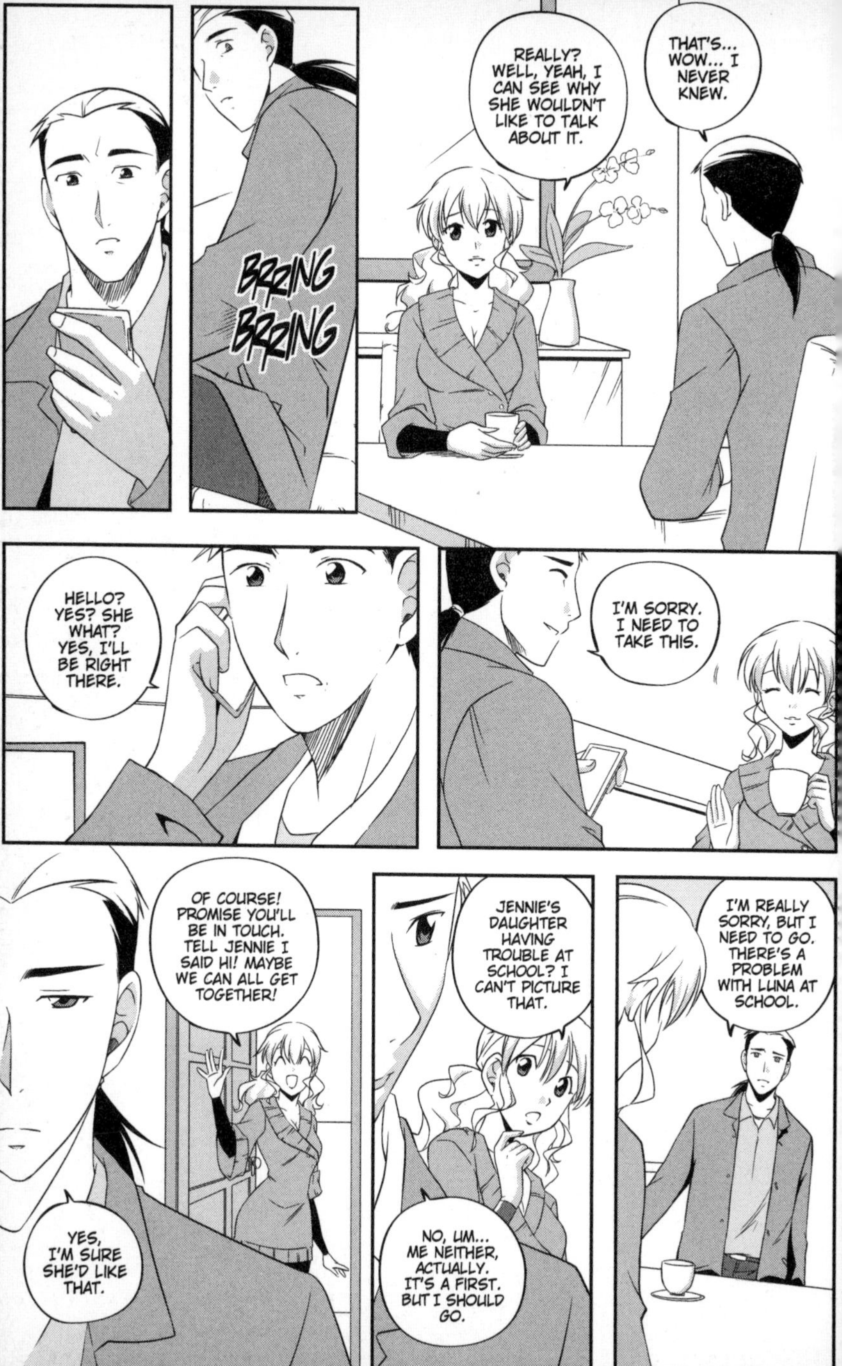
THAT'S... WOW... I NEVER KNEW.
REALLY? WELL, YEAH, I CAN SEE WHY SHE WOULDN'T LIKE TO TALK ABOUT IT.
BRRING BRRING
I'M SORRY. I NEED TO TAKE THIS.
HELLO? YES? SHE WHAT? YES, I'LL BE RIGHT THERE.
I'M REALLY SORRY, BUT I NEED TO GO. THERE'S A PROBLEM WITH LUNA AT SCHOOL.
JENNIE'S DAUGHTER HAVING TROUBLE AT SCHOOL? I CAN'T PICTURE THAT.
NO, UM... ME NEITHER, ACTUALLY. IT'S A FIRST. BUT I SHOULD GO.
OF COURSE! PROMISE YOU'LL BE IN TOUCH. TELL JENNIE I SAID HI! MAYBE WE CAN ALL GET TOGETHER!
YES, I'M SURE SHE'D LIKE THAT.

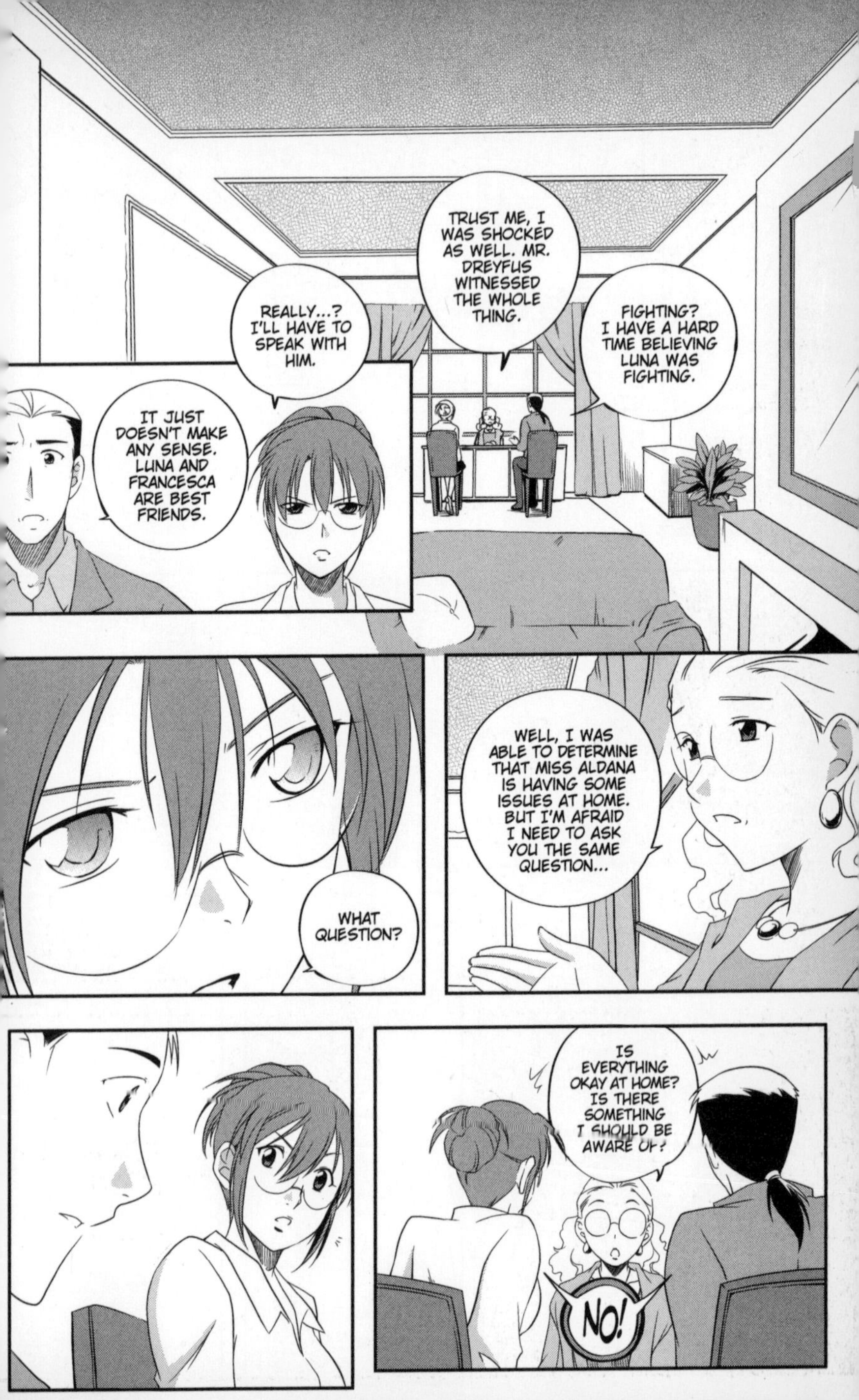
FIGHTING? I HAVE A HARD TIME BELIEVING LUNA WAS FIGHTING.
TRUST ME, I WAS SHOCKED AS WELL. MR. DREYFUS WITNESSED THE WHOLE THING.
REALLY...? I'LL HAVE TO SPEAK WITH HIM.
IT JUST DOESN'T MAKE ANY SENSE. LUNA AND FRANCESCA ARE BEST FRIENDS.
WELL, I WAS ABLE TO DETERMINE THAT MISS ALDANA IS HAVING SOME ISSUES AT HOME. BUT I'M AFRAID I NEED TO ASK YOU THE SAME QUESTION...
WHAT QUESTION?
IS EVERYTHING OKAY AT HOME? IS THERE SOMETHING I SHOULD BE AWARE OF?
NO!

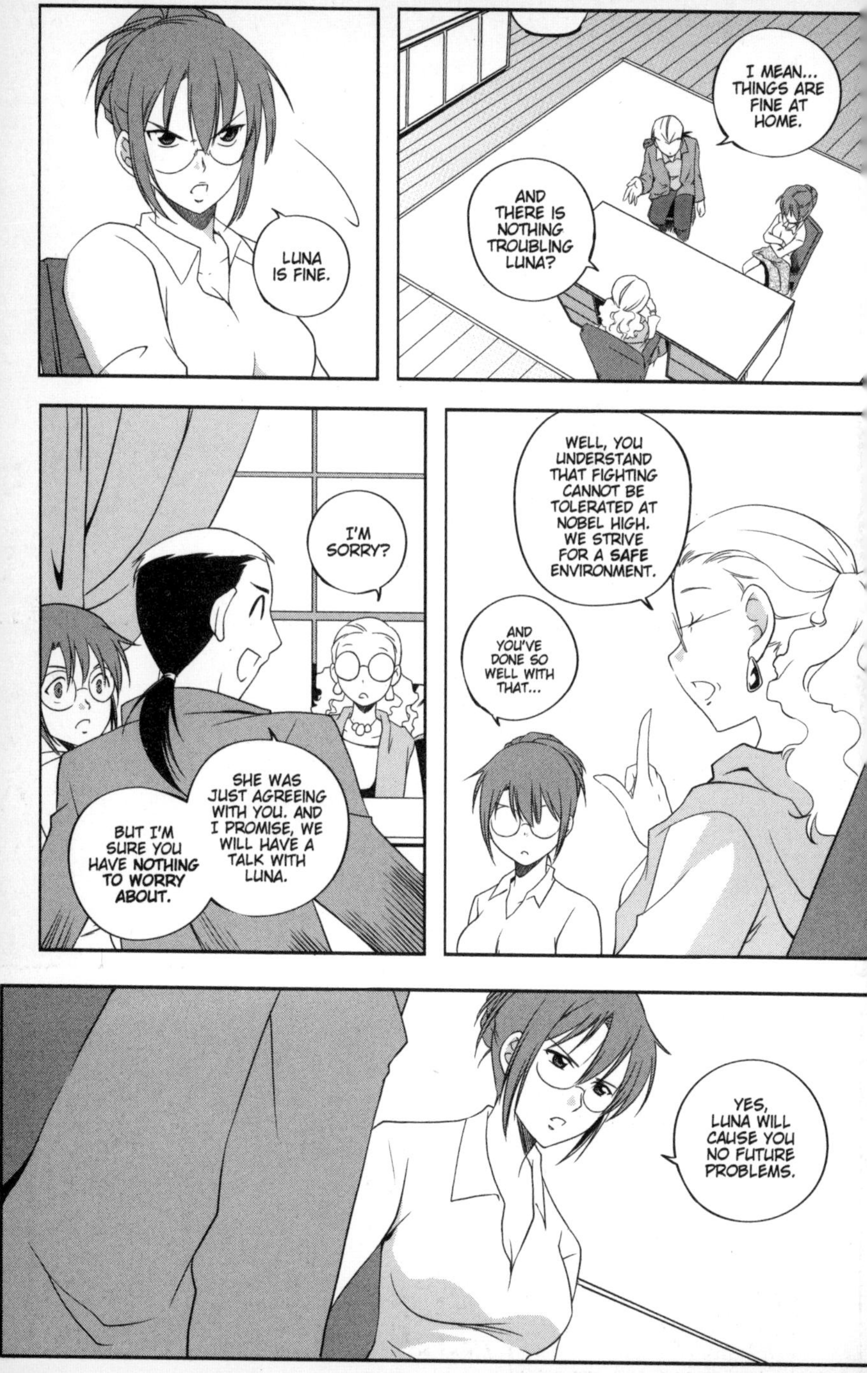
I MEAN... THINGS ARE FINE AT HOME.
AND THERE IS NOTHING TROUBLING LUNA?
LUNA IS FINE.
WELL, YOU UNDERSTAND THAT FIGHTING CANNOT BE TOLERATED AT NOBEL HIGH. WE STRIVE FOR A SAFE ENVIRONMENT.
AND YOU'VE DONE SO WELL WITH THAT...
I'M SORRY?
SHE WAS JUST AGREEING WITH YOU. AND I PROMISE, WE WILL HAVE A TALK WITH LUNA.
BUT I'M SURE YOU HAVE NOTHING TO WORRY ABOUT.
YES, LUNA WILL CAUSE YOU NO FUTURE PROBLEMS.

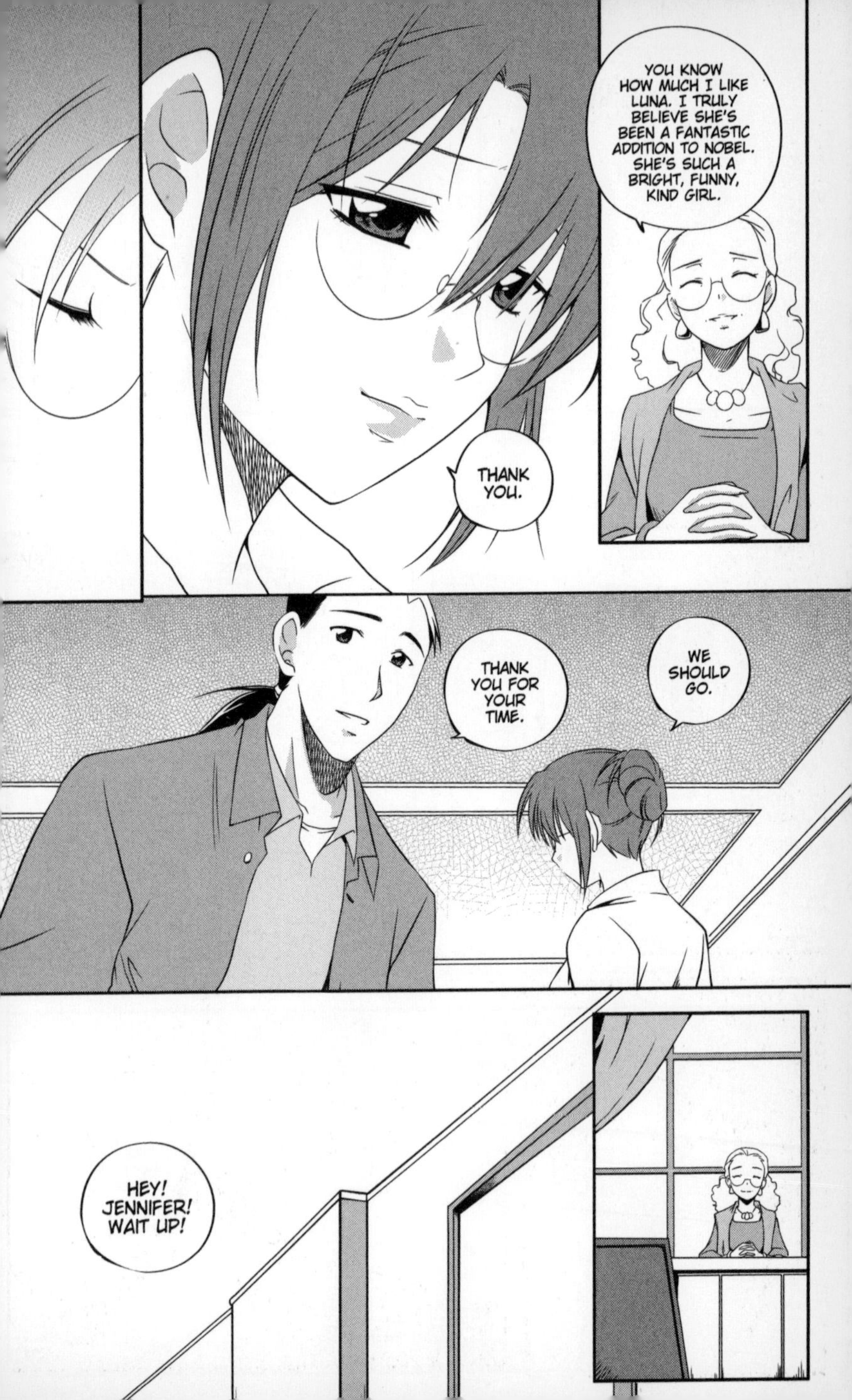
YOU KNOW HOW MUCH I LIKE LUNA. I TRULY BELIEVE SHE'S BEEN A FANTASTIC ADDITION TO NOBEL. SHE'S SUCH A BRIGHT, FUNNY, KIND GIRL.
THANK YOU.
WE SHOULD GO.
THANK YOU FOR YOUR TIME.
HEY! JENNIFER! WAIT UP!

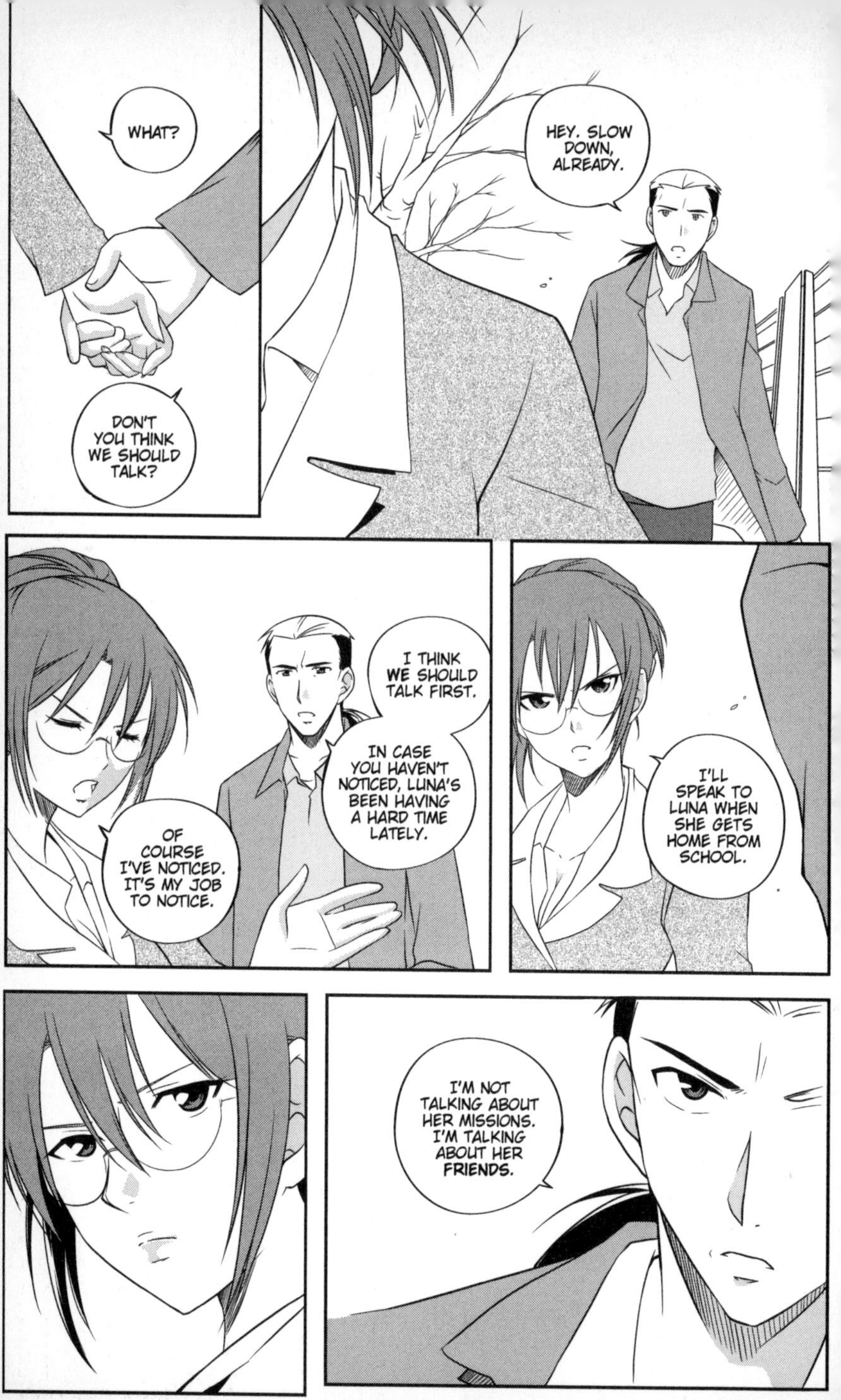
HEY. SLOW DOWN, ALREADY.
WHAT?
DON'T YOU THINK WE SHOULD TALK?
I'LL SPEAK TO LUNA WHEN SHE GETS HOME FROM SCHOOL.
I THINK WE SHOULD TALK FIRST.
IN CASE YOU HAVEN'T NOTICED, LUNA'S BEEN HAVING A HARD TIME LATELY.
OF COURSE I'VE NOTICED. IT'S MY JOB TO NOTICE.
I'M NOT TALKING ABOUT HER MISSIONS. I'M TALKING ABOUT HER FRIENDS.

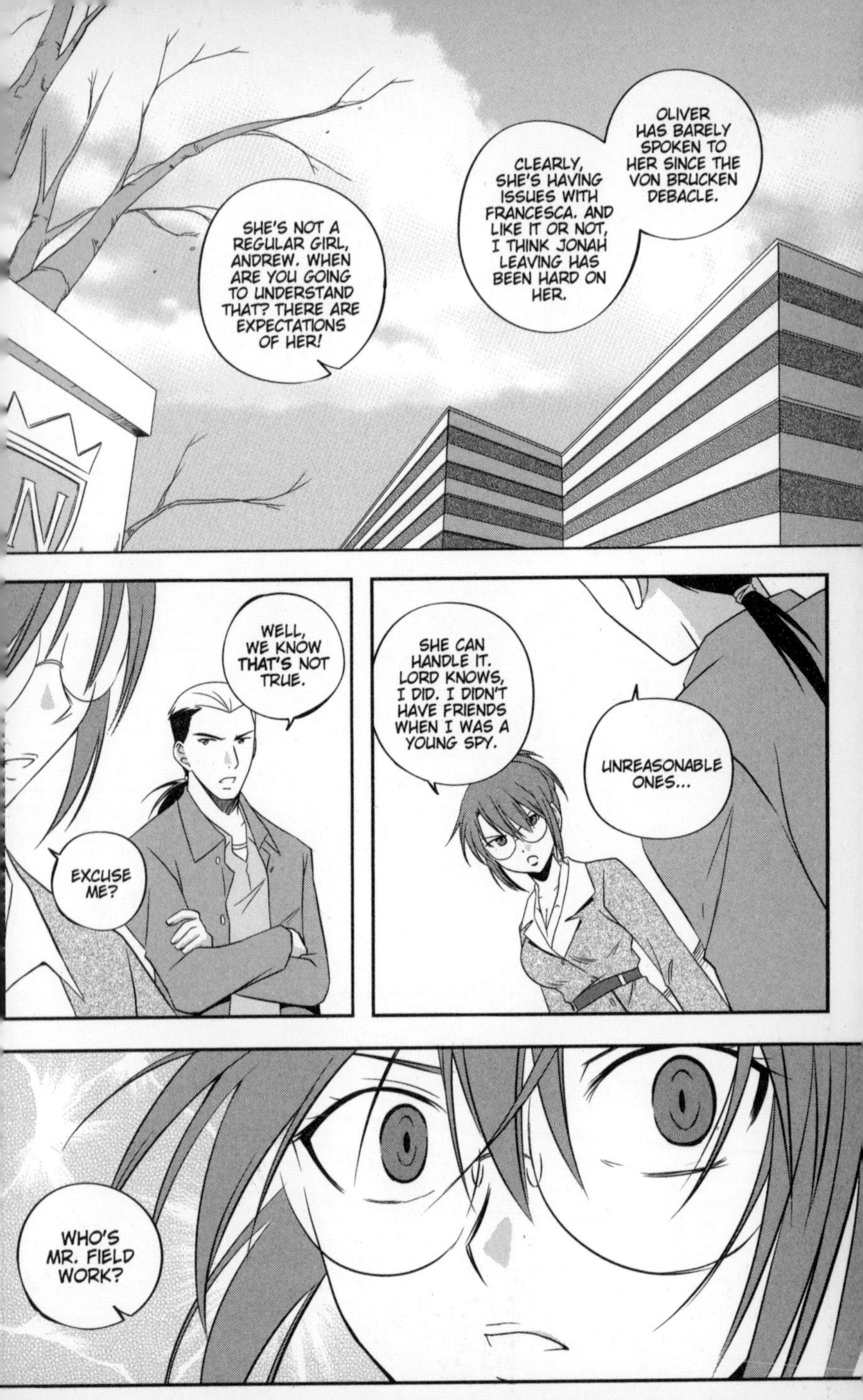
OLIVER HAS BARELY SPOKEN TO HER SINCE THE VON BRUCKEN DEBACLE.
CLEARLY, SHE'S HAVING ISSUES WITH FRANCESCA. AND LIKE IT OR NOT, I THINK JONAH LEAVING HAS BEEN HARD ON HER.
SHE'S NOT A REGULAR GIRL, ANDREW. WHEN ARE YOU GOING TO UNDERSTAND THAT? THERE ARE EXPECTATIONS OF HER!
UNREASONABLE ONES...
SHE CAN HANDLE IT. LORD KNOWS, I DID. I DIDN'T HAVE FRIENDS WHEN I WAS A YOUNG SPY.
WELL, WE KNOW THAT'S NOT TRUE.
EXCUSE ME?
WHO'S MR. FIELD WORK?

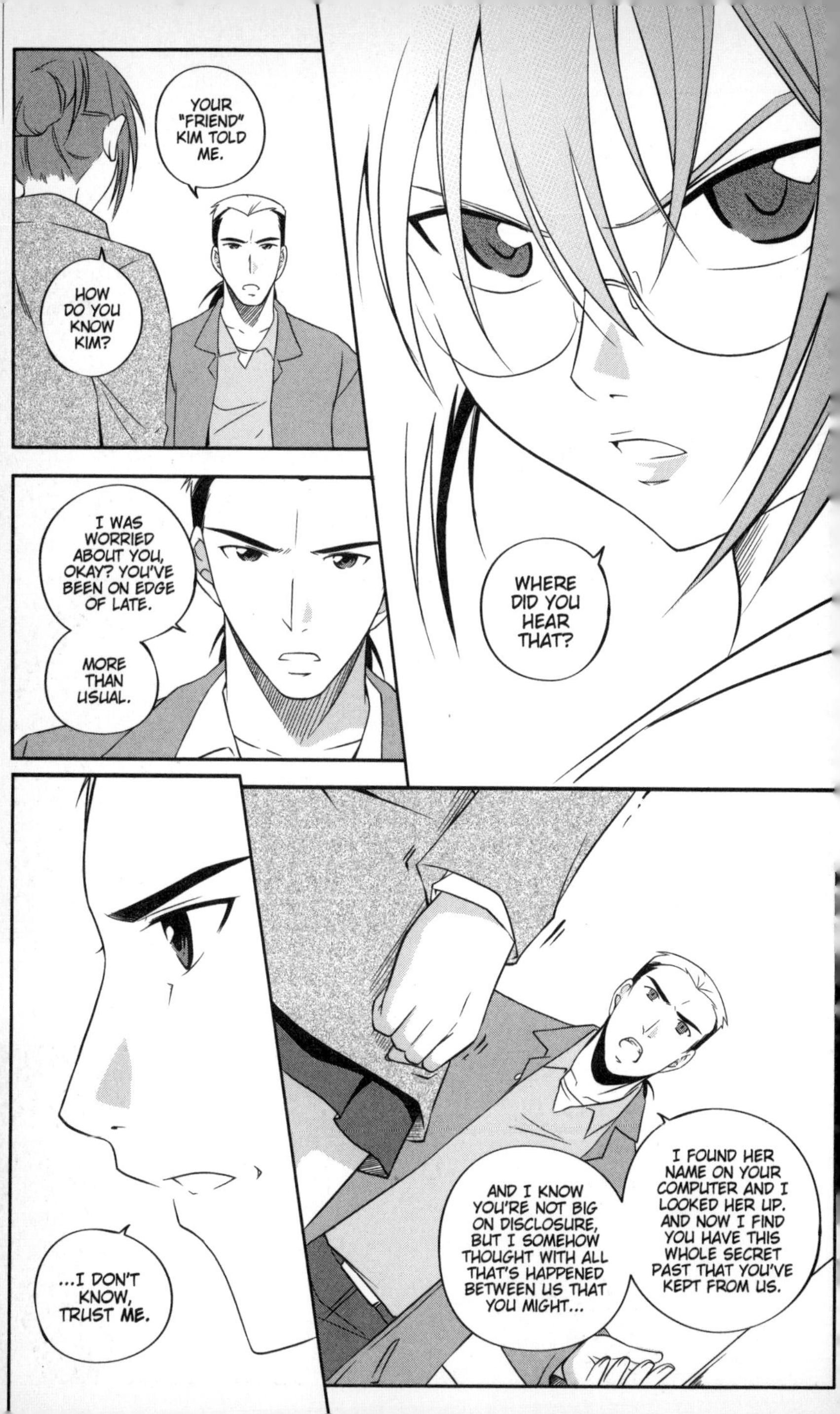
WHERE DID YOU HEAR THAT?
YOUR "FRIEND" KIM TOLD ME.
HOW DO YOU KNOW KIM?
I WAS WORRIED ABOUT YOU, OKAY? YOU'VE BEEN ON EDGE OF LATE.
MORE THAN USUAL.
I FOUND HER NAME ON YOUR COMPUTER AND I LOOKED HER UP. AND NOW I FIND YOU HAVE THIS WHOLE SECRET PAST THAT YOU'VE KEPT FROM US.
AND I KNOW YOU'RE NOT BIG ON DISCLOSURE, BUT I SOMEHOW THOUGHT WITH ALL THAT'S HAPPENED BETWEEN US THAT YOU MIGHT...
...I DON'T KNOW, TRUST ME.

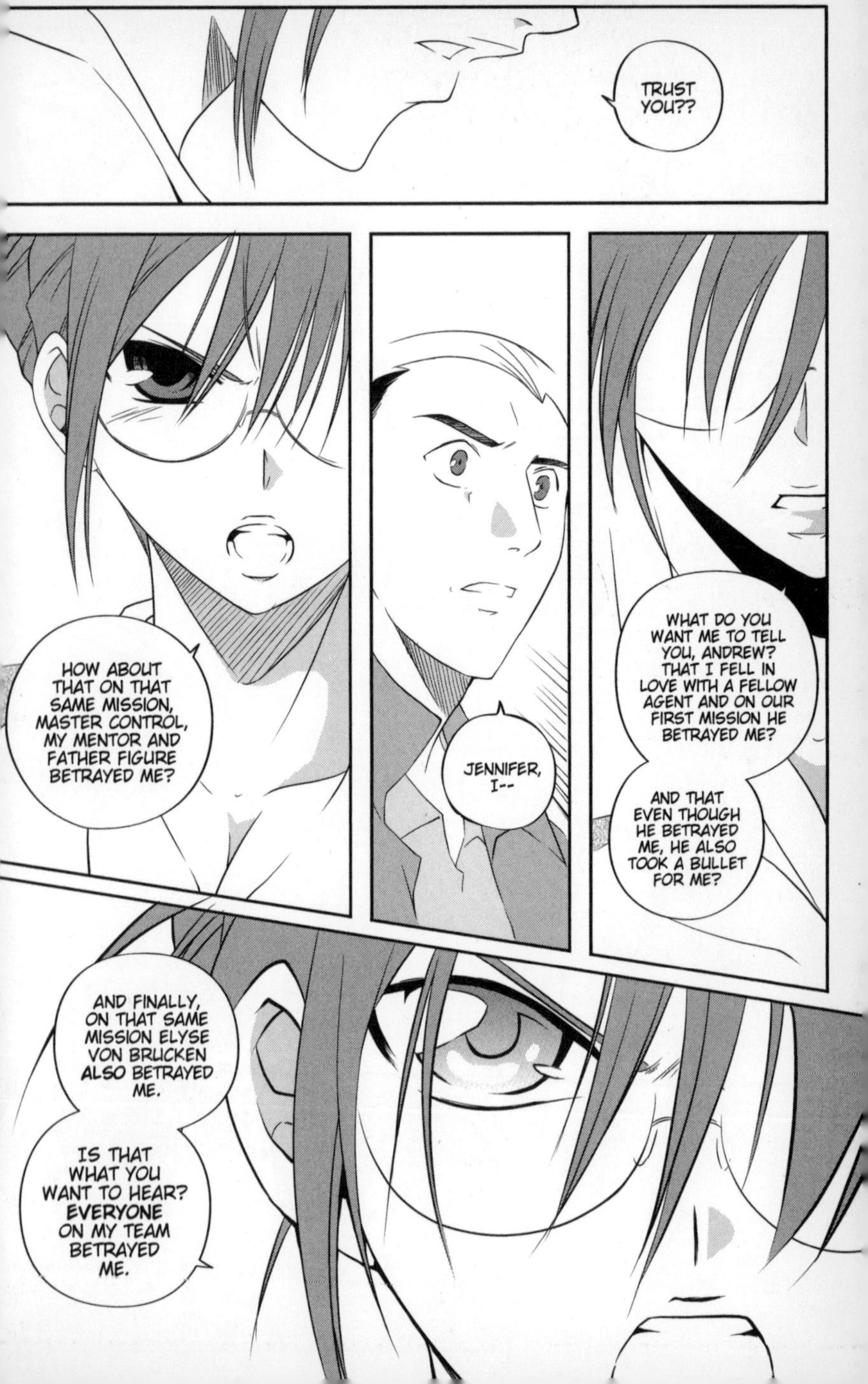
TRUST YOU??
WHAT DO YOU WANT ME TO TELL YOU, ANDREW? THAT I FELL IN LOVE WITH A FELLOW AGENT AND ON OUR FIRST MISSION HE BETRAYED ME?
AND THAT EVEN THOUGH HE BETRAYED ME, HE ALSO TOOK A BULLET FOR ME?
JENNIFER, I--
HOW ABOUT THAT ON THAT SAME MISSION, MASTER CONTROL, MY MENTOR AND FATHER FIGURE BETRAYED ME?
AND FINALLY, ON THAT SAME MISSION ELYSE VON BRUCKEN ALSO BETRAYED ME.
IS THAT WHAT YOU WANT TO HEAR? EVERYONE ON MY TEAM BETRAYED ME.

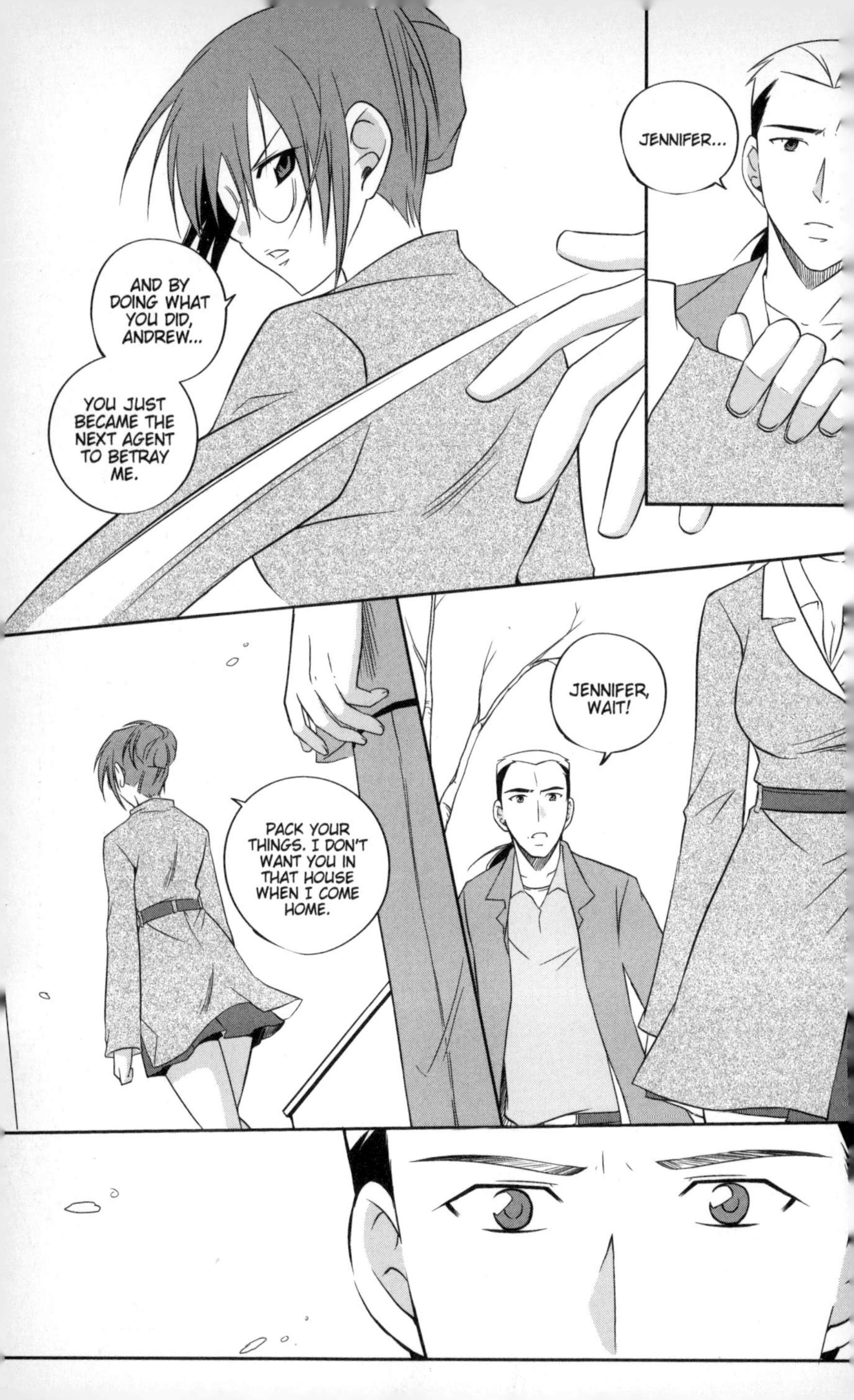
JENNIFER...
AND BY DOING WHAT YOU DID, ANDREW...
YOU JUST BECAME THE NEXT AGENT TO BETRAY ME.
JENNIFER, WAIT!
PACK YOUR THINGS. I DON'T WANT YOU IN THAT HOUSE WHEN I COME HOME.

File 44
DEFECTION

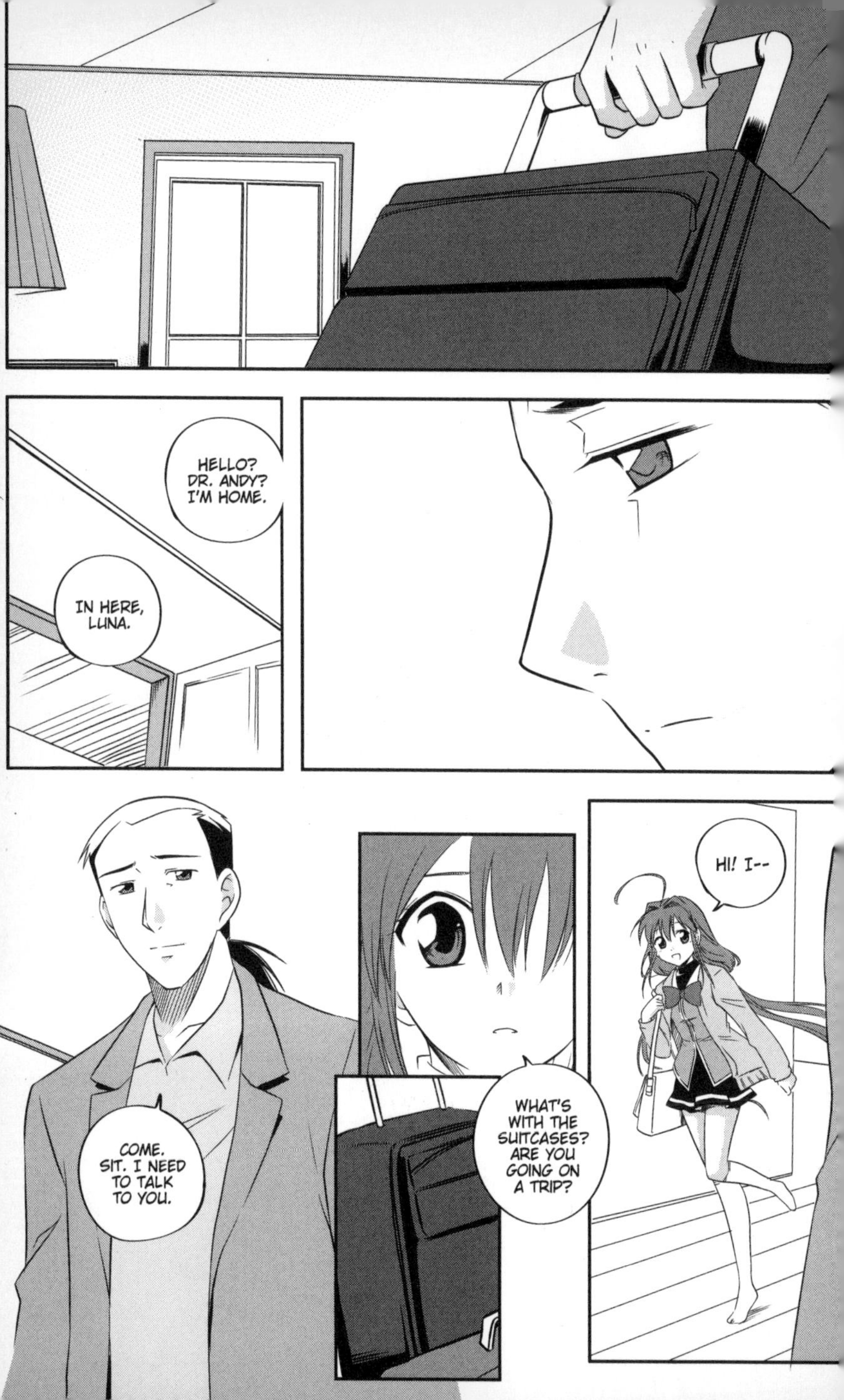
HELLO? DR. ANDY? I'M HOME.
IN HERE, LUNA.
HI! I--
WHAT'S WITH THE SUITCASES? ARE YOU GOING ON A TRIP?
COME. SIT. I NEED TO TALK TO YOU.

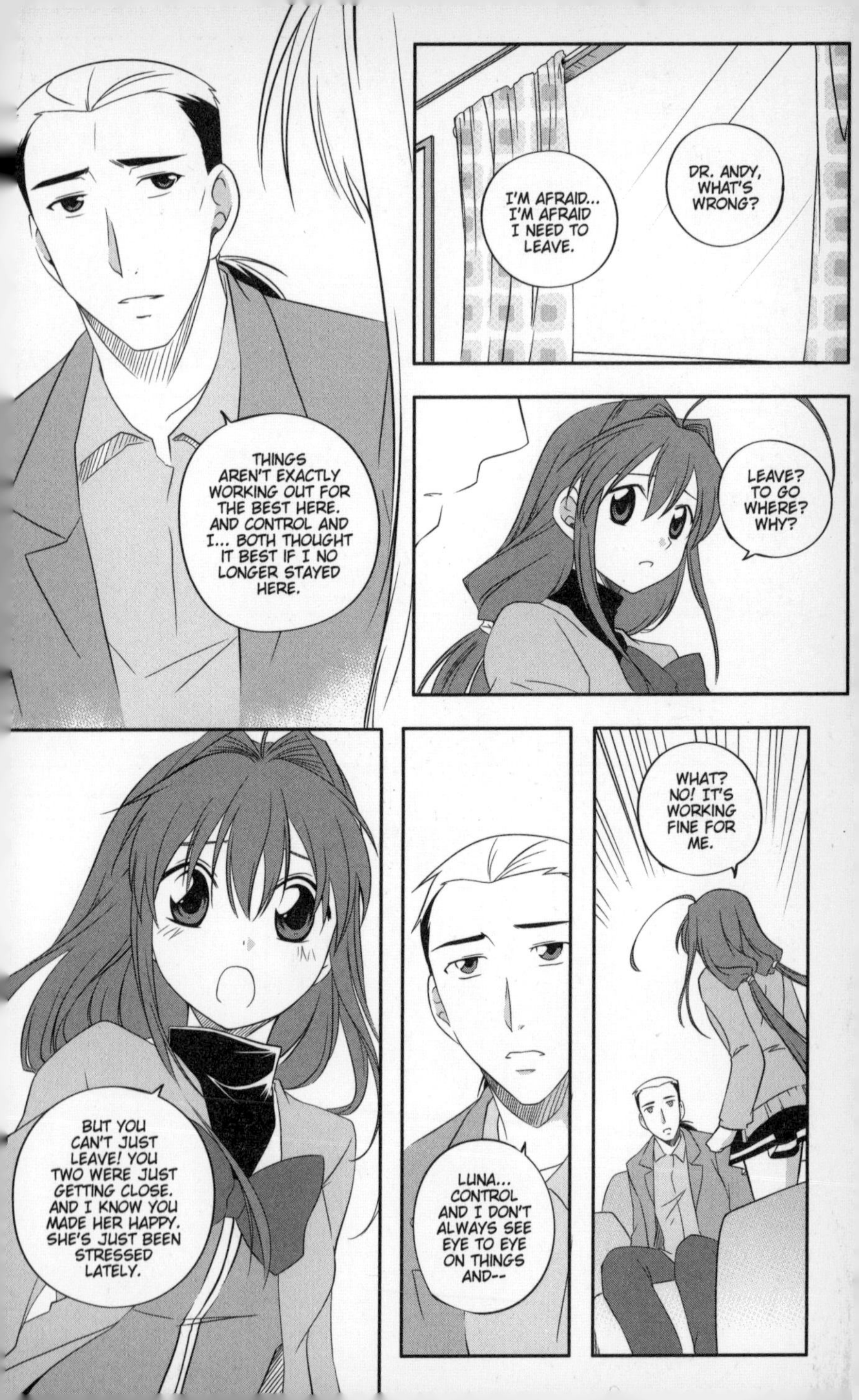
DR. ANDY, WHAT'S WRONG?
I'M AFRAID... I'M AFRAID I NEED TO LEAVE.
LEAVE? TO GO WHERE? WHY?
THINGS AREN'T EXACTLY WORKING OUT FOR THE BEST HERE. AND CONTROL AND I... BOTH THOUGHT IT BEST IF I NO LONGER STAYED HERE.
WHAT? NO! IT'S WORKING FINE FOR ME.
LUNA... CONTROL AND I DON'T ALWAYS SEE EYE TO EYE ON THINGS AND--
BUT YOU CAN'T JUST LEAVE! YOU TWO WERE JUST GETTING CLOSE. AND I KNOW YOU MADE HER HAPPY. SHE'S JUST BEEN STRESSED LATELY.

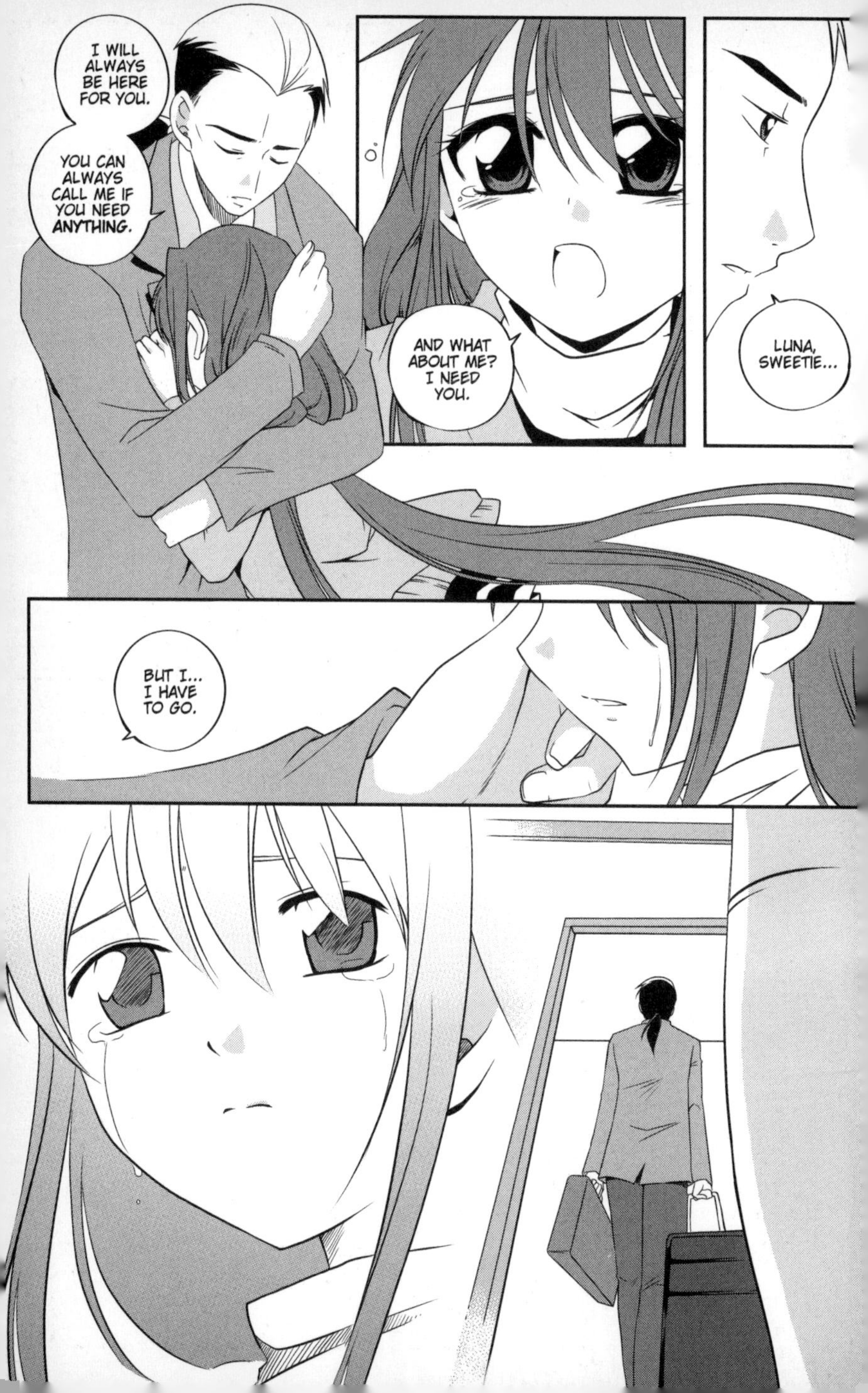
LUNA, SWEETIE...
AND WHAT ABOUT ME? I NEED YOU.
I WILL ALWAYS BE HERE FOR YOU.
YOU CAN ALWAYS CALL ME IF YOU NEED ANYTHING.
BUT I... I HAVE TO GO.

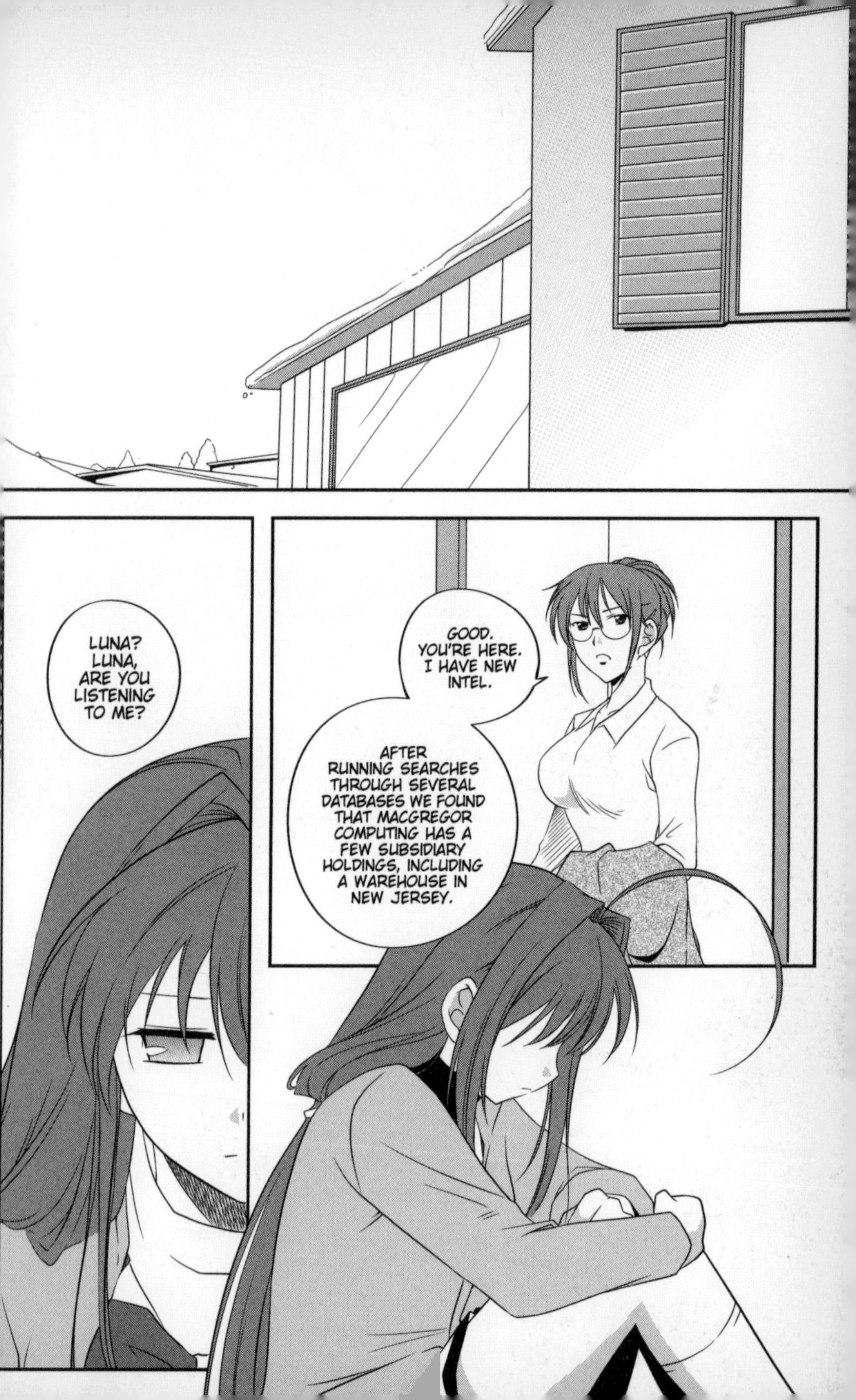
GOOD. YOU'RE HERE. I HAVE NEW INTEL.
AFTER RUNNING SEARCHES THROUGH SEVERAL DATABASES WE FOUND THAT MACGREGOR COMPUTING HAS A FEW SUBSIDIARY HOLDINGS, INCLUDING A WAREHOUSE IN NEW JERSEY.
LUNA? LUNA, ARE YOU LISTENING TO ME?

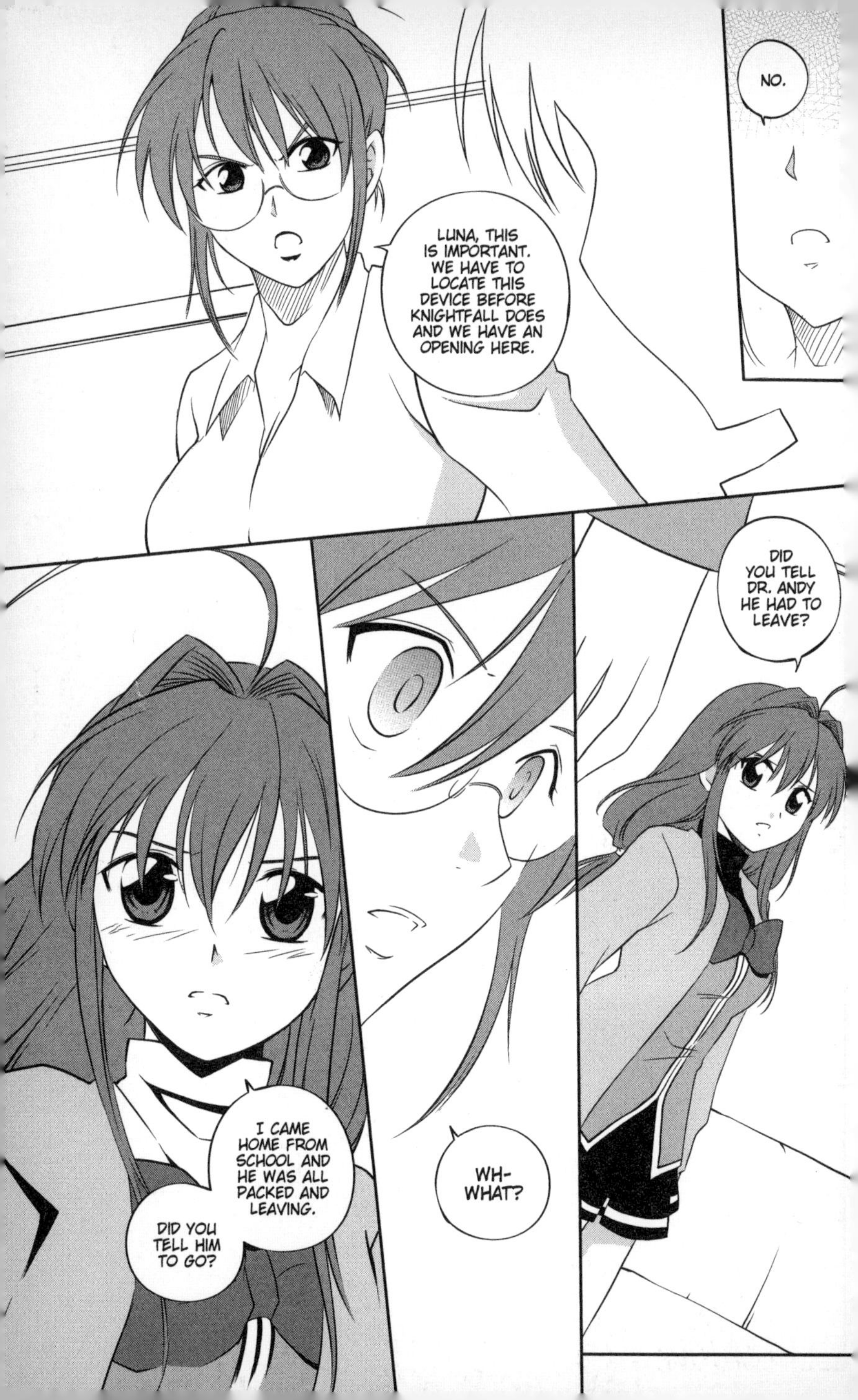
NO.
LUNA, THIS IS IMPORTANT. WE HAVE TO LOCATE THIS DEVICE BEFORE KNIGHTFALL DOES AND WE HAVE AN OPENING HERE.
DID YOU TELL DR. ANDY HE HAD TO LEAVE?
WH-WHAT?
I CAME HOME FROM SCHOOL AND HE WAS ALL PACKED AND LEAVING.
DID YOU TELL HIM TO GO?

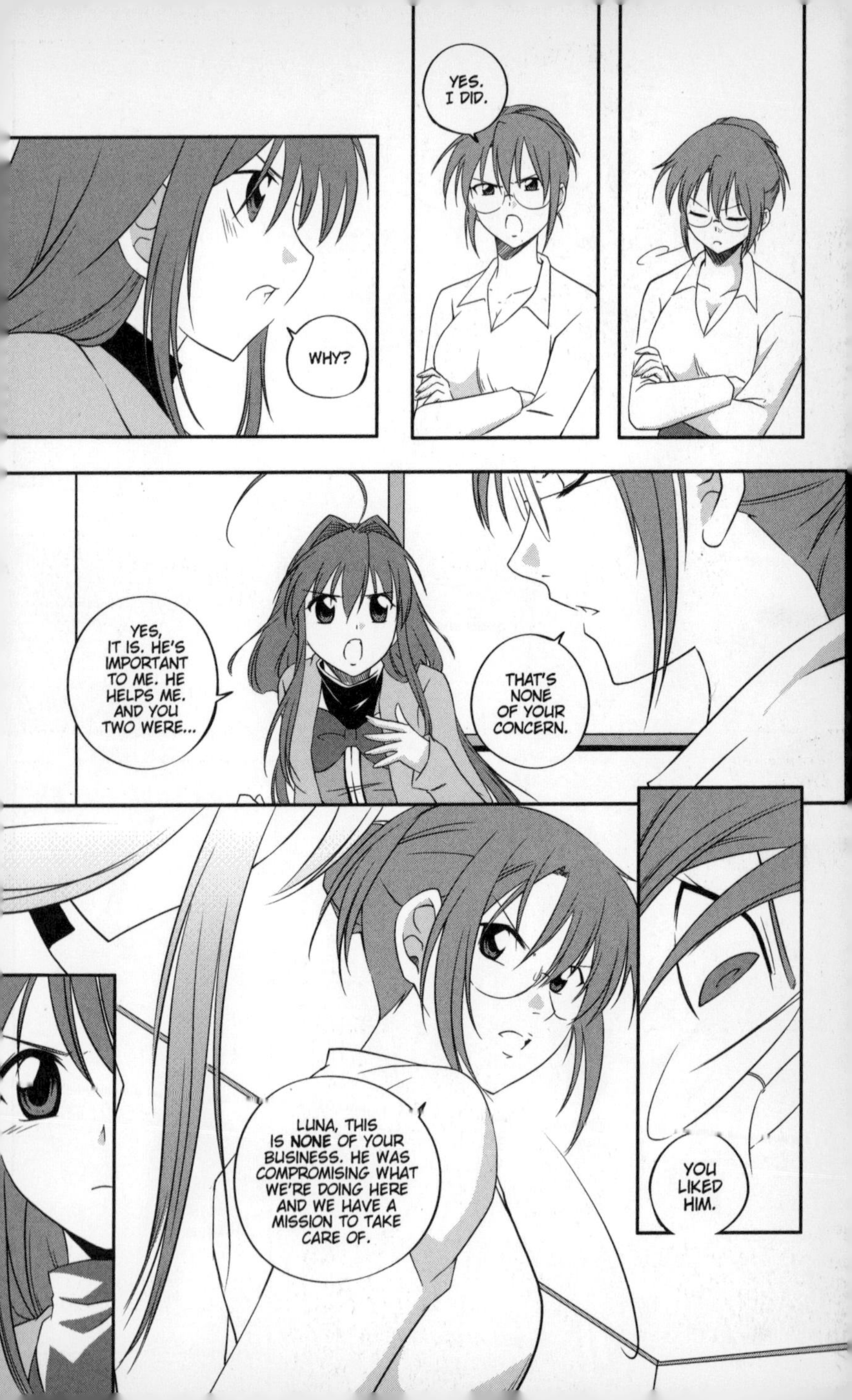
YES. I DID.
WHY?
THAT'S NONE OF YOUR CONCERN.
YES, IT IS. HE'S IMPORTANT TO ME. HE HELPS ME. AND YOU TWO WERE...
YOU LIKED HIM.
LUNA, THIS IS NONE OF YOUR BUSINESS. HE WAS COMPROMISING WHAT WE'RE DOING HERE AND WE HAVE A MISSION TO TAKE CARE OF.

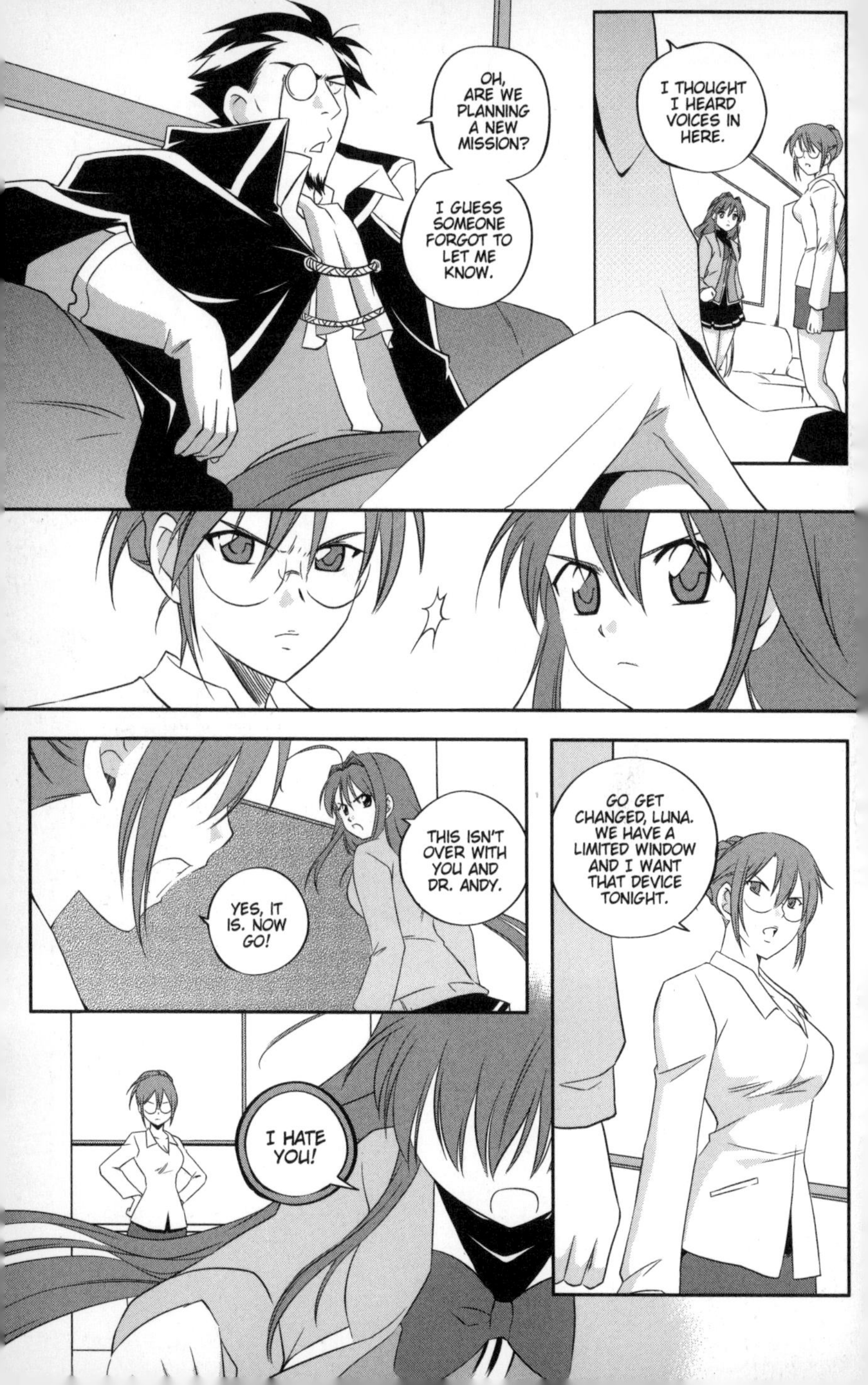
I THOUGHT I HEARD VOICES IN HERE.
OH, ARE WE PLANNING A NEW MISSION?
I GUESS SOMEONE FORGOT TO LET ME KNOW.
GO GET CHANGED, LUNA. WE HAVE A LIMITED WINDOW AND I WANT THAT DEVICE TONIGHT.
THIS ISN'T OVER WITH YOU AND DR. ANDY.
YES, IT IS. NOW GO!
I HATE YOU!

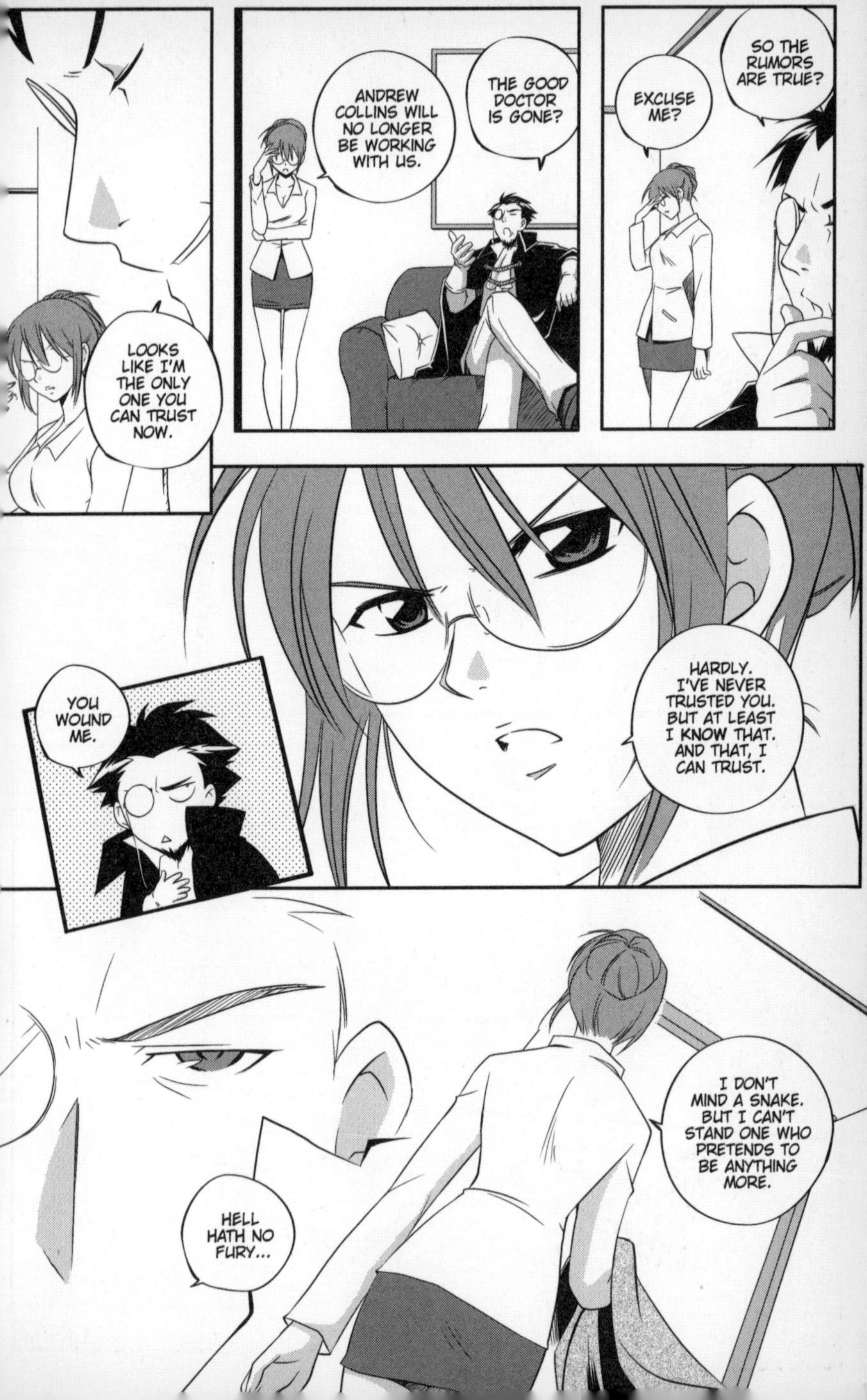
SO THE RUMORS ARE TRUE?
EXCUSE ME?
THE GOOD DOCTOR IS GONE?
ANDREW COLLINS WILL NO LONGER BE WORKING WITH US.
LOOKS LIKE I'M THE ONLY ONE YOU CAN TRUST NOW.
HARDLY. I'VE NEVER TRUSTED YOU. BUT AT LEAST I KNOW THAT. AND THAT, I CAN TRUST.
YOU WOUND ME.
I DON'T MIND A SNAKE. BUT I CAN'T STAND ONE WHO PRETENDS TO BE ANYTHING MORE.
HELL HATH NO FURY...

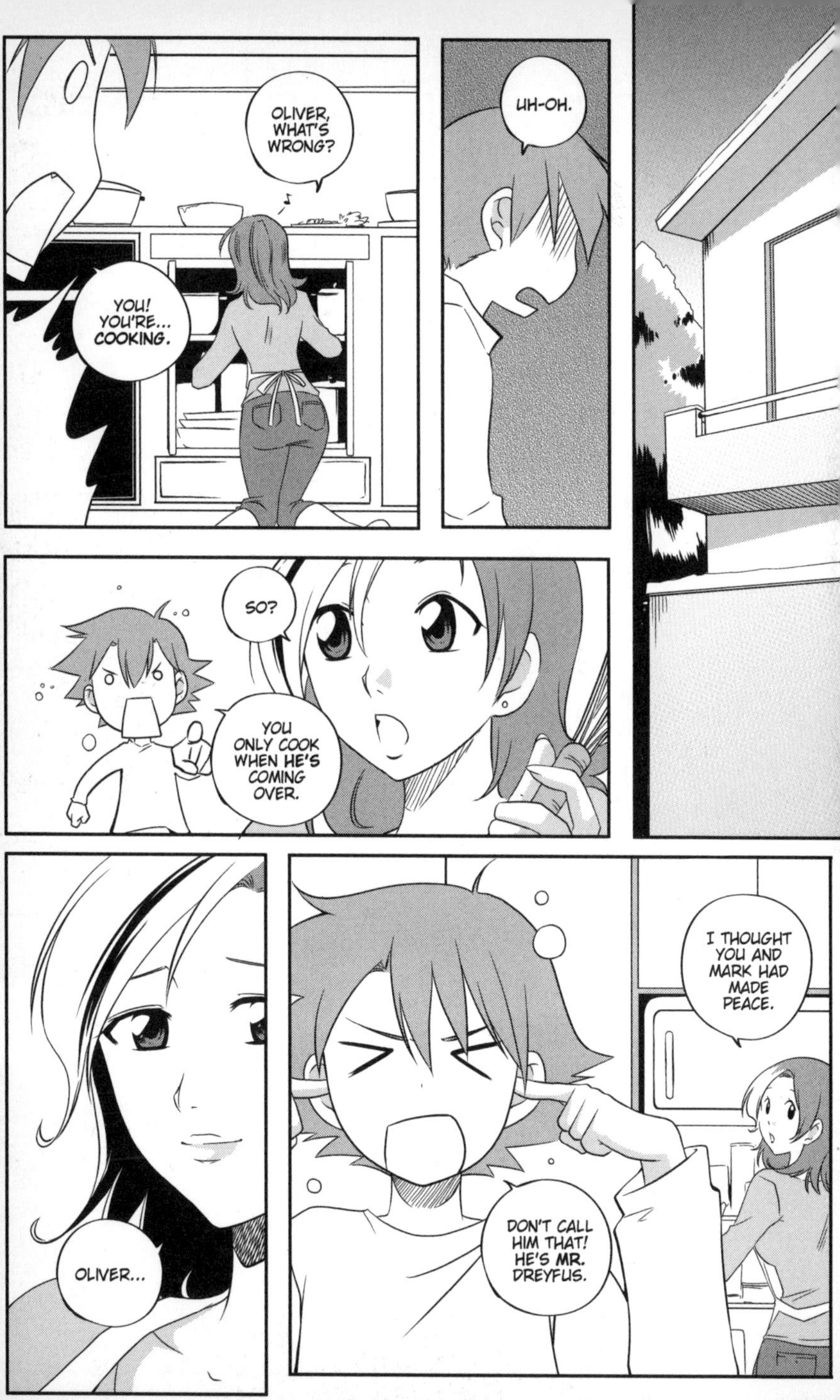
UH-OH.
OLIVER, WHAT'S WRONG?
YOU! YOU'RE... COOKING.
SO?
YOU ONLY COOK WHEN HE'S COMING OVER.
I THOUGHT YOU AND MARK HAD MADE PEACE.
DON'T CALL HIM THAT! HE'S MR. DREYFUS.
OLIVER...

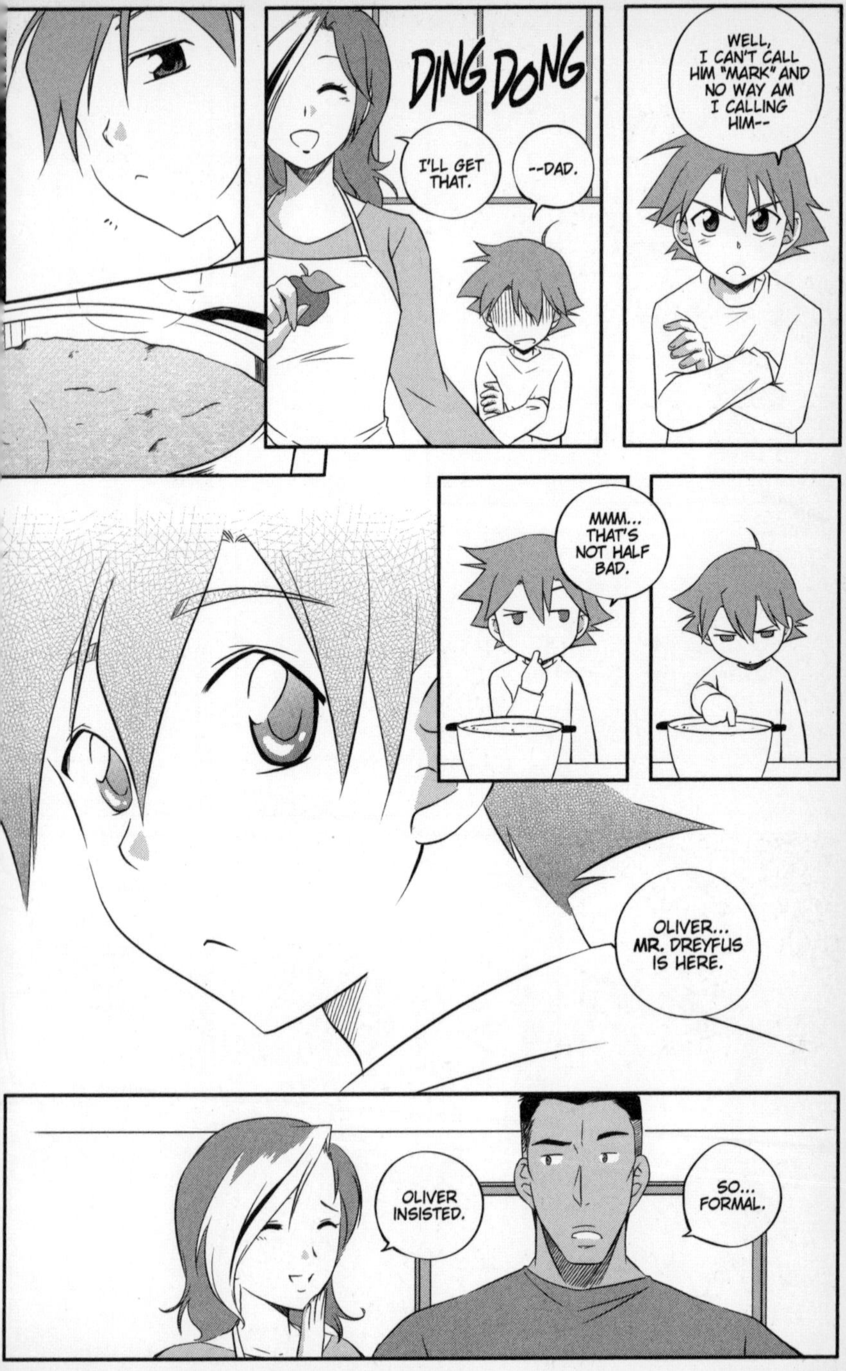
WELL, I CAN'T CALL HIM "MARK" AND NO WAY AM I CALLING HIM--
DING DONG
--DAD.
I'LL GET THAT.
MMMM... THAT'S NOT HALF BAD.
OLIVER... MR. DREYFUS IS HERE.
SO... FORMAL.
OLIVER INSISTED.

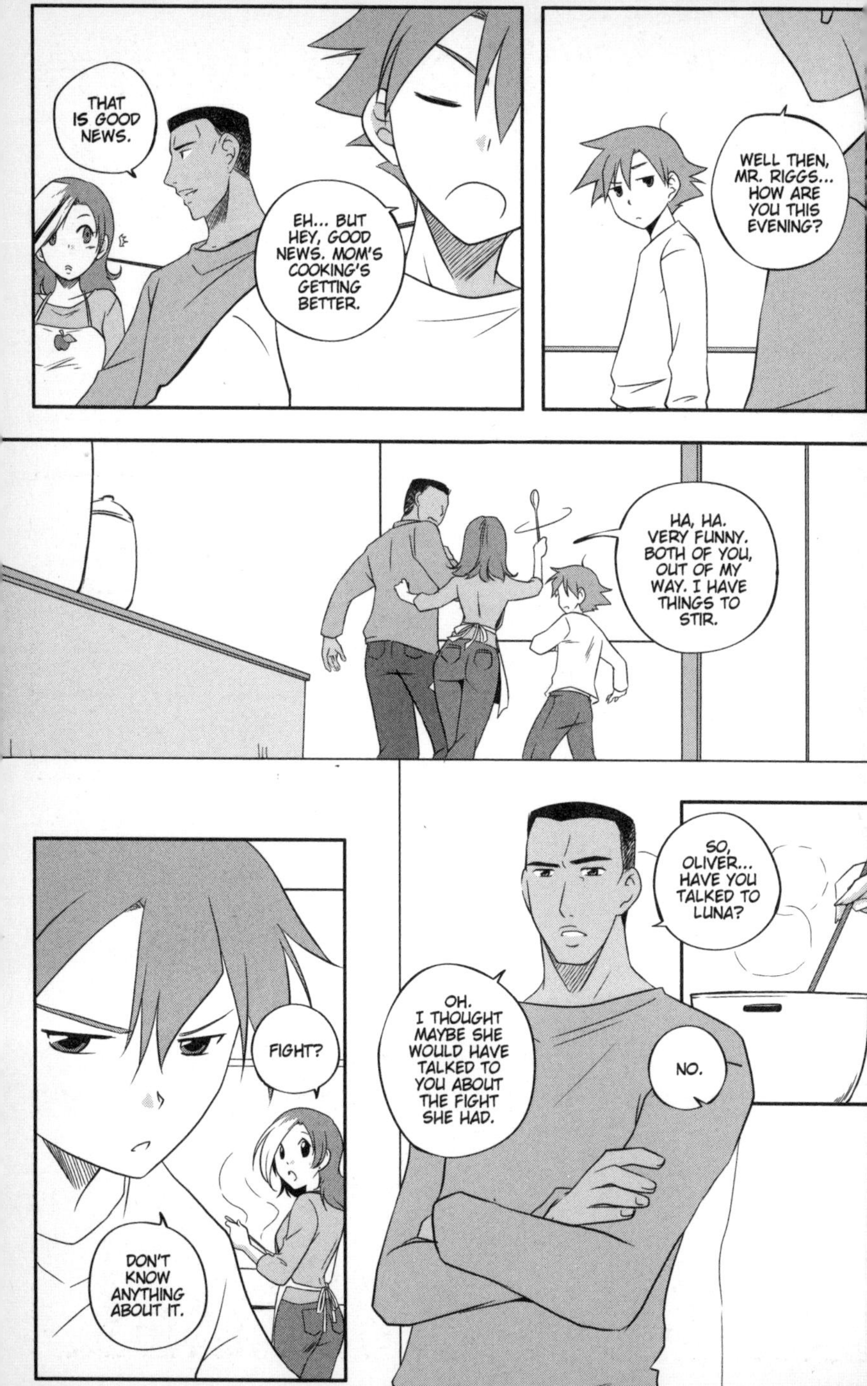
WELL THEN, MR. RIGGS... HOW ARE YOU THIS EVENING?
EH... BUT HEY, GOOD NEWS. MOM'S COOKING'S GETTING BETTER.
THAT IS GOOD NEWS.
HA, HA. VERY FUNNY. BOTH OF YOU, OUT OF MY WAY. I HAVE THINGS TO STIR.
SO, OLIVER... HAVE YOU TALKED TO LUNA?
NO.
OH. I THOUGHT MAYBE SHE WOULD HAVE TALKED TO YOU ABOUT THE FIGHT SHE HAD.
FIGHT?
DON'T KNOW ANYTHING ABOUT IT.

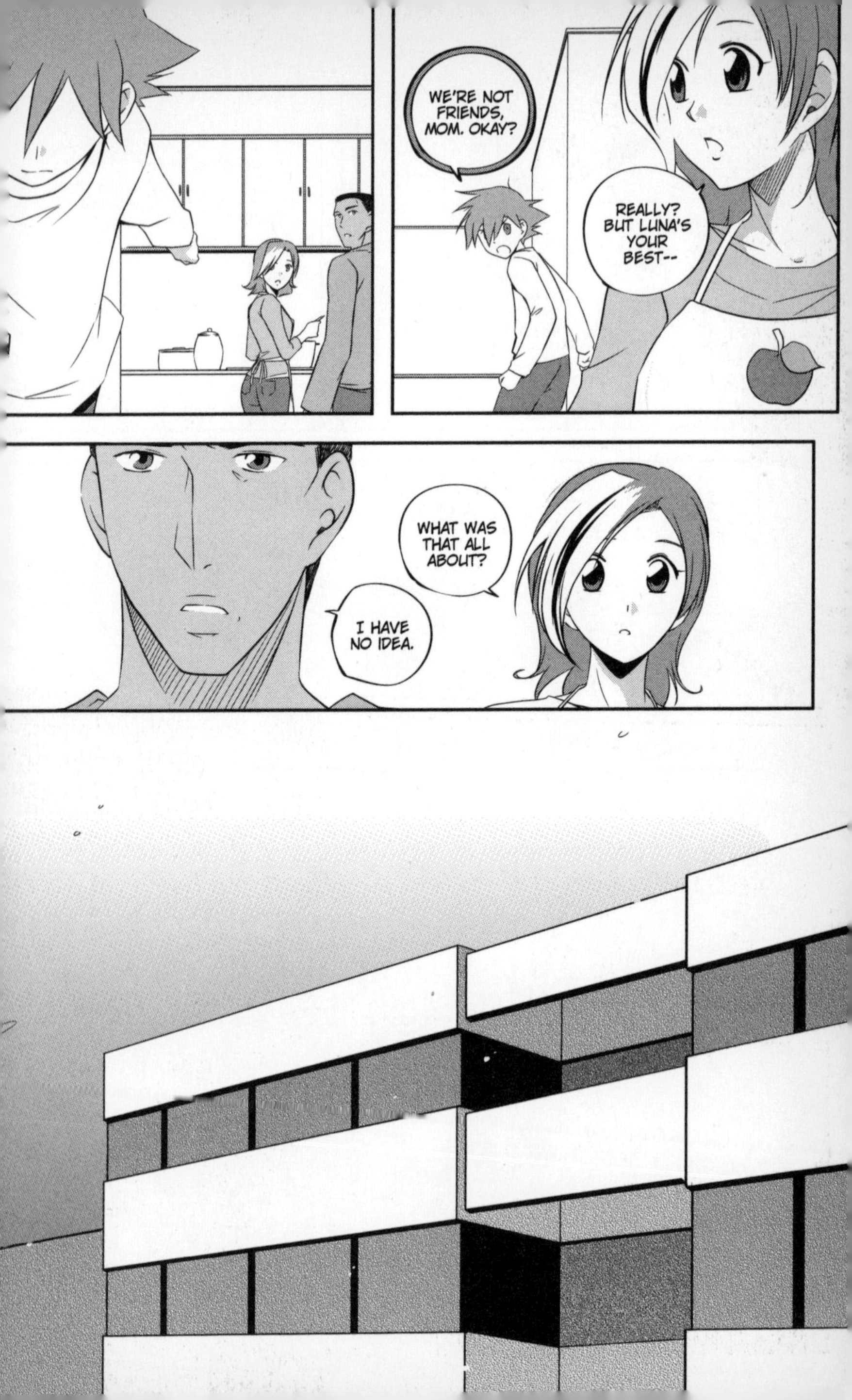
WE'RE NOT FRIENDS, MOM. OKAY?
REALLY? BUT LUNA'S YOUR BEST--
WHAT WAS THAT ALL ABOUT?
I HAVE NO IDEA.

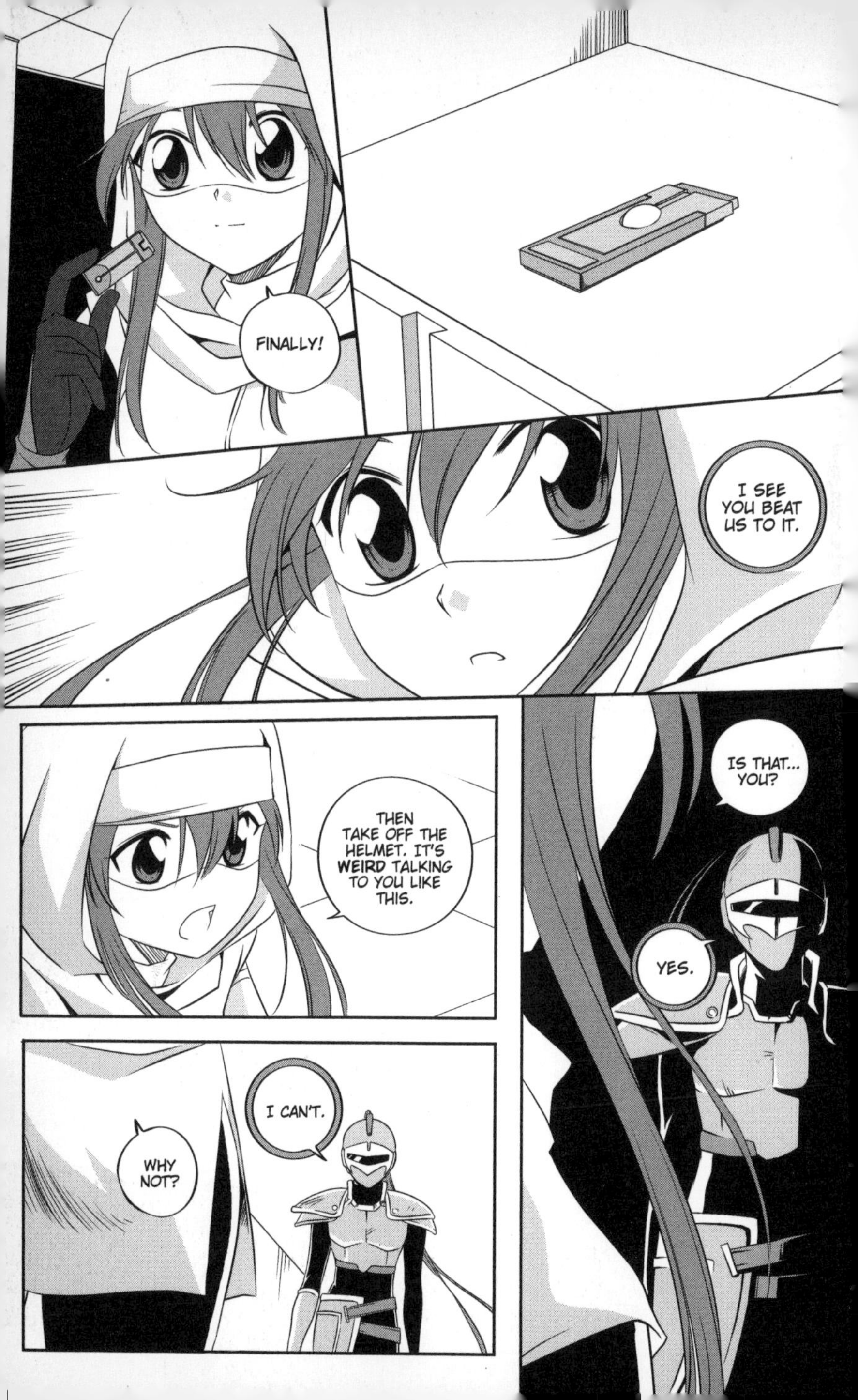
FINALLY!
I SEE YOU BEAT US TO IT.
IS THAT... YOU?
YES.
THEN TAKE OFF THE HELMET. IT'S WEIRD TALKING TO YOU LIKE THIS.
I CAN'T.
WHY NOT?

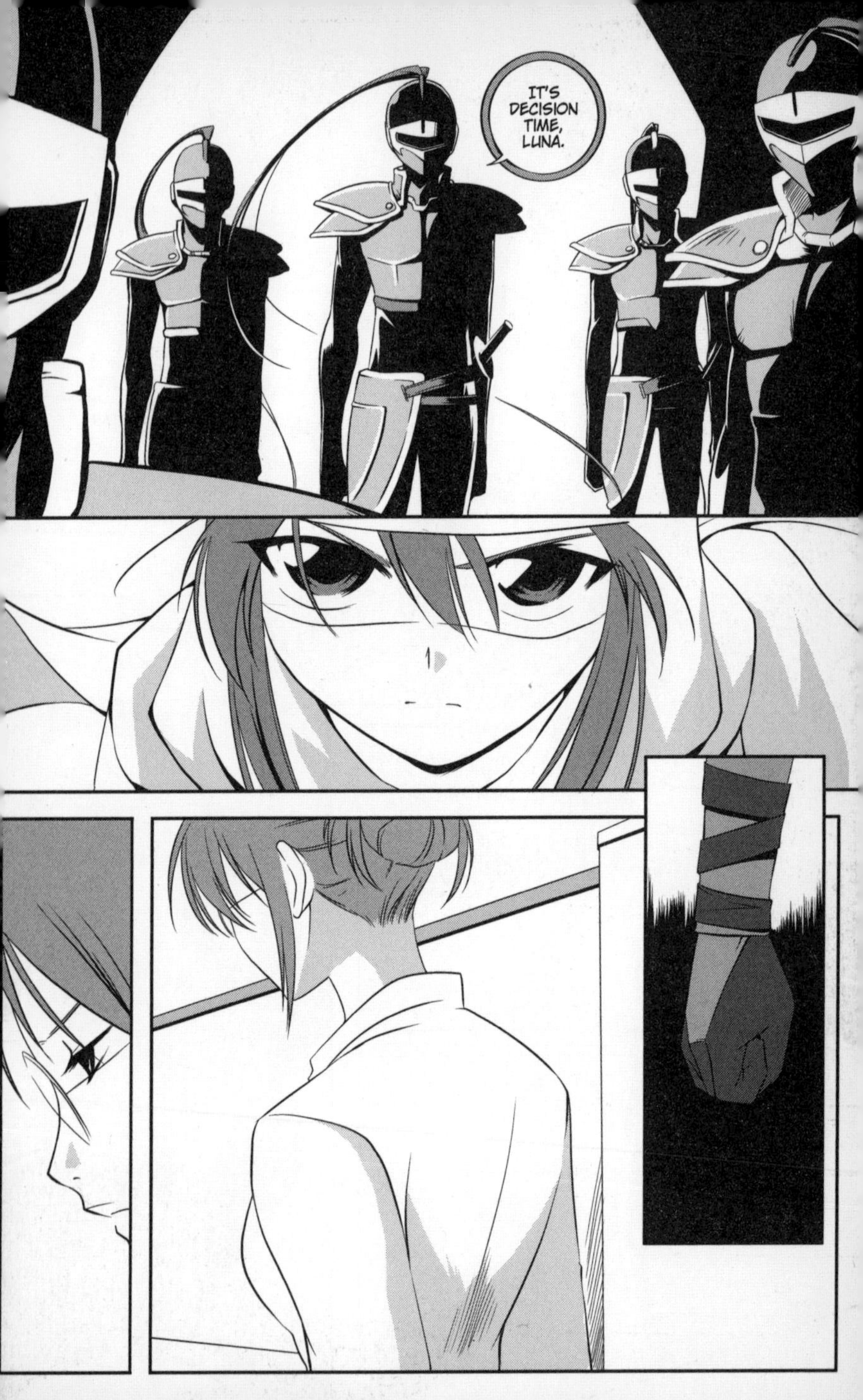
IT'S DECISION TIME, LUNA.

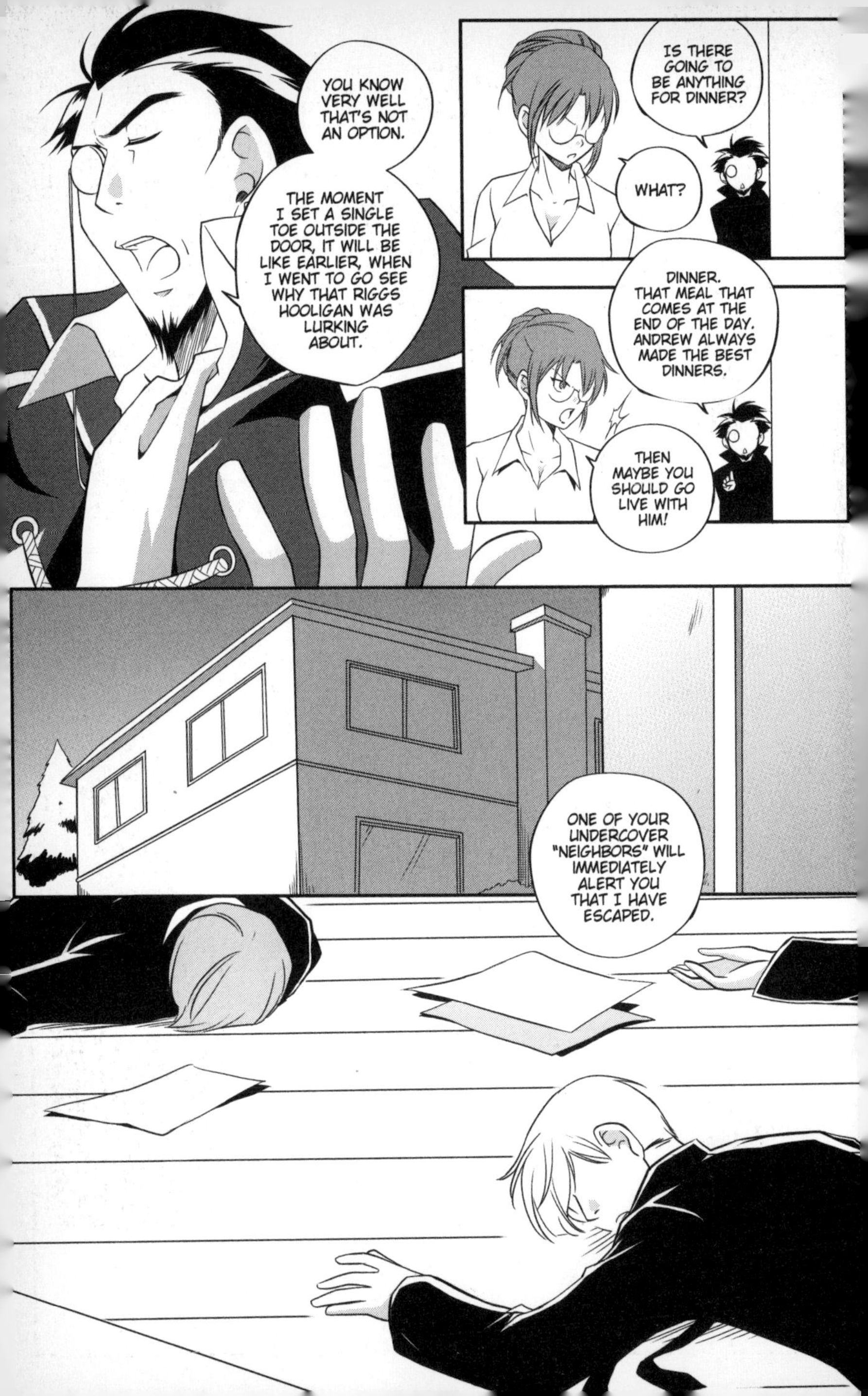
IS THERE GOING TO BE ANYTHING FOR DINNER?
WHAT?
DINNER. THAT MEAL THAT COMES AT THE END OF THE DAY. ANDREW ALWAYS MADE THE BEST DINNERS.
THEN MAYBE YOU SHOULD GO LIVE WITH HIM!
YOU KNOW VERY WELL THAT'S NOT AN OPTION.
THE MOMENT I SET A SINGLE TOE OUTSIDE THE DOOR, IT WILL BE LIKE EARLIER, WHEN I WENT TO GO SEE WHY THAT RIGGS HOOLIGAN WAS LURKING ABOUT.
ONE OF YOUR UNDERCOVER "NEIGHBORS" WILL IMMEDIATELY ALERT YOU THAT I HAVE ESCAPED.

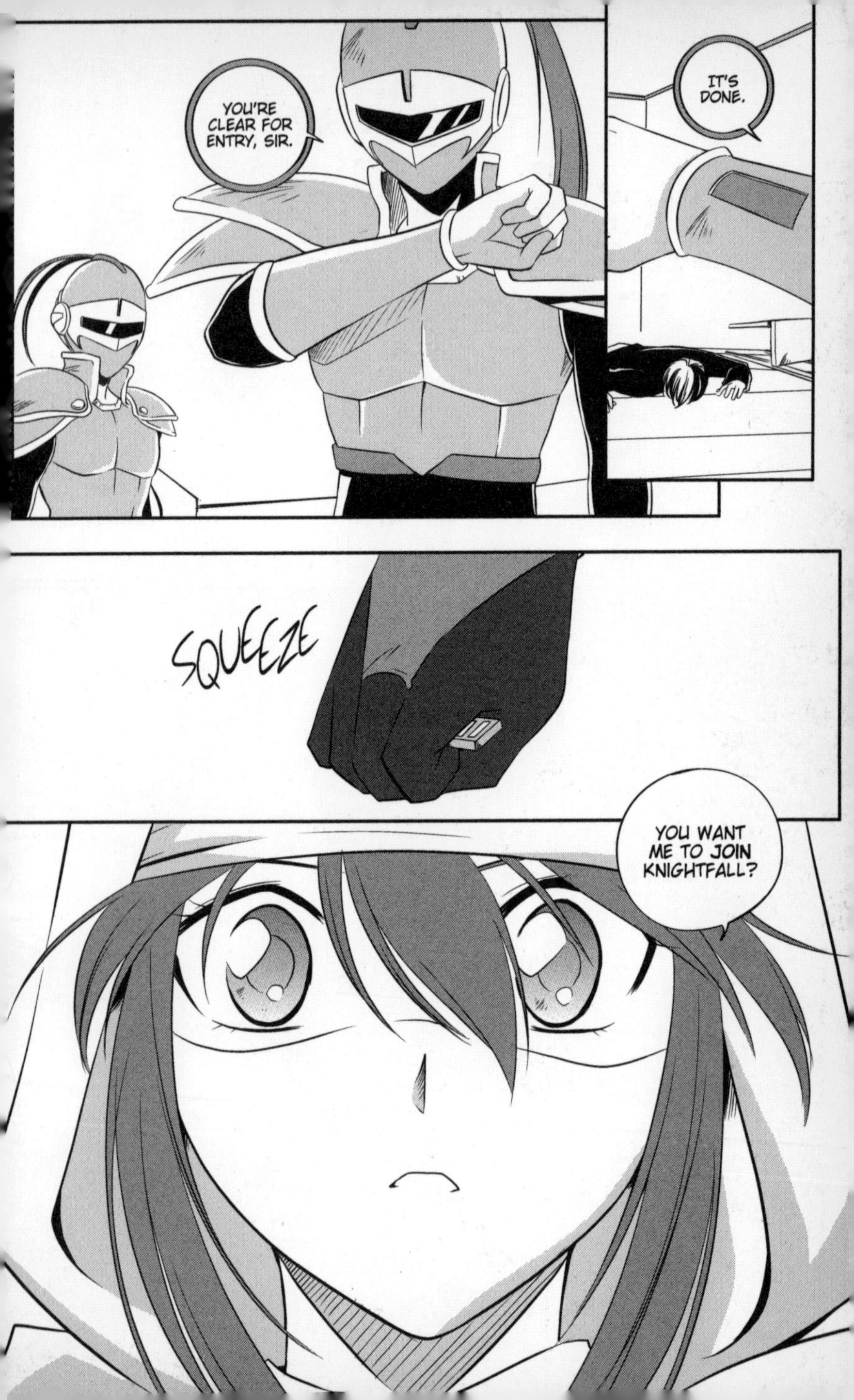
IT'S DONE.
YOU'RE CLEAR FOR ENTRY, SIR.
SQUEEZE
YOU WANT ME TO JOIN KNIGHTFALL?

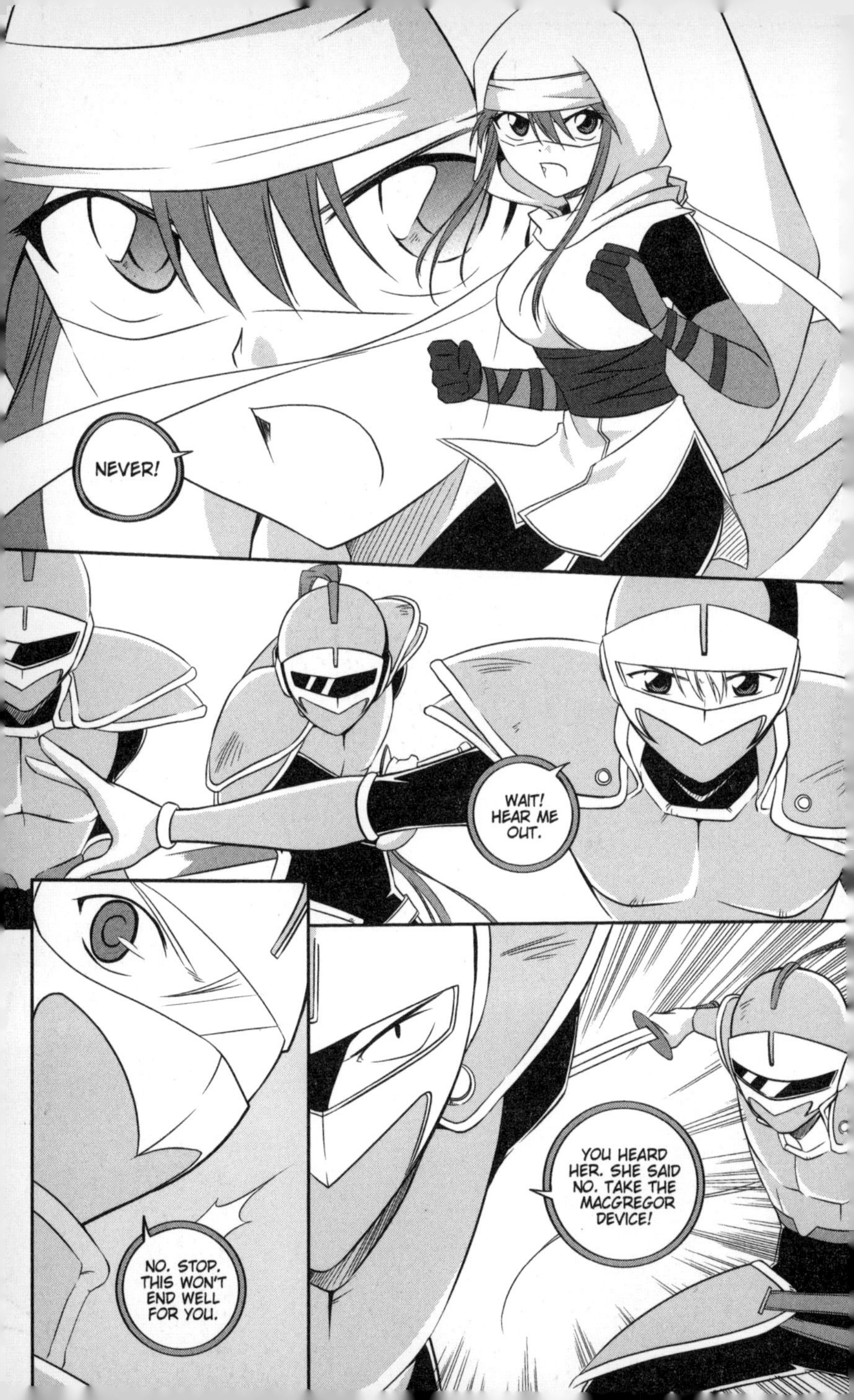
NEVER!
WAIT! HEAR ME OUT.
YOU HEARD HER. SHE SAID NO. TAKE THE MACGREGOR DEVICE!
NO. STOP. THIS WON'T END WELL FOR YOU.

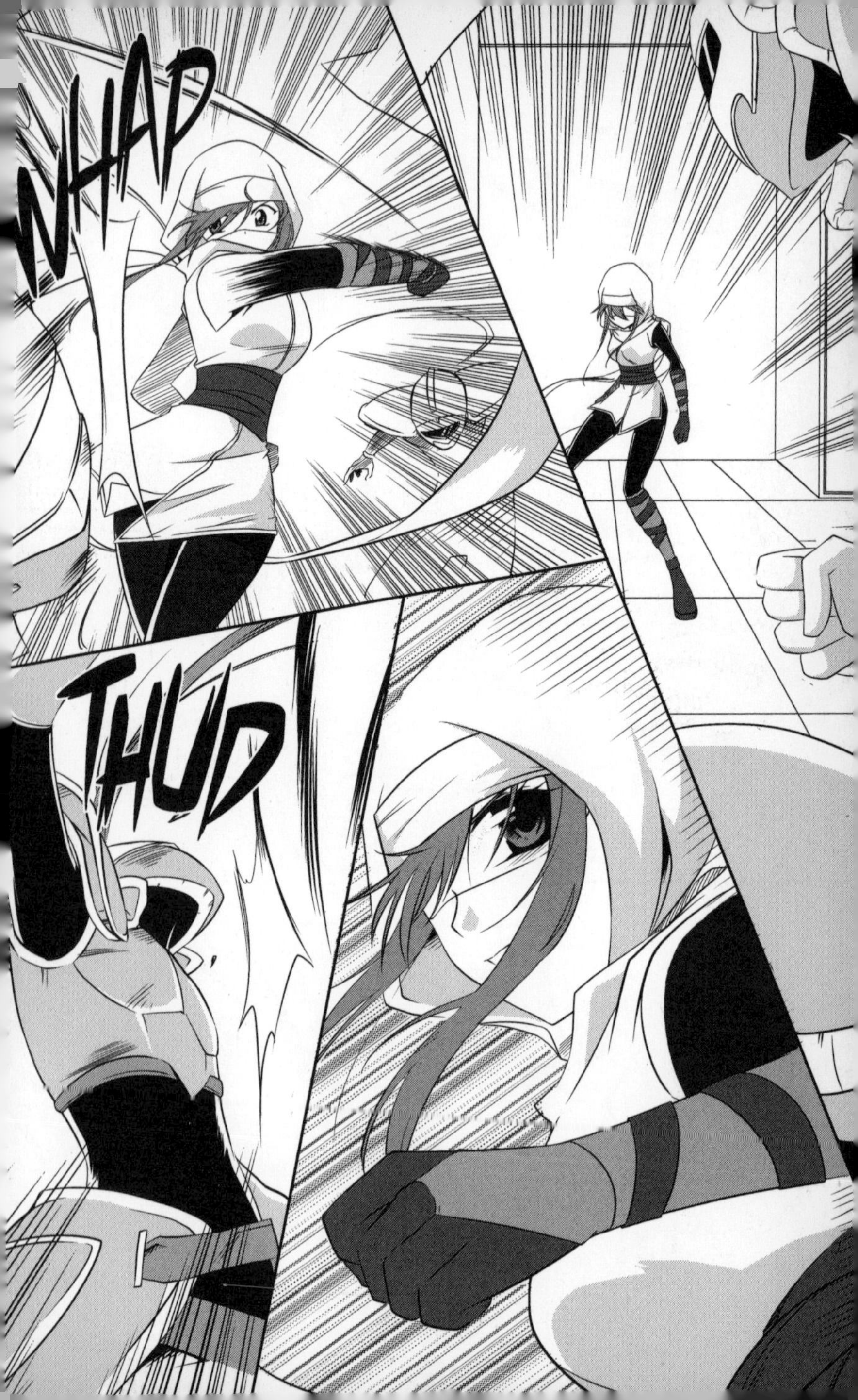
WHAP
THUD

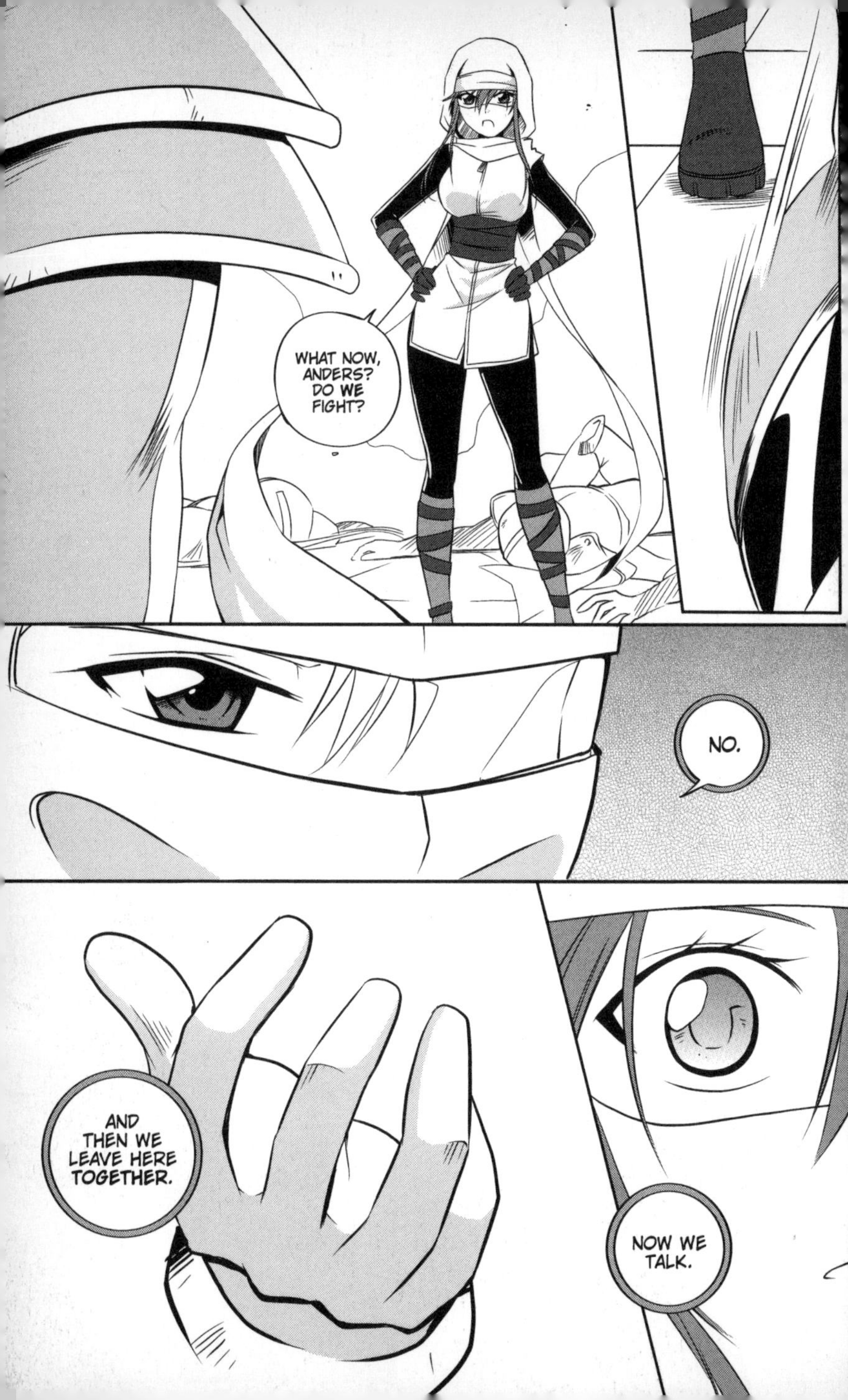
WHAT NOW, ANDERS? DO WE FIGHT?
NO.
NOW WE TALK.
AND THEN WE LEAVE HERE TOGETHER.

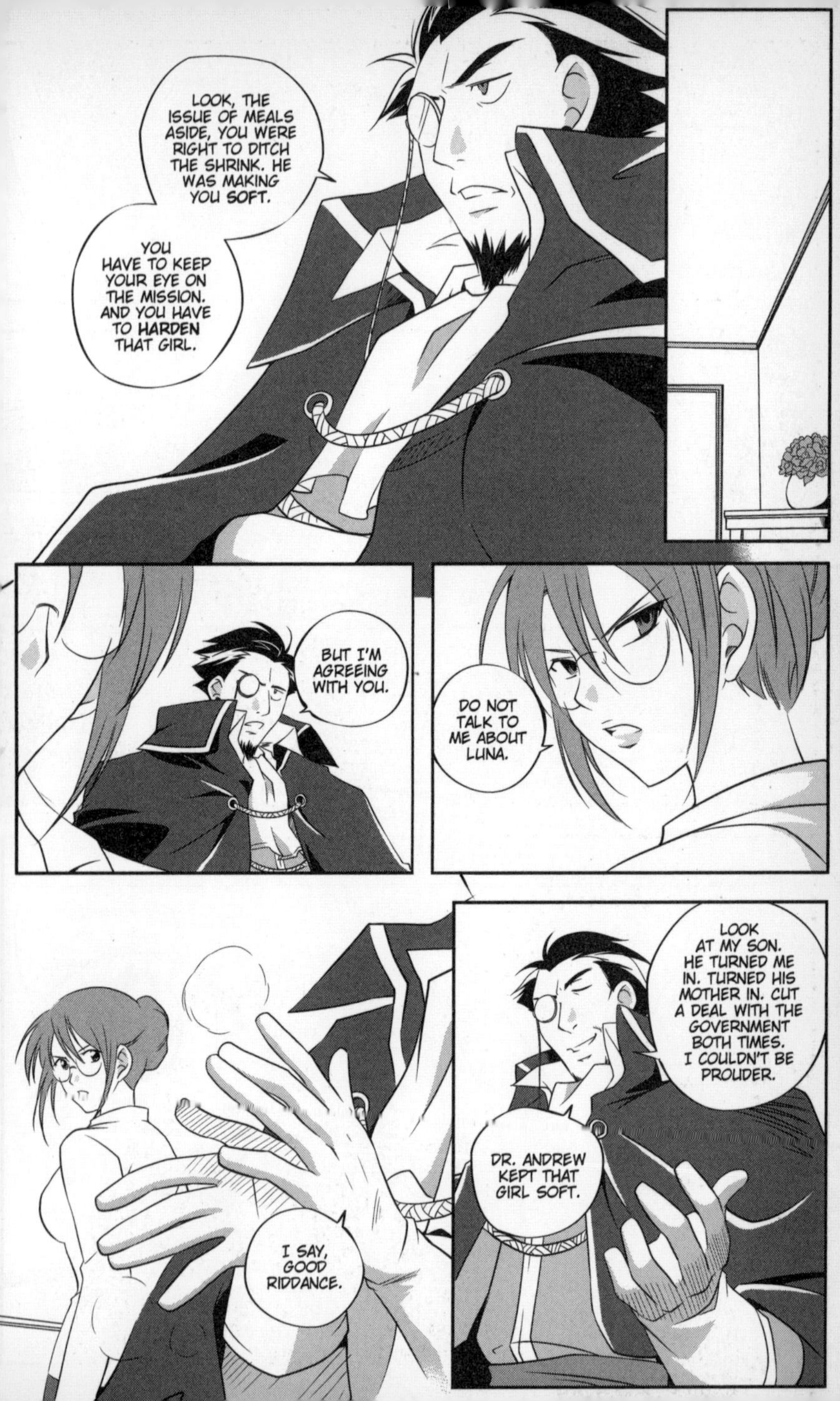
LOOK, THE ISSUE OF MEALS ASIDE, YOU WERE RIGHT TO DITCH THE SHRINK. HE WAS MAKING YOU SOFT.
YOU HAVE TO KEEP YOUR EYE ON THE MISSION. AND YOU HAVE TO HARDEN THAT GIRL.
DO NOT TALK TO ME ABOUT LUNA.
BUT I'M AGREEING WITH YOU.
LOOK AT MY SON. HE TURNED ME IN. TURNED HIS MOTHER IN. CUT A DEAL WITH THE GOVERNMENT BOTH TIMES. I COULDN'T BE PROUDER.
DR. ANDREW KEPT THAT GIRL SOFT.
I SAY, GOOD RIDDANCE.

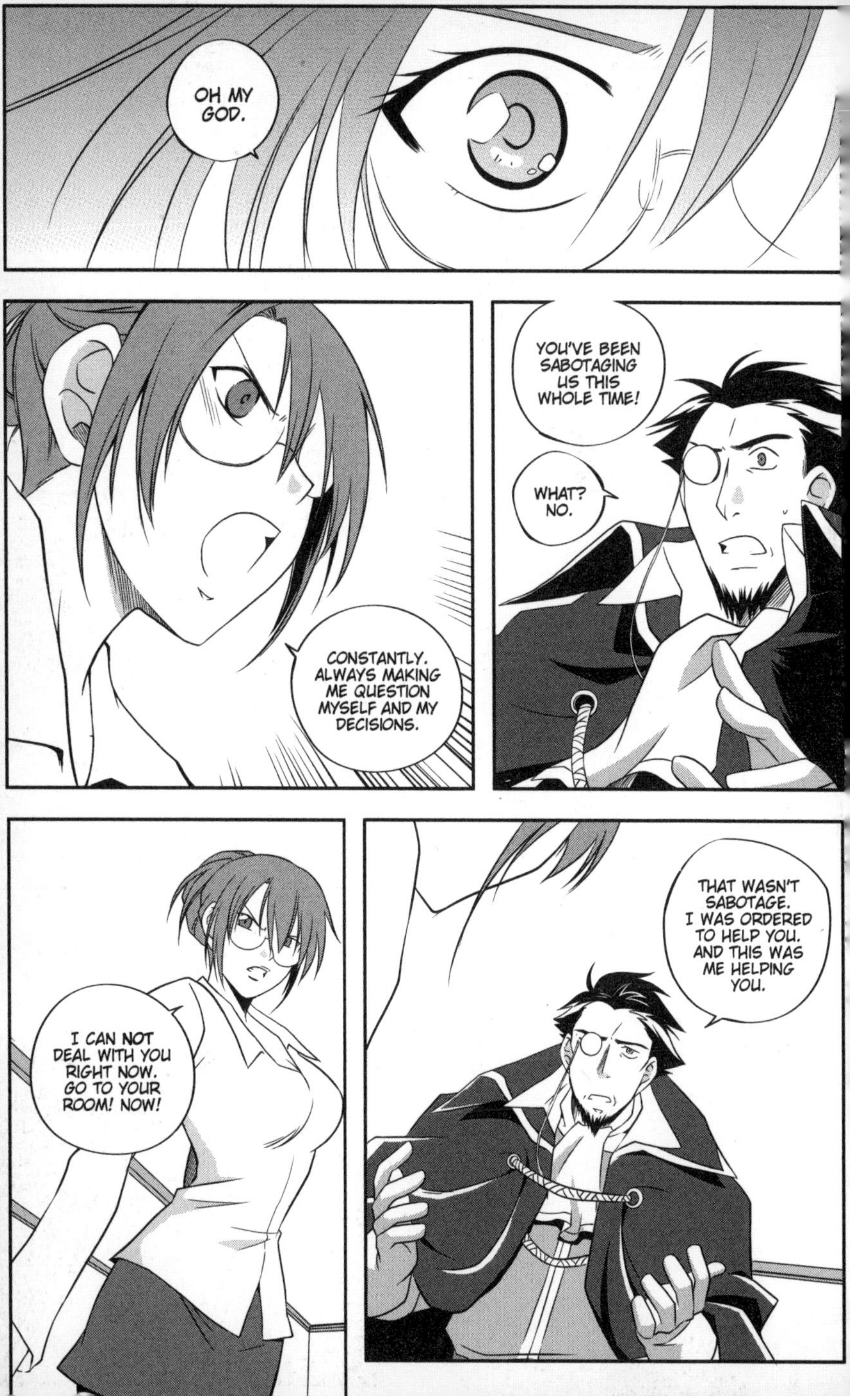
OH MY GOD.
YOU'VE BEEN SABOTAGING US THIS WHOLE TIME!
WHAT? NO.
CONSTANTLY. ALWAYS MAKING ME QUESTION MYSELF AND MY DECISIONS.
THAT WASN'T SABOTAGE. I WAS ORDERED TO HELP YOU. AND THIS WAS ME HELPING YOU.
I CAN NOT DEAL WITH YOU RIGHT NOW. GO TO YOUR ROOM! NOW!

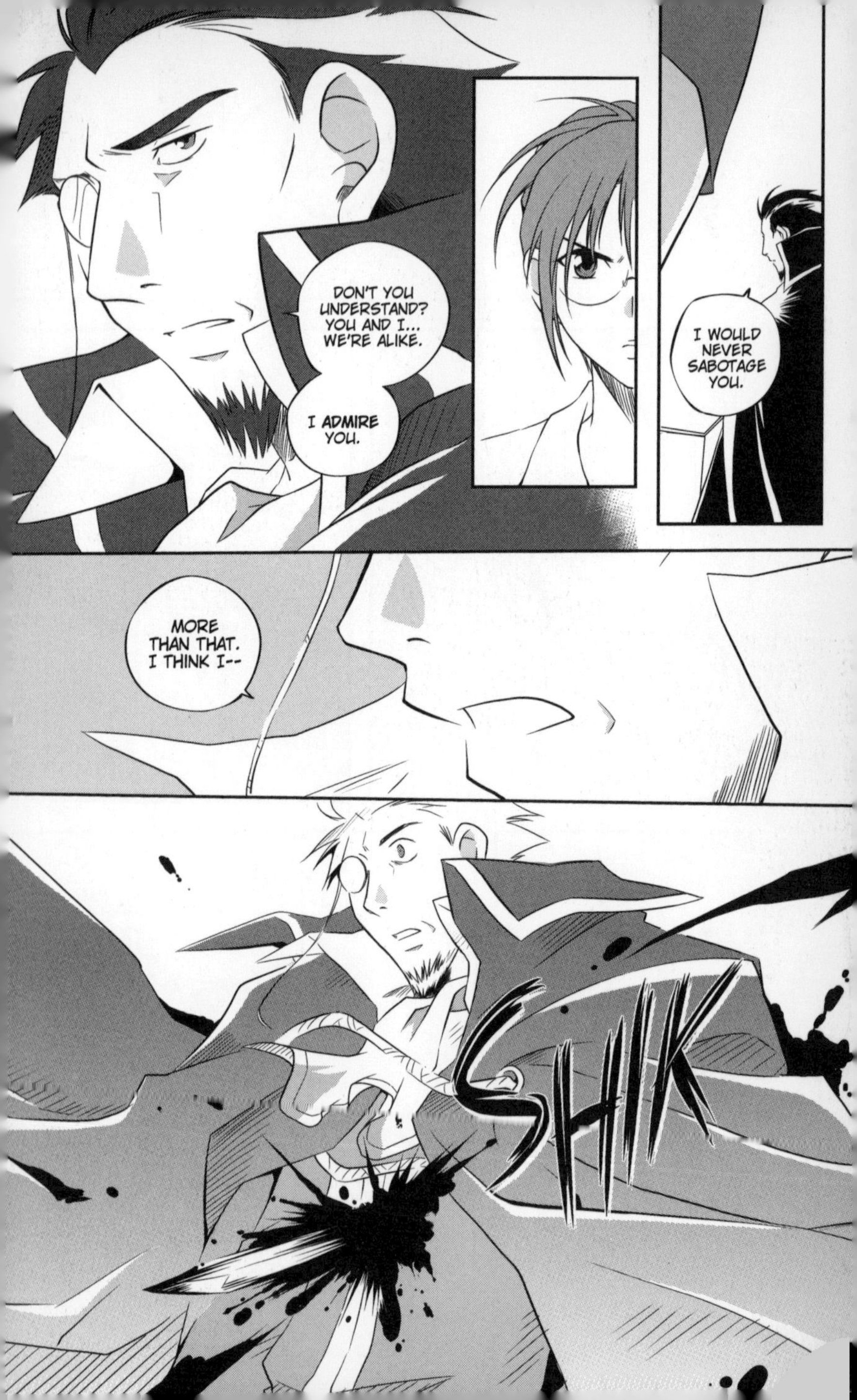
I WOULD NEVER SABOTAGE YOU.
DON'T YOU UNDERSTAND? YOU AND I... WE'RE ALIKE.
I ADMIRE YOU.
MORE THAN THAT. I THINK I--
SHIK

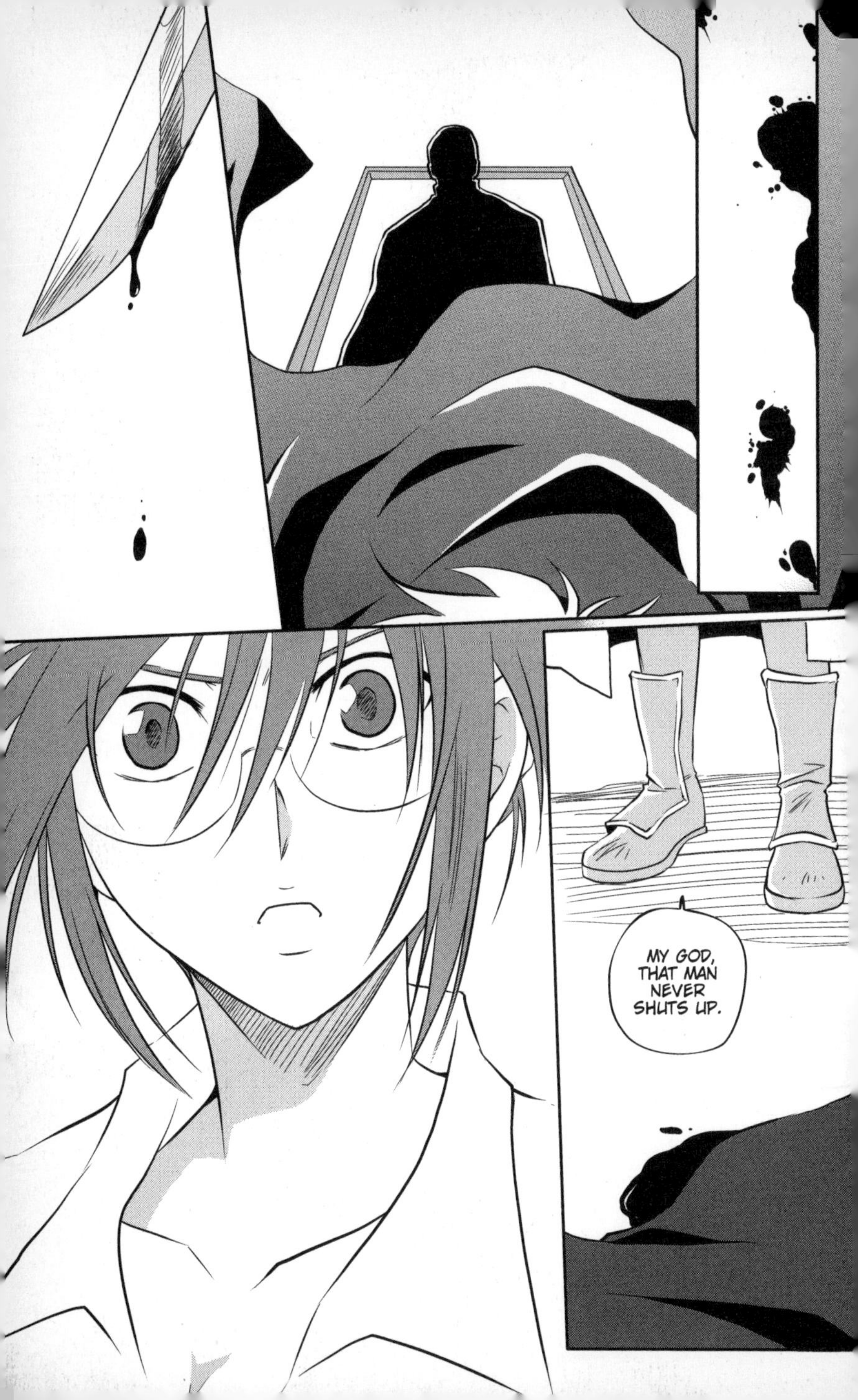
MY GOD, THAT MAN NEVER SHUTS UP.

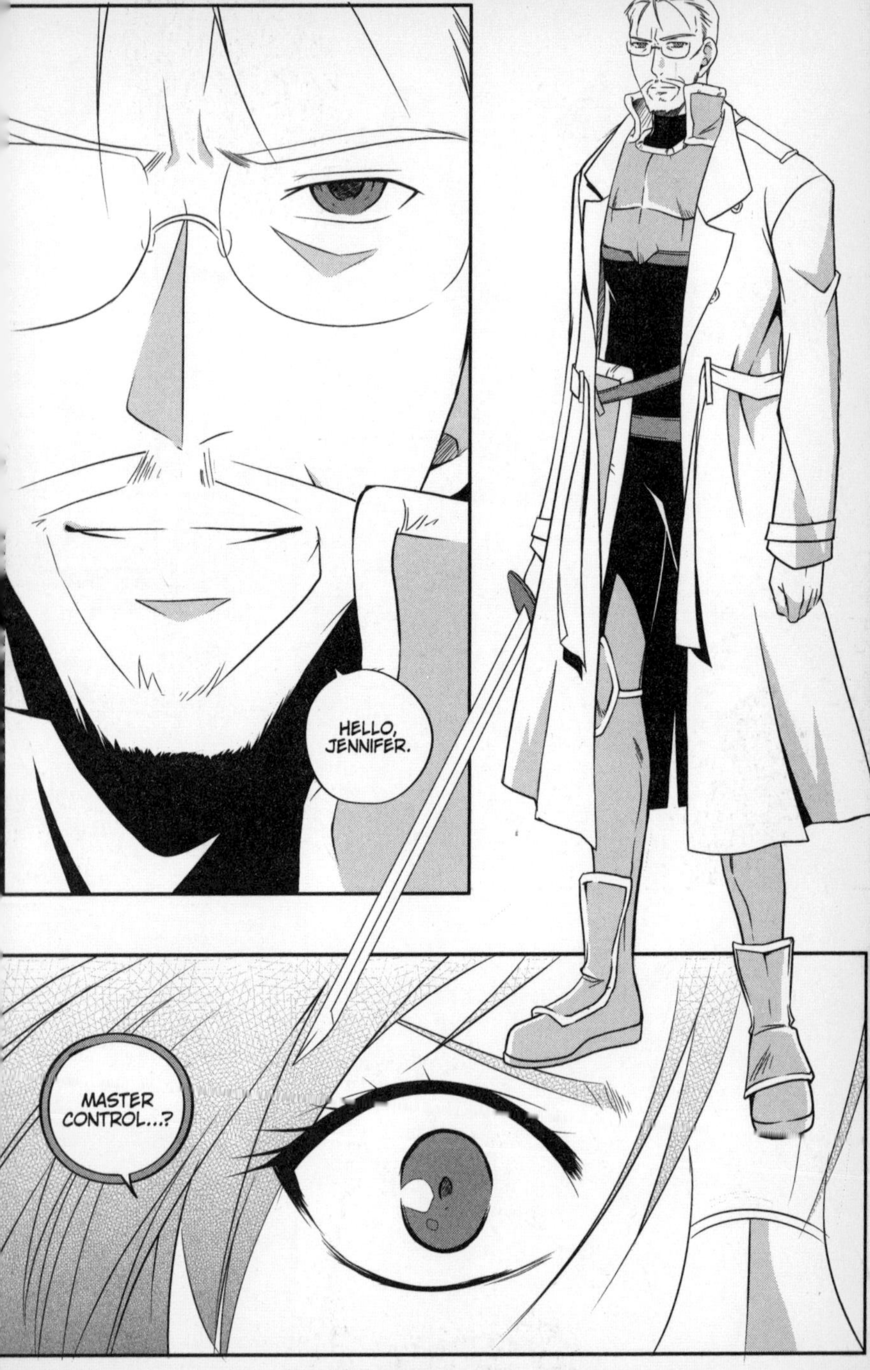
HELLO, JENNIFER.
MASTER CONTROL...?

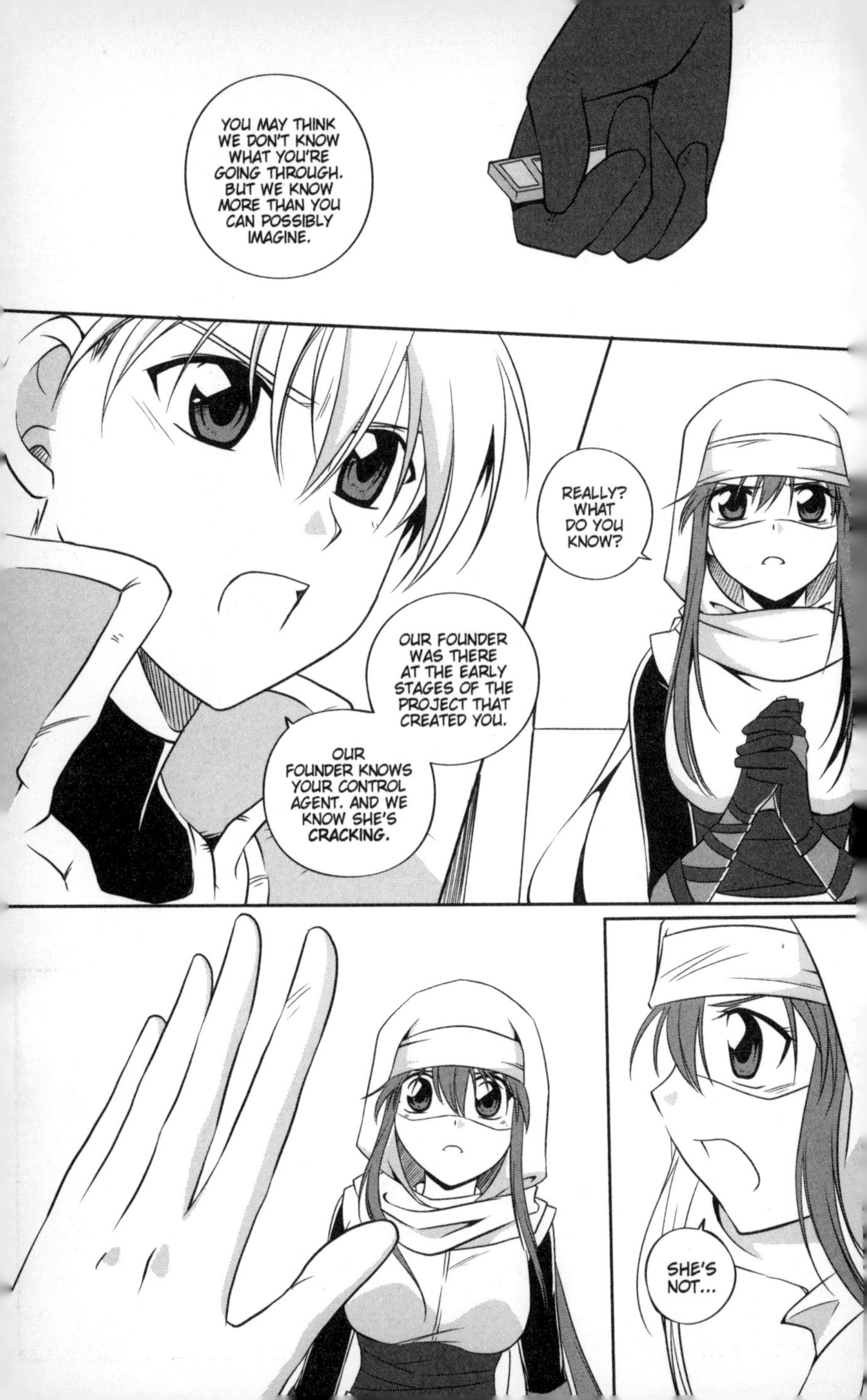
YOU MAY THINK WE DON'T KNOW WHAT YOU'RE GOING THROUGH. BUT WE KNOW MORE THAN YOU CAN POSSIBLY IMAGINE.
REALLY? WHAT DO YOU KNOW?
OUR FOUNDER WAS THERE AT THE EARLY STAGES OF THE PROJECT THAT CREATED YOU.
OUR FOUNDER KNOWS YOUR CONTROL AGENT. AND WE KNOW SHE'S CRACKING.
SHE'S NOT...

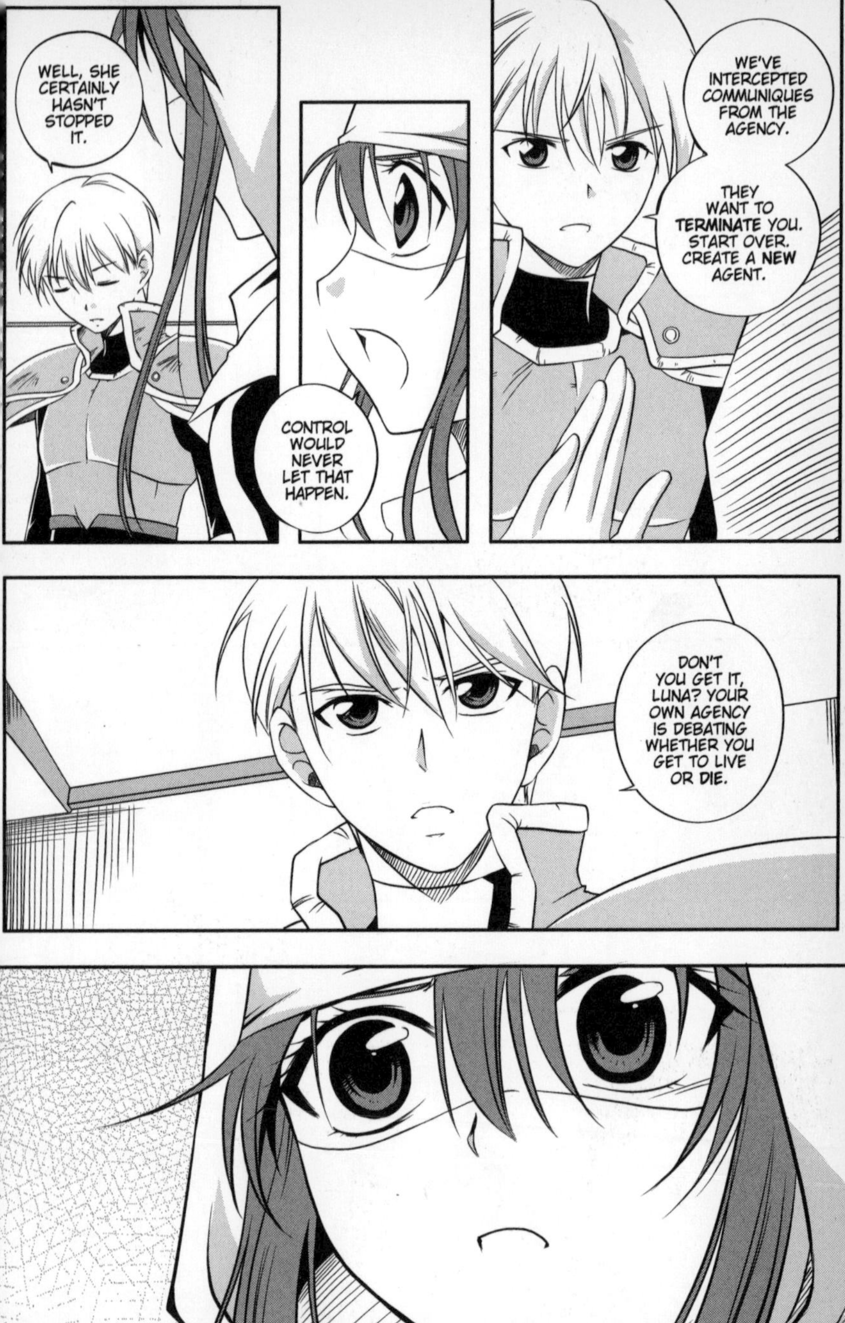
WE'VE INTERCEPTED COMMUNIQUES FROM THE AGENCY.
THEY WANT TO **TERMINATE** YOU. START OVER. CREATE A **NEW** AGENT.
CONTROL WOULD NEVER LET THAT HAPPEN.
WELL, SHE CERTAINLY HASN'T STOPPED IT.
DON'T YOU GET IT, LUNA? YOUR OWN AGENCY IS DEBATING WHETHER YOU GET TO LIVE OR DIE.

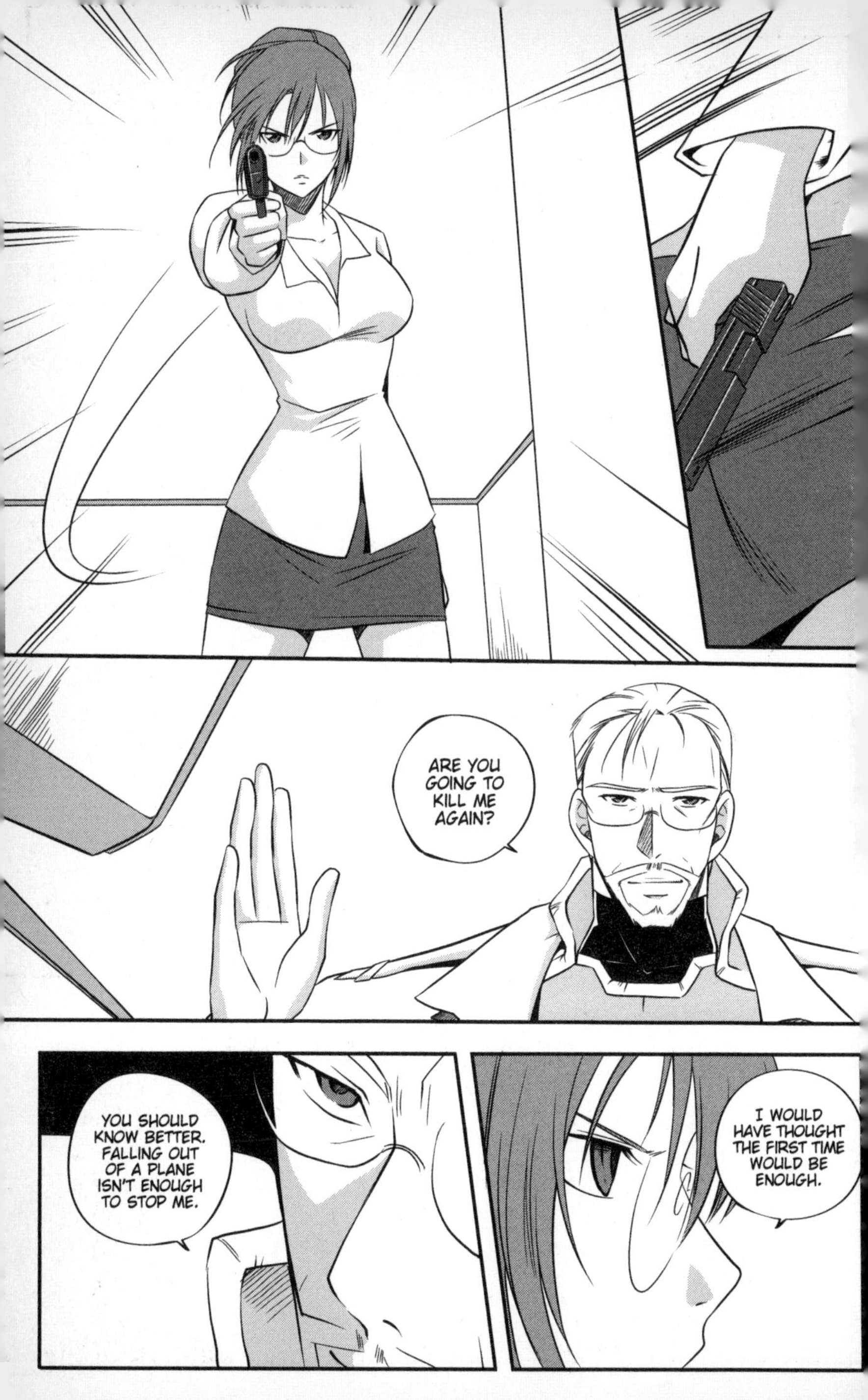
ARE YOU GOING TO KILL ME AGAIN?
I WOULD HAVE THOUGHT THE FIRST TIME WOULD BE ENOUGH.
YOU SHOULD KNOW BETTER. FALLING OUT OF A PLANE ISN'T ENOUGH TO STOP ME.

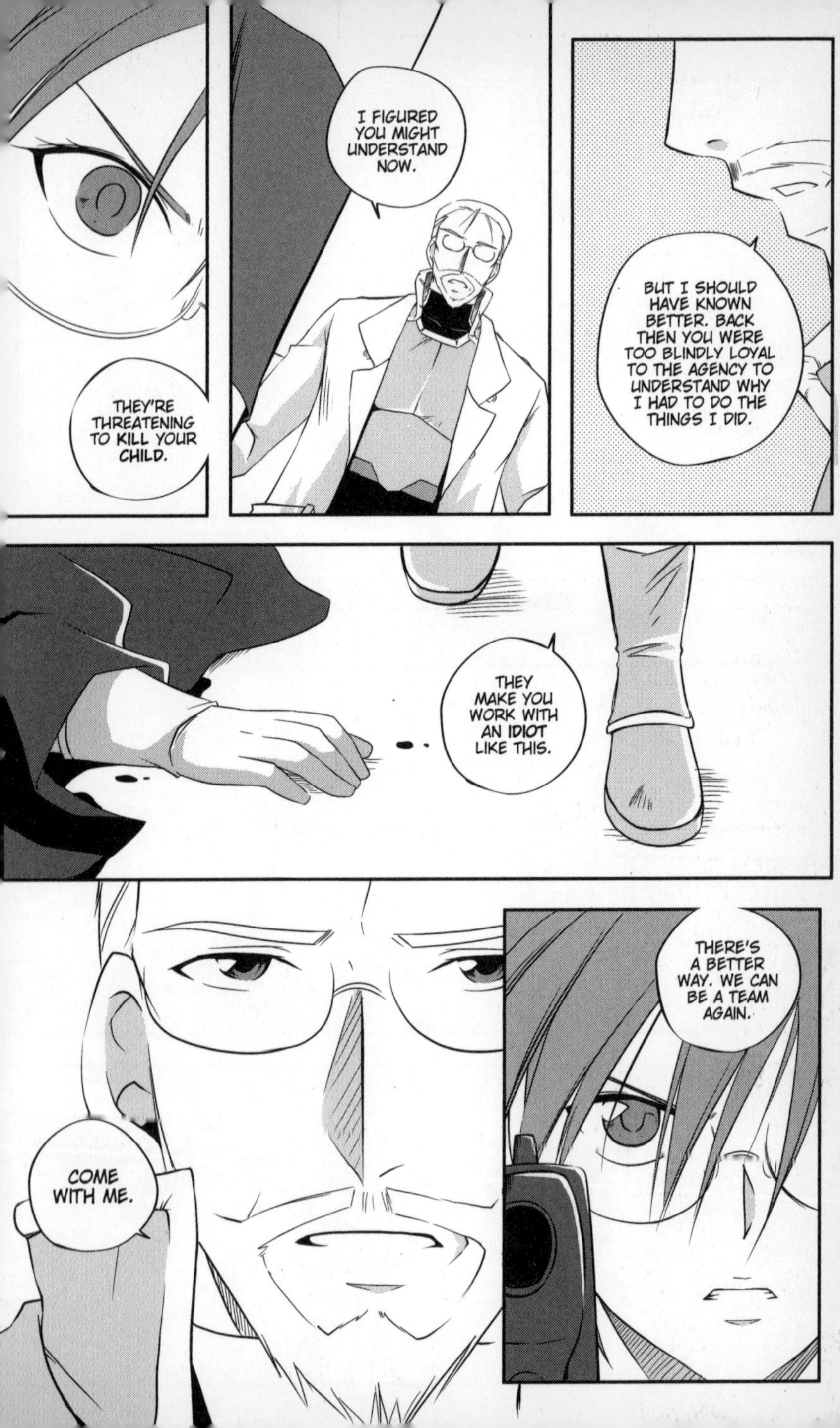
BUT I SHOULD HAVE KNOWN BETTER. BACK THEN YOU WERE TOO BLINDLY LOYAL TO THE AGENCY TO UNDERSTAND WHY I HAD TO DO THE THINGS I DID.
I FIGURED YOU MIGHT UNDERSTAND NOW.
THEY'RE THREATENING TO KILL YOUR CHILD.
THEY MAKE YOU WORK WITH AN IDIOT LIKE THIS.
THERE'S A BETTER WAY. WE CAN BE A TEAM AGAIN.
COME WITH ME.

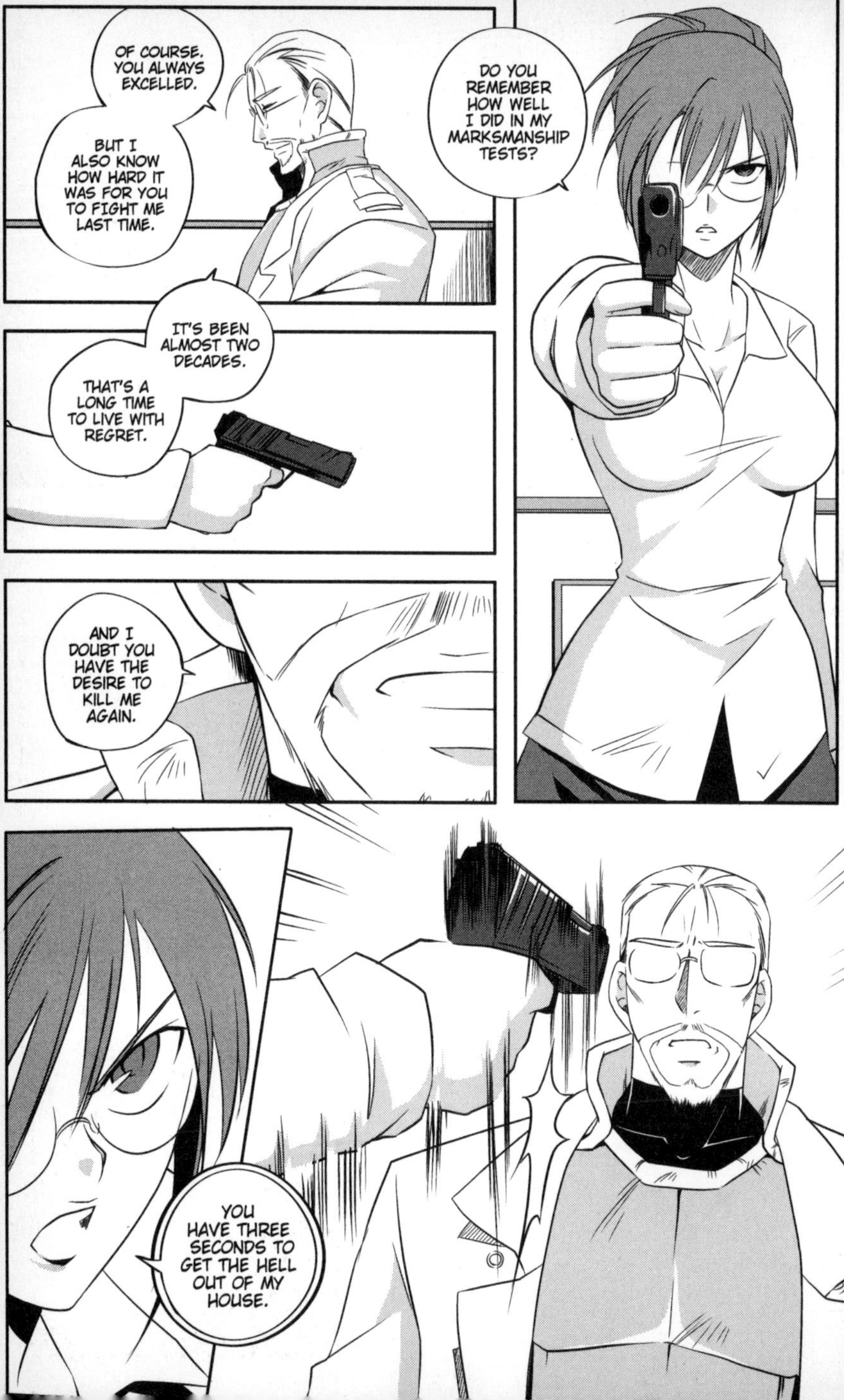
DO YOU REMEMBER HOW WELL I DID IN MY MARKSMANSHIP TESTS?
OF COURSE. YOU ALWAYS EXCELLED.
BUT I ALSO KNOW HOW HARD IT WAS FOR YOU TO FIGHT ME LAST TIME.
IT'S BEEN ALMOST TWO DECADES.
THAT'S A LONG TIME TO LIVE WITH REGRET.
AND I DOUBT YOU HAVE THE DESIRE TO KILL ME AGAIN.
YOU HAVE THREE SECONDS TO GET THE HELL OUT OF MY HOUSE.

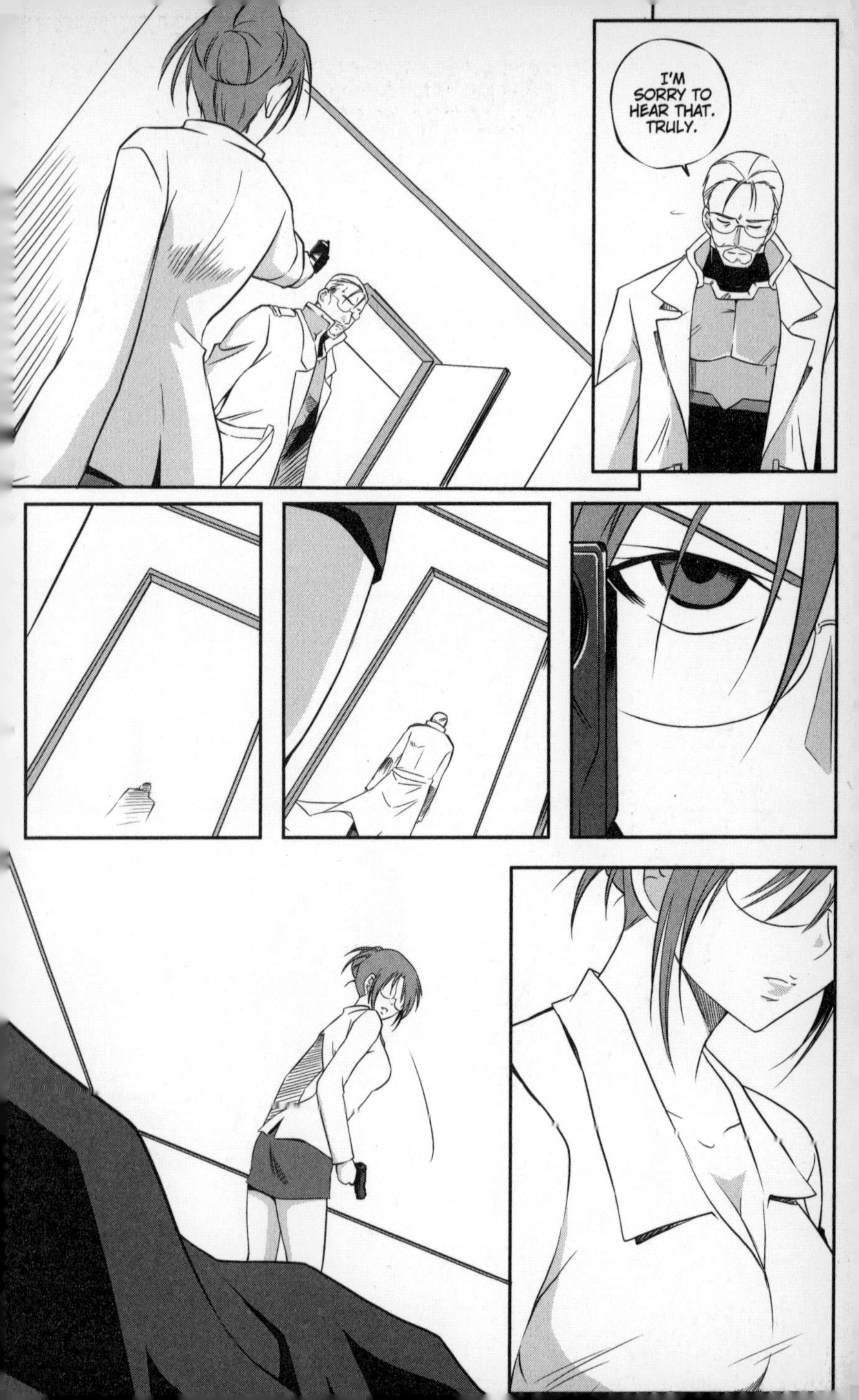
I'M SORRY TO HEAR THAT. TRULY.

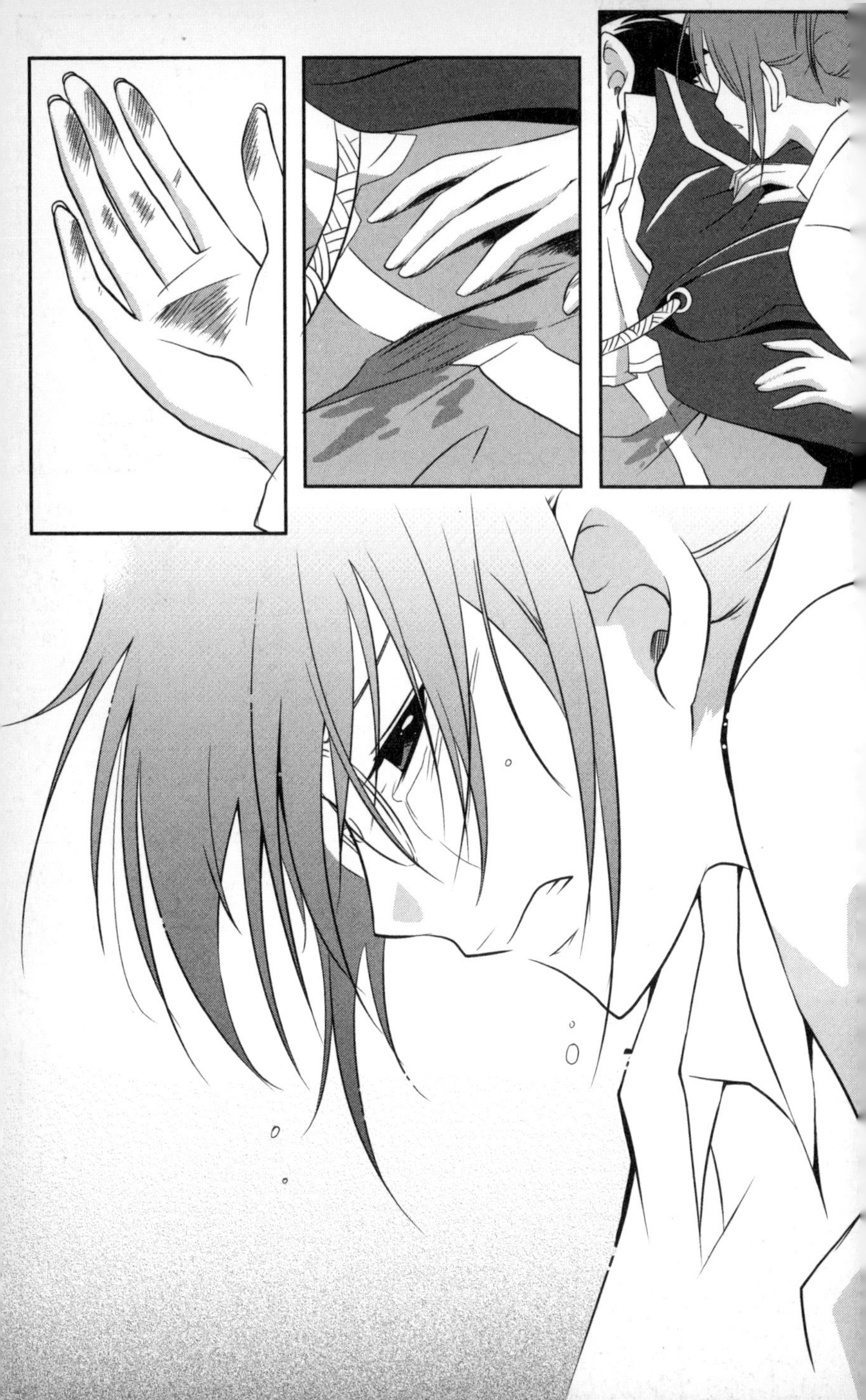

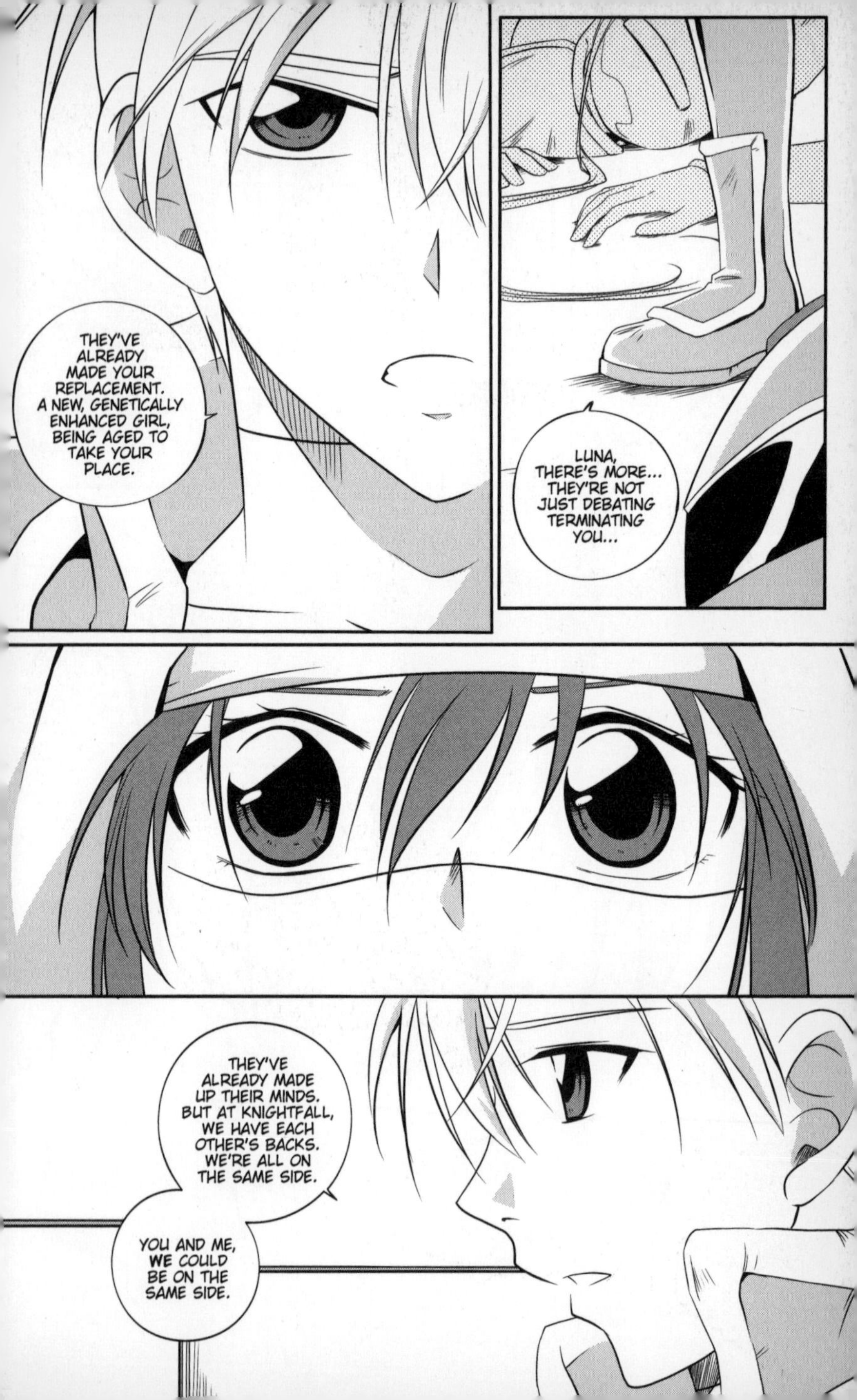
LUNA, THERE'S MORE... THEY'RE NOT JUST DEBATING TERMINATING YOU...
THEY'VE ALREADY MADE YOUR REPLACEMENT. A NEW, GENETICALLY ENHANCED GIRL, BEING AGED TO TAKE YOUR PLACE.
THEY'VE ALREADY MADE UP THEIR MINDS. BUT AT KNIGHTFALL, WE HAVE EACH OTHER'S BACKS. WE'RE ALL ON THE SAME SIDE.
YOU AND ME, WE COULD BE ON THE SAME SIDE.

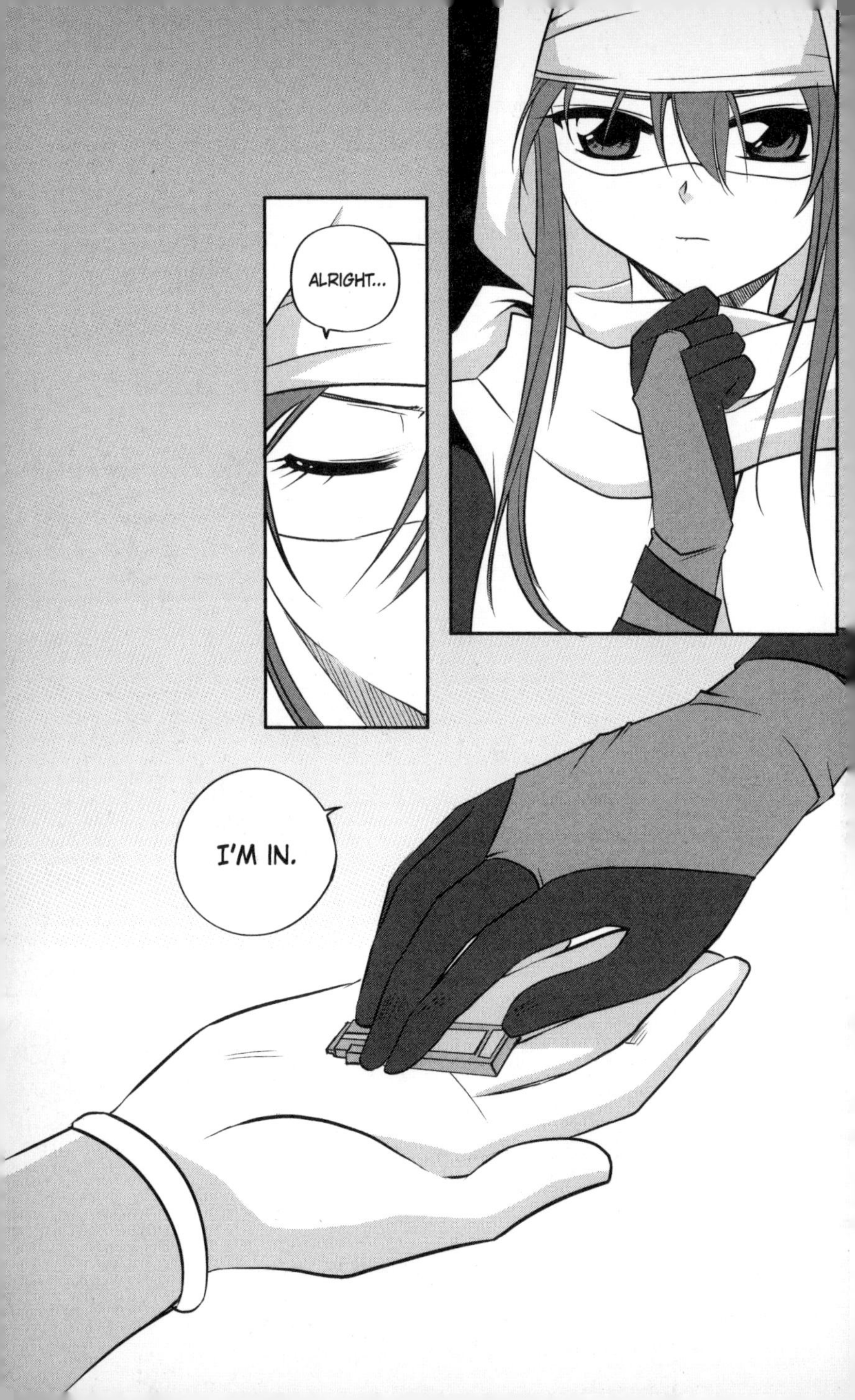
ALRIGHT...
I'M IN.

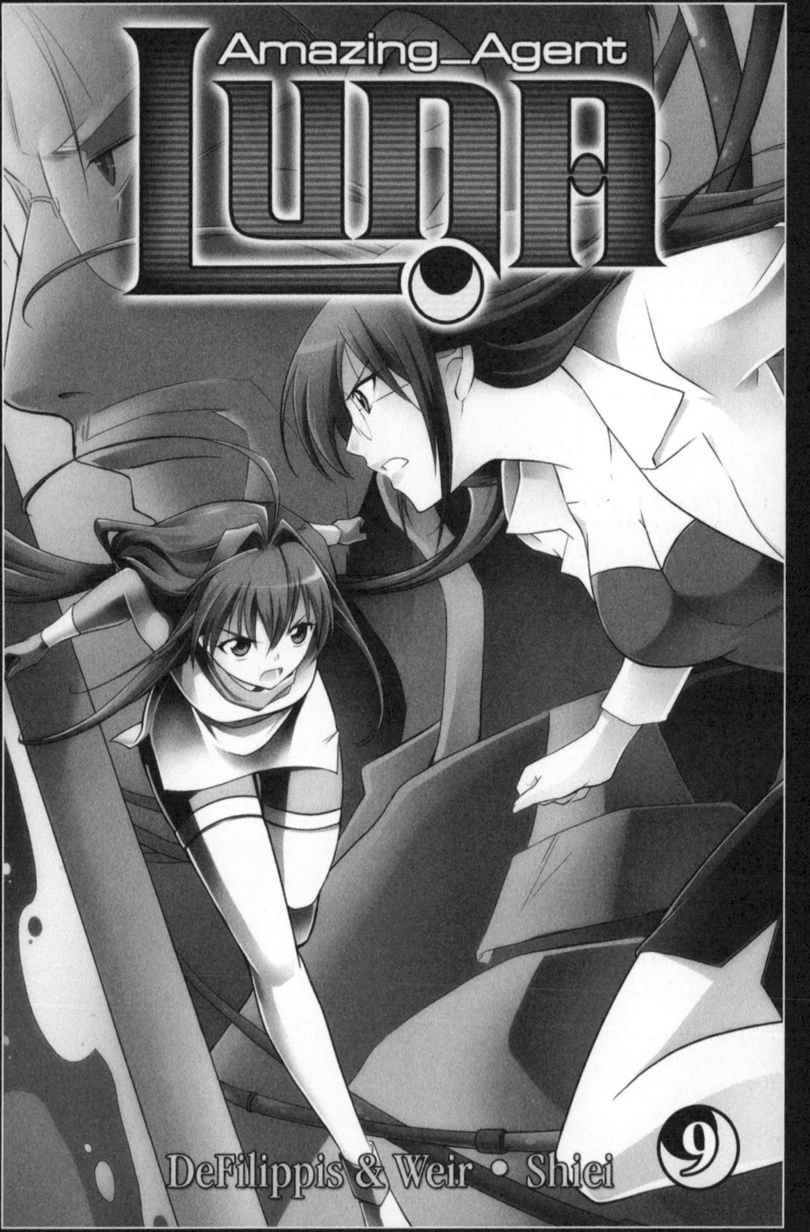
Amazing Agent
Luna
9
DeFilippis & Weir • Shiei

MEMORANDUM

TO: OUR READERS
FROM: NUNZIO DEFILIPPIS AND CHRISTINA WEIR
RE: AMAZING AGENT LUNA

"This is Luna's 'Empire Strikes Back.'"

That's how we pitched this story arc to Jason DeAngelis and Adam Arnold.

STAR WARS was a great movie. But it wasn't a saga. Not yet. Not until THE EMPIRE STRIKES BACK. It's the perfect Star Wars movie.

But it's dark. Really dark. Secrets revealed. Betrayals from friends. Villains triumphant.

It was time for Luna to be tested in the same way.

We had planned this Knightfall story for a while (more on that in next Volume's Memorandum), and we put them into the story with this development in mind.

But the closer we got to writing it, the more the Empire metaphor took over. Jason and Adam suggested setting this story in winter, to visually connect this story to the Hoth segments of that film. They also thought Luna in a winter ninja outfit would be cool, and we agreed with that!

Then they asked about ideas for cover design, so we sent them an image of one of the great movies posters of all time: Empire's 'Gone With The Wind' One-Sheet, which earned that name by having the Han-Leia kiss pay homage to the poster for GONE WITH THE WIND.

We asked for Control & Andy as the kissing lovers; Luna placed where Luke was on his Tauntaun; Aristotle flying where there had been an X-Wing; Anders, Oliver & Francesca where the droids and Chewie had been. And then lastly, we asked for a shadowy Agency Director where Darth Vader's head had been.

And it's that last one that really speaks to what's going on for Luna. The Agency isn't heroic. Luna is. For Luna to confront this, she's going to have to make some big decisions.

And go to some very dark places. Secrets. Betrayals. Villains.

Stay tuned.

AMAZING AGENT LUNA: DESIGN FILES

EYES ONLY
CLASSIFIED
TOP SECRET

REPORT PRODUCED AT	DATE PRODUCED	FILE PROCESSED BY	NATURE OF REPORT
CHQ B-2			

KIM DONOVAN

Kim Donovan was a supporting player in the Amazing Agent Jennifer prequel, and very quickly, we fell in love with her. When the decision was made to bring her back, we tried to imagine how she'd aged, and what kind of woman she'd become. We think Shiei's redesign makes sense. Kim still looks good, but she's matured, slowing down her chattering (a little, not much!) and taking some responsibility in her life. More on Kim next volume, but needless to say, this design wouldn't work if Kim were suddenly dour and serious. Never fear, she's as fun and goofy as ever. She just has a better job and a few other responsibilities.

AMAZING AGENT LUNA: DESIGN FILES

EYES ONLY
CLASSIFIED
TOP SECRET

REPORT PRODUCED AT	DATE PRODUCED	FILE PROCESSED BY	NATURE OF REPORT
CHQ D-6			

MASTER CONTROL

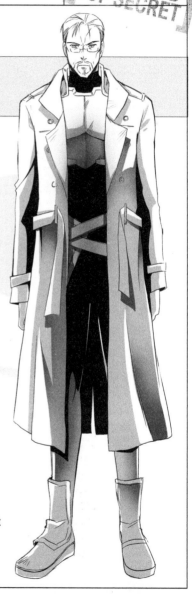

Our second returning character was saved for an end-of-volume reveal. Shiei didn't change much about him, and with good reason. This is not a man who lets the world change him. He plans to change the world. We did want Shiei to test him out in the Knightfall armor. Looks good, doesn't he? Especially for a 'dead man.'

AMAZING AGENT LUNA: DESIGN FILES

EYES ONLY CLASSIFIED TOP SECRET

REPORT PRODUCED AT	DATE PRODUCED	FILE PROCESSED BY	NATURE OF REPORT
CHQ B-2			

THE CONTROLLER

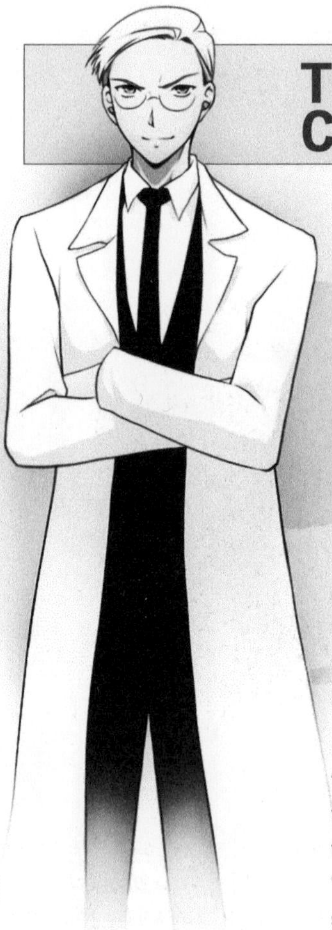

Most Control Agents simply call themselves Control Agent F or whatnot, following the naming convention we established for the Agency in Amazing Agent Jennifer. There are, however, exceptions. Jennifer calls herself Control, but this is for clear reasons. Luna needs a title to call her, something that could take the place of Mom. This guy, however, has reasons for his unique title that tell us more about him. He is the Controller. He likes being in charge and likes how that lets him treat people.

In this volume, he's little more than a tease for future storylines. But we needed a look that let people know: he's going to be trouble down the line. We asked Shiei for "someone with glasses, good looking. He should wear a lab coat, like Control does, but with a tux underneath it. Picture a cross between Neil Patrick Harris and Daniel Craig (if that's even possible)." What do you think?

REPORT PRODUCED AT	DATE PRODUCED	FILE PROCESSED BY	NATURE OF REPORT
CHQ D-6			

EYES ONLY
CLASSIFIED
TOP SECRET

THE MACGREGOR DEVICE

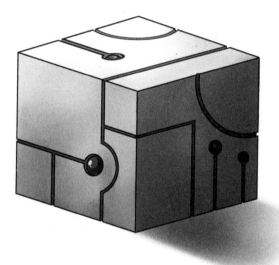

The MacGregor Device is our MacGuffin—the thing everyone is after that simply exists to set our characters in motion. We wanted it to do something cool, but not literally take over the story the way, say, a fusion hearted robot girl or army of clones would. While the device itself is a small chip, the storage device that houses it needed to really jump off the page. We wanted something that looked very Silver Age Comics, as if Jack Kirby would have designed it. We think Shiei got that down perfectly.

OPERATIONAL UPDATE

OPERATION: PROJECT TERRA
OPERATIVE: None yet
CONTROL AGENT: Eugene Marlow (The Controller)

■ As Project Luna continues to flounder, great strides have been made in Project Terra. Unhindered by the so-called 'ethical' concerns of previous Control Agents and with embryos in sealed, adjustable environments, testing can be conducted as the actual test subjects gestate.

The most recent subject has survived all such testing. It should be stronger and faster than previous agents created in this manner, though the level of improvement can not be assessed until the subject is activated.

Should the levels be unsatisfactory, subject can be terminated and a new one created.

Project Terra awaits your activation order.

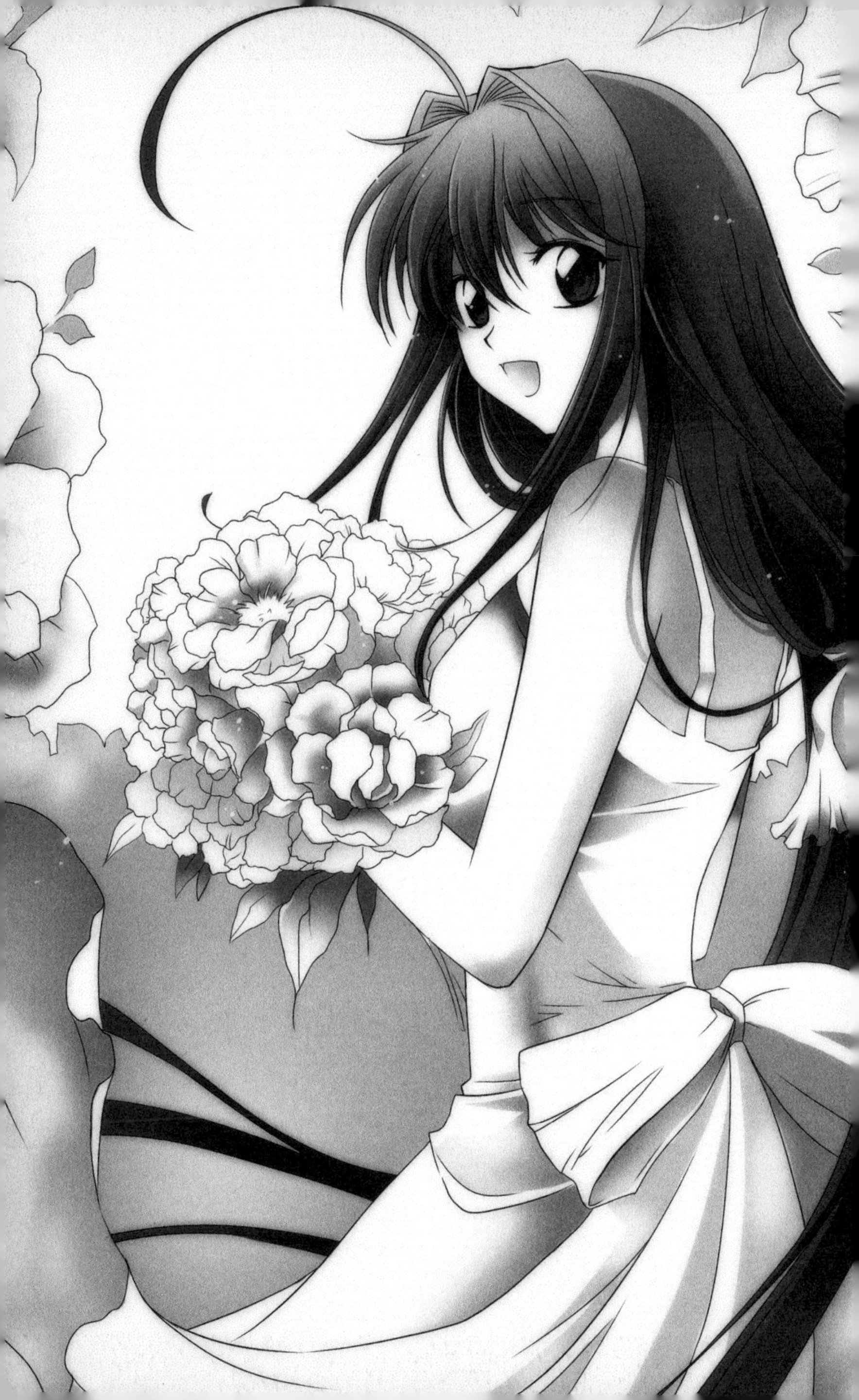

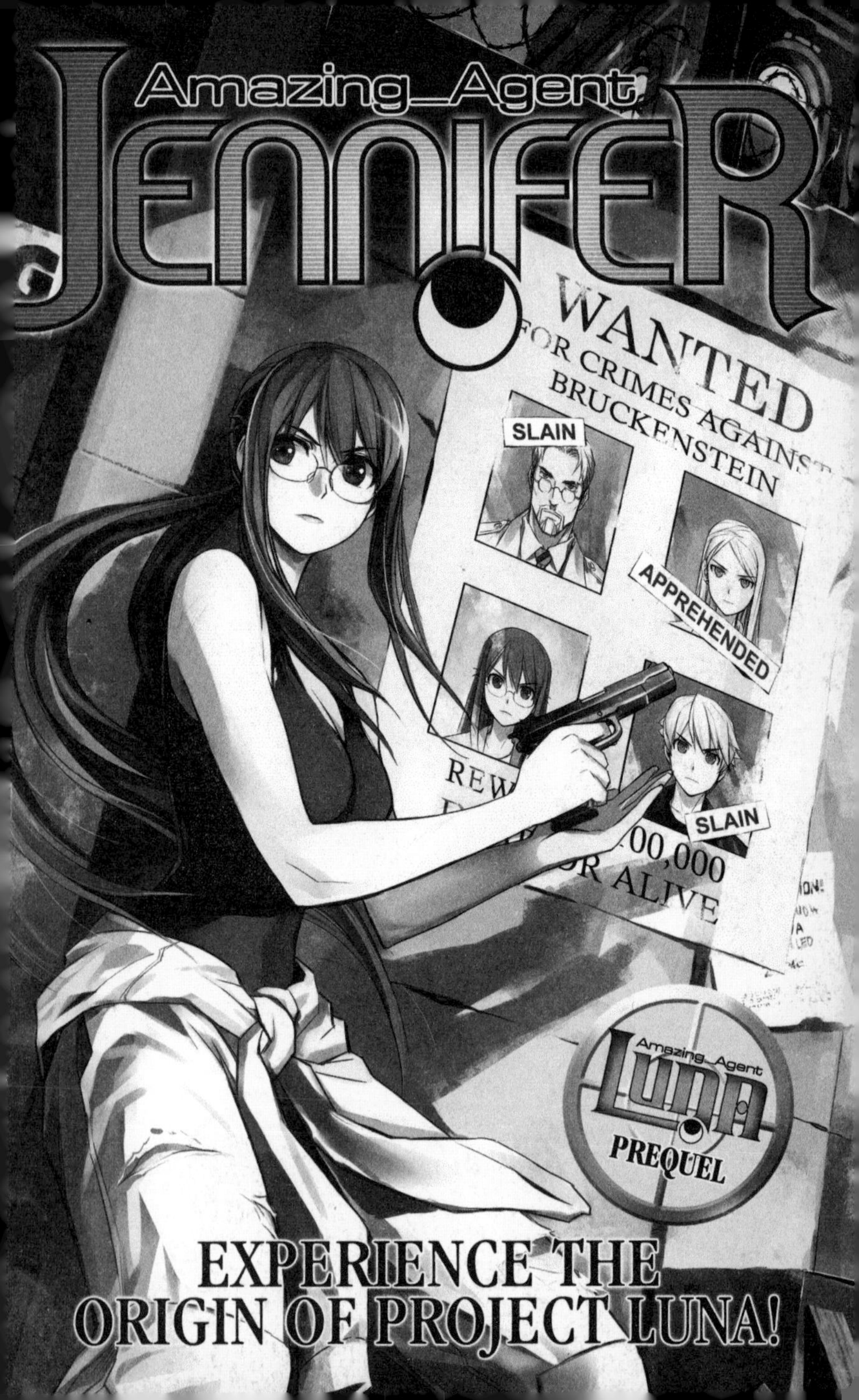
Amazing_Agent
JENNIFER
WANTED
FOR CRIMES AGAINS
BRUCKENSTEIN
SLAIN
APPREHENDED
SLAIN
Amazing_Agent
LUNA
PREQUEL
EXPERIENCE THE
ORIGIN OF PROJECT LUNA!

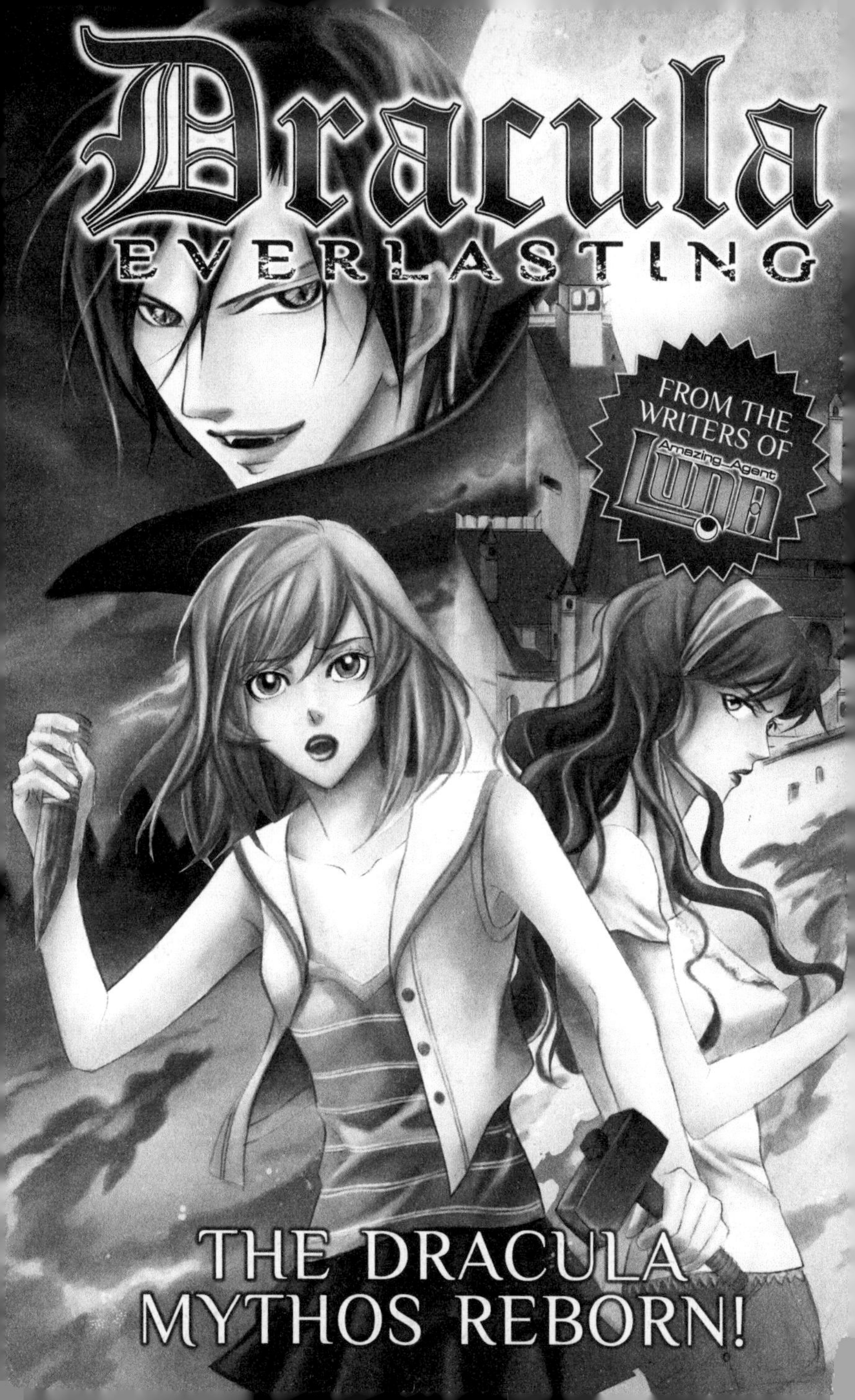
Dracula
EVERLASTING
FROM THE WRITERS OF
Amazing Agent
Luna
THE DRACULA MYTHOS REBORN!